The Skills of Management
Fourth edition

WITHDRAWN

This book is the fourth edition of a highly successful introduction to management. Starting with the transition to a managerial role, it deals with core skills involved in management. These include delegation, appraisal, staff development, disciplinary handling, employee relations, negotiation, and chairing and conduct in meetings. These are discussed alongside the key themes of time management and the need for thorough identification of objectives and diagnosis of problems before action.

This edition has been considerably amended to take account of recent developments in management theory and practice. These include changes in the private and public sectors, including the role and operation of 'quangos'. Also discussed are managerial competences, the impact of globalisation and developments in information technology on organisations and managers' jobs, Total Quality Management, managerial stress and the impact of European law on employment protection. Real-life examples are offered throughout, with the variation in styles of management required by different organisations and countries taken into consideration.

W. David Rees draws on his wide experience as an academic, manager, consultant and arbitrator to provide a sound blend of theory and practice which is useful and highly readable.

W. David Rees was, prior to early retirement, a Principal Lecturer at the University of Westminster's London Management Centre. He has extensive experience in management consultancy in the UK and abroad in both the private and public sectors.

The Skills of Management
Fourth edition

W. David Rees

INTERNATIONAL THOMSON BUSINESS PRESS
I(T)P An International Thomson Publishing company

London • Bonn • Boston • Johannesburg • Madrid • Melbourne • Mexico City • New York • Paris
Singapore • Tokyo • Toronto • Albany, NY • Belmont, CA • Cincinnati, OH • Detroit, MI

The Skills of Management, 4th edition

Copyright © 1996 W. David Rees

First published 1996 by International Thomson Business Press

I ⏀ P   A division of International Thomson Publishing Inc.
The ITP logo is a trademark under licence

British Library Cataloguing in Publication Data
A catalogue record for this book is available from the British Library

First edition 1996, reprinted 1999

Typeset in Baskerville by Keystroke, Jacaranda Lodge, Wolverhampton
Printed in Croatia by Zrinski d.d.

ISBN 1-86152-482-X

International Thomson
Business Press
Berkshire House
168-173 High Holborn
London WC1V 7AA
UK

Contents

List of figures   vii

Preface to fourth edition   ix

Acknowledgements   xiii

Introduction   xv

1   **Managers and their background**   1

2   **Identifying the manager's job**   25

3   **The manager and the organisation**   52

4   **Managerial style**   97

5   **Delegation**   123

6   **Motivation**   136

7   **Payment systems**   158

8   **Communication**   177

9   **Selection**   202

10   **Appraisal, training and counselling**   227

11   **Disciplinary handling and dismissal**   263

12   **The manager and employee relations**   295

13   **Meetings and chairing**   328

Conclusion   350

Index   353

Figures

1.1	The managerial cycle	2
1.2	The managerial escalator	3
2.1	Role set analysis for head of personnel of a professional organisation	33
2.2	Critical path analysis: launching a new product	43
4.1	A continuum of leadership styles	106
4.2	John Adair's action-centred model of leadership	109
6.1	Maslow's hierarchy of human needs	140
6.2	The skill pyramid	147
6.3	Job distortion	149
7.1	The long-term pattern of incentive schemes	161
8.1	Communication exercise	181
11.1	The disciplinary pyramid	278
13.1	Chair-centred discussion	341
13.2	Group-centred discussion	342

Preface to fourth edition

Perhaps the best way of explaining the rationale for this edition is to liken the writing of the book to the production of a motor car. Car design has to take place within a changing environment – particularly in the technological and market areas. However, if a car is to be produced, at some stage the design has to be frozen so that production can start – even though opportunities for improvement continue to emerge. Note is taken of these opportunities for further improvement, however, so that they can be incorporated into the next model. This is just the process that has taken place with this book. It has been repeated with each new edition. Also – just as with car production – there is all the information about the performance of the product after it has been launched. A particularly important source of information in this respect has been discussions about the content with mature students who are in managerial jobs.

Much has changed since the third edition was published in 1991. The overall framework of the book has been retained but every chapter has been revised in the light of recent developments. A considerable amount of new material has been added but other material has been reduced or deleted to help contain the increase in size of the book. The scale of the changes has been particularly great in Chapters 3, 10 and 12. The changes in Chapter 3 particularly relate to the impact of both globalisation and developments in information technology, trans-national organisations, Total Quality Management and the use of mission statements. The chapter has also been amended to take account of the major changes in the way much of the public sector is managed, including the use of performance indicators and the role and operation of 'quangos'. The changes in Chapter 10 have been mainly about developments in the training area and include the concept of the learning organisation, National Vocational Qualifications (NVQs) and modular course design, Training and Enterprise Councils (TECs), and mentoring. The issue of performance management and its links to appraisal is also included. The issue of competences and their relevance to management are also examined in Chapter 10 as well as other chapters. The changes in Chapter 12 relate to the concept of human resource management, pressures to reduce unit labour costs, major changes in the labour market, the impact of inward investment on working practices and the changed role of trade unions. Legal developments in this area are also examined relating to health and safety, the reduction of collective trade union rights under domestic law and the increases in collective and individual employee rights because of developments in European law.

Having taken early retirement from the University of Westminster, although I still work there as Visiting Lecturer, I have been able to undertake a range of new activities. These have included a range of consultancy activities, including those undertaken on behalf of the Institute of Personnel and Development, and a period in the voluntary sector as a Director of the Westminster Children's Society. My greater freedom has also enabled me to do justice to the major task of writing this fourth edition.

The general tendency for authority and decision-making to be devolved lower down in flattened organisational structures in both the public and private sectors and its implications with managerial responsibilities is a recurring theme. Other topics that have been introduced or expanded include gender issues, which also covers the increasing phenomenon of dual-career couples, the impact of culture on management, empowerment, managerial stress, the response of managers and employees to organisations which offer reduced levels of security, the impact of electronic developments on communications, presentation skills and assessment centres.

There are some important issues with regard to writing style. I have dealt with the issue of the use of the personal pronoun 'he' this time by simply not using it unless it refers to a specific person. Language conventions have changed so that I have followed the practice of some other writers by using the term 'they' in a singular as well as a plural context to avoid sexist connotations. I have preferred to stay with the term 'skills' rather than use the term 'competences'. This is because the term 'competences' refers to a particular approach to the identification, development and assessment of skills and I believe the term skills is more generic. Also I have always been determined to express myself as clearly as possible and to avoid using long words if there are shorter alternatives. The consistent feedback I have received about the previous editions has been that they have above all else been readable and I have been determined to keep it that way.

W. David Rees

Acknowledgements

Particular acknowledgement is due to the countless number of management students who, in different classes and organisational workshops, have allowed me to test out and develop my ideas and have contributed both ideas of their own and many invaluable illustrative examples which appear in this book. The classes have been on a wide variety of courses – especially at the University of Westminster's London Management Centre. Particular thanks are due to students on the MA in Human Resource Management and to those on the MA in Diplomatic Studies who have given me very useful insights about management in a variety of cultural settings. Further cultural insights were gained from the students on the various management development workshops I have run in Malaysia and Indonesia. Thanks are also due to the many students I have taught at the City University Business School. I have gleaned innumerable valuable ideas from former colleagues at the University of Westminster and also by 'in-house' training and consultancy in a wide variety of organisations, especially the Bass Group and the London Borough of Hackney. Mention should also be made of the students I have met at the Royal College of Nursing – particularly those who first prompted the idea of my writing a book about basic management skills. I also gratefully acknowledge *Private Eye*, for allowing me to reproduce the cartoon that appears on p. 218.

I have received direct help in writing the various editions of the book from a wide range of people. Whilst it is perhaps invidious to name just some of them I must pay particular thanks to Kath Brady, Laurence Campbell Reece Evans, Robin Evans, Les Galloway, Sue Miller and Roger Woodley. Emma Westcott's help in inputting edition three onto a disc has enabled me to improve the quality and topicality of edition four considerably. The contribution by Fraser Tuddenham, formerly of Unilever, was substantial. Finally and most of all I must thank my wife and colleague Christine Porter who gave substantial and continuous help over the whole range of the activity – from the conceptual and creative to the grammatical and data inputting. She also gave me great emotional support and encouragement whilst 'living through' all four editions.

Introduction

During the time that I have taught management subjects I have become aware of the dearth of books that address a reasonable range of core issues, let alone tackle such topics in an appropriate way. Most books about management are written from the perspective of a particular discipline or function and are intended for a specialist rather than a person with a range of management responsibilities. A further complication has been that the language in many of these books is not particularly user-friendly. Through taking a marketing approach to my teaching and trying to establish the areas those who had management responsibilities actually needed help in I built up a fund of relevant material. I also sought to use clear language and practical illustrations to facilitate learning. After prompting from some student groups I eventually converted some of this material into a book about practical management skills and, as explained in the Preface to this edition, the book has been systematically developed through various editions. In revising the book once more I have endeavoured to keep to the original idea of writing one that was intended to be of practical benefit to those who had acquired, or who expected to acquire, a range of management responsibilities and which was user-friendly.

Over the years I became fascinated with the way in which people in widely different organisations and countries seemed to be grappling with similar basic issues and problems. This enabled me to identify a core of basic issues that match the syllabus requirements of a wide range of courses as well as being relevant to the non-student practitioner. I have been able to draw on the contributions made in hundreds of classroom discussions and 'in-house' workshops to provide appropriate practical examples to illustrate and help explain the relevant theoretical concepts and practical skills. Such examples, and a constant reminding of what the real agenda is by those facing management problems on a day-to-day basis, has enabled me to write a book that is relevant, with an appropriate blend of theory and practice. Providing a blend is critical, as this book is not intended to supply a set of prescriptive remedies. Action needs to be preceded by careful diagnosis. Mary Parker Follett's concept of the 'law of the situation', explained in Chapter 1, is all important. Decisions and action need to take account of the variables in a situation. By providing both a basic theoretical analysis of concepts and an explanation of the skills that are likely to be useful, the intention is to provide readers with the ability to judge when and how to use specific skills and remedies and not to apply them as a knee-jerk reaction to problems.

It is increasingly recognised that people who train as specialists are likely to accumulate considerable managerial responsibilities in the course of their career. As explained in Chapter 1 few people start their careers as managers. Organisations usually have a departmental structure. The normal career progression is for people to start off as a specialist and then progressively acquire responsibility for supervising or managing other specialists. Even business studies graduates usually find they have to be placed initially in a specialist job, despite the general nature of the training they have received. If that is the pattern, it is just as well to prepare people for what is to come. If the specialism requires training why not also the managerial aspects? The trend to devolution of authority and decision-making within both private and public sector organisations, accompanied by flatter organisational structures, has emphasised this by increasing the range of responsibilities and the speed with which people acquire them. Recognition of this phenomenon made me first consider naming the book 'Management – for those thrust into it'. Logically the syllabuses of most professional and specialist courses have now been adapted to include management. Many people, however, do not have the benefit of training in this area and it is hoped that this book will be of assistance to them as well as those who are engaged in the formal study of management.

I have generally not made a distinction between management and supervision, although I have referred to the role of the first-line supervisor in Chapters 11 and 12. I have used the term 'management' generically to incorporate supervision. My general scepticism of the value of the distinction has been reinforced when I have run management courses or workshops for people at different levels within the same organisation. On one occasion I was involved in running management courses simultaneously at three different levels in the National Health Service. These were for ward sisters, middle managers and senior nursing officers. The, perhaps heretical, conclusion I came to was that many of the basic management problems facing the people employed at these different levels were the same. Status issues required that the programmes be written up in distinctly different ways and there were some genuine differences. However, it was the common nature of the problems rather than the differences which was the more noticeable. People in senior positions may perceive their management development needs as being very sophisticated, by virtue of their position, when the reality often is that they, for whatever reason, can't or don't get the basics right. The general problem is not one of establishing new insights but of getting people to convert basic concepts into effective action. This applies to management syllabuses on formal courses. Any introduction to the basic concepts is going to have to cover much the same general ground, whether it be on an undergraduate, professional or postgraduate course, or a National Vocational Qualification (NVQ) at any level. It is only when the basics have been mastered in practice as well as theory that it is appropriate to consider identifying and meeting advanced needs.

The range of topics covered includes general management and the management of people. The range does not extend to areas such as finance and marketing. These areas are not only outside my own particular area of expertise but are also subjects where there is likely to be considerable variation of responsibility between managers. What I believe I have done is to identify a core range of topics that is of relevance to all persons studying or involved in management. The potential scope of managerial responsibility is so wide that the coverage cannot be exhaustive. However, no person with managerial responsibilities can escape the need, for example, to consider such issues as the identification of objectives, prioritisation, managerial style, delegation, motivation, remuneration, communication, selection, training, disciplinary handling, employee relations and chairing and conduct in meetings.

In writing this book I have taken into account the needs of managers and students in and from countries other than the UK. I have for a long time been concerned that teaching and writing should be understandable to people from other countries without detracting from its value to British students. The avoidance of long words when short ones will do is very much in keeping with the theme of the chapter on communication. It means that readers, whether from the UK or from other countries, do not have to translate unnecessary jargon in order to understand the contents of the book. The aim is to help, not to impress.

In considering the needs of readers from other countries I have been able to capitalise on my experience in teaching and discussing management issues in the UK with people from a wide variety of countries. This has particularly included diplomats on the MA in Diplomatic Studies at the University of Westminster. I have also been able to capitalise on my own overseas working experience. This approach is also of benefit to British readers because of the increasing likelihood of their working or dealing with people from different cultural backgrounds or working in different cultural environments. These issues are particularly addressed in the sections dealing with culture in Chapters 3 and 4. The places where I have worked, and thus gained insights into other cultures, include the University of Guyana; a range of private and public sector organisations in Malaysia, including the Mara Institute of Technology; Ngee Ann Technical College in Singapore, where I was external examiner in Business Studies; and Pertamina – the national oil company of Indonesia. My exposure to different cultures and to different nationalities has led me to the conclusion that the bulk of the material in this book is about skills that are needed in a wide range of cultures. Globalisation has increased the international relevance of the material.

Chapter 1

Managers and their background

INTRODUCTION

'Management' has been defined by Mary Parker Follett as 'the art of getting things done through people'.[1] A shorter way of saying the same thing is perhaps that management is 'getting work done through others'. The elements involved in the process of management were identified by Henri Fayol as 'to forecast and plan, to organise, to command, to co-ordinate and to control'.[2] Synthesising this view with later writers, one can identify the basic elements in terms of the 'managerial cycle' as shown in Figure 1.1.

A more recent view of the role of the manager and of the skills involved was provided in a study of management in local government. There is a general relevance in their observation that:

> Management is best defined not as a limited number of 'top' or 'leading' positions, but as a set of competences, attitudes, and qualities broadly distributed throughout the organisation. Management skills are not the property of the few. Effective local authorities will recognise that many jobs which have not conventionally borne the tag 'manager' rely none the less on that bundle of actions – taking charge, securing an outcome, controlling affairs – which amounts to 'managing'.[3]

Many people embark upon their careers without expecting to become involved in management. Nevertheless, they may well find that they gradually accumulate managerial responsibilities. Such people may find that, although they may be designated as specialists, a critical and increasing part of their job is the management of other people. In other cases people may be promoted

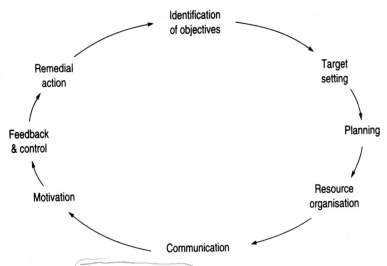

Figure 1.1 The managerial cycle

from a specialist job and given the title 'manager'. They may still be required to make a specialist contribution. The difference between these two sets of people may be that the recognition of the managerial element is gradual in the first instance and more sudden in the other. The actual balance of the activity may be much the same in both instances.

Whatever route people take into management, they still need to discharge their responsibilities effectively. They are much more likely to be effective if they clearly recognise the range and nature of the responsibilities they have acquired. Having identified their responsibilities, the next step is to develop the skills that are necessary to handle them. This first chapter is about the route most people take in entering management. The hybrid nature of many managerial jobs is considered in that they tend to be part specialist and part managerial. The dilemma of the specialist-manager is examined along with the problems this can generate. The causes of these problems are identified, as are remedies and recent developments.

HOW PEOPLE BECOME MANAGERS

The structure of organisations is usually such that most of the employees are engaged on a specialised activity. The number of general jobs involving, for example, the co-ordination of the work of a number of different specialist departments tends to be very limited. The entry into organisations is, I would argue, essentially into specialised activity. People may be engaged at a lowly level in a specialised department. Alternatively they may have advanced specialist skills – that they have acquired either by experience or training, or by a combination of both. This specialist background is the pedigree of the vast majority of managers. This can be demonstrated by probing into the background of almost anyone you know who has managerial responsibilities. Engineering managers come from the ranks of specialist engineers. Bank managers will have previously been engaged in specialist banking activities. Ward sisters or nursing officers will inevitably have a professional nursing qualification. A head teacher will have a teaching qualification. Football managers are invariably ex-professional players. Small business entrepreneurs are usually running a business based on their initial technical skill – for example, in the building trade or as a motor mechanic. In Figure 1.2 I have shown, in a rather simplified form, how specialists can, and often do, become managers.

The amount of time spent on managerial activity is indicated by reading off the level of the shaded area on the vertical scale on the

Figure 1.2 The managerial escalator

left-hand side of the diagram. The balance of activity, much of which may be of a specialist nature, is calculated simply by subtracting the managerial element from 100 per cent. The difference between the amount of time that a person should be spending on managerial activities and the amount of time that they actually spend on these activities is defined as 'the managerial gap'. Initially a specialist may be employed 100 per cent of the time on specialist activity. This may well be after professional training as an accountant, engineer or whatever. The competent specialist may gradually acquire minor supervisory responsibilities – perhaps quite informally. For example, this could be helping newcomers with their job. After five years of competent performance it would not be unusual for a specialist to be promoted. Given the structure of organisations, this usually involves an element of managerial responsibility. An engineer could become a section leader or a bank cashier an assistant officer. After a further five years there could be a further formal promotion, either within the same or another organisation, which could have been preceded by a certain amount of accumulation of managerial responsibility on an informal basis. People tend to be carried along this 'escalator' and may finish with most or even all of their time on the managerial side of the axis. The exact course of progress will vary widely from one person to another. However, the escalator-type progression is a very common way in which people become managers. The managerial activity may well be in a specialist context, but the crucial change is that former specialists may have to spend most of their time managing other specialists, rather than engaging directly in specialist activity themselves.

THE CONFLICT BETWEEN SPECIALIST AND MANAGERIAL ACTIVITY

Nature of the problem

The possession of specialist skills is normally an asset and in many cases quite indispensable. If the person who manages in a specialist environment does not understand it, they will be under a great and perhaps insurmountable handicap. *Management does not take place in a vacuum but in a particular set of circumstances – usually requiring specialist knowledge.* This may be necessary so that instructions are sensible but also to inspire respect in others. However, this specialist pedigree of most managers is at the root of many of the problems that confront them, *particularly the danger of getting the wrong balance between specialist and managerial activity.*

Some of the problems which are likely to arise may now be obvious. A person may have embarked on a career and acquired specialist skills that they are increasingly less able to use. A person may have an emotional commitment to their specialist area and a confidence in that area which may be backed up by several years' formal training. Conversely, the commitment to, and training and aptitude for, the managerial side of the job may all be low. *It would not be unusual for a manager in a specialist environment to have had years of specialist training but only days of management training.* Few managers have a formal management qualification and the managerial content in specialist courses is usually small or non-existent. This inexorably creates the temptation for managers to adjust the balance of their activity so that they concentrate on what they like doing and what they feel equipped to do, at the expense of the managerial aspects of their job. This dilemma can sometimes be revealed by the job titles people use. A colleague of mine, who used to do personnel management advisory work in the civil engineering industry, found that the approach of the senior person on site was often indicated by whether they used the title 'site engineer' or 'site manager'. Job titles can be revealing in many other occupations as well – for example, the choice of the term 'buyer' or 'department manager' in a department store. It could also be that the use of the term 'head teacher' indicates a traditional orientation around teaching rather than the management of other teachers. *The specialist culture that exists in so many organisations is perhaps the biggest single obstacle to effective management.*

The problem has existed in a different form in the British Civil Service. Management in the Civil Service is examined specifically in Chapter 3. However, it is useful at this stage to refer to one of the findings of the Ibbs Report of 1988 which was to the effect that the senior civil servants also had a specialist orientation and background – that of giving policy advice to ministers.

Consequently, very few (top) civil servants have had direct experience of management in large executive organisations. This is reflected when senior civil servants are suddenly put in positions which do have management responsibilities. Either they neglect management, because the immediate pressures are to deal with day-to-day ministerial business, or they go about the management task in a way which shows a lack of confidence and conviction. Many people commented to us that too few senior civil servants showed the qualities of leadership which would be expected from top managers in organisations outside the Civil Service.[4]

Specialist career structures and their limitations

The dilemma of the specialist who is forced into management is accentuated by the difficulty that organisations have in providing alternative career progressions. In some cases it may be possible to get around the dilemma by providing the opportunity for specialist career progression. However, the extent to which this can be done seems to be severely limited in practice as it frequently proves impractical to separate out managerial and specialist duties.

One attempt was made with the non-commissioned ranks in the British Royal Air Force. Separate technical and supervisory career structures were established for the other ranks. Those on the technical side could work their way through the ranks of junior technician up to chief technician. The conventional non-commissioned officer (NCO) ranks were retained. The theory was that those with the technical expertise should concentrate on that side, leaving the supervisory tasks to those within the conventional non-commissioned officer ranks. Problems did, however, arise with this breakdown, in that it was a lot more difficult to disentangle the technical and supervisory roles in practice than in theory. The various levels of technicians still had to brief, instruct and control their subordinates in technical matters. These aspects could not be farmed out to a distant NCO who had no technical knowledge. The non-technical NCOs had their problems too. They tended to accumulate the residual and unpopular supervisory duties to do with parades, guards and general orderly duties. Consequently, the division between the two structures was largely abandoned.

Some companies, such as Imperial Chemical Industries, have found that they have been able to create technical career structures for some people at least. This can provide a means of retaining high-calibre technical personnel and allowing them to concentrate on what they are good at. Another instance in which there has been an attempt to develop a specialist career structure is in the nursing profession, but this also has met with only very limited success. Nurses used to have a clinical career structure, but this created problems of imbalance in that the managerial tasks tended to be ignored. Consequently, drastic changes were made in the nursing career structure.[5] Job descriptions were introduced defining the managerial element in jobs and, once nurses moved from ward sister to the next grade of nursing officer, their jobs were exclusively managerial. Partly as a reaction to this there has been some attempt to recreate senior clinical jobs for nurses. This led to a clinical grading structure that began to be introduced in 1988. However, this scheme has not been without its problems. The constraints include the fact that nurses have to be managed by someone, which means that the senior nurses have to be involved in managerial activity. Also, the demarcation line between the medical work undertaken by doctors and nursing activities means that despite some relaxations of medical boundaries, the scope to develop the clinical nursing role is still quite limited. Consequently, the dilemma of many nurses remains. They will have trained at length for a job for which they have aptitude and emotional commitment. In order to gain promotion they have increasingly to move away from direct clinical involvement. At least in their case, though, these often unpalatable truths are explicitly recognised. The career path is clear and the use of job descriptions and training in nursing management clarifies what nursing officers should be doing.

In some occupations, particularly academic ones, specialists can be required to undertake research as part of their specialist activity. However, meritorious though research is, this can create problems of balance between research and managerial activity. This in turn can generate problems of whether people are to be rewarded for their specialist activity, their research or managerial work. The more senior a person, the greater is the likelihood that their knowledge and expertise is needed to help manage the organisation effectively. Sometimes specialists can develop their own alternative career progression by developing private work. However, this option is not usually available and even in those instances where it is it can cause problems of availability, commitment and promotion blockages for the host organisation.

The essential point is that there are limits to the extent to which specialist and managerial activity can be disentangled. There is undoubtedly room for much more experiment in this area. Also, there is obviously a strong case for giving senior specialists as much clerical and secretarial-type assistance as is practicable. A diary study of the work of head teachers interestingly showed that they spend much of their time on boring, irrelevant or trivial tasks.[6] However, even if appropriate support is given, the dilemma of specialists needing to manage is going to remain. When the separation of managerial from specialist activity is suggested in group discussion on management courses as a solution to the dilemma, I often respond by asking whether the people without specialist knowledge could supervise the people present. The standard answer is 'no', whether it be a high-technology industry like electronics or not. The clear implication of this is that a large part of management activity must be undertaken by specialists.

General consequences

One reason why managers sometimes engage in an inappropriate balance of activities may simply be that they have failed to identify the fact. If the general style is for overconcentration on specialist activity, an imbalance may not be easily recognised by others either, far less be the subject of constructive comment and advice. Sometimes managers can find out the right balance by accident. One who did was the football manager Colin Addison when he was player-manager of Hereford United. He broke his leg and found that, although the team was deprived of a player, overall they benefited because of his enforced concentration on management. The gains that this concentration brought more than compensated for the loss of a member of the first-team squad. It is easy, though, to see why professional footballers may try to combine the daunting tasks of playing and managing. Their reputations will be as players and, if they step down a division or two, they may find that for a while they can cope with both tasks. However, there is a danger that they will fail in both directions. Their playing ability will be on the decline because of age, just as technical specialists moving up the managerial escalator will find that their technical skills are declining. Their selection and support by club directors may be such that they have limited help, and perhaps limited aptitude, for the jobs for which they have been chosen. Under these pressures, and those of trying to learn a new job, probably with a new club, they may 'regress' into doing what they have been historically good at. The more they try in this direction, the more may be their physical exhaustion and retreat from the key area of management. Perhaps a few player-managers can cope with this for a while; others try and fail and still others accept that they have to 'cross over the line' and concentrate full time on management. The same logic applies when players move into the more restricted role of coach.

The example given concerning football management is meant to help explain a general problem. This is that when people are experiencing strain in the managerial part of their job they may seek to avoid this by 'regressing' into their former specialist role. This may provide a temporary refuge, or 'comfort zone' and restore confidence by enabling the person concerned to do what they feel good at. However, like much avoidance behaviour, it is likely to make matters even worse in the long term. A symptom of this may be the eagerness with which a manager insists on 'acting down' when a subordinate is away.

The issue remains that employees, especially those who are likely to acquire management responsibilities, need to have specialist skills in order to be absorbed into the specialist departmental structure that characterises most organisations. A whole host of problems can arise though if the 'weaning' process, whereby those with managerial responsibilities get the right balance of specialist and managerial activity, is not satisfactorily accomplished. This is the recurrent theme of the whole of this chapter. Further examples of what can go wrong if the 'weaning' does not happen abound. A general theme is the propensity of managers to show favouritism in the allocation of resources to their own area of interest and historical specialisation. One example is of the cost accountant who was promoted to a general management position. He continued to give the issue of cost control overriding priority and was unable to adjust to the need to concentrate instead on the need to optimise the difference between income and expenditure. When income-generating opportunities emerged he had great difficulty in authorising even modest expenditure on promising initiatives because he had become conditioned to keeping costs down almost as an end in itself. Another unfortunate and dramatic example concerned the senior officer who 'persuaded' the pilot of a sophisticated military aircraft to allow him to land the plane. As can so often happen with occupational regression, the senior officer did not have the up-to-date expertise nor the recent practice of his junior, and crashed the plane killing two of the crew.

Experience elsewhere

The problem of imbalance between specialist and managerial roles is not confined to any one country. The issues and examples already covered are mainly British. However, some of the material later in the chapter is derived from other developed countries – particularly that relating to the problem of the way managers are selected and trained. I have also tested out these ideas with senior managers from developing countries and found that they have reported an even more alarming pattern. This may be because the inherent problem is accentuated by other factors. These other factors include the rapid promotion that many specialists enjoy in developing countries. This can be caused by the shortage of staff with appropriate skills, the speed with which newly independent countries had to assume responsibility for managing their own affairs and the tendency for employees in state and parastatal organisations to be obliged to retire when they reach 55. This early retirement age not only reduces the pool of available talent, but encourages managers to retain their specialist skills for a post-retirement career.

There are clearly dangers in generalising on the basis of dramatic examples, but it does seem reasonable to suggest that the basic causes of imbalance between specialist and managerial activity operate at least as strongly in developing countries. In the absence of a systematic study to quantify the scale of the problem I invite readers to reflect on the importance of the issue in the light of their own experience and the following examples. In two countries, medical doctors were appointed as Permanent Secretaries to the Minister of Health. There was nothing inherently wrong in that, but there was in their subsequent behaviour – which was to spend about 90 per cent of their time on clinical work. In both cases the Permanent Secretaries had to be removed from their positions. There were many more examples of the same type of imbalance with medical doctors appointed to run hospitals. The managing director of one national airline was an ex-pilot and frequently flew passenger aircraft – especially if there were prestigious people on board! A commissioner of police would patrol the highway checking for unroadworthy vehicles, leaving the staff, who should have been doing it, free to take advantage of the lack of supervision. A scholar who was appointed ambassador continued his scholarly work, leaving the embassy to run itself. The military background of many political leaders can be one of the reasons why preferential treatment is often given to defence budgets. The lack of general management expertise can be particularly unfortunate on large development projects because of the huge sums involved. The way forward for developing countries is for the more effective allocation and management of available resources, which is particularly important given the increasing difficulty of maintaining, yet alone increasing, external aid.

THE CAUSES OF IMBALANCE

The causes of imbalance between managerial and specialist activity have already been partly explained. It is more appropriate, however, to examine the causes in greater detail so that the problem can be more fully understood and strategies for dealing with it identified. There will be factors other than imbalance that lead to poor managerial performance. However, the issue of imbalance has been singled out for detailed examination because of its central importance, the relative lack of attention paid to the issue and the need to avoid ending up with a long list of the largely self-evident other factors that might lead to poor managerial performance. The specific causes of imbalance that will be considered are: selection, personal preference, personality factors, rewards, pressure from subordinates and inadequate training.

Managerial selection

The easiest way to choose a manager is to look at their historical performance and appoint or reject on that basis. The danger in this approach is, however, that there may be critical differences between the duties that a person has performed in the past and those that they may be expected to perform in the future. This is over and above the problems of judging historical performance anyway. If a person is moving from specialist to mainly managerial activity it could mean that they are appointed on the basis of their specialist performance. Whilst this is a legitimate and necessary area to investigate, the person's managerial potential may be more important. Unfortunately, this point may not be properly grasped and, in any case, it is so much easier to assess historical performance rather than speculate about a person's managerial potential. It is, for example, far easier to count the number of international caps that a professional footballer has acquired than judge whether they have the appropriate range of skills to manage a football club. This is no doubt why there are so many disastrous appointments to football management! Experience as a professional footballer may be vital, but there are other factors that may be vital as well – even if they are more difficult to identify – either in the job or in the person. The likelihood of this happening is increased if selectors view an appointment as a reward for past specialist achievements, instead of a need to choose the right person for the future. This syndrome had long been recognised in the engineering industry by the adage that 'it is easy to lose a first-class skilled worker and gain a third-rate supervisor'.

The appointment of managers may prove to be a fairly random affair – the competence of the selectors may mean that it is often a question of luck as to whether the people with the right mix of skills and potential are appointed in the first place. However, those who find that they have emerged through the selection system as managers need to address themselves to the behaviour that will be appropriate, even if those appointing them did not. A further obstacle to appointment on the basis of 'fit' with the job in the UK has, historically at least, been the importance of social class. According to Scase and Goffee the 'skills' that have been traditionally, but perhaps erroneously, associated with leadership

> may be difficult to acquire, if only because they are derived through particular child rearing patterns, education and class-based experiences. The persistence of such styles results from the tendency for senior managers to recruit successors with similar personal characteristics. Such processes militate against the career opportunities of those from working-class origins, of women and of others who have been unable to acquire the intangible but *real* personal attributes of class privilege.[7]

The material in Chapter 9 on selection, particularly the section on equal opportunities, gives practical guidance on how to appoint on the basis of 'fit' with the job.

The problems that can arise as a result of selecting on the basis of historic performance are satirically and amusingly explained in the book *The Peter Principle* by Peter and Hull.[8] Their observations contain more than a germ of truth. The basic concept explained in the book is that if one looks backward in time instead of forward when selecting, people will rise up through organisational hierarchies until they pass their threshold of competence. Only when that has happened will there be no basis for appointment at a higher level of responsibility. The basic Peter Principle is stated to be that 'In a hierarchy every employee tends to rise to his level of incompetence'.[9] Corollaries are that 'in time, every post tends to be occupied by an employee who is incompetent to carry out its duties'[10] and that 'work is accomplished by those employees who have not yet reached their level of incompetence'.[11] This issue is examined further in Chapter 9 in the context of the selection process generally.

Rewards and work preferences

The propensity for people to strive to obtain positions that they cannot or will not handle properly needs some explaining. A basic cause is that the structure of most organisations is such that this may be the only way for employees to gain promotion with the associated increases in pay, status and authority. A further pressure to take promotion may be an antipathy to being supervised by any of the other people who may be appointed to the 'boss' job. Some people may be reconciled to this shift and be able to cope with it. Others may not be reconciled to it and/or may not be equipped to handle it. This may lead to them overconcentrating on the specialist area – either through conscious design or, more likely, because they have never really reasoned it through. The problems may be compounded by the actions and perceptions of their bosses. If the boss has not reasoned it through either, a pattern may be created down the line. Alternatively, even if bosses have reasoned it through for themselves, the appointment of subordinate managers may still be faulty.

Frequently managers concentrate unduly on what they simply enjoy doing. This can happen in many, if not all, managerial environments. On one occasion I was explaining this problem to a group of transport managers; they grasped the point and told me in return that not only did they recognise the phenomenon, but they had a name for it. Supervisors who insisted on driving, ostensibly to 'keep their hand in', were described by them as being 'cab happy'. Ex-pilots are notorious for this and the tendency is reinforced by the requirement that a minimum number of hours must be flown to retain a licence. If this type of activity only happens occasionally perhaps one should not worry unduly – it is when it forms a regular pattern that there is likely to be a serious problem. Sometimes, however, it may be a calculated strategy of having 'the penny and the bun'. The most extreme example I came across of this concerned the head of an educational institution. The gentleman who obtained this job had been attracted to it by the many tangible benefits. Once he had been appointed he announced that as he was an academic he would only undertake academic work. He deemed managerial work to be beneath his intellectual status. The position then arose that the only work he would do he was not given and the only work he was given he would not do! Needless to say the subordinates in this case were not at all amused by this blatant contract violation – particularly as they had to do their boss's job whilst he effectively did nothing. The head did, however, at least provide a perfect example of how a person could get his role completely the wrong way around as far as everyone else was concerned. One has rather more sympathy for people who are sucked into management but who are concerned that, if for any reason they lose their jobs, they will have difficulty in returning to their specialist sphere unless they have kept up to date.

Underlying all this behaviour can be powerful psychological factors relating to individual personalities. Some people may strive for the power that managerial authority can give, regardless of whether or not they are competent to exercise that authority wisely. Sometimes people may actually be in flight from their specialism because they are not very good at it or because they have 'burnt out' in that area. This does not mean that there are not also perfectly valid reasons why people aspire to positions of greater responsibility. The point being made is that it is necessary at the selection stage to try and identify the real reason why people want a particular job and to distinguish between the valid and the invalid.

The fundamental nature of some of the personality factors that may discourage people from applying for managerial positions or 'regressing' when they are in such jobs needs examination. One basic possibility is that extroverts prefer the managerial role, and introverts the specialist activity. To appoint or not to appoint on that basis would be somewhat naive. However, the value system that specialists develop in their formative occupational years and their self-image may be much more bound up with specialist rather than managerial activity. This in turn may conflict with organisational values. Keenan points out that

several authors have noted how the professional values of engineers and scientists, emphasising technical accomplishment, autonomy and public availability of knowledge, are at a variance with the goals of profitability, marketability of products and safeguarding of knowledge which might be useful to competitors.[12]

The conflict between these sets of values may be precipitated by promotion and create considerable stress. Blackler and Shimmin comment that promotion to supervisory or management positions of specialists 'may reduce or remove the opportunity to do the work for which they were trained and with which they identify. Professional and skilled manual workers are particularly prone to this type of conflict, for example, nurses whose contact with patients lessens with increasing seniority and engineers for whom advancement means abandoning technical work for management'.[13] Blackler and Shimmin add that

> The perfectionist, for example, whose self-esteem is tied closely to the idea of a job well done, is likely to be more subject to stress of this kind than someone who is happy go lucky in his or her approach. As Keenan (1980) says of professional engineers 'the successful accomplishment of meaningful technical work is at the centre of their perception of themselves in their jobs.' Consequently, neither work that under-utilises their technical skills nor work that is so demanding that they feel unable to complete it successfully is satisfactory from their point of view.[14]

Those with a professional or scientific training may also, according to Pedler and Boydell, have developed norms of carefulness and certainty, and learnt to avoid conflict rather than develop skills to handle it.[15] There may also be little in their specialist culture to equip them to deal with that key variable – people.

These personality factors can in turn be reinforced by the uncongenial aspects of many managerial roles. This has led Scase and Goffee to coin the phrase *Reluctant Managers*.[16] They refer to the 'emotional hardening' that may be necessary to handle managerial roles. They also comment about changing social values and the increasing desire of managers to balance their work and domestic roles. The stereotype of the male manager with the family's interests subordinated to his career is decreasingly representative. What is more common for managers, as for others, are dual career couples, dependent aged relatives, single parents and divorce (or the danger of it).[17] Additionally, the actual work may be fragmented, managers can be expected to reconcile a mass of conflicting pressures, be poorly serviced and supported and in some cases even receive less than their subordinates. These un-enviable aspects are considered further in Chapter 12 under the sub-heading 'supervisory control'. Unfortunately, there are still more reasons why those with managerial responsibilities might wish to shy away from the managerial aspects of their work. Pressures to reduce overall spending, particularly in the public sector, are another disincentive. Two further factors to be examined in detail are pressure from subordinates and inadequate training.

Pressure from subordinates

The traditions of a particular occupation may influence a manager's behaviour. In teaching, for example, there may be considerable pressure, direct and indirect, by junior teachers, for senior teachers, or for head teachers, to concentrate on teaching. The person in a supervisory position may have to be prepared to resist the pressures of subordinates which could lead to them striking the wrong balance. Such a person may also feel that 'they should not give a job to a subordinate that they cannot do themselves' – a popular but dangerous maxim. There may also be the fear that, unless a direct specialist involvement is retained, the manager will become out of date and perhaps ultimately unable to manage at all. The problem is that, if a person responds to these pressures, they may make matters worse. This can happen in two ways: by interfering in the work of subordinates and also by neglecting the critical managerial aspects of a job.

The pressures by subordinates for a manager to demonstrate competence and interest in their specialist activity can be real enough. However, subordinates may also quite fail to comprehend the other aspects of a boss's job. Additionally, they may resent the 'creaming-off' of the more interesting parts of the job by a boss who wants 'to keep their hand in'. This may be particularly annoying if the boss does this on a random basis so they never quite know what their job is. Situations where you have 'two cooks in the kitchen' may generate more friction than where one cook leaves the other to get on with it and puts up with any adverse comments about the lack of specialist involvement. Specialist knowledge in the work situation is a means to an end and not an end in itself. Managers are likely to be judged ultimately by their results – not by specialist knowledge. The specialist knowledge that managers require is that which enables them to supervise others. If subordinates can do a particular job better than the manager, the manager's skill is in arranging just that state of affairs. To compete with the subordinate, and then fail, is hardly to be recommended. There is a world of difference between a manager having no specialist competence and having sufficient specialist knowledge to supervise subordinates. The latter may be quite sufficient. It would be very nice if all managers knew more about every aspect of the subordinate's job than the subordinate, but it is not very realistic – particularly with changing technology. It may also not do a great deal for the esteem of subordinates. The manager may have to face up to being confronted by a specialist issue that they cannot deal with. Rather than have nightmares about this, it may be that this is simply an issue where the manager re-routes the subordinate to a source where they may get the right information. The emphasis needs to be on seeing that the specialists maintain and develop their skill base rather than on the manager trying to do this.

Ironically this seems to be less of a problem for those operating at the top of an organisation: managing directors are not likely to try to compete with their various specialists. It may be that the structure at the top of an organisation – with, for example, the work of various departments being synthesised by one person – makes it much clearer just what the top manager should be doing. Managers at this level seem to be able to move more easily to a different type of organisation compared with those managers who are at the middle level and managing in a very specific specialist environment. The options for this latter group may be restricted, for example, to managing similar specialist activity elsewhere, but on a larger scale. The freedom to appoint people without detailed specialist knowledge may be subject to considerable variation between different industries. Managing directors in high-technology industries can perhaps only come from within that industry. Even at this level, though, there may be a temptation for the person at the top to devote too much of their time to their favourite area. Managing directors, for example, will invariably have started off by acquiring a specialist skill, even if they have subsequently moved into a career path of running progressively larger companies.

The training of managers

In view of the problems of getting those with managerial responsibilities to discharge them effectively, it is somewhat astonishing to find how little training is given to managers before or after they are appointed. According to Charles Handy this has much to do with the British amateur tradition:

> Management, after all, was held by the British to be akin to parenting, a role of great importance for which no training, preparation or qualification was required: the implication being that experience is the only possible teacher and character the only possible qualification.[18]

This lack of provision was highlighted in two studies published in 1987, one by Constable and McCormick[19] and the other by Handy.[20] Whilst the amount of management qualification training provided by universities and other colleges has undoubtedly increased significantly since these studies were undertaken, it is most unlikely that there has been a comparable increase in in-house provision because of the sustained economic recession since the studies were undertaken. In Constable and McCormick's study it was estimated that as little as one day's formal management training a year was received by managers in post, and that most managers received no formal training.[21]

The situation is made even more gloomy by the problems of providing effective management education and training. Technical and other specialist skills are in general more easily integrated with people's behaviour. The acquisition of knowledge about management does not automatically mean that people become better managers. The personality factors already explained can be a potent reason for people failing to apply what they have learned at an intellectual level. This is often aggravated by the expectation that there are easy prescriptive solutions to most management problems, however complex they may be. A further problem is that a wide range of topics can be passed off as falling within the definition of management education and training. Training can switch to being about management instead of being for managers, and be taught as a set of unrelated theoretical disciplines which can aggravate the problem of the compartmentalisation of management activity. Also, the skills of effective teaching are sophisticated and in short supply and the effectiveness of teaching in this area is difficult to validate. These problems are further considered in the section on management development in Chapter 10.

Another issue that needs comment is the problem of integrating those who have received general management training into organisations. As previously explained, most organisations can only easily accommodate people with specialist skills, because of their departmental structure. Thus, people with general management qualifications find it difficult to gain entry into organisations unless they have also acquired specialist skills. The general pattern remains one of grafting general management skills onto those who already have specialist skills. Ways of dealing with the problem vary, but this has also been an issue in Germany and Japan.[22] In some Japanese organisations the concept has been developed of 'the horizontal fast track in which people of managerial potential are deliberately routed through a variety of functions in their early years'.[23] This is a practice also used in oil companies such as Shell and even in the British Civil Service. However, the 'mandarin' approach in the UK is still based on the concept of the gifted amateur, as explained in Chapter 3. The Japanese approach is more structured and reinforced with analysis of learning and the provision of mentors. Another feature about Japan is that loyalty is to the organisation rather than the specialisation. For a variety of reasons, this included, there is relatively little inter-company movement of managers, which also facilitates a return on investment in management training.

REMEDIES AND DEVELOPMENTS

The lengthy examination of the problem of securing effective management performance goes a long way towards identifying just what needs to be done. The rest of the book is devoted to explaining some of the specific skills that have to be acquired. Of particular importance are the need for careful role definition, selection, training and monitoring, all of which are dealt with in later chapters. It is appropriate, however, at this stage to say a little more about the training and monitoring of managers and developments in the area of management education and training.

Training and monitoring

A key feature of any strategy for correcting imbalance in the job is for those likely to experience the problem to be made more aware of it. They may manage to do this for themselves by learning, perhaps on a trial and error basis. However, training and monitoring of performance, as well as careful selection, can help to ensure that people do not have to learn everything the hard way – or even not at all. The trend towards including a management component in vocational undergraduate and professional courses is a welcome development in this respect. However, any such undergraduate training needs to be reinforced by further training once those concerned have had greater exposure to management problems. Such exposure is likely to lead to an increased awareness of what the problems really are and the concepts and skills that may assist in their resolution. Such further training is not just a matter of going on courses. There is a considerable responsibility for bosses to see that those who are given managerial responsibilities are also given help through appraisal, counselling and coaching. This is particularly necessary when people make critical moves up the managerial escalator. So often people are 'thrown in at the deep end' by managers who have not handled the transitional problems themselves and who blame subordinates for their shortcomings in a new job. These issues are further developed in Chapter 10.

Further developments

The need for effective managerial performance is now becoming more appreciated. Changes within organisations, examined in Chapter 3, particularly pressures for the devolution of financial responsibility, are leading to more explicit recognition of the nature of managerial roles. Areas where this has happened include education, the National Health Service and those organisations which have been privatised. Organisation de-layering is causing significant changes. In police forces, for example, the tradition of rewarding staff for faithful service with nominally supervisory jobs is under attack and the convention of regarding sergeants as 'constables with stripes' is disappearing. With fewer supervisory layers, those remaining are forced into undertaking more managerial activity.[24] De-layering may also force a broadening of roles as the number of specialist advisers is also reduced. This in turn may be contributing to a breakdown of conventional managerial boundaries with managers becoming more multi-skilled, just as skilled manual workers have often had to become multi-skilled. The development of more generic managers has also been precipitated by more flexible management structures and initiatives such as Total Quality Management. This also has the effect of making managers more occupationally mobile.

Sometimes the response to more explicit management pressures has been to give more administrative support to professionals. An example of this is the introduction of 'partnership administrators' in professional partnerships. However, partners cannot expect the administrators to determine policy, future strategy, financial priorities, to resolve conflict between partners and to supervise specialists in the professional aspects of their work. More competitive market conditions, including the emergence of more multi-professional partnerships, mean that effective management is bound to become an increasingly important factor in determining success or failure.

Another, mainly private sector, development has been a great reduction in the number of people employed and their replacement by expensive and sophisticated equipment. However, if this new balance of people and equipment is to be utilised effectively the skilful handling of staff may be just as important. The major need is the wider adoption of the good practices that are evident in the better-managed organisations. The gap between good and bad practice is enormous. The need is not for dramatic breakthroughs in managerial thinking, but for the general application of existing knowledge.

The publication of the 'Handy Report'[25] helped focus attention in the UK on the need for urgent action. This helped precipitate a lively debate about the improvements that were necessary. One of the developments was the Management Charter Initiative. Many of the proposals contained in the original Charter Initiative were welcome and generally supported, such as the need for employers, and the government, to invest more in management education and training. Employers associated with the initiative were also committed to developing networks to achieve this. The mission of the MCI became clarified 'as to improve the performance of UK organisations by improving the quality of UK managers'.[26] The establishment of the MCI also precipitated the competence approach to management development. The term 'competence' is more specific than skill, as it is restricted to job performance standards based on an occupational analysis of the kind used in the National Vocational Qualification (NVQ) approach. What was controversial, however, was the concept of a 'chartered manager' and a regulatory scheme of courses and assessment as the route to membership. There is less talk now about 'chartered managers' and difficulties have been encountered in the attempts to define and assess management competences. The Management Charter Initiative body now has a particular responsibility for developing standards which form the basis of NVQs. Its work and related issues are considered further in the section of Management Development in Chapter 10.

Whilst the case for improving the standards of management is overwhelming, there are specific problems involved in defining standards and in checking that they have been achieved. The concerns about the assessment of management competences include the need for theoretical underpinning, the need for a holistic approach to management, the variety in managerial roles and expectations, the volume of assessments and the problems of making valid assessments anyway. However, there are positive gains to be made by sensible use of the competences approach. The applications will be dealt with further in relation to job evaluation (Chapter 7), selection (Chapter 9) and training and performance-related pay (Chapter 10). The issue is also referred to in examining traditional and situational approaches to leadership in Chapter 4.[27]

The ways in which people need to or do prepare for and enter management are diverse, and the appropriate strategies may need to be diverse. Despite plenty of examples of good practice there is also uncertainty and debate about the ways in which managers are best developed. Whilst it may prove practicable to effect some rationalisation of management education and training, in an age of deregulation it seems highly unlikely that much in the way of a regulated entry into management can make much headway. Specialists who have acquired management responsibility may also not see the need nor be prepared to study for management qualifications. The effective conversion of specialists into being managers of specialists, however, needs to be seen in the context of the need for much more and much better management training generally. Specific strategies for improving managerial performance form the content of the other 12 chapters of this book.

CONCLUSION

The theme of this chapter has been that, at all levels of management, managers are likely to have the task of managing particular activities when there are other things they would prefer to be doing. They will not always realise it if they neglect the managerial aspects in favour of what they like doing. There are a variety of reasons why this should be so. They include poor selection, personality factors, pressure from subordinates, and poor training and monitoring. These issues have been dealt with at length because it is important to understand the causes of ineffective managerial performance if appropriate remedial action is to be taken. It is by an understanding of these problems that one can then go on to develop the appropriate skills to manage effectively, and the rest of this book is intended to give just that help, in a practical and interesting way. The four key issues in this first chapter are the need for the proper definition of managerial roles, selection, development and monitoring. Having identified the need for the proper definition of managerial roles as the first in this sequence it is appropriate that this forms the subject matter of Chapter 2.

NOTES

1   For an account of Mary Parker Follett's work see Pauline Graham, *Dynamic Managing – The Follett Way*, Professional Publishing, 1988.
2   For an account of Henri Fayol's work see Fayol, *General and Industrial Management*, revised by Irwin Gray, Pitman, 1988.
3   Local Government Management Board, *Managing Tomorrow*, Panel of Inquiry report, Local Government Management Board, 1993, p. 8.
4   K. Jenkins et al., *Improving Management in Government: The Next Steps* (the Ibbs Report), HMSO, 1988, p. 24.
5   *Report of the Committee on Senior Nursing Staff Structure* (the Salmon Report), HMSO, 1966.
6   D. Lever and D. Blease, 'What Do Primary Headteachers Really Do?', *Educational Studies*, October 1992.
7   Richard Scase and Robert Goffee, *Reluctant Managers: Their Work and Lifestyles*, Unwin Hyman, 1989, pp. 185–8; emphasis in original.
8   Lawrence Peter and Raymond Hull, *The Peter Principle*, Pan, 1970. Alternatively, see the Souvenir Press edition, 1969, reissued in 1992.
9   Ibid., p. 22.
10 Ibid., p. 24.
11 Ibid.
12 Frank Blackler and Sylvia Shimmin, *Applying Psychology in Organisations*, Methuen, 1984, p. 23. This paraphrases T. Keenan's (1980) work, which is contained in 'Stress and the Professional Engineer', in C. A. Cooper and J. Marshall (eds), *White-collar and Professional Stress*, Wiley, pp. 23, 24.
13 Ibid., p. 25
14 Ibid.
15 M. Pedler and T. Boydell, *Managing Yourself*, Fontana, 1985.
16 Scase and Goffee, op. cit.

17 Ibid.
18 Charles Handy, *The Age of Unreason*, Business Studies Books, 2nd edn, 1991, p. 122.
19 *The Making of British Managers*, a report for the British Institute of Management and the Confederation of British Industry into management, training, education and development, prepared by Dr John Constable and Roger McCormick, BIM, April 1987, Summary, p. 3.
20 Charles Handy et al., *The Making of Managers* (the Handy Report), NEDO/HMSO, 1987.
21 Constable and McCormick, op. cit.
22 Handy et al., op. cit.
23 Ibid., p. 172.
24 Jane Goodsir, 'A New Beat for HR in the Police', *Personnel Management*, December 1993.
25 Handy et al., op. cit.
26 Management Charter Initiative, 'MCI's Mission', *MCI'S 5th Anniversary Review*, 1993.
27 John Constable, 'The Test of Management', *Personnel Management*, November 1990, p. 6; 'Training News: HR Director Doubts Value of NVQs in Professional Jobs', *Personnel Management Plus*, April 1994, p. 9.

Chapter 2

Identifying the manager's job

INTRODUCTION

It follows from the previous chapter that the first essential requirement for managers is to define their job carefully and accurately. Effectiveness depends upon the accomplishment of appropriate objectives rather than just being busy. Consequently, the methodology of objective setting is considered. The technique of role set analysis is also explained. This can be a very effective way of identifying the priorities in a job and it enables comparisons between model and actual time allocations. The technique can also be used on a departmental or organisational basis. Establishing performance indicators can be a useful way of seeking to measure organisational effectiveness. Careful identification of the job is also a necessary foundation for effective time management. The basic elements of time management are covered. It is not enough for managers to plan just their own work systematically. If this is to be accomplished they also need to help develop a rational framework within which to operate. Consequently, the need for effective long-term and corporate planning is considered.

ACTIVITY VERSUS EFFECTIVENESS

One of my own earliest observations about managers was that they tend to fall into two groups: those who define what has to be done, get on with it and then go home; and those who create a flurry of physical activity and seek to justify their positions by the demonstrable effort they put into a job, rather than by the results they achieve. The latter group also tends to be reactive rather than innovative in their responses. The emphasis on effort tends to combine neatly with a reactive 'management by crisis' approach. There can, perhaps, be some of this in most managers but it is still useful to consider the different approaches. Sometimes the attempts at self-justification are a combination of humour, pathos and ineffectiveness. I have in mind here such managerial games as: never going home until the chief executive has left, working overtime for the sake of it and seeking to demonstrate to colleagues that you have worked later than them. Such stratagems may or may not work in the short term. It may even be that in some cases they are necessary political ploys, given that there will be political activity in any organisation. However, the great danger is that, if managers spend too much time simply justifying themselves, they may actually fail to diagnose what they should be doing and therefore fail to do it. Ultimately, managers are much more likely to be judged by results than by anything else. Activity-centred behaviour is in any case much more likely to spring from incompetence and/or insecurity rather than adroit political behaviour. This type of behaviour is likely to aggravate the position of the manager in the long run rather than ameliorate it.

What is work?

One point that needs to be established at this stage is just how people define 'work'. A notion that I have repeatedly come across is that work is synonymous with physical activity. This misconception can have most unfortunate consequences, particularly in the job of a manager. One manifestation of this misconception is when shop-floor workers have applied for various white-collar positions. The mental activity of a clerk or rate-fixer or supervisor simply may not be perceived by a person used to manual work, because such mental activity is not overt. A person who applies for a white-collar job, labouring under this delusion, may find out too late that the mental activity may be far more demanding than the physical activity to which they have been accustomed.

I remember one occasion when a steelworker in a television interview referred to a particular Secretary of State and complained that 'she had never done a day's work in her life'. This is a criticism that is often levelled at people in such positions. However, whatever one thought of that particular Secretary of State, one could hardly sustain an argument that she was not hard working. A further example, to illustrate this point, was volunteered by one of my students on a course in hospital ward management. She related an incident when she had noticed a patient fall into a coma. At the time she was the staff nurse on that particular ward and knew that this patient was on a special diet. She stopped what she was doing to try to puzzle out if the staff who would administer drip feeding to the patient would be aware of his special dietary needs. Her mental activity was soon interrupted by the ward sister, who brusquely asked her what she thought she was doing, just standing there, and told her to get on with her work!

The recurring problem is that it is obvious when people are working at a physical level, but less obvious when they are engaged in what is likely to be more crucial mental activity. This is compounded by the fact that you can have staff just standing around day-dreaming and not engaged in mental problem-solving activity. Also, the tradition of judging manual workers by their rate of physical activity is something which can carry over into judgements about whether managers are working or not. It may be that managers have, to some extent, to respond to this type of pressure by demonstrating physical activity. It may be crucial though to their effectiveness that they do not overreact to such pressure. Managers need also to make this distinction when they are assessing, and perhaps pressurising, their own subordinates.

THE IDENTIFICATION OF THE MANAGER'S JOB

Perhaps the first thing that any manager needs to do is actually to identify their job. This should be seen as a continuous process rather than a one-off activity. Organisations have to change in order to survive and the jobs of managers need to alter accordingly. This is why, if a manager has a job description, it should be seen as a starting point for identifying the job rather than a definitive unalterable document. Job descriptions, whilst being useful, may leave considerable room for interpretation; they will also need updating. They suffer too from the deficiency that they usually do not give a clear indication of the priorities in a job. There are likely to be other ways in which managers identify and adjust their jobs. They are hardly likely to be left completely to their own devices – there will obviously be instructions from superior managers. In some cases the remit for a manager will be very specific and the problem will primarily be one of doing the job rather than of identifying what needs to be done. In other cases – perhaps where there is significant internal and external change – the manager may need to spend a considerable amount of time defining and redefining what needs to be done. A further guide may be the way the work was performed by a previous incumbent. It would be folly to ignore the way a previous incumbent had performed a job, but perhaps equally foolish not to review their interpretation of a job nor to allow for changed circumstances. There can in any case be considerable misunderstanding about just what is done before one gets to the question of just what needs to be done. In my own experience I have found that it is usual for there to be significant surprises when the purpose and content of jobs are actually clarified. Usually the job holder will find that they are undertaking some tasks of which their boss is unaware. It is also likely that there will be some tasks that they are expected to do of which they are unaware. One of the reasons for these misunderstandings is that the boss may have never fully appreciated the demands of the job. Alternatively, they may have appreciated these demands at a previous time, or even have done the job at one stage, but may be basing their view on what was historically done rather than what is subsequently needed.

Short-term pressures and long-term needs

Much of a manager's time will be devoted simply to responding to pressures and demands from other people. The in-tray tends to dominate the daily pattern of activity. Whatever a manager wants to do in the long term is all very well, but often cannot be contemplated until the short-term pressures have been dealt with. However, there are dangers that a manager will simply react to short-term pressures and not think out what they should be doing from a long-term point of view. This problem can be exacerbated by developments in information technology such as e-mail. These can make the manager too available – whether at work or at home. Managers are less likely than before to have personal secretaries to act as filters or, if they still do, it may be possible for people to bypass the secretary electronically. Consequently, there may be an even greater need for managers to consciously prioritise. Managers may also fall into a particular pattern of responding to certain short-term pressures and ignoring others. It is necessary to periodically review such patterns to see if they match the needs of the situation.

Responding to a predetermined selection of short-term issues can become a way of life for some managers. In some cases this may be because of the sheer pressure on a manager, in other cases because they want to avoid certain issues. One problem with this approach is that some of the issues that are left are important; moreover, if the manager thought things out on a long-term basis then some of the short-term pressures might be reduced or eliminated. Managers have to react to some, at least, of the short-term pressures. However, it can be very easy to fall into a pattern of just doing this, with possibly disastrous results on long-term effectiveness. Managers need to compare what they are doing in the short term with what they should aim to be doing. This issue is one that managers are not always prepared to face.

In a study of the way 160 managers actually performed their jobs, Rosemary Stewart observed that:

> A fragmented day is often the laziest day; the day that demands the least in terms of mental discipline, though the most in nervous energy. It is easier to pass from one subject to a second when the first requires a difficult or unpalatable decision, or sustained thought. It is easier to respond to each fresh stimulus, to hare after the latest query, than to set an order of priorities and try to keep to it. This, of course, includes knowing when the latest query has priority. It is easier to be a grasshopper jumping from one problem to another, than a beaver chewing away at a tough task.[1]

The identification of objectives

As has already been indicated, the reverse of the reactive activity-centred approach of managers is one where objectives are carefully identified and then, hopefully, achieved. A consequential benefit can be that the manager's time is allocated in proportion to the priority of a task. Reactive managers may find, assuming they ever think in these terms, that they have failed to match the time available to the key elements in their jobs. Management writers who have made historically important contributions to this issue include Peter Drucker[2] and John Humble.[3] Peter Drucker appears to be the first person who used the term 'management by objectives', whilst John Humble developed the idea into a systematic method of management, not just for the individual manager but for the total organisation.

'Management by objectives' was very fashionable in the late 1960s and early 1970s. However, it was very often applied in a simplistic manner. There was little stress in the literature on how to handle the conflicts that can emerge between individual and organisational objectives. There may also have been exaggerated expectations of what could be achieved when all managers were required to participate in a 'total' scheme.

Despite the demise of 'management by objectives' there is still merit in examining the concepts on which it was based. The crucial, and still very relevant, question it invited managers to ask was just *why* they were doing a particular job or task. It is all too easy to say what one is doing rather than why. Answering the question 'why?' can produce surprising results. The following *Evening Standard* report, whilst not an example of a managerial job, makes the appropriate point:

> Night watchmen at Westminster Council House in Marylebone Road protecting the Council's silver plate, cost ratepayers £21,000 last year. Clever economists at the Council now think that the resident caretaker may be able to handle the job alone. They have discovered that the silver was moved elsewhere years ago.[4]

The identification of the key tasks that are contained in a job does present some advantages over the conventional type of job description. Job descriptions can, by their length and detail, obscure the key elements in a job. Humble also advocated that every manager needed to define the six to eight key tasks that needed to be accomplished if the overall job objective was to be achieved. It was argued that if this was done the residual detail in a job would fall into place. The minimum acceptable standards of performance were also specified. These were accompanied by quantitative and qualitative standards including cost limits and time deadlines. It may still be a useful exercise for managers to go through this type of exercise on an individual basis. Such a methodological approach needs to form the basis of performance management, as the essential first step is to have some criteria for judging what performance should be and then measuring it, either on an individual or collective basis. The concept of performance management and its links with appraisal are dealt with in more detail in Chapter 10.

The 'management by objectives' approach also has relevance,

and in some ways broad similarities, to the establishment of organisational 'performance indicators'. These are increasingly used, especially in the public sector. The special relevance to the public sector is because of the absence of the criterion of profit or loss. As is explained in the next chapter, there is much more emphasis now on ensuring that public services are customer-orientated. Consequently, key criteria are measures of customer satisfaction, e.g., with regard to service response times and the achievement of appropriate quality standards. Total Quality Management (TQM) initiatives also need to start from the basis of clearly defined objectives and they involve the specification of product and, where appropriate, customer service performance standards. This topic is also covered in the next chapter. Another similar approach is for organisations to produce mission statements. This involves defining the purpose of an organisation, where it plans to go, and the principles that will enable it to achieve its purpose. This may be supplemented by a statement of the organisational core values that underpin the mission statement.

At this point it is appropriate to make some comment about the way in which these various ways of defining objectives, priorities and measures of performance may operate in practice. As has previously been explained, a basic reason why 'management by objectives' schemes failed was that they were applied in a simplistic manner. Many managers make the naive assumption that employees will automatically subscribe to the organisational objectives, strategies and priorities that are pronounced by senior management. This is in line with a 'unitarist' view of organisations. Alan Fox very lucidly explains how, if one takes the pluralistic view of organisations, one sees that policies that may be to the advantage of an organisation as a whole may not always be to the liking or in the interests of particular groups or individuals within that organisation.[5] If, for example, labour-saving economies can be achieved, then those people who are going to be the subject of those economies may say that it will be all very well for those who remain in an organisation but what about those who are made redundant as a consequence?

Other conflicts may be less obvious and dramatic, but nevertheless important. Staff may not, for example, co-operate in reorganising their work to accommodate new organisational priorities if that conflicts with individual priorities. This means that attempts to focus organisational activity, so that it is more effective, may be limited by the ability of managers to resolve such conflicts. This is going to be particularly difficult to do if managers, because of their unitarist philosophy, can't see the potential conflict of interests. Admittedly, in a hostile economic climate there may be some lee-way to coerce employees into accepting change, but organisational initiatives usually need active co-operation if they are to succeed, not minimalist grudging acceptance. When 'management by objectives' was introduced it was usually accompanied by systematic attempts to involve the individuals concerned. Whilst this is a feature of the TQM approach, other attempts to refocus organisa-tional activity may be attempted with little or no regard on how to win the active co-operation of the staff. Consequently, many of the statements relating to organisational purpose may just be the pious expression of what senior management *hopes* will happen, rather than effective planning tools to ensure that aspirations are actually achieved. Another technique for identifying the priorities in a job or organisation is that of role set analysis. This technique is explained in the next section. The related concept of long-term and corporate planning is explained in the final section of this chapter.

ROLE SET ANALYSIS

An alternative or additional technique that may help managers check whether they are using time effectively is role set analysis. The technique involves using a market research approach to one's job. The raw data consists of the expectations of the main individ-uals and interest groups with whom one has to interact. Instead of identifying one's job by saying 'what should I be doing?' the starting point is to say 'what do others expect of me?'. In order to do that one first of all has to identify just what the main elements in the role set are. The process of identifying the expectations of the members in the role set may be undertaken by analysing data already available and, where appropriate, actually checking out with people what the expectations are. The next stage is to synthesise this raw data, and the often conflicting pressures, into a coherent form. This is done by presenting the information in chart form, as shown in the example of the head of personnel (Figure 2.1).

The key activities, people and groups with whom a manager has to work have to be identified. The chart needs to indicate the volume of work that is appropriate for each constituent part and

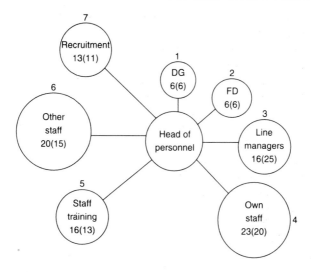

Key: DG = Director-General
     FD = Finance Director

Figure 2.1   Role set analysis for head of personnel of a professional organisation

also the priorities. It needs to be remembered that there may be some particularly influential members of the role set with whom contact is infrequent but very important when it does occur. The diagram should be drawn so that the more important a member of the role set, the closer they are located to the person at the centre. The next step is to see that the time and priority allocated to the elements in the role set are in line with what is actually needed. To do this effectively it is best for the person concerned to keep a diary of how they really spend their time over a few representative days. The actual time allocation to the individuals and groups in the role set can then be compared with what is considered desirable (see specimen figures in Figure 2.1).

Actual time spent is shown as a percentage with the model time given in the accompanying brackets. The model percentages add up to 96 per cent, as 4 per cent is planned 'slack'. Alternatively, time can be shown in hours and minutes. This will enable reductions or increases in the total working time to be shown. The other numbers represent the rank order of importance of the individuals, groups or activities to the head of personnel.

The above example is based on the job of head of personnel of a professional organisation employing approximately 500 people. Two personnel officers are also employed. Contact with external visitors has been subsumed under the subject of their visits, namely, recruitment and training. The head of personnel reports to the finance director. The analysis prompted a series of basic questions, which was the purpose of the exercise. The appropriateness of the head of personnel reporting to the finance director is one such question. Others include whether the head of personnel is spending enough time with the line managers and too much with his own and other staff. Proposed adjustments in time allocation are shown in the new model allocations. Time spent working on the head of personnel's own was allocated according to whose behalf it was on. However, what also emerged was the need for some time for general reflective thought about the job.

Whilst a role set diagram may reveal misjudgments about the model time allocations it may, as in the case of the head of personnel, reveal that the actual time allocations need reviewing. That this should often be the case is not very surprising, particularly bearing in mind some of the points made in the previous chapter about managers and their backgrounds. Additionally, it is all too easy, for example, for those who have easy physical access to a manager to claim a disproportionate share of their time. A manager may also find the people have expectations of them which they do not perceive as being legitimate. It may then be up to the manager to renegotiate this situation or to use their political guile to alter the expectations, or even ignore them. Managers may also prefer spending their time with some individuals or groups because their social and/or professional company is found to be more enjoyable than that of other individuals or groups. Role set analysis may demonstrate the need for the manager to make a conscious effort to give an appropriate share of their time to those people who work outside their department or to clients or other people who are external to the organisation. It may be found particularly necessary to spend time building bridges with individuals or groups with whom one tends to be thrown into conflict rather than just taking the short-term solution of avoidance.

In estimating the amount of time that other individuals or groups require of your attention it is necessary to remember that one can allocate too much time, as well as too little. Subordinates can feel 'over-supervised' and those in senior positions to oneself may have as their objective not spending too much time with you! However, having said this, it is obviously potentially damaging to spend less time with one's boss in particular than they deem appropriate. It is also necessary to consider what time one needs for oneself – particularly for reflective thought. Diary analyses by managers usually reveal that it is very difficult for them to arrange periods when they can engage in concentrated work or reflective thought without interruption. Such time may, however, be essential if one is to do long-term thinking about a job. Appropriate refinements to the role set diagram are to allow a percentage of time for oneself as well as for 'others', who will invariably take up a share of one's time.

Amongst the benefits that can be obtained from this method of analysis is that it may show whether or not a job is viable as currently structured. There may be so many individuals and groups the manager has to interact with that the job may be impossible. Alternatively, the manager may be tackling their job in an inappropriate way. One example of this was the manager who, having used this technique, revealed that he was dealing directly with his subordinate's subordinates instead of just with his own subordinates. Whether problems are organisational or of the manager's own making there may also be health implications if the manager has a pattern of interaction which is just too much to cope with. For example, on a management development workshop a participant revealed that he suffered from angina. His role set analysis demonstrated that he was grossly overloaded and that his part of the organisation needed restructuring – a factor which cannot have helped his health problems and may have even precipitated them.

The emphasis in this section has so far mainly been about working out appropriate time allocations. The technique can also be used though to consider how other resources should be allocated. Managers can also review their budget distribution in this way. An interesting example of the application of this type of thinking with regard to organisational priorities concerns a change in strategy by the London Metropolitan Police Service announced in 1987. Faced with the dilemma of limited resources to deal with an increasing amount of crime, the Commissioner reviewed the allocation of resources to the various types of crime. He judged that the public were particularly concerned about acts of violence against the person, such as sexual assault and mugging and, in comparison with these crimes, less concerned about car thefts. Consequently, the deployment of police resources was adjusted in line with these perceived public priorities. Subsequently, a points scheme was developed to help decide which of the less serious crimes were investigated and which were not. Offences that might realistically lead to successful detection and conviction were allocated resources in preference to cases where this was less likely. The amount of available evidence was considered particularly important in allocating points. Consequently, aspects such as the quality of the description of a person, the noting of a car number or the possibility of forensic evidence could be crucial in determining whether a crime was investigated or not. The method of prioritisation was essentially a formalisation of the general way in which the Metropolitan Police had previously allocated resources.[6]

However, there were particular problems in operating this policing system, especially as it was made so explicit, and it was formally abandoned in 1989. Factors leading to this change were public concern about the high volume of crime which was 'screened out' and the danger that crime could increase if it was generally known that most crimes would not be fully investigated. There was also the need to recognise the importance of the public in the role set because of the critical need for their co-operation with the police. The experiment, however, is of interest as it shows both how the technique can be applied and, in this case, its limitations. Additionally, it shows the need for discretion in revealing the results of one's role set analysis. In whatever area the technique is used, those who emerge low down on the list of priorities are likely to feel disgruntled, however powerful the arguments for a particular scale of priorities. The point also needs making that even given the formal abandonment of the points system by the Metropolitan Police Service a basis still has to be found of allocating scarce resources to deal with an overloaded service.

A blunt way in which individual managers can identify priorities is to ask themselves who is in the position to do them the greatest damage? The leader of an architectural group, when asked to do a role set analysis on this basis, likened it to the theory of 'damage limitation', which is one way of viewing it. The value of doing this is to see that those who can do one the greatest damage are top of the list in getting their share of the time. It is also of value, as will shortly be explained, in working out what to do if one comes under conflicting pressures. Alternatively, the question can be asked 'who can help the manager most?', and time allocated accordingly – though it is to be hoped that this approach is not used too opportunistically.

Establishing the order of importance in the role set is not always as easy as it seems. One training officer gave the example of how he mistakenly thought the most important member of his role set was the managing director of a company he once worked for. The training officer had numerous differences of opinion with his immediate boss and sought to overcome the bad working relation-ship by going over the head of his boss, the company secretary, to the managing director. The company secretary became aware of this and as a counter-measure started giving bad reports about the training officer to the managing director. Consequently, the more the training officer went to the managing director the greater the number of bad reports there were of him. The managing director, faced with a choice, understandably preferred to accept the view of the more strategically placed company secretary. Ideally, of course, he should not have allowed the training officer to bypass the company secretary, but that is what actually happened. Eventually the training officer, prompted by good advice from other colleagues, came to realise that the most important person in his role set was the company secretary. In the end he did what he should have done in the first place, in his particular case, which was to work on improving his relationship with his immediate boss! This illustrates the important point that it is not the most senior person in an organisation who is necessarily the first in importance in one's role set. The view senior people have of you may well be important, but it is necessary to work out whose word they take into account when forming their opinion of you. It isn't however just people of high status who may be in a position to inflict 'damage' on a manager. Often people in low-status positions, but who control important and perhaps scarce services, can do the same. So too may those who control access to important information or who act as 'gatekeepers' to senior managers.

Informal members of role sets may also need to be identified, assessed and handled in terms of their importance. A failure to do this effectively allegedly contributed to the enforced resignation of President Reagan's Chief of Staff, Donald Regan, in 1987. The informal member of the role set was said to be the President's wife, Nancy Reagan, and press reports suggested that on one occasion Donald Regan 'put the phone down on her'. It was also suggested that Donald Regan relied too much on his relationship with the

President and not enough on the other powerful political figures in the role set. The other members may not have been individually as important as the President but collectively their influence was considerable, especially if it was reinforced by the views of the First Lady.[7] The extent to which these reports are true or untrue is unimportant as far as the basic point is concerned – the need for careful identification of the role set and appropriate responses based on that analysis.

There are further ways in which information can be collected about role sets. The technique can be a very useful device for getting people to talk about common problems on in-house management workshops. If syndicates of managers doing similar jobs are arranged they can critically cross-examine one another about the appropriateness of one anothers' role set analysis. I have found that this invariably generates a searching discussion of issues that need airing. Workshops can provide a climate in which basic issues, which would not otherwise be discussed, are brought out into the open. The technique of role set analysis can have a powerful catalytic effect in this context. Another method of collecting information is for a manager to take a market research approach and ask colleagues just what their expectations of them are. Care has to be taken, however, about who is approached and the manner of the approach. One of the potential problems is that expectations are aroused which cannot be met. As a minimum, though, one should reflect on just what are the expectations of you by the other individuals and groups in your role set. This may reveal a variety of misunderstandings about what you expect from others and what they expect from you.

What also may be revealed is that some of the expectations are contradictory. This may happen if the manager is given incompatible tasks or if the sheer volume of work they are expected to do is unrealistic. The most practical way of handling such a dilemma is often for managers to try to gauge what the real priorities are amongst the welter of instructions they are given. They also need to be sensitive to changes in organisational priorities. Those senior to a manager may be reluctant to admit that the various requests are in conflict. Therefore, the reality may be that the individual manager has to work out what the real priorities are at a given time. To do this the manager may need to judge just what the priorities are with others in the role set and the ways in which they may be changing. In an ideal world one would work only in organisations where job demands were compatible and all legitimate expectations could be met. However, as we live in an imperfect world it is just as well to have a method of resolving contradictory pressures. It is also as well to recognise that when changes in priorities occur it is often politically too difficult for policy-makers to say that a certain priority has been abandoned, or even downgraded. The most one may get is an admission that a certain objective has been 'put on the back burner'. However, managers ignore these shifts in priority at their peril, as otherwise they may be failing to adjust their pattern of activity to a new scale of priorities.

The pressures for competitiveness in the private sector and for economy in the public sector are putting managers under increasing stress. Consequently, they usually cannot do all that is expected of them and have to develop some basis for deciding how their own time and the resources under their control are allocated. If not everything can be done, it seems far more logical to consciously and systematically prioritise rather than do things on a random basis. Individual survival and organisational effectiveness are both likely to be served by conscious prioritisation. The best way of coping with managerial stress is to try and reduce the stress rather than dealing simply with the symptoms. Techniques of prioritisation can be enormously useful in this context and also in relieving managers of guilt feelings about not meeting what may be impossible demands. The issue of managerial stress is dealt with further in Chapter 6, and the organisational problems caused by the mismatch between expectations and resources in the public sector in Chapter 3. The issue of individual prioritisation is dealt with further in the next section of this chapter.

What has been explained is a progressively more sophisticated method of gathering data and developing insight about how to identify one's job. After all this has been done, it is up to the manager to evaluate and synthesise the material and stamp their own personality on the job. There is more to identifying a job than working out what those in strategic positions want of you – but it is, to say the least, prudent to take that into account before then adding the essential ingredient – one's own personality.[8] The concept of role set analysis also stresses the interdependence of managers with others. The importance of the manager's role in creating and energising teams is examined in the context of organic structures in Chapter 3, with regard to managerial style in Chapter 4 and in handling meetings in Chapter 13.

TIME MANAGEMENT

When the overall objective key tasks and role set have been clarified it may then be appropriate for a manager to consider how effectively their time is used. One view of the manager's job is that the only real resource is their time. There appear to be enormous variations in the ways in which managers either use their time effectively or squander it. Consequently, this topic deserves specific attention. Issues of particular importance are the identification of priorities, the logical sequencing of work and the need for managers to avoid wasting other people's time.

Identifying priorities

The reactive or 'grasshopper' manager may fail in their management of time in the first instance by failing to identify the priorities in their job. Perhaps the worst way of prioritising work is to deal with the last request first, whether it be made in person or be the item just received in the in-tray! Sadly, there are many examples of people who do this regularly. The priorities of a job need to be established quite consciously. To do this it may be necessary to write them down and then either to rank the priorities over a particular time period or to group them into bands of varying urgency. Even well-organised managers will find that they have to react to the short-term crises and pressures that they meet in their day-to-day jobs, but they should have as a constant reference point a clear grasp of the priority issues that are accumulating and which merit attention.

The identification of the priorities in a job may reveal fundamental issues about the appropriate balance of activity. Some interesting examples of this at an organisational level concern police and medical work. The police have consciously looked at the balance between crime detection and crime prevention. The same type of issue arises with medical work in trying to strike the right balance between health cure and health care.

Finding the time to think about the job may itself constitute a problem, particularly for managers who are already heavily involved in 'fire-fighting' activities. However, unless they somehow find the time to think their way through to a more rational pattern of activity, they are unlikely to be effective. One of the problems in organisations is that managers find that they have to cope with so many interruptions that it is difficult to find time to think in a concentrated and systematic way about the job. It may be necessary to do this away from one's normal place of work or to use a secretary or other person as a screen to prevent interruptions. It may also be necessary to have a clear idea of who those people are who make unproductive claims on one's time with a view to reducing the time spent with them. It is one of the ironies of organisational life that so often the people with the most time to waste are those who insist on spending long periods telling you how busy they are! In such cases it may be particularly necessary to tell people at the start of a discussion how much time you have available for them.

Establishing the priorities in a job may well involve a careful look at the conflict between what a manager prefers to do and what they actually need to do. This is a necessarily recurring issue in this book. I found that I had to face up to much the same issue when I was an undergraduate student preparing for my examinations. The subjects which I enjoyed revising were those at which I was good but where the scope for improvement was consequentially least. After much anguish I decided that I really had to spend most of my time working on those subjects which I liked least, but where the potential for improvement was greatest.

The personnel policies of organisations unfortunately do not always help people take a balanced approach in their job. In one local authority building department all the charge-hand craft-workers were upgraded to be general trades supervisors. The idea was sound enough in principle – which was to avoid having a charge-hand craft-worker on every site where craft-workers of that particular trade were working. Unfortunately, the idea was poorly implemented. There was no attempt to select who should be upgraded and who should not. Neither was there any attempt to train the newly appointed general trades supervisors, either in management or in the technical aspects of the new trades that were nominally under their control. Consequently, most of the newly appointed general trades supervisors were too frightened to supervise craft-workers in trades other than their own. This meant that, for example, the person who had previously been a charge-hand bricklayer spent nearly all their time with the bricklayers and rarely tried to supervise the craft-workers in the other groups such as the electricians, plumbers and carpenters.

Sequencing work

Once the priorities of a job have been clearly identified, it is then necessary to consider whether or not they need to be tackled in a particular sequence. This will be particularly necessary if time may run out. The domestic example, which illustrates this point, is that it is more appropriate for people pressured for time in the morning to get dressed before they eat breakfast. It is much more practicable to run down the road for the train fully clothed but with breakfast unfinished rather than the other way around!

The need for careful sequencing was brought home to me by the simple but apt example of two delivery drivers. One driver would look at the first address and drive off and then look at the next address and so on. In the course of a day he was likely to retrace his route several times. The other driver would spend about an hour each morning planning his route so that, although he started his deliveries later, he covered his route with the minimum mileage. Another issue that needs to be taken into account is the need to give time for ideas to be mulled over. It is not just the speed at which issues are dealt with that is important, but also the quality of any decisions. Some managerial judgements are likely to be better if preceded by reflective thought. The thought may not even need to be conscious, as ideas can suddenly fit into place after subconscious mental activity. Students can also find this when answering examination questions. A difficult question that is put on one side, whilst an easier one is tackled, may appear much simpler when it is read for the second time a while later. However, the manager needs to recognise the difference between mulling over difficult issues, so that an appropriate decision is eventually taken, and procrastination.

Critical path analysis

The concept of logical work sequencing can be developed further by the use of the technique of 'critical path analysis'. This is of particular use in planning and controlling tasks where a number of activities need to be carried out simultaneously. The technique has been developed particularly for use on construction projects and production planning. The benefits of this technique did not live up to early expectations because of the unforeseen variables, failures in communication and competing agendas that can affect any project and frustrate mechanistic planning systems. However, the technique, if used carefully, can be and often is a powerful planning tool. It can also be of value for individual work planning. It is often used intuitively by people who have never heard of the term 'critical path analysis' – for example, when the Sunday joint is put to roast whilst the rest of the dinner is prepared. Alternative titles for the same concept are 'network planning' and 'network analysis'.

An example of how the technique can be used in launching a new product is shown in Figure 2.2. One assumes that the starting point is the announcement and launch of the new product; the market research and design having been previously undertaken. The packaging would then be designed, and the dealers could be contacted at the same time to prepare them for the new product. When the packaging is designed it can then be ordered from the supplier. The publicity material can then be designed (not before, as one would want to see the packaged product first). When the packaging is received and orders received from the dealers the product can be delivered. A further step in the planning can be to show the time period during which each step of the process needs to be completed. Although the example is simple, the written explanation is complicated and difficult to follow. In contrast, the diagram is very clear – as in the proverb 'a picture tells a thousand words'.[9]

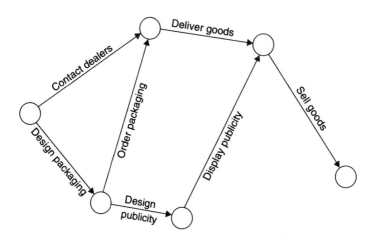

Figure 2.2   Critical path analysis: launching a new product

Fatigue

It is also necessary for managers to take into account their own physical limitations in planning their workload. Individuals vary considerably in their propensity to fatigue, and fatigue also depends on the commitments a manager has outside the workplace. It can be very tempting to compare oneself to a person with an unusually high degree of energy, but the consequences may be disastrous if workload is planned on an over-optimistic assessment of what one's physical capabilities really are. If this happens it seems likely that in the long term the quality and rate of work will suffer and the likelihood of illness increase. This is certainly the evidence of studies on long hours of work for manual workers, and it would seem a common sense step to assume that the same pattern would affect managers. Maier reports on an interesting British Medical Research Council study of the effects of an increase in the working week in 1940 after the Dunkirk evacuation.

> Under the pressure of the World War II emergency, England increased its work-week. Before Dunkirk, the work-week was 56 hours; after Dunkirk it was increased to an average of 69.5 hours in the war industries. The first effect of this increase was a 10 per cent rise in production, but then production declined, and sickness, absenteeism, and accidents increased. By the end of a couple of months, the average work-week was 68.5 hours, but the average amount of time actually worked was only 51 hours, as compared with the period before Dunkirk when the average time worked per week was 53 hours. As a result, production was 12 per cent below that preceding Dunkirk. Six months later, the shorter week was restored, with the result that production steadily rose to a higher point than ever before.[10]

Maier also reports on Angela Masso's studies on fatigue. The results of these studies may have considerable implications for the way people, including managers, pace themselves at work. One concerned the ability of a person to move a six-kilogram weight attached to a free finger by a length of string. It emerged that if the movement was repeated every two seconds an individual would cease to be able to lift the weight at all after about a minute. However, if the movement was only repeated every 16 seconds the weight could be raised and lowered almost indefinitely.[11] A particular point that needs stressing is that recovery time from fatigue tends to increase exponentially with the amount of the fatigue. What this means is that when practicable, one should rest as soon as there are signs of fatigue, otherwise recovery can take so much longer. Performance may be unduly affected if one continues working once there are signs of fatigue.

General

In planning one's activity it is also necessary to recognise that people meet social as well as work needs when they are doing their job. An overplanned approach to the job may be too inflexible, and it can also make life dreadfully dull. Additionally, it may be necessary to spend some time maintaining working relationships by a certain amount of social conversation. There are obviously limits to the extent to which this should be done, but it could be foolish to ignore this aspect. Managers also need to pace themselves at work and it may be necessary to have some periods in the working day when they relax a little. However, relaxation needs to be done in such a way that it does not interrupt those who are working effectively. Managers also need to help others use their time productively, as well as organising their own time management. This can, for example, mean careful preparation for discussions and interviews so that the time of the other people involved is not wasted.

Prior preparation is particularly important if one has to chair a meeting, as will be explained in more detail in Chapter 13 on meetings and chairing. Let it suffice at this point to give the example of a local government body where 23 people from different parts of London were called to a meeting that had to be aborted because it had not been properly planned. One's potential to waste the time of colleagues can, therefore, be even greater than the potential to waste one's own. A final point that needs making is that at times the volume of activity confronting a manager can seem quite overwhelming. However, they cannot tackle everything simultaneously. A careful assessment of just what has to be done, and in what order, may help the manager cope far more than if they rush in and do the first thing that comes to hand without having a clear idea of the total picture.

LONG-TERM AND CORPORATE PLANNING

The concepts explained so far in this chapter have focused mainly on how the individual manager can do their own job more effectively over a relatively short-term period. However, managers also need to take a long-term and corporate perspective. Long-term strategies also need to be developed and this inevitably means co-operating with other managers in order to anticipate and, where appropriate, shape the future. If an individual manager can help develop rational long-term policies this can not only make their own job easier to perform but may also lead to improvements in other parts of an organisation that are even more important. It has already been explained how the techniques of objective setting and role set analysis can be applied on a departmental or organisational basis as well as an individual basis.

Basic concepts and issues involved in corporate planning consequently need to be explained. Even though most managers will not be involved in board level planning, long-term and strategic planning is also needed at departmental level. For this to be done, it is necessary to involve the key decision-makers. Experience with corporate planning groups made up of specialists outside the main power structure suggests that they are likely to fail because they do not have the 'clout' or often even the information and expertise with which to fashion long-term policies. The problem that has to be overcome with the key decision-makers is that they are invariably busy people. To complicate matters, such people may be reluctant to commit themselves to long-term strategies, particularly if there are sectional rivalries. However, the potential gains should outweigh these drawbacks. The problem of creating time for such planning with key, but busy, people can be reduced by having a chair who is under less pressure and by the provision of specialist reports for consideration at corporate or long-term planning meetings. It is inappropriate to include long-term planning with the business discussed at ordinary departmental or board meetings, as this inevitably leads to the short-term issues 'crowding out' the long-term ones. Sadly, in practice, often the only long-term planning that takes place is that associated with planning the annual financial budget.

In considering long-term planning, it is necessary to identify what the potential changes are in both the external and internal environments. Changes may be imposed on an organisation from outside, but opportunities for shaping the future through internal developments, such as product improvement, may also exist. It may be appropriate to establish what degrees of freedom are open to a unit or organisation in planning its future and what will happen if no positive decisions are taken. The lead time needed to alter activities also needs to be identified. It may also be useful to identify what an organisation's primary activity should be and to carry out an audit of its main strengths and weaknesses.

Other issues that will need consideration are the dangers of simply identifying the future by extrapolating from the past and also how to avoid developing a parochial view of the future. The analysis of what competitors are doing may help in this respect. Examination of changes in customer or client needs may also be needed. A further dimension is to identify the main ways in which an organisation is at risk or is likely to become at risk. One simple model that incorporates some of these key issues is the 'SWOT' analysis. The internal factors to be analysed are the strengths (S) and weaknesses (W). The external factors are opportunities (O) and threats (T).

Long-term planning can be a 'top-down' or 'bottom-up' process. In the former, the attempt is made to change the organisation in line with a centrally conceived master plan. With bottom-up planning, information is sought much more from the grassroots to help shape evolutionary development. In practice, there usually needs to be a fusing of these two approaches. Ideally, a long-term plan will be established and short-term plans integrated with it. This may involve 'gap-analysis' to establish what has to be done to bring an organisation's activities into line with that which is planned. Any long-term plan will, however, need continuous adjustment, especially in turbulent environments.[12]

Another framework for undertaking long-term planning or establishing corporate strategy that has become popular is that of 'business process re-engineering' (BPR). This has been defined as:

> the fundamental rethinking and radical redesign of business processes to achieve dramatic improvements in critical measures of performance such as cost, quality, service and speed.[13]

Key features of this approach involve discussions with no boundaries about the future of an organisation, the attempt to gain major (as opposed to incremental) improvements, a recognition that a change in corporate culture is likely to be a pre-requisite of major change, the involvement of human resources specialists as change agents and a critical appraisal of every policy and activity to see if they add value or not. The essence of the process is that it involves strategic decision-making that is linked to the core objectives of an organisation. Successful implementation of a change is likely to yield major benefits. Critics complain that this approach has led to an undue emphasis on cost reduction rather than opportunities for growth, and some have added that BPR stands for 'big people reductions'. Such emphasis on cost reduction may be because of the way the approach has been implemented or because it has often genuinely been the main option. Sometimes the term is devalued when it is used to describe operational changes that are not strategic.[14]

It is important to mention some of the other trends and potential dangers in attempting to undertake long-term and corporate planning, necessary as that process may be. As is explained in the next chapter, commercial organisations are faced with ever-increasing turbulence caused particularly by the impact of computer technology and the globalisation of markets. Consequently, there has been a reaction against detailed centralised planning because such a process is too cumbersome to react quickly and effectively to changing market conditions. The emphasis is much more now on semi-autonomous business units which can react more quickly. Charles Handy has argued strongly for this 'federal' concept and for the associated idea of 'subsidiarity' of business in organisation.[15] The Hanson organisation is a prime example of a conglomerate organised on this basis with a minute head office. However, this approach can be taken too far. The Hanson model may be particularly appropriate for a large and diversified group. Shell UK rethought its approach to decentralisation after finding it led to worsening performance. Consequently, whilst retaining a decentralised approach, a greater steer was given from the centre to avoid too much fragmentation and to retain the basic elements of a coherent company culture.[16] Another problem can be that devolution to business units and the setting of financial targets can be an over crude way of just seeking to control the financial dimension, without giving any consideration to the key variables.

One UK conglomerate, centred on the brewing industry but with interests in many other areas, found that when they analysed the reasons for sometimes quite astonishing turn-arounds in the performance of subsidiary companies they found that the key variable was the managerial talent that had been injected into these companies. At whatever level long-term and corporate planning is undertaken the process needs to be reasonably broadly based – even if the lesson has been learned that one should avoid centralised prescriptive approaches that are too detailed. Many corporate plans revolve just around the financial and marketing dimensions. The whole move to strategic human resource planning, explained in more detail in Chapter 12, necessitates considering the human resource dimension *before* and not after strategies are determined.

There is a great danger in planning processes that revolve too much around that which is relatively easily quantified. Denis Healey learned this lesson when he was Chancellor of the Exchequer. Admittedly, he was involved in planning on a grand macro scale, but his reflections are worth remembering with regard to smaller scale planning:

> Economics has acquired a spurious respectability through the use of numbers, which appear to many people, like my old friend McNamara (Head of the World Bank), much more meaningful than mere adjectives or adverbs, because they appear to be precise and unambiguous. Unfortunately I soon discovered that the most important numbers were nearly always wrong.[17]

Denis Healey was even more forthright in commenting on the dangers on an overreliance on numbers with regard to defence planning. Referring to an earlier stage in his career when he was Defence Secretary in the UK and Robert McNamara was his counterpart in the USA, and whilst acknowledging what he had learned from him about the control of defence projects, he said:

> McNamara, like the whizz-kids who had so much influence on his strategic thinking, demonstrated what I call the 'lamp-post fallacy' in its purest form. Late one night a policeman found a man on his knees under a lamp-post. 'What are you doing?' he asked. 'I dropped my keys at the bottom of the street,' was the reply. 'But that is a hundred yards away. Why are you looking here?' 'Because there's no light at the bottom of the street.'[18]

Denis Healey's concerns about the limitations and dangers of 'rational' numerically orientated strategic plans echo the concerns of the American consultants and writers Peters and Waterman whose views are explained and examined in the next chapter in the section on theories of organisations.

CONCLUSION

There have been two interlocking themes in this chapter. One is whether managers are simply going to be dictated to by events or whether they are going to develop a strategy for influencing events, as well as being influenced by them. The other is whether managers are going to seek to justify themselves by looking busy or by their results. It is to be hoped that readers will opt for exerting some influence over events and will try and justify themselves by their performance rather than by mere activity. Good management is like good medicine – the starting point is accurate diagnosis. One would not think much of a doctor who prescribed treatment before they had diagnosed the patient's condition. Sadly, this latter approach can be all too common in management. Managers can implement prescriptive action before they have defined their objectives or the problem areas.

A diagnostic approach needs to be taken to the job as a whole, as well as to the individual problems that present themselves. For greatest effectiveness it is also necessary to influence the policy and planning framework within which a manager has to operate. There needs to be conscious resistance to action for action's sake or the adoption of prescriptive solutions just because they are fashionable. If managers are able to develop a diagnostic approach they are likely to find that the gains are not just confined to improved performance in the immediate job. The development of initiatives and the acceptance of responsibility may be associated habits. Managers who behave in this way are preparing themselves for further promotion as well as cultivating a positive approach to life in general.

NOTES

1 Rosemary Stewart, *Managers and Their Jobs*, Macmillan, 2nd edn, 1988, p. 130.
2 Peter F. Drucker, *Practice of Management*, Heinemann, 1955.
3 John Humble, *Improving Business Results: The Definitive Work on Management by Objectives*, McGraw-Hill, 1967. See also John Humble, *Management by Objectives in Action*, McGraw-Hill in association with the British Institute of Management, 1979.
4 *Evening Standard*, London, 10 January 1977.
5 Royal Commission on Trade Unions and Employers' Associations/Alan Fox, *Industrial Sociology and Industrial Relations*, Research Paper No. 3, HMSO, 1965.

6 *Evening Standard*, London, 14 April 1988.
7 Donald T. Regan, *For The Record*, Arrow, 1988.
8 For a further account of this little-documented technique see W. David Rees, 'A System for Assessing Work Priorities', *Personnel Management*, December 1989, pp. 46–9.
9 For a comprehensive account of the technique see Keith Lockyer, *Critical Path Analysis (and other Project Network Techniques)*, Pitman, 4th edn, 1984.
10 Norman R. F. Maier, *Psychology in Industry*, Harrap, 1955, p. 447.
11 Ibid., pp. 425–8.
12 For a basic but comprehensive account of corporate strategy see Gerry Johnson and Kevan Scholes, *Exploring Corporate Strategy*, Prentice Hall, 3rd edn, 1993.
13 M. J. Hammer and J. Champy, *Re-engineering the Corporation: A Manifesto for Business Revolution*, Nicholas Brealey, London, 1993.
14 For a useful critique see Michael Oram and Richard Wellins, *Re-engineering's Missing Ingredient: The Human Factor*, Institute of Personnel and Development, 1995.
15 Charles Handy, *The Empty Raincoat*, Hutchinson, 1994.
16 'Shell UK Pulls Responsibility Back to Centre', *Personnel Management Plus*, April 1992, p. 1.
17 Denis Healey, *The Time of My Life*, Penguin, 1990, pp. 379–80.
18 Ibid., p. 307.

Chapter 3

The manager and the organisation

INTRODUCTION

Managers have to operate in the situations in which they find themselves. They may have a long-term aim to alter the situation they are in or to transfer to another one, but that may be little help in dealing with their immediate problems. Complaining about the situation as it is may invite a riposte similar to that of the soldier depicted in the famous *Punch* cartoon sheltering from shell fire during the First World War – 'if you knows of a better 'ole, go to it'. In other words, one has to make the best of things as they are, at least in the short term, and not as one wishes they were. The nature of the problems will be greatly influenced by the type of the organisation in which a manager works. In turn, the nature of that organisation will be influenced by the environment in which it exists. Managers will find that they have to work in a great variety of different situations. If they move to another organisation, or to a different part of the same organisation, they may find that the behaviour that was previously appropriate is quite inappropriate in their new position. They may also find that the situation they are in changes and this may also necessitate change in their managerial behaviour. It is therefore important that managers carefully assess the situations which they are in with a view to matching their behaviour with the circumstances. This issue is also of relevance to the next chapter on managerial style.

In this chapter some of the basic organisation theories are explained. The key factors which can determine the structure of an organisation are examined. These include the impact of technology – especially information technology – size, the need to identify the critical factor and function, and national culture. The problems involved in integrating the work of different departments are also considered. So is the importance of 'role' in determining people's behaviour and the need to distinguish between personality and role behaviour. The final section is about general organisational developments in the private and public sectors and the contrasts between them. Particular attention is given tó some of the specific and radical developments in the public sector, especially in the Civil Service, local government, the National Health Service and the increased importance of independent unelected 'quangos'.

THEORIES OF ORGANISATION

The historical approach to management was that it consisted of a set of principles which were capable of definition and universal application. This was the approach of writers such as F. W. Taylor[1] and Henri Fayol[2] early this century. Taylor, along with Gantt and the Gilbreths, was a member of the 'Scientific Management School' which conceptually overlapped with the 'Classical Management' theorists, including Fayol. Those in the Scientific Management School concentrated on the organisation of manual work, production planning and time and motion study. Taylor advocated the systematic analysis of work and for management to take over decision-making about which methods of work were used, based on the principle that the average worker preferred a well-defined task and clear-cut standards. The classical theorists developed these ideas into a framework of organisational principles. The collective view of the classical theorists was that work could be so organised that the objectives of organisations could be accomplished with great efficiency. Organisations were viewed as the product of logical thought concerned largely with co-ordinating tasks through the use of legitimate authority. Employees were seen as rational beings whose interests coincided with those of the organisations in which they were employed. They were also seen as being capable of working to high levels of efficiency, provided they were properly selected, trained, directed, monitored and supported. Indoctrination and coercion would be used if necessary to achieve a rational approach by employees. This was presumed to lead to employees behaving exactly as they were told. Great emphasis was also placed on the need for careful and detailed explanation of organisational structure.

Later, the limitations of the classical writers became apparent, particularly their simplistic approach to people. The Hawthorne experiments conducted at the Western Electric Company in Chicago in the 1920s and 1930s revealed that groups can have a powerful effect on the way organisations work and that people did not always do what employers wanted, nor did they always act in a way that was considered rational. The existence of informal networks and working relationships was also observed.[3] This led to the evolution of the Human Relations School of organisational thought with which Elton Mayo in particular was associated. The work of occupational sociologists has subsequently emphasised the need to view organisations as social entities. As explained in the previous chapter, it is also necessary to recognise that there can be considerable conflict between the objectives of the organisation and those of the individuals employed in it. As is explained in Chapter 12, informal and formal employee organisation can also lead to the sharing of power in organisations, so that there are limits to the authority of management.

A further school of thought which has emerged is the systems concept of organisations. This views organisations as dynamic organisms with interconnecting parts. Each part is dependent on integration with related parts if objectives are to be accomplished. Each part, however, has to operate in an environment which influences what the employees in that section want to achieve and are capable of achieving. An overlapping concept is that of 'socio-technical systems', according to which theory technical systems need to be effectively integrated with the social organisation at work, not simply imposed on it. The approach taken in this book is consistent with the systems theory of organisations.

It will be seen that organisational theory has gradually evolved. The formulation of one school of thought has facilitated the testing of that approach with actual organisational behaviour and the development of further schools of thought. The valid aspects of a particular approach have then been integrated with later views. The approach of the classical writers, in particular, needs to be seen in this light. Apart from its pioneering nature, much of what they have to say about organisations is still worth considering. However, their principles of organisations need to be seen as possible guidelines rather than definitive rules. The variety of managerial and organisational situations is such that it is impossible to set down universal principles. In any such list, the 'principles' are platitudinous or have clear exceptions.

It is also necessary to have some understanding of the various approaches to management so that one can understand the views that colleagues may have about the way in which organisations should work. Such approaches may be reinforced, or be caused, by an individual's cultural background. People tend to have beliefs and make value judgements about the ways organisations should operate. Even if these are never formally expressed, they may nevertheless be held with considerable conviction. Hopefully, such views will match the situations that arise. However, there are likely to be occasions when they do not, and it may be as well to recognise when a situation demands particular organisational arrangements that are in conflict with the beliefs of colleagues. It may even be appropriate to reflect on one's own ideology and the extent to which it is appropriate to the current situation.

Mechanistic and organic structures

A particularly useful classification of organisational structures is the extent to which they are mechanistic or organic. The ideas of the classical theorists were, and to a large extent still are, particularly appropriate to large-scale organisations operating in stable environments. Burns and Stalker have since suggested that such circumstances lend themselves to 'mechanistic' systems.[4] This is in contrast to more rapidly changing environments where more adaptive 'organic' systems may be necessary. Although the research conducted by Burns and Stalker took place 40 years ago, it is still of great relevance. Later writers in this area have generally either used Burns and Stalker's work as a foundation or independently confirmed their conclusions, even if they have identified further issues.

The features of mechanistic systems include: a clear hierarchy of control, a high degree of specialisation of labour and reference upwards for the reconciliation of differences within the organisation. This type of arrangement may be entirely appropriate where there is sufficient time to prescribe organisational arrangements and procedures in this type of detail, so that they match the environment in which the organisation operates. Where the technology and market are rapidly changing, however, it could be a recipe for disaster. A mechanistic system would simply not be adaptive, or its responses fast enough, to enable an organisation to remain competitive. Hence the need in some situations for 'organic' systems. These are characterised particularly by greater room for initiative, and for contact, co-operation and decision-taking to be in accordance with the needs of particular situations rather than the formal organisation.

The work of Burns and Stalker was based on research into certain Scottish companies, particularly in the electronics industry, in the period 1953–7. Considerable success had been achieved in the application of scientific research findings within the Royal Air Force in the Second World War. This had been accomplished by the creation of particular (organic) structural arrangements that contrasted sharply with the mechanistic relationships between scientific departments and the Luftwaffe in Germany. The aim of Burns and Stalker's research was to investigate the extent to which organic arrangements needed to be, and could be, introduced into organisations in peacetime.

A particular problem found in the firms in the Burns and Stalker study was that they often had arrangements for co-ordination between the research and development departments and production that had more in common with the German wartime procedures than the British. However, it was clear that certain types of technical innovation, where know-how was diffuse and rapidly changing, demanded the reverse type of arrangements. I subsequently witnessed a research and development failure for just these reasons. It concerned the unsuccessful attempt to introduce an improved version of the existing product in an engineering firm. When this failed, the design and research and development staff blamed the production staff for having been technically incompetent, whilst the production staff blamed the design and research and development staff for having been impractical, unrealistic and failing to communicate all their requirements. The company's response was not to create more organic relationships in this area (no-one was aware of this concept) but to establish three competing design teams. The view was that the best design would then be chosen for production. However, as the basic issue of the working relationships between the groups involved was not addressed, this approach did not prove to be very satisfactory either.

These mechanistic and organic approaches should be seen as different ends of a continuum rather than straight alternatives. Few, if any, organisations will be completely mechanistic or completely organic. However, it is important for the individual manager to be able to recognise the difference between the two. It is also necessary to recognise that greater market turbulence is likely to increase the emphasis needed for organic-type structures. Factors causing this are especially the increasing pace of technological change and the increasing globalisation of markets.

A variation of organic arrangements is the matrix structure. Essentially, this involves the setting up of more or less permanent project-type groups to which people are allocated from resource centres. The line, or command, structure is retained on the resource group side but the appropriate mix of specialists can then be allocated, full time or part time, to 'product-type' teams. This arrangement is very often found necessary in high-technology organisations. It is also often found in colleges. It can assist in seeing that clients' needs are properly identified and met. If you have resource groupings only, as is often the case in universities, for example, the danger is that activity is focused on the development of the discipline alone without regard to the needs of clients. A feature of behaviour in many organisations, though, is that in any conflict between project groupings and the line structure it is the latter that usually wins. This is because of the power base of the command structure rather than because it necessarily has the better arguments.

A later writer who commented on the various different types of organisational structure was Charles Handy. He identified four main organisational cultures – which he classified as power, role, task and person.[5] The power culture is explained as being frequently found in small entrepreneurial organisations led by a dominant personality. The role and task cultures have broadly similar characteristics to, respectively, mechanistic and organic structures. The person culture is described as being a loose grouping of individuals who find it convenient to co-operate with one another without sacrificing too much of their independence, e.g., barristers' chambers or architectural practices.

Other writers to comment on the importance of the organic type of organisation are Peters and Waterman. Their book *In Search of Excellence*, published in 1982[6] attracted much international attention. They based their work on the business practices of a number of leading American companies which they had been able to study whilst working for the management consultants McKinseys. They identified eight key attributes common to most of these excellent companies which were:

1   A bias for action;
2   Close to the customer;
3   Autonomy and entrepreneurship;
4   Productivity through people;
5   Hands-on, value driven;
6   Stick to the knitting (i.e., avoiding diversification into un-con]nected areas of business and technical specialisation);
7   Simple form, lean staff;
8   Simultaneous loose–tight properties (the coexistence of firm central direction and maximum individual autonomy).

This account by Peters and Waterman was of value in that it was an empirical attempt to explain what was actually happening in successful American companies. Their approach encouraged managers to beware of 'rational' planning models, to rely more on their subjective judgement, to consider the human element in organisations and be aware of the virtues of organic-type struc-tures. The book had considerable appeal in the business world, but there has been criticism by academics about the evidential base for the conclusions. These criticisms include the subjectivity of the data, its selective interpretation, the lack of a control group of less successful companies and the fact that many of the companies quoted as models of excellence fared badly in the subsequent economic downturn.[7] Also, there is no consideration at all of management issues in the public sector. It may be that the type of characteristics described by Peters and Waterman tended to be particularly appropriate to large private sector organisations during a period of economic growth, but some of these attributes may actually have been handicaps when there was a recession. This illustrates a continuous theme of this chapter – that organisational structures need to 'fit' with their objectives and circumstances. Whilst acknowledging the merits in the account by Peters and Waterman, it could have become a trap for those managers who based organisational structure on a prescriptive fashionable solution rather than undertaking the patient and intellectually demanding exercise of establishing which structure was right for their particular purposes.

Tom Peters's views have evolved further since *In Search of Excellence* was published. Subsequently, he claimed that the really key attributes were concern for customers, innovation, attention to the people in the organisation and, above all (a new explicit attribute), leadership.[8] Later, Peters emphasised the need for constant, rapid change to survive in a rapidly changing world. He also embraced much of the philosophy of Total Quality Management – explained later in this chapter.[9] Subsequently, he has stressed the crucial importance of the impact of computer technology – particularly its effects on world markets – and globalisation.[10] Waterman has subsequently emphasised the importance of companies using their staff effectively and developing customer orientation even further.[11] To reject the work of both Peters and Waterman because of its methodological limitations could well be a case of 'throwing the baby out with the bath water'. The issues that they identify are of fundamental importance. However, particularly given the increasingly Messianic approach of Peters, managers should be aware of taking 'their eye off the ball' as far as their own particular circumstances are concerned. The contingency approach of matching behaviour with the situation you are actually in is a topic that is considered further in Chapter 4 on managerial style. The impact of information technology on organisational structure and behaviour is considered later in this chapter.

The flexible organisation

An extension of the concept of the organic organisation may be provided by the concept of the flexible organisation, and Atkinson has provided a theoretical model of this type of organisation.[12] It is particularly evident in Japan, where security of employment is often guaranteed only to a core of permanent employees. Other employees are engaged on a temporary basis. Potentially, an organisation is more likely to be able to adapt and survive if the outer core can be shed or replaced easily. This also enables the security of those in the inner core to be more easily guaranteed. Whilst people usually prefer to work in the inner core, those who are unemployed may regard a job in the outer core as better than no job at all. Employment in the periphery may anyway provide opportunities for promotion to the core, and this can be a very useful way for employers to screen potential core employees. The requirement for some specialist skills may not be on a full-time basis, so a cost saving is made by employing some specialists part time. These arrangements give the organisation *numerical* flexibility. The emergence of chronic unemployment in the labour market enables employers to be much more innovative, as a result of their bargaining advantage, in recruiting staff for non-standard contracts. Some of those with specialist skills may anyway prefer to exploit the new options in the labour market by having non-standard working arrangements, particularly if that gives them tax advantages as well as greater freedom, so in some cases employees may prefer not to be part of the core. This may include those who, having taken early retirement, are amenable to the idea of having their skills bought back in, for example, on a consultancy basis. Where specialist skills are in short supply, however, employers may prefer to try and lock people with those skills into the organisation by employing them in the core.

Technological developments, such as those in electronic data processing, mean that practices such as working at home and subcontracting are possible in entirely new areas. Teleworking can be another option.[13] Organisations that can predict their likely pattern of activity may also offer annual hours contracts so that employees' work attendance varies with, for example, the seasonal demand for their products.[14] The greater availability of labour may also create the option of having some people to work at peak periods of the day only. Such arrangements could enable banks, for example, to have their counters fully manned at lunchtime, and thus overcome the problem of leaving some counters vacant at a peak time so that staff can have their lunch. Numerical flexibility can also be achieved by employing people on short-term contracts. Another aspect of the flexible organisation is the benefits that may be derived in terms of *functional* flexibility. Staff may be contracted to perform a variety of different jobs and even to operate at varying levels of responsibility in accordance with the fluctuating needs of an organisation. Japanese companies in particular place much emphasis on multi-skilling and generic job descriptions, and developments such as these are increasing functional flexibility within organisations. The attempts by the government to create more contracting out of public sector work, explained later in this chapter, have been a further impetus to the development of flexible organisations.

Having explained the greater tendency for numerical and functional flexibility within organisations it is necessary to say also that if taken too far this can create drawbacks. A sizeable core is needed to retain reasonable continuity and generate organisational synergy. Some able people may be discouraged from applying to organisations if, for example, only a fixed-term contract is on offer. Not all activities can be neatly packaged up and subcontracted. It is more difficult to develop an integrated organisational approach with a subcontractor who is only paid for what is strictly defined in the contract. Those in the peripheral work-force also need to be strategically managed. Inadequate attention to their supervision and training can easily lead to the alienation of the customers or clients on which the organisation depends. One of the cost advantages of employing part-time staff has been eliminated by the House of Lords decision in 1994 that statutory rights regarding unfair dismissal and redundancy shall be the same for part-time staff as they are for full-time staff, so as not to be discriminatory against women.[15] In the same year, and for the same reason, The European Court of Justice ruled that organisational pension schemes must not discriminate against part-time employees.[16] It is probably prudent to view any trend towards more flexible working arrangements as a series of *ad hoc* responses to labour market conditions rather than as an attempt to establish a conceptually different structure. This view is confirmed, at least with regard to the UK, by a 1992 study.[17] The key variable that has probably more to do with such changes than anything else is the greater availability of labour on such terms as it can get.

Quality circles

An organisational development that has links with the organic system and project and matrix structures is that of quality circles. They have been defined as:

> A small group of between three and twelve people who do the same, or similar work, voluntarily meeting together regularly for about an hour per week in paid time, usually under the leadership of their own supervisor, and trained to identify, analyse, and solve some of the problems in their work, presenting solutions to management, and where possible, implementing solutions themselves.[18]

Quality circles, although American in origin, have attracted considerable attention because of their popularity in Japan since the 1960s and the economic success of that country. Consequently, they have been introduced into manufacturing and service activities in other industrial countries. The potential benefits are mainly improved quality, cost savings and the improved morale

created by these achievements and the increased employee participation that is the essence of the process. Whilst the idea may be
capable of useful application in other countries, one must always
be wary of attempts to transplant management practices from
one country to another – as is explained later in this chapter in
the section on national culture. The greater emphasis on the
group in Japan, compared with the emphasis on the individual in
the West, is of particular importance It is also necessary to beware,
as is repeatedly stressed in this book, of management panaceas
that so often turn out to be simplistic attempts to deal with
complex issues. It is not surprising to learn that quality circles
often fail and that even in Japan, according to one study, only one
in three work.[19] However, many apparently succeed and it may be
that the concept can work in selected situations, provided the conditions are right. The way in which quality circles are implemented
is also crucial, and the seven critical factors in their introduction
have been identified as:

1 Commitment by the board and senior management;
2 Involvement of middle management and supervisors;
3 Trade union support;
4 Delegation of decision-making;
5 Adequate training; -
6 Use of a pilot study;
7 Monitoring.[20]

Total Quality Management

A more recent development, Total Quality Management (TQM),
adopts a broader approach to the continuous improvement of
quality. TQM seeks to obtain everyone's commitment to satisfying
customer expectations and its originality lies in identifying the
organisation as a set of linked processes with internal customers
and suppliers all driven by what the external customer wants. The
intention is to build-in quality at the earliest stages when designing
a product or service – to 'get it right first time' instead of relying
on 'end of line' activities such as inspection, quality control and
assurance to remedy errors after they have occurred. The philosophy
is of error prevention through careful specification of how to meet
customer requirements, bringing to bear the knowledge and ideas
of all the people involved in the process working as a team and

accepting responsibility for a quality output. Quality does not mean 'top of the range' excellence – a Mini car or a Rolls-Royce will both be quality products if they meet the specification, including price. In defining the quality standard, the question to answer is 'what does success look like?' Any gap between the quality standard and the quality actually achieved can then be identified. Organisational activity then needs to be directed towards eliminating this gap.

TQM, properly applied, involves a major shift in organisational culture and a new decision-making structure so that all staff understand the strategic direction of the organisation and are empowered to 'own' problems and take actions to solve them and avoid recurrence. This can involve a fundamental organisational restructuring which is at variance with the traditional nature of so many organisations with strong functional and hierarchical boundaries, as explained in Chapter 1. The potential benefits of TQM include cost reductions arising, for example, from the need for less inspection and rectification, and quicker introduction of innovative new products and services, leading in turn to greater market share and increased revenue. However, these benefits are only likely to be achieved if appropriate organisational adjustments and training investments are made. The key preconditions for success are generally seen to be:

1 Sustained commitment by the board and senior management, especially if the TQM initiative seems to be losing its momentum;
2 Strong emphasis on communication to the work-force;
3 A determined attempt to improve and structure lateral communication and co-operation between departments;
4 Sound mechanisms for employee involvement and skills development with particular emphasis on problem solving through team work.

It is also necessary to identify the specific qualitative standards and improvements that are required, mount a programme for their accomplishment and measure and communicate progress. The development of skills by front-line staff is critical, and in turn necessitates careful selection and appropriate training. An example of this thinking is the redefinition of the role of a delivery driver to that of a representative of the company who drives and who accepts responsibility for developing and maintaining a good relationship with the customer. The role of front-line supervisors and managers is particularly important and involves a change from keeping all authority and knowledge in their hands to one of developing the skills of their team.

The concept of TQM was developed in Japan after the Second World War, particularly by an American industrial adviser, W. Edwards Deming. Deming used as a base the statistical process control techniques developed earlier by Walter Shewhart and promoted a method of review and improvement applicable to all activities (the 'plan–do–check–act' cycle). Other important exponents of TQM were Juran and Crosby. Japan's quality revolution and export success caused organisations in other countries, especially competitors, to begin to look closely at what the Japanese had been doing. By the 1980s interest was widespread. Ignored initially in the USA, Deming had found that Japan was a fertile ground for the development of TQM. Industry needed to be rebuilt, there was an adequate supply of labour and raw materials were short, so waste urgently needed to be avoided. The Japanese culture particularly lent itself to TQM. The emphasis was on teams, not individuals, and organisation cultures were generalist rather than specialist. Trade unions had become weak and were organised on a company basis. Loyalty to the company and the work ethic were both high and labour stability helped social control. Economic growth meant that work rationalisation did not create redundancies and the employment of a core work-force further guaranteed security for those with permanent jobs. Sophisticated long-term relationships evolved with suppliers so that quality was not threatened by supplies of faulty components. The concept of *kaizan* was developed too so that continuous improvement became part of organisational culture with work teams geared to constantly improving methods in order to produce innovative products attractive to customers.

There was not the same impetus for improvement in the West after the war. Manufacturers operated in a sellers' market and some even developed cynical approaches to quality. The technique of 'just-in-time' production, which the Japanese developed so well, wouldn't work in overheated economies where the main concern was avoiding disruption to the production system. This could be caused by late or poor-quality deliveries or industrial action. Consequently, components were often hoarded rather than only being fed in at the appropriate moment. When Western economies found that they had to operate much more in buyers' markets many of their companies found it very difficult to compete with Japanese manufacturers, particularly on quality and price. The concept has also been applied in many parts of the public sector. This is in keeping with the increasing emphasis on consumerism and the increasing amount of work contracted out to internal or external clients.

One important element of TQM is to have robust systems that ensure continuous measurement of the achievement of quality standards and the basis for targeting improvements to close the quality gap discussed earlier. Development of quality standards requires working with customers to help clarify their needs. Having defined the standards, the supplier needs to establish procedures to ensure that these standards are consistently achieved. This has led to a wave of organisations seeking external accreditation that they have done this and produced the appropriate operating quality manual. The most common British accreditation is BS 5750. There is also a European standard ES 2200 and an international standard – ISO 9000, both of which are based on BS 5750. Accreditation does not involve any judgement about the quality level, just that the organisation has detailed documented procedures to demonstrate that it is consistently meeting the standards it has set for itself. There is clearly felt to be a commercial advantage in gaining a quality kitemark, and some customers, including many government departments, indicate that they expect this in organisations tendering for business. The process can be bureaucratic, though, and the costs of producing manuals, gaining accreditation and paying for this and follow-up visits can be expensive. Critics claim that, in contrast to TQM, accreditation does not focus on improving quality or exploiting new market opportunities.[21] It remains to be seen if possession of a kitemark is a worthwhile investment leading to quality improvements or simply a rigid bureaucratic on-cost. The answer will vary according to the nature of the organisation and industry or service.

The potential gap between aspiration and achievement with regard to quality standards is also an issue for the process of TQM as a whole. If organisations see it as a quick cure for fundamental problems they are likely to be disappointed. Organisational cultures are not that easily altered, and so often one sees one 'quick fix' tried after another and all failing because the scale of the adjustment is not understood. There is also the specific constraint in the public sector that, whilst TQM may reduce some costs and improve service, it may not be easy to generate the revenue that would finance it. The concept of TQM envisages all interested parties having a shared interest in organisational success, but for this to happen it is necessary to recognise sectional interests when they arise and to address rather than ignore any potential conflict.

The difficulties that many organisations have encountered are documented in research studies. Voss and O'Brien reported that many schemes were foundering because of a lack of leadership by senior and middle management, and this was exacerbated by a failure to understand customer needs. They also reported that cost-cutting measures precipitated by the recession were undermining quality initiatives and that organisations often failed to realise the level of commitment and adjustment that needed to be made by the whole organisation.[22] The last failing featured prominently in a study led by Binney, which also commented that change could be provoked but not imposed and that in the best examples TQM was working well.[23] A further problem may be that organisations introduce what Deming would have seen as contradictory initiatives, such as performance-related pay (emphasising the contribution of the individual) and TQM (with its emphasis on team work). There is also the need, especially in the public sector, to carefully balance any measures of throughput with quality standards. However, there seems little doubt that TQM has the potential to release the energies of employees to regenerate and improve the effectiveness of their organisations considerably. Whether that potential is realised or not is clearly up to individual managements. If they do take it seriously, they will continually ask questions about whether a TQM initiative is working, paying back on the investment and moving the organisation forward.

FACTORS THAT DETERMINE THE STRUCTURE OF ORGANISATIONS

There are many variables that will affect the structure and operation of an organisation. These may be within the organisation, outside it or a combination of the two. Managers need to work out which factors in their particular situation are likely to be important. These could include the impact of technology, the size of their organisation, the identification of the critical function at a given time, and culture.

The impact of technology

One of the most critical factors is that of technology. Particular attention will be given in this section to information technology because of its enormous importance. However, organisational structure has probably always been influenced by the technology it deploys. One of the writers who made a historically important contribution to understanding this relationship was Joan Woodward.[24] She reported that organisations with mass-production technologies were found to lend themselves to mechanistic-type systems. Firms with process-type technologies appeared to be at that time best managed by less formal and more organic-type systems. The absence of the sheer physical effort involved in making items and co-ordinating thousands of small decisions, characteristic of large-batch and mass-production technology, meant that managers were left with much more time to initiate and co-operate with others. Consequently, the need for specialisation was found to be reduced in the process-type industries. The organic type of structure was also found to be more appropriate with small firms which were not making standard products. Some small organisations, though, were informal and mechanistic – the routines being so well known that there was no need to formalise them. Technological developments since then, however, such as robotic technology, have enabled some of the traditional mass-production industries to acquire some of the characteristics of the process-type industries. The important point that emerged from the Woodward studies was the link between organisational structure and behaviour and technology, and the empirical support this gave for the contingency approach. Related to this was her observation that many managers had as their model of organisation structure the old classical beliefs. As is explained in the next chapter, on managerial style, a mismatch between style and the needs of the situation can have unfortunate consequences. Given the general lack of management training, as explained in Chapter 1, it is still likely that the options in organisational structure and behaviour are not fully understood by many managers.

The impact of technology on organisational structure and behaviour also has to be considered in relation to information technology. The rapid processing and retrieval of data can have a major impact. So too can computer-controlled production and other operational processes. Despite the increasing sophistication of information technology equipment, costs are falling and the general levels of computer literacy are rising.

Rapid information access may increase an organisation's ability (and need) to respond quickly to market changes. It may also facilitate meeting individual customer requirements. This may necessitate flexibility within the organisational structure and also means that, especially in commercial organisations, the stakes are much greater. The gains to be made by a rapid response may be high and the penalties for a slow response correspondingly high as well. Many markets are becoming much more 'perfect' as information is more easily obtained and analysed and as the barriers of time and distance are reduced. This in turn means that product life cycles are tending to be shorter and international and market boundaries less important. The greater volatility of markets and knowledge about their behaviour means that customer and brand loyalty is likely to be less. Organisations may find that they have the knowledge and capacity to enter new markets but, conversely, this may mean that they have to face new sources of competition.

A related development is the use of software packages to automate many processes previously done manually (e.g., many accountancy procedures and calculations), more effective organisation and use of organisational memories, common databases throughout organisations (and consequentially fewer internal barriers to effective communication) and electronic conferencing. The use of electronic mail (e-mail) enables rapid and simultaneous transmission to any number of colleagues. Linking of e-mail to a wide area network enables messages to be exchanged and material accessed throughout the world. Other external contacts may involve more effective collaboration (as well as competition) with other organisations, shared information with buyers and sellers, and electronic market broking arrangements. Access is also available to an increasing number of public databases, e.g., of copies of newspapers, magazines, journals and other archive material. Electronic Data Interchange (EDI) enables ordering to be done on a daily basis. Overnight orders to suppliers may reduce turn-around time. The same system also gives very accurate stock control. These internal and external developments may in turn mean that information is more readily available about new options and services that can be provided. Information technology may facilitate 'business scope redefinition'. An example of such redefinition was the introduction by American Airlines of its computer reservation system (Sabre). This on-line system enabled reservations to be made direct from travel agents' offices. It also created the opportunity for the company to lease out the facilities to other airlines.

The developments described above may enable organisations to use their expertise in information technology to creatively influence strategy rather than simply using technology in a supportive role. A dramatic example of this was how the Italian authorities were able to analyse the previously impenetrable wall surrounding many financial transactions involving the Mafia and then use the evidence obtained to secure criminal convictions. The information now available within the British National Health Service enables comparisons to be made about the cost and quality of services at different locations and to identify delays in treatment and the availability of space for those requiring treatment. Surprising spin-offs may be generated by new data. An example of this occurred in the social services directorate of a local authority. Details of external phone calls became available when all calls were electronically logged. Analysis of the data revealed, amongst other things, the times when home helps rang in to liaise with office staff. This was because they had been given charge cards to use on clients' phones. It emerged that the offices were overmanned with support staff early in the morning, as the home helps generally rang in later than had been realised.

The changes so far identified may precipitate further internal organisational changes. The rapid access to data can have a centralising effect and may enable senior managers to directly manage more people, leading to a flatter organisational pyramid. The electronic storage of and access to information can also generate significant space savings. These developments can reduce the need for middle-level managers and in turn lead to organisational 'de-layering'. Sometimes, though, it can lead to overcentralisation as managers may centralise because they can do it more easily rather than as the result of a considered judgement as to whether decisions are better taken locally or not. The overall scale of the organisational pyramid may also be shrunk in terms of the number of people employed, as many front-line tasks are automated or made easier. An example of how front-line jobs may be eliminated in the service sector is the increasing use of electronic surveillance by the police to deter motorists from speeding and jumping traffic lights, and the possibility of using this method to detect illegal exhaust emissions. Other effects are likely to include a large increase in capital equipment per employee. Inventory costs may also be reduced by programmed stock control and purchasing procedures, and 'just-in-time' production methods may be further facilitated. The increased availability of information may indicate the logic of greater vertical integration with suppliers or distributors. Conversely, comparative cost information may also give clear indications as to when it would be more appropriate to subcontract some activities. The ease with which data can be transmitted may make geographic dispersion of an organisation's physical locations much easier and cheaper.

Whilst there are dangers of overgeneralising about the impact of information technology on organisational structures and behaviour, especially as not all information technology acquisitions are major, the issue is so crucial that further consideration of its impact and of the necessary adjustments is needed. Technological forecasting may help in working out what future changes are both likely and necessary. Analysis of what new skills need to be acquired is also clearly required. This involves more than exhortations that everyone become computer literate. A mix of skills will be needed, including systems design, programming, data inputting and retrieval, the facility to use a keyboard and the ability to make use of the information. The acquisition of these skills needs to be matched to individual requirements. However, the changes precipitated by information technology will necessitate a range of other skills as well. A particular danger is that computer specialists will only recognise the need for new skills in their area and not the range of managerial and other skills that will also be necessary if information technology is to be harnessed effectively.

The constraints of information technology also need to be recognised. Whilst there may be general qualitative gains in decision-making and product reliability, the cost and consequence of systems and programming errors may be greatly increased. One major systems failure was experienced after the introduction by the London Ambulance Service of a computerised system for despatching vehicles to emergencies in 1992. This had to be quickly abandoned and the manual system reintroduced.[25] Another failure, documented by the Public Accounts Committee in 1994, was the expenditure of £20 million by the Wessex Health Authority on a computer system for storing patient data; this also had to be abandoned.[26] Also, not all important information is readily quantifiable – a point stressed in the previous chapter. Sometimes expensive systems are not integrated and are used on top of existing systems rather than instead of them. On other occasions systems may be acquired that do not do the job any more effectively than previous arrangements, leading to a low or negative pay-off on the investment. If the right equipment is acquired, a further adaptation that may be necessary is that of shift-working, so that full use is made of the new facilities. The dehumanising impact on certain jobs may also require consideration – e.g., the even greater impersonalisation of relationships between staff and customers in supermarkets caused by new technology – and thought should be given as to what remedial action can be taken in such cases. It also needs to be recognised that some jobs may significantly increase in importance, as so often power is where the information is. Sometimes this can mean that people in relatively lowly positions can have considerable influence. As has been previously explained, many front-line jobs are made much easier by information technology. However, in other cases the ready access to data enables front-line staff to take decisions that would have not previously been possible. The ability of others to maintain power by their control of and ability to filter information will be correspondingly reduced. A further impact is the blurring of traditional distinctions between blue and white-collar employees, as new skills replace old ones and the shape of an organisation changes.

The general implication of the change precipitated by information technology is that management needs to learn to live not only with continuous change, but with change that may accelerate in pace. The use of fibre-optics to enable massive amounts of information to be transmitted may be of particular importance in actually accelerating the rate of technological change. This will facilitate the development of information superhighways. Central to the need to capitalise on these developments is the need for managers, especially in the private sector, to learn to keep abreast of developments in information technology, so that they can take advantage (before their competitors) of the new applications as they come on stream. At present, though, there is a tendency for the technology to race ahead of the ability of organisations to identify areas of application. Even when applications are identified organisations may lack the ability to use them productively.[27] A key need is for organisations to invest in technical support and in the training of managers and others so they can make good use of the equipment that is available.

Size

Another important factor that will affect the structure and operation of an organisation is size. You do not need much formality if you are engaged in building, for example, a small boat, as to a large extent people can see what needs to be done for themselves. The mass-production of motor cars requires much more formality because, amongst other things, people cannot easily grasp what has to be done. The number of variables that has to be co-ordinated in that situation creates enormous organisational problems. It may well be that these problems increase on an exponential rather than a linear basis. The solution of breaking the units down into a manageable size may not be an option if your technology dictates that you need a large integrated plant.

Identifying the critical function

Another factor that needs to influence the structure of an organisation is the recognition of what is the critical function at a given time. Joan Woodward defined commercial success as, in part, stemming from the ability of those in organisations to identify the *area* where it was most important to get the correct decisions.[28] If necessary, the views of the management in the critical function need to take precedence over the views of managers in less important areas. The critical function can vary over time, and in mechanistic structures especially such movement of influence from one function to another may be inhibited. The managers in a traditionally powerful function are not likely to take kindly to having a reduced say in major decisions in order to allow a rival function a greater say. The managers in the traditionally powerful function may, in any case, not fully appreciate that the critical focus of decision-making has moved. The success of managers in solving problems may be their very un-doing in this respect. If, for example, difficult design problems are overcome, this removes a constraint. The problem then can be how to increase production or sales. However, a 'critical' function is still interdependent with the other functions in an organisation.

National culture

Organisations also need to mesh with the culture of the country in which they operate. Organisations such as multi-national corporations are tending to operate more and more on a global basis, but we also have the increasing emergence of trans-national organisations in both the private and public sectors. These organisations are structured so that they do not have their roots in any one country. Some discretion needs to be given to local managers to be able to adjust the organisation, as well as their managerial style, to suit national conditions. The issue of achieving an appropriate managerial style, including the issue of cultural adjustment, is dealt with further in the next chapter.

The customs and values of a country clearly need to be taken into account as well as the increasingly necessary cultural diversity within organisations. Management practices which appear to work well in a particular country may not be easily exported because the environment in which they work cannot be transplanted. This also applies to the importing of practices from other countries. At present there is often much emphasis on what other countries have to learn from the Japanese. However, Japanese industrial success owes much to their highly developed work ethic, cultural homogeneity, outstanding technical achievements, long-term financing, effective and sophisticated system of government support for industry and import barriers. The social traditions of conformity and obedience, and the importance of the group or wider organisation compared with the individual are also relevant. Some of these features are noticeable, too, in some of the other economic successfully countries in the region, such as South Korea, Taiwan and Singapore. The importing of particular management practices and customs is not going to radically change organisational cultures in the West. That is not to say that some Japanese practices will not work elsewhere – the point is that much of their success stems from more fundamental causes. The point needs to be made, too, that the Japanese also need to adapt their organisations' structures and style when they have to operate in different cultures. The very success of countries such as Japan is also likely to precipitate social changes in their own societies.

THE INTERRELATIONSHIP OF ORGANISATIONAL ACTIVITY

As well as considering the nature of the organisation they are in and how appropriate that organisation is to its environment, managers need to consider how they relate to the other functions within their organisation. Organisations may be arranged on neat departmental lines, but many of the problems that will have to be dealt with will not conveniently correspond to a departmental structure. Such structures, although usually necessary, are artificial. Problems may contain many different interactive dimensions. Managerial approaches to such problems will need to be integrated if they are to succeed. True, some problems may confine themselves to departmental boundaries, but this will not always be the case. Unfortunately, there are often considerable barriers to lateral contact between departments, especially in mechanistic-type organisations. Rivalries, role conflicts, different values and differing types of expertise may all act as impediments. Staff may prefer the security of contact with like-minded people within their own department to the often more hostile encounters with other departments. A lopsided approach to organisational problems may develop as a result. This may have a detrimental effect on the work of departments. It may also lead to problems that straddle departmental boundaries being ignored. It is all too easy for an 'ostrich'-type managerial style to develop in organisations. Managers may keep their heads down and just deal with what is clearly in their own patch. This tendency may be reinforced by their initial specialist training – as explained in Chapter 1. Managers may be much more able to identify the problems that correspond with their specialism than those outside it.

The problem of boundary-crossing can be particularly acute in the public sector, and it follows that there are many examples. The old-established boundaries which define what is medical work and what is nursing work do not facilitate organisational change in the National Health Service. The attempt to introduce corporate management in local government has been hampered by the 'professional' orientation of individual departments and officers. The development of a corporate approach necessitates officers at all levels, not just those at the top tier, taking a wider approach. The legal profession provides a particularly glaring example of where well-established professional traditions that have led to fierce opposition to suggestions for change in working arrangements. The older-established the profession, the greater seem to be the problems of altering occupational roles and associated training in line with changing organisational and societal needs.

Interdepartmental problems

To understand broader problems – particularly those which fall between different departments – managers need to have some understanding of overall activity in their organisations. Attempts to bring departments together may be frustrated, however, because of the conflict this can generate. The objectives of departments may not always be complementary nor will they all operate at the same level of performance. Consequently, much time and effort can go into justifying to others the activity of a particular department rather than developing common problem-solving approaches. The hidden agenda at interdepartmental meetings can be that nothing is to be proved wrong about one's own department. However, if everyone takes that approach the real issues to be discussed simply get lost in smoke screens. One has only to look at the annual report of a company which has made a loss to see the standard smoke screen that can be put out for public, if not internal, consumption. The list of causes for poor performance is likely to include inappropriate legislation, national and international trading conditions, unfair competition, government policy, failures by suppliers, acts of God, bad luck, trade unions and a deterioration in the standards of society. It might include incompetence by previous executives but is most unlikely to include admissions of failure that were within the current management's control.

The magnitude of this issue is compounded by the fact that the very nature of problems can often be identified only by an interdepartmental group with complementary skills and expertise. If the current objectives of an organisation, or the major constraints impeding the achievement of those objectives, are to be defined, this may be accomplished only by a pooling of knowledge. Even when the nature of a problem is identified, the causes may be far from obvious. One of the traps that people can fall into is to assume that the problems which emerge in particular departments have their causes in those same departments. In analysing 'personnel' problems in organisations, I have often found that the causes are numerous and may involve many different departments.

Productivity levels may be influenced, for example, by production control, organisation structure, investment policy and personnel management policies. It may be pointless trying to recruit more and more labour to boost production if the production process or planning is inadequate. In some cases, problems, causes and solutions may all exist in the same department, but it is dangerous to assume that this is always the case. That is why the importance of the systems approach to organisations has been stressed earlier in this chapter.

A further point of which managers need to be aware is the implications of their decisions for other departments. An example of how one department, in trying to improve its own performance, created greater problems elsewhere concerns a change in sales policy. The limit on the size of small orders in a soft drinks company was reduced and sales increased as a result. Unfortunately, the extra revenue was not sufficient to cover the extra transport costs involved!

The poet John Donne's observation that 'no man is an island' might equally be applied to managers. They need to see their experience as something to be shared, to help identify and deal with problems facing the whole organisation, rather than simply a means of justifying the activity of their own department. They may not be capable of resolving the problems facing their own department alone anyway. This point is explained further in Chapter 12 and illustrative examples are given from the field of employee relations. This is a function where the root cause of problems very often lie in other areas of management activity. Unfortunately, this is frquently not appreciated. Consequently, attempts to improve matters can erroneously take place entirely within the employee relations function when often the need is to remedy weaknesses elsewhere.

There are, however, preventive strategies which can reduce the problems created by poor interdepartmental liaison. As has previously been indicated, the most important strategy is to have the right fit between organisational structure and purpose. Whatever the formal structure, though, other means can be found to improve co-operation. As has also been previously indicated, TQM and developments in information technology usually help interdepartmental co-operation. Positive steps can be taken to encourage team work by the creation of joint departmental teams or project groups containing staff from a range of departments. Contacts made in this way can help develop informal networks which are often the glue that holds organisations together and facilitates coherent activity. The geographic arrangement of work can also have an important and constructive impact if this dimension is given attention. Colleagues, especially those who are not in regular contact with one another, may find it very useful to meet in accessible communal areas such as coffee points. Unfortunately, this idea is often missed, with the consequence that work is physically arranged on the 'battery hen' model, with no thought given on the need to promote informal, and sometimes even formal, interaction. Even open-plan offices may be counter-productive in their effect, as relaxed or confidential exchanges may be discouraged by the 'goldfish bowl' atmosphere they can generate.

ROLE BEHAVIOUR

Personality versus role behaviour

When interacting with colleagues it is important for managers to be able to distinguish between personality behaviour and role behaviour. Role behaviour occurs when a person acts in accordance with the requirements of the position that they hold. Managers may meet with opposition from colleagues that can be wrongly attributed to personality factors. It would be foolish to pretend that personality factors never have an influence on people's behaviour, but it can be all too easy to miss the point that a person may feel obliged to behave in a particular way because of the demands of their job. The danger is that the issue can become personalised. Real role conflicts can thus be exacerbated by personality conflicts. Traditions of hostility can develop and spread through whole departments. It is, unfortunately, so much easier, and often more satisfying, to blame a particular dispute on the actual personality of a protagonist. Sometimes this will even be true – a role may be clumsily or wrongly interpreted by a particular person. It can be very difficult, in the heat of the moment, to reflect that there is nothing personal in the perhaps crucial conflict in which you are involved. The basis of the conflict, however, may be entirely to do with roles and it may be possible to contain the area of conflict by putting one's case assertively, not aggressively. The concept of assertiveness is explained in detail in the next chapter. It is as well to remember, too, that whilst role conflicts can be incorrectly identified as personality clashes, it is rare for the mistake to be made the other way around. The constant danger is that conflict is wrongly attributed to personalities, rather than the reverse.

Failure to recognise that people's behaviour stems from their roles, rather than their personality, is particularly likely when the roles are informal. Often people adopt positions because, for example, they have particular information to hand which is not generally available or its significance may not be generally appreciated. This may drive them into conflict with others, even though their formal roles appear to be compatible.

Reducing conflict

The reason for distinguishing between role and personality behaviour that has been stressed so far is the need to contain the area of conflict to the minimum. It is also important to get the diagnosis right if one is attempting to resolve the conflict. If one makes the mistake of assuming that a conflict is personality-based, when it is in reality because of roles, the false solution may emerge of changing the personalities involved. Thus, an 'awkward' person may be transferred or dismissed, only for the same 'awkward' behaviour to re-emerge with the next job holder. The original solution, as well as having been wrong from an organisational point of view, may also constitute a grave injustice to the person who is removed. In some cases it may even be that a person is only doing their job correctly if they are being awkward. It is partially the understanding of this issue which led to the establishment of traffic wardens. The police had, and to some extent still have, the contradictory tasks of maintaining good relationships with the public and enforcing road traffic legislation. The problem is that the more the public is in conflict with the police about their driving habits the less likely they are to co-operate with the police in other areas. The area of conflict was reduced, and the possibilities of co-operation increased, by the hiving off of the enforcement of parking regulations to traffic wardens. Traffic wardens are much less in need of co-operation from the public than the police. If the public has a hostile attitude to traffic wardens this could even be advantageous, in that it may mean motorists are more likely to adhere to parking regulations. There is the further advantage that the police can be released from routine activity and put on to more demanding work.

It follows from this example that, as well as working out whether behaviour is a product of the role or the person, it is important to ensure that people are given viable roles. If people in managerial positions are expected to issue brickbats, but no bouquets, to their employees, it is unreasonable to expect them to have an easy working relationship with the same people. There is an inevitable tendency in organisations for there to be competition for the handing out of bouquets – like wage rises, good news and perks – and a great reluctance to get embroiled in, for example, disciplinary matters. A way of making it easier for a person to handle the disciplinary aspects is to allow them to take the credit for distributing rewards when these are available.

The task of distinguishing between role and personality behaviour can demand considerable intellectual effort and emotional discipline. However, the rewards can be considerable – starting with the more accurate diagnosis of organisational problems. This can, in many situations, lead to real instead of false solutions. The amount of personal injustice can be reduced and last, but not least, the amount of personal aggravation for oneself diminished.

GENERAL DEVELOPMENTS IN THE PRIVATE AND PUBLIC SECTORS

Most of the major developments in the private sector have already been covered in this chapter. Developments relating to long-term and corporate strategy, including the relationship between operational units and the centre, were covered at the end of the pervious chapter. Many of the issues covered also have considerable significance for the public sector. However, it is appropriate at this stage to explicitly cover important issues which apply to the private sector and which may also be relevant to the public sector. Developments specific to the public sector will then also be examined. A recurring theme in the section on the public sector is how the changes in its framework and operation are creating a much more managerial, as opposed to administrative, culture.

The private sector

Competitive pressures have caused many private sector organisations to 'downsize' and sometimes the concept of being 'lean and mean' has been carried to such an extent that organisations have become 'anorexic'. There has been a general tendency to move towards semi-autonomous business units with financial performance targets. This has reduced the potential for cross-subsidisation within organisations. (These two developments have also been noticeable in the public sector.) The concept of added value has been prominent, with units and individuals expected to justify themselves more in terms of their profitability. These developments in turn have led to a trend to much smaller head offices. There has been a reaction, too, to the Taylorist scientific management approach of division of labour, functional control and non-involvement of the work-force. This has partly been a consequence of more volatile markets. There is more emphasis now on flexibility and work-force involvement in process and product and service improvement. This in turn has necessitated more emphasis on training and creative human resource management, which issues are considered further in Chapters 10 and 12. Of particular importance is the trend to relocate manufacturing processes away from high-cost economies. There is also likely to be increasing competition for the design work to be done in countries with low wage costs. One example of this is the use of satellite transmission to enable computer programming to be undertaken in Eire for American customers. The search for new markets and cost reduction opportunities is also causing more collaborative ventures. The collaboration between the Rover car unit of British Aerospace with Honda is one of many such examples. The subsequent acquisition, in 1994, of Rover cars by the German car manufacturer BMW is also an example of the trend towards more international take-overs as well as the volatility of international markets. Another development has been for companies to plan international marketing strategies. As markets have become globalised so it has become more possible and appropriate to market global or regional, as opposed to national, products.

The changing shape of the public sector

In the UK and many other countries there has been a systematic attempt to redraw the boundaries between the public and private sectors so that many of the activities that were previously in the public sector could be run privately instead. As is so often the case, the shift in emphasis away from direct state spending and control seems to have started in the USA. Many of the interventionist and regulatory policies of the 1960s and before in America and elsewhere were seen not to have worked and had often become prohibitively expensive. Rising public expectations and reduced economic growth were further factors forcing a rethink of the role of the state, including an attempt to reduce the expectations of what the state should do for individuals. President Reagan in America and Margaret Thatcher in the UK were principal exponents of the need to roll back the frontiers of state ownership and regulation. One development of deregulation or divestment tended to lead to another until it became a flood. Associated developments were the opportunities this created for private business, the revenue generated by the sale of state assets and tax cuts. This is a route many countries in both the West and the developing world have followed. It has been given further impetus by the collapse of communism in the former Soviet bloc.

In the UK successive Conservative administrations since 1979 have sought to create an 'enterprise' as opposed to a 'dependency' culture. Privatisation has been one important element in the UK government's strategy. State divestments have included British Telecommunications, British Airways, the British Airports Authority and the steel, coal mining, aerospace, shipbuilding, gas, ports, water supply, and electricity power generation and distribution industries. The state has also divested holdings in various 'private' companies including the Rover Group, Rolls-Royce, Jaguar, Cable and Wireless and much of its holding in British Petroleum. Ordnance factories and naval dockyards have been privatised and the armed services and Ministry of Defence scaled down as a result of the end of the cold war, particularly in administrative and support areas. The railways have been restructured, rolling stock sold and some activities put out to franchise, in preparation for privatisation. Constraints on the way the private sector operates have also been reduced.

The more administratively orientated parts of the public sector have also undergone major changes. Some administrative elements have disappeared completely. In local government the Metropolitan Authorities, the Greater London Council and the Inner London Education Authority have been abolished, thus eliminating the concept of a two-tier system in the areas concerned. There are also proposals to extend this logic to the county council–district council arrangement by abolishing some of the county councils and replacing them with unitary authorities. An alternative scenario is envisaged by the Labour Party, however. They propose to reverse the trend of increasing national government control of local issues, including the hiving off of activities to quangos, by creating Scottish and Welsh assemblies, and possibly regional assemblies in England.

The administrative tier of Area Health Authorities in the National Health Service has been abolished and there are plans to either greatly reduce or eliminate the further tier of Regional Health Authorities. Changes in the Civil Service include the development of the agency concept, which distances services from central government. This issue is examined in more detail later in this chapter.

Comparisons with the private sector

As a corollary of reducing state ownership and control there has been a strong trend to the more effective use of those activities still financed or run by the state. There have been attempts to make the public sector operate more like the private sector. Whilst the public sector has undoubtedly had lessons to learn from the private sector, it would be a mistake to imagine that the differences between the two sectors can be ignored. It would also be a mistake to ignore the considerable variations within the private and public sectors. Public bodies are democratically accountable, have statutory obligations and often have to operate in a sensitive political environment – for example the National Health Service and local government. The aims of public sector bodies often cannot be easily defined and quantified. Often public sector organisations are very large. Much of the private sector, by contrast, is in small units with clear commercial goals. These differences enable private sector organisations often to behave in a way that would be quite inappropriate in the public sector, particularly with regard to risk taking. The overall need can perhaps best be described as for the various elements of the public sector to become more businesslike without trying to operate as businesses.

Having defined the distinctive nature of the public sector it is appropriate, however, to examine the way in which it is adopting a more commercial approach. One way of explaining this is to examine the historic differences between management and administration. This has been done by a British civil servant associated with the Treasury Centre for Administrative Services. The emphasis, with 'management', is on results and on taking calculated risks; with 'administration' it is on procedures, accountability and risk avoidance. These are not complete opposites but rather the ends of a continuum. The general thrust in the public sector has been to shift it more to the managerial end of the continuum. The full list is included as an Appendix to this chapter.

Another basic change is that policy and budgeting is now much more finance-led instead of being on a needs or demand basis. This in turn has meant that managers have to make the best use of a given level of funding, which may necessitate making conscious priorities as explained in the previous chapter. Often the level of funding is geared to 'performance indicators'. There are also attempts to generate cash from the private sector for the public sector, as for example with major transport projects. Publicly funded organisations are now expected to take less of a 'custodial' approach to their assets and more of a market orientation of matching resources with demand. This is in keeping with greater customer orientation and focus on service delivery. A number of organisations have been required to produce 'citizens' charters' guaranteeing standards of service to the public, and in some cases being obliged to make penalty payments if the standards are not met. An increasing amount of work is organised on a contract basis, with public sector bodies being partly or totally financially dependent on the winning and retention of contracts, sometimes in competition with the private sector. The practice has now come to be known as 'market testing'. This concept has also been applied to employment contracts, especially for senior positions. Renewal is logically likely to depend on performance. There has also been a general application of the concept of performance-related pay in the public sector, though, as explained in Chapter 10, the results have been rather disappointing. The new market freedoms have enabled much more generous payments to be made to senior managers. The issue of pay for directors and senior managers in the private and public sectors is considered further in Chapter 12, including the issues of market rates, the control of pay for directors and senior managers and whether the scale of the increases in privatised utilities in particular has been necessary.

One area where a contrast is provided with developments in the USA concerns the use of government purchasing power to influence business behaviour. The federal government has increasingly sought to impose ethical business practices on government contractors. This practice was adopted by some local authorities in Britain with regard to employment policies until their powers to do this were drastically curtailed during Mrs Thatcher's last administration. The Fair Wages Resolutions of the House of Commons, which were applied to those businesses and services receiving government contracts or economic concessions, were rescinded under a previous Thatcher administration. However, experience in the USA especially suggests that the growing sensitivity of customers is likely to create a commercial pressure on an increasing number of private organisations to demonstrate that they have ethical business practices and also that they are behaving responsibly with regard to the local community and the environment.

The massive shift in activity that was envisaged by opening up work from the Civil Service and local government in particular to competitive tendering has been inhibited by the European Community's Acquired Rights Directive. This means that those who win contracts may assume responsibility for the work-force previously undertaking the work at their existing terms and conditions of employment. The extension of these rights to cover non-commercial trades or businesses was incorporated in the Trade Union Reform and Employment Rights Act of 1993. This, and the case law relating to the Acquired Rights Directive, means that these rights generally affect the public as well as the private sector, although there is still some uncertainty about the precise circumstances when contract work is similar enough to the previous activity for these rights to be inherited. A rough guide is to distinguish between the disposal of an economic *entity* (which may involve acquired rights obligations) and an *activity* (which might not).

Quangos and Government agencies

As part of the reshaping of the public sector, work has been systematically removed from direct government control and given to supervisory bodies run by political appointees. These are primarily government-appointed trusts, advisory committees and funding agencies. Some would classify all these bodies as 'quangos' but the Government uses the term more strictly. In a 1994 report in the *Observer* it was reported that 'according to Whitehall there are no quangos at all – although it does not object to the use of the term for some bodies. It prefers "Non-Departmental Public Bodies".'[29]

In the same article it was reported that the government stated that there were 1,389 such quangos and that these excluded Hospital Trusts. According to the *Observer*, though, in 1994 there were 5,521 bodies responsible for almost every aspect of life in Britain, spending £46 billion of taxpayers' money and 70,000 'quangocrats'.[30]

Such bodies are not directly accountable for their activity in the way that elected members of central and local government are. According to a 1993 *Guardian* survey there were 3,000 unelected unaccountable boards and 40,000 appointees, but by 1996 this number was due to rise to 7,700. It was estimated that £24 billion of former local authority-controlled work had been transferred and that already these boards spent more than local authorities on local services. It was also estimated that £30 billion was spent by health boards.[31] Part of the reasoning behind this massive change was that the boards, freed from direct control, would be more enterprising and cost-effective. It also enabled politicians to distance themselves from arguments about funding and the difficult and often sensitive issues of prioritisation, operation and remuneration.

Whatever the advantages, such as greater enterprise and 'value for money', of the removal of so much of public spending from direct democratic supervision, problems have inevitably arisen. The greater freedom has not always been exercised prudently and the Public Accounts Committee in 1994 identified 26 cases where financial systems and controls had been ignored and money was wasted or improperly used. Examples included £65.6 million lost by the Property Services Agency because of a breakdown in invoicing and £48 million spent by the Employment Department on an inefficient computer system.[32] Not everyone is satisfied with the lack of direct democratic accountability of the work undertaken by the boards and the way they have operated in secret. It is also argued that the ethic of honest and impartial public service is being undermined and that a great source of political patronage has been created. The evaluation placed on these developments in the *Observer* article was:

> Earlier this year the all-party Commons Public Accounts Committee declared that standards in the conduct of public business were at their lowest ebb since 1850 when the civil service was cleaned up and patronage eliminated. Now it's back and those involved are doing their utmost to ensure the public has no idea what is going on.[33]

A further issue has been the politicisation of the quangos. Although it was not publicly acknowledged, it would seem that discreet but rigorous checks were regularly undertaken to ensure the 'political acceptability' of those appointed as 'quangocrats'. This not only reduced the pool of available talent, dramatically in some parts of the country, but also caused tensions where there was a divergence of political beliefs between those running quangos and the local community. Such tensions became particularly noticeable in Scotland and Wales.

Another basic issue has been the danger of conflicts of interest between appointees and their commercial interests. This may also have provided an unwelcome incentive for people to use the 'old-boy' network' to try and become members of quangos. 'Fewer than six in every hundred people joining quangos last year [1994] were appointed via the Cabinet Office body set up to identify suitable candidates.'[34] However, in 1995 the government agreed to implement a recommendation made in the first of the Nolan Reports that a Public Appointments Commissioner be appointed to ensure high standards and fair play in appointments to quangos.[35]

FURTHER CHANGES IN SPECIFIC PARTS OF THE PUBLIC SECTOR

The Civil Service

Part of what has been said in the previous section applies to the Civil Service. A particularly important change has been the development of semi-autonomous agencies. The case for this was made in The Next Steps (Ibbs) Report, in 1987.[36] The main thrust of the Ibbs Report was that the Civil Service was too large to be managed effectively and that most of its work should be hived off to semi-autonomous executive agencies. The remaining core would concentrate on giving policy advice. The first executive agency, the Vehicle Inspectorate, was established in 1988 and since then the process has gathered pace. In 1979, when Mrs Thatcher became Prime Minister, there were 732,000 civil servants, but it is estimated in a report in the *Observer* in 1994 that 440,000 of the remaining 546,000 civil servants (81 per cent) will be in executive agencies by the middle of 1995. The *Observer*'s political correspondent went on to say:

That will leave about 54,000 'core' civil servants concentrating on policy advice, strategic management, central purchasing and financial and personnel functions, together with another 49,000 who work in areas too small or too sensitive to be viable or suitable for agency status.[37]

John Garrett MP, a member of the Treasury and Civil Service Select Committee estimated in 1994 that the new structure would 'shortly consist of 30 ministerial headquarters; 150 agencies; hundreds of quangos and thousands of contracts with private contractors'.[38]

Further changes were announced in a Government White Paper in 1994.[39] These included more autonomy in budgeting and staffing arrangements in individual departments or agencies, delayering and a targeted reduction in total staff of 50,000, to less than 500,000, over four years. Changes in accounting practices were also announced, particularly arrangements to monitor capital expenditure more effectively and to ensure that capital resources were used to good effect.[40] The 'mandarin' system was also reviewed by the Cabinet Efficiency Unit. It was recommended that the system be retained but that there should be more internal and external competition for top jobs.[41] The combined impact of these latter recommendations and the White Paper are intended to encourage more movement between the Civil Service and outside employment for senior jobs, individual contracts of employment and some link between pay and performance. The use of fixed-term contracts on a regular basis was not recommended for senior jobs. These planned changes were reinforced by a review of the operation of the Treasury. It was announced in 1994 that delayering would take place, that less detailed control would be exerted over other departments and agencies and that some activities would be scaled down or transferred. One estimate was that the example the Treasury was setting would lead to a reduction of 100,000 jobs in the Civil Service as a whole by the end of the decade.[42]

Clearly, a dramatic restructuring of the Civil Service has taken place. The way in which the agencies actually operate will also be important. A basic issue will be how far the moves to give freedom from Ministerial and Treasury control are taken. The old 'Whitley' system of detailed and centralised pay determination is clearly changing, but pay arrangements in one agency can have a knock-on effect in other agencies, so some restriction of freedom in this area may continue. Another issue will be the extent to which staff can move from one agency to another. One obvious change has been geographical – it was estimated that in 1993 over three-quarters of the agency headquarters were outside London.[43]

Local government

The issues of size and cost-effectiveness have also been of major concern with regard to local government in the UK. Attempts to introduce a greater managerial orientation met with limited success. The scale of local government spending increased substantially in the 1970s and early 1980s. The 'needs-led' policy-making and, hence, budgeting of many local authorities led to large rate increases. The scale of the local government spending problem was such that a whole series of central government counter-measures was instituted, particularly with the aim of creating a tighter financial framework within which local authorities would have to operate. One of the earliest measures was the Local Government Planning and Land Act of 1980 which required direct labour (building) organisations to make a notional 5 per cent return on the capital involved in their activities or close down. In 1982 the Local Government Audit Commission for England and Wales was established; previously local authorities had internally appointed auditors. The Commission was modelled on the central government's 'efficiency unit' and half of the Audit Commission's work was 'value for money' investigations. Other general controls included the reduction or withdrawal of financial assistance from authorities that exceeded spending limits. Rate-capping was also introduced to prevent authorities continuing to balance their books by passing the cost on to the ratepayers. Councillors who set illegal budgets were surcharged and disqualified from office. This all helped create a pattern of finance-led policy and budgeting, with increasing national control.

The pressure to contain local authority spending continued, particularly by the use of compulsory competitive tendering for local authority services and the introduction of the community charge (or poll tax). Under the Local Government Act of 1988 local authorities are obliged to offer designated services to outside competitive tender. The Secretary of State for the Environment is empowered to add to the list of designated services and has used these discretionary powers to extend the range of services that must be put out to tender. There is also a prohibition on taking into account non-commercial matters when awarding contracts. The aim of this is not necessarily to secure privatisation of services, but to ensure that those services councils run themselves are provided on a cost-effective basis. The Act also included further controls to prevent local authorities from using creative accounting to circumvent control of their spending. The introduction of the community charge, first in Scotland in 1989, and then in England and Wales in 1990, was also intended to tighten the financial framework within which local authorities operated. One of its prime purposes was to make local voters more conscious of the need to vote according to the size of the community charge rather than on the basis of party political labels. The unpopularity of the community charge, together with the administrative costs and problems involving collection, led to it being replaced by the council tax in 1993. This combined the concept of payment according to the value of accommodation and the number of adults living in a property.

The cumulative effect of these measures has been fairly dramatic in containing the previous 'runaway' pattern of local authority spending. This has been reinforced by the transfer of major activities to quangos, as previously explained in this chapter. The main thrust of the changes has been to try and inject more financial discipline into local government. Work and remuneration packages are, for example, more likely to be critically reviewed if the choice has to be made between improving performance or reducing services. The concept of local authorities being responsible for the funding and direct delivery of an increasing range of services has been directly challenged. The emerging role model is more an American one of local authorities being simply the providers or co-ordinators of basic services. This concept has been enthusiastically pursued by 'flagship' Conservative-controlled boroughs such as Wandsworth and Westminster. However, as previously explained, local authorities' ability to contract out by market testing has been constrained by the European Acquired Rights Directive. Already, though, local authorities generally are being forced into a more co-ordinating role. The Local Government Management Board in 1993 commented that:

> direct local authority control over services may diminish, as new, appointed bodies assume power in parts of primary and

secondary as well as further eduction, the administration of the police and possibly other areas. Local authorities will have the task of bringing together a fragmented set of (unelected) public service providers.[44]

This emerging role is within the context, not only of increasingly tight national financial control but of increasing central direction about the way in which councils must operate. Examples over and above those already given include the 'freezing' of the revenues generated by the sale of council houses and the introduction of the National Curriculum in schools. A further erosion of local authority discretion has taken place with the local management of schools and the even greater independence of 'opted-out' schools. Another feature is the requirement to publish performance indicators and national league tables of how, for example, schools perform with regard to criteria such as examination results and truancy.

The relentless pressure to improve the cost-effectiveness of local government has led to internal changes in the way authorities are managed. These include de-layering, more generic management (as opposed to specialist management hierarchies) and the development of the purchaser–provider relationship between departments. This latter development involves the creation of 'service level agreements' between departments. This may bring advantages, particularly if it leads to a serious consideration of the needs of users. There can also be advantages in developing agreements so that 'providers' are dependent on the income they generate from internal purchasers. This may also facilitate contracting out if the internal services are found to be uncompetitive. However, there are also considerable dangers in developing service level agreements in this way. Once budget allocations are involved, the focus may be on maximising the gain to a particular department rather than concentrating on the benefit to the organisation as a whole. There are some common features between service level agreements that involve interdepartmental payment and wage incentive schemes. The disadvantages that the latter arrangements can generate are explained in detail in Chapter 7. There is also the issue that in devising service level agreements not all the activities of an organisation can be neatly compartmentalised. The essence of approaches like TQM is in breaking down interdepartmental barriers, not reinforcing them.

The trend of getting better value for money will inevitably

continue, given the low rate of national economic growth and the demands placed on local authorities. These demands are likely to increase because of the problems created by chronic unemployment, continuing urban decay, an ageing population, the level of statutory obligations, and debt repayment. A further development is direct links by local authorities with the European Union, where cases can be made for regional aid.

The National Health Service

The need for the systematic identification of priorities became particularly necessary in the National Health Service and it became obvious that the open-ended commitment to meeting the medical needs of the nation could not be sustained. Advances in medical knowledge, the ageing of the population and rising expectations of what should be provided meant that there were clearly not the resources to do everything. A radical attempt to ensure that the available resources were used to greatest effect was the phasing in of an internal market from 1991 onwards. This involved the establishment of the purchaser–provider relationship. The purchasers are the district health and family health service authorities. They buy services from where they can get the best deal, which includes the private sector. Principal providers are hospital trusts and general practices. The system is still financed by the state and is free at the point of delivery. The concept of value for money is central to the change, particularly given the 'cost-plus' system that operated previously. It is intended that resources will now go to the 'efficient' providers and that all providers will examine ways in which they can provide a more cost-effective service. The new system, and information technology, has helped generate basic performance data such as comparative costs of treatment, comparative waiting times, length of hospital stays and quality indices. There is now greater pressure for providers to examine their working practices. This includes the 'skill mix' of those involved in providing services, in case the 'mix' is unnecessarily costly. It is intended to run down national bargaining, partly to facilitate new local working arrangements. Local bargaining machinery has been established for trust hospitals and other service providers.[45] However, progress in shifting the focus of bargaining to the local level may need to be gradual, given the need to develop the local skills to handle it and the fact that regional and national labour markets also exist for some of the required skills. Other important issues are the targeting of resource allocation, the cost of 'heroic' medicine and whether hospital provision has in some cases become too specialised and fragmented. The system has had its critics, especially as change has been introduced within a wider context of controversy about the level of overall funding. Administrative costs were estimated to have increased from 6 per cent to 11 per cent,[46] and change on this scale has provoked fierce in-fighting between the sectional and vested interests involved.

Other public sector changes

Another part of the public sector to experience the same pattern of change is further and higher education. Intercity and municipal bus services have been deregulated and major change is planned with the provincial police forces. In 1988 29 polytechnics and 35 other major educational establishments were removed from the control of the local authorities and became independent higher education corporations. In 1990 the polytechnics were redesignated universities and the Council for National Academic Awards was abolished. Further education colleges were also removed from local authority control in 1993 to also become independently managed bodies with funding provided nationally. It is also proposed to transfer control of provincial police forces from local authorities to independent bodies. Related proposals are to replace chief constables with 'chief executives' with control of their own budgets, de-layering, the introduction of performance indicators, change from a militaristic to a managerial culture, more 'civilianisation' and greater flexibility in the employment and control of staff.[47] The Home Office is also identifying 'core' and 'ancillary' activities with a view to seeing if more work can be civilianised or contracted out. The extent of the possible change is causing anxiety with some Chief Constables, however, because of the danger, as they see it, that their services become law enforcement agencies rather than being concerned with general policing, which involves a closer and more constructive relationship with the public.

CONCLUSION

The basic theme of this chapter has been that there is no one way of designing an organisation. Organisational structures are means to ends and not ends in themselves. The structure that may be ideal in one situation can be disastrous in another. Managers need to examine the fit between what is appropriate in terms of organisational design and operation and what actually exists. They also need to do what they can to make the fit as close as possible. The parameters within which managers have to work need to be understood, as does the trend of organisational change. The interrelated developments generated by information technology and the globalisation of markets are having a massive impact on the private sector. Whilst there are and will continue to be differences between the private and public sectors, it is illuminating to see the similarities in many general trends common to both sectors. These have been for more market-, or client-, orientated structures with generally greater devolution of authority for decisions in financial and other matters. The tight control of some local government activities is, though, an exception to this general trend. Amongst the effects of the structural and operational changes in the public sector is the identification of much more explicit managerial roles than before. This in turn means that there is a much clearer need for those in positions of authority to develop managerial skills.

Hopefully, individual managers find that they are working in organisations with structures that are congruent with the objectives being pursued. The next issue for managers to consider is whether or not their style is appropriate to the situation they are in. Just as with organisational structure, there is no one pattern that will always guarantee success. The topic of managerial style requires detailed consideration and it logically follows that it should be dealt with in the next chapter.

NOTES

1 F. W. Taylor, *Scientific Management*, Greenwood Press, 1972; first published 1911.
2 Henri Fayol, *General and Industrial Management*, translated from the French Dunod edition by Constance Storrs, Pitman, 1967; first French edition published 1916; the Storrs' translation first published 1949.
3 F. J. Roethlisberger and W. J. Dickson, *Management and the Worker*, Harvard University Press, 1939.
4 T. Burns and G. M. Stalker, *Management of Innovation*, Tavistock Publications, 1972; first published 1961. For a summary of this work, see Honor Croome, *Human Problems of Innovation*, Ministry of Technology, Pamphlet, 1970, reprint.
5 Charles Handy, *Understanding Organisations*, 4th edn, Penguin, 1993.

6 Thomas J. Peters and Robert H. Waterman Jr., *In Search of Excellence, Lessons from America's Best-run Companies*, HarperCollins, 1982.

7 David Guest, 'Right Enough to be Dangerously Wrong: An Analysis of the *In Search of Excellence* Phenomenon', in Graeme Salaman (ed.), *Human Resources Strategies*, edited by Sage Publications in association with the Open University, 1992.

8 Tom Peters and Nancy Austin, *A Passion for Excellence*, Random House, 1985.

9 Tom Peters, *Thriving on Chaos*, Pan Books in association with Macmillan, 1988.

10 Tom Peters, *Liberation Management*, Macmillan, 1992; also Pan, 1994.

11 Robert H. Waterman Jr., *The Frontiers of Excellence (Learning from Companies that Put People First)*, Nicholas Brealey, 1994.

12 J. Atkinson, *Flexibility, Uncertainty and Manpower Management*, IMS Report no. 89, Institute of Manpower Studies, 1985.

13 John Stanworth and Celia Stanworth, *Telework: The Human Resource Implications*, Institute of Personnel Management, 1991.

14 Chris Brewster and Stephen Connock, *Industrial Relations: Cost Effective Strategies*, Hutchinson, 1985.

15 *Equal Opportunities Commission v Secretary of State for Employment* [1994] 1 All ER 910.

16 *Vroege v NCIV*, IRLR, vol. 23, no. 12, December 1994 (C/57/93), pp. 651–62, *Fisscher v Voorhuius Hengelo*, IRLR, vol. 23, no. 12, December 1994 (C/128/93), pp. 662–6.

17 Alan McGregor and Alan Sproull, 'Employers and the Flexible Workforce', *Employment Gazette*, May 1992, pp. 225–34.

18 David Hutchins, *Quality Circles Handbook*, Pitman, 1985, p. 1.

19 Ron Collard and Barrie Dale, 'Quality Circles: Why They Break Down and Why They Hold Up', *Personnel Management*, February 1985, pp. 28–32.

20 Ibid.

21 Stephen Halliday, *Which Business: Tested Ideas for Profitable Businesses*, Kogan Page, 1994.

22 R. C. Voss and R. C. O'Brien, *In Search of Quality*, London Business School, 1992.

23 Economist Intelligence Unit/George Binney, *Making Quality Work*, Economist Intelligence Unit, 1992.

24 Joan Woodward, *Industrial Organisation: Theory and Practice*, Oxford University Press, 1965. For a summary of this work see Joan Woodward, 'Management and Technology' (Ministry of Technology pamphlet, 1970), reprint.

25 Alan Cane, 'Failure of Computers "May Kill"', *Financial Times*, 14 June 1993.

26 House of Commons Public Accounts Committee, *Proper Conduct of Public Business*, House of Commons Paper 154, HMSO, 1994.

27 For a particularly useful account of the impact of information technology on organisations see Michael S. Scott Morton (ed.), *The Corporation of the 1990s*, Oxford University Press, 1991.

28 Joan Woodward, *Industrial Organisation*.

29 Barry Hugill, 'Invisible Army of the Quangos Marches On', *Observer*, 3 July 1994.
30 Ibid.
31 *Guardian*, Leader, 29 January 1994.
32 House of Commons Public Accounts Committee Report, op. cit.
33 Barry Hugill, op. cit.
34 Response to a parliamentary question reported in *Independent*, 18 May 1995.
35 Committee on Standards in Public Life, *Volume 1 Report*, Book no. 0101285027, HMSO, 1995.
36 K. Jenkins et al., *Improving Management in Government: The Next Steps* (the Ibbs Report), HMSO, 1988.
37 Anthony Bevins, Political Editor, 'Mandarins in Whitehall Counter-revolution', *Observer*, 22 May 1994.
38 David Rose, 'A Dangerous State of Irresponsibility', *Observer*, 30 January 1994. See also, John Garrett, *Westminster: Does Parliament Work?*, Gollancz, 1992.
39 *The Civil Service: Continuity and Change*, HMSO, 1994.
40 *Better Accounting for the Taxpayer's Money: Resource Accounting and Budgeting in Government*, Cmnd. 2626, HMSO, 1994.
41 *Review of Fast Stream Recruitment*, HMSO, 1994.
42 *Independent*, 20 October 1994.
43 Susan Corby, 'One More Step for the Civil Service', *Personnel Management*, August 1993, p. 31.
44 Local Government Management Board, *Managing Tomorrow*, Panel of Inquiry report, Local Government Management Board, 1993, p. 10.
45 'NHS Trusts Told to Establish Local Pay Machinery by February 1995', *Personnel Management*, July 1994, p. 5.
46 *Evening Standard*, London, Leader, 13 January 1994.
47 Jane Goodsir, 'A New Beat for HR in the Police', *Personnel Management*, December 1993, pp. 34–6, 57.

APPENDIX TO CHAPTER 3 THE DIFFERENT CHARACTERISTICS OF ADMINISTRATION AND MANAGEMENT

	Administration	Management
Objectives	Stated in general terms and reviewed or changed infrequently.	Stated as broad strategic aims supported by more detailed short-term goals and targets reviewed frequently.
Success criteria	Mistake-avoiding Performance rarely measurable.	Success-seeking Performance mostly measurable.
Resource use	Secondary task	Primary task
Decision-making	Has to make few decisions but affecting many and can take time over it.	Has to make many decisions affecting few and has to make them quickly.
Structure	Roles defined in terms of areas of responsibility. Long hierarchies; limited delegation.	Shorter hierarchies; maximum delegation.
Roles	Arbitrator	Protagonist
Attitudes	Passive: workload determined outside the system. Best people used to solve problems.	Active: seeking to influence the environment. Best people used to find and exploit opportunities.
	Time-insensitive	Time-sensitive
	Risk avoiding	Risk accepting but minimising it
	Emphasis on procedure	Emphasis on results
	Doing things right	Doing the right things
	Conformity	Local experiments: need for conformity to be proved.
	Uniformity	Independence
Skills	Legal or quasi-legal	Economic or socio-economic
	Literacy (reports, notes)	Numeracy (statistics, figures)

Chapter 4

Managerial style

INTRODUCTION

Leadership and effective management are confused with the concept of 'charisma'. Whilst there are situations in which charisma can be important, the main theme of this chapter is that managers need to try to match their style to the situation. The effective manager is likely to be the one who can do this. Obviously, the greater the range of skills managers have, the more potential they have for being effective – provided they can adapt in such a way that they use the right skills at the right time.

A number of factors have tended to reduce the extent to which managers can rely on the exercise of formal authority for getting their job done. These factors include social, technological and organisational developments. This has put a premium on the more political styles of management, with formal authority being used as a last rather than a first resort, although changes in economic circumstances have sometimes caused a reversion to more authoritarian managerial styles. Issues covered in the previous chapter have also had an impact on managerial style. These include the trend towards more organic-type organisations, which puts a premium on managers co-ordinating the expertise necessary to undertake tasks that may be widely distributed. Managers may need to develop, and also be dependent on 'sapiential authority' – a concept that is explained in this chapter. Initiatives such as TQM depend for their success on employee involvement and often managerial philosophies have changed to those recognising the need for such involvement.

There is still considerable variety in the types of situation in which managers find themselves. There are many factors which can have a bearing on the style that will be appropriate in a given situation. Some of these factors are examined in this chapter, including the effect of cultural differences and the problems that may be faced by managers working abroad. The concept of assertiveness and its relevance to management is also covered. Finally, guidance is given on how managerial style can be evaluated, bearing in mind that ultimately it is effectiveness that matters, with style being a means to an end and not an end in itself.

THE AUTHORITY OF THE MANAGER

Managers will normally have a certain amount of formal authority. This will entitle them to issue instructions, distribute rewards and administer discipline to help them accomplish the work for which they are held accountable. Often, however, managers have to look less to their formal authority and more to other means of influencing the behaviour of their subordinates and colleagues. In some cases they may be in a powerful position with regard to the distribution of rewards and administration of discipline. In other cases managers will have much less in the way of formal control over rewards and penalties. This is often still true in the public sector, despite the many changes explained in the previous chapter. Managers may have relatively little influence over the remuneration or promotion of subordinates. They may be able to make recommendations about promotion but only subject to checks and balances such as promotion boards. The same may be the case with discipline, especially given the requirement, explained in Chapter 11, that dismissal should not be effected by the immediate superior.

The authoritarian styles of past periods are generally less acceptable today. Despite chronic unemployment, managers often need to achieve a large measure of consent for their actions. The social and other pressures that subordinates can put on bosses may be reinforced by union organisation. Managers may also have to deal with unions amongst white-collar employees in the private sector, as well as in the more traditional areas of union organisation amongst manual workers and employees at all levels in the public sector.

All this does not mean that managers should never give orders or that they should opt out of the disciplinary side of their jobs. The point is that these are usually best employed as a last rather than a first resort. Managers who feel that they cannot do anything unless there is consensus, will in, fact be opting out of management. Conflicts are inevitable; unpalatable decisions have to be taken and, if necessary, imposed – otherwise organisations will die through paralysis. Resolving such issues is likely, though, to require careful diagnosis and patient navigation rather than the often traditional approach of issuing a diktat. Organisations, as well as society, have tended to become more complex. In a technologically sophisticated age the expertise necessary to cope with particular problems is often widely distributed within organisations. This is reinforced by the growing, and often increasingly specialised, developments in education, training and experience. Managers are more likely to be focal points for assembling the right mix of information and personnel to deal with particular problems. If employees are mishandled they may withhold their co-operation and expertise or it may be that they are simply not given the opportunity to contribute. The manager thus has to behave much more as a facilitator. In commenting on organisations that depend on the effective use of Intelligence, Ideas and Information (the 'Triple I Organisation') Handy says that:

> It is this type of organisation which has given rise to what has been called the post-heroic leader. Whereas the heroic manager of the past knew all, could do all and could solve every problem, the post heroic manager asks how every problem can be solved in a way that develops other people's capacity to handle it.[1]

This underlines the dangers of the charismatic approach. Whilst it is foolish to suggest that charisma is not a potential asset, it needs to be clearly understood that it can also have a downside. Charismatic leadership can be reassuring and exciting, but it is heavily dependent on the judgement of the leader and the results can be disastrous if that judgement is flawed. The gap between followers and leader can become too great, rendering upward communication difficult and encouraging subordinates to surrender responsibility and independent thought. This in turn may create further opportunities or pressure on the charismatic leader to behave as though omniscient, thus further increasing the likelihood of failure.

These views are underlined by the Local Government Management Board who predict that:

Among future management roles are those of the honest broker, and negotiator, requiring qualities of peacemaking and peacekeeping between conflicting interests, and a temperament which maximises agreement, and mutual benefits. Vital management skills, in short, include dealing with, leading, motivating, handling people. Good management will more and more be seen as unlocking barriers to performance by colleagues and subordinates, enhancing their contribution, and releasing their potential. Management involves simultaneously playing as a team member while pushing the team forward – not least in conveying a sense of direction, by successfully painting a picture of the future.[2]

Sapiential authority

In piecing together the permutations of people and expertise needed to solve organisational problems it should be remembered that managers will also be contributing their own expertise. Just as managers are going to be dependent on subordinates and colleagues, so others are likely to be partly dependent on them. Much of the manager's contact with others will be when the manager helps them to accomplish tasks or, indeed, when others help the manager to accomplish tasks. This may lead to the development of sapiential authority by the manager, i.e., leadership by virtue of their particular expertise. Such expertise will not just be specialist knowledge but often, significantly, a knowledge of organisational procedures and processes. The critical skill of managers is likely to be knowing how decisions are taken or can be taken. As much as anything, managers may be facilitators. This will not just be within a department but will also involve contacts with other parts of an organisation. It is perhaps only when this facilitating, problem-solving approach breaks down that managers need resort to their formal authority, and even then it may be inappropriate.

In some situations it may be appropriate to try to develop a sapiential-type relationship with new subordinates as soon as they start. Newcomers may, especially in professional-type jobs, be resentful of too much formal guidance about how they should do their job. If the manager gives them enough rope, so that they realise their limitations for themselves, after a little while they may then be glad enough to come to the manager for help. I have encountered this issue particularly with new lecturing staff. They may be very indignant if it is suggested that they need advice, especially if the formal reporting lines are blurred, and thus they find it fairly easy to 'fob' off suggestions about how they should do their job. The knack in establishing an effective working relationship in this type of situation seems to be to avoid souring the relationship by giving advice when the person is not ready for it. It may be necessary to make a general statement about being willing to help should it be necessary. It may then be best, provided the damage done is not too great, to let a person find things out the hard way. If they then admit to being in difficulties, that is the time to offer help, with the newcomer's face being saved by them being the one who has initiated the request for help. The pattern may then be set for a long-term effective working relationship.

Relationships with people in other departments

Managers need political skills to negotiate, not only with subordinates but also in a more general context within the organisation. Managers will find that, just as their formal authority is in fact restricted by the attitudes and behaviour of subordinates, so will it be restricted by the behaviour of colleagues in other departments. Colleagues in other departments may have formal functional control over part of the manager's job. Even if they do not, the reality of many line and staff relationships is such that it is often very difficult for the manager to resist advice from specialist advisers. Managers may not have the knowledge to argue with the specialists on a particular topic. If they argue, there is the danger of being proved wrong in the face of advice; if they refrain from argument and things go wrong, they can rely on the protection of saying they have followed specialist advice. In any case, specialist advisers can always threaten to take an issue up the organisation to someone superior if managers indicate they are going to ignore the advice. In some cases the managers themselves will be specialist advisers. The comments about managerial style already made may be particularly appropriate to them. They may rely on their formal relationship and perhaps emphasise this with claims to a professional level of expertise not necessarily accepted by those on whom they wish to impose their advice.

As was explained in Chapter 3, organisation problems are often highly interactive, even when organisation charts suggest that the various parts of an organisation are largely autonomous. Specialist advisers may find that they make much more progress by trying to find out the problems that colleagues have, and then trying to help them with them, rather than by making extravagant and perhaps quite unjustified claims about their special knowledge and right to interfere. This may have considerable implications for the training of specialists. It may well be that specialists need training sufficient for them at least to comprehend the nature of the various parts of the organisation they are in. Training that is a combination of this and specialist expertise may enable them to integrate with their colleagues far more effectively than training which concentrates only on their specialist area. (This is explained further, with particular reference to the specialism of employee relations, in Chapter 12.) Managers are likely to be most effective if they concentrate on the influence they can develop by political skill and patient negotiation with those around them, rather than by the use of formal authority. This is not to say that formal authority should be ignored but, when it is invoked, it should be as part of the political judgement of the manager, that is, invoked only in such a way and at such a time that it is likely to be effective rather than counter-productive.

TRADITIONAL AND SITUATIONAL APPROACHES TO LEADERSHIP

Having suggested that there is likely to be an increasing need for, and emphasis on, the role of the manager as a facilitator, it is also necessary to state that there will always be a wide variety in the nature of managerial jobs. Factors such as the specialist expertise required, the extent of the manager's formal authority and discretion, and the rate of change will vary from place to place and over time. This variety is such that traditional approaches to leadership, often called 'trait' theories, have often not proved helpful in the selection or guidance of managers. An exercise that demonstrates this is to ask a person or group what characteristics are necessary for an effective leader or effective manager. Inevitably one gets a list which includes such attributes as honesty, intelligence, consistency, integrity, firmness, ruthlessness, flexibility, imagination, technical excellence, charisma, and so on. It can then emerge that the list could go on for ever and that the requirements be so demanding that no mortal could fulfil them. There are other problems: the attributes may overlap, be controversial and in some cases plain contradictory. So we are left with the question of what attributes make an effective leader or manager, and the answer, of course, is that it all depends on the situation. The attributes that may be essential in one situation may be disastrous in another. One looks at the managerial situation first and then at the person who is in that situation or who is being considered for that situation. What is important is that they possess the key attributes relevant to that situation.

The key attributes will vary over time as well. There is no guarantee that a productive matching of manager to situation will be permanently effective – situations can change, as can managers. One sees this particularly in the world of politics. Great leaders can be thrown up in times of war who might otherwise have remained in obscurity – 'cometh the hour, cometh the man'. They may replace leaders whose skills might have been entirely appropriate for conditions of peace. Conversely, at the end of a war, further new leaders may emerge with attributes more appropriate to peacetime again. Great revolutionary leaders may similarly prove disastrous in the period when consolidation is required – all the more so as their prestige may enable them to pursue quite the wrong policies for a while when the revolution is over. Chairman Mao Zedong appears to have been but one example of this, as was later admitted in China. Another example concerns the many failures of successful businessmen trying to make a career in politics. Whilst there are exceptions, so often businessmen fail to be able to cope with the quite different power relationships, particularly the fact that power tends to come from 'grassroots' in politics and not simply because one is at the top of an executive chain of command.

The significance of this situational view of management and leadership has major implications for the basic training and assessment of managers. This issue is considered in depth in Chapters 1 and 10. 'Although there may be a common core of management skills, it is necessary to take into account the variety of situations managers may have to confront.' Supplementary training may be necessary for the specific situations managers find themselves in. The definition of skills (or competences) required may help in this respect, as long as the problems relating to transferability are understood.

ALTERNATIVES IN MANAGEMENT STYLE

Just as the attributes required by a manager vary from situation to situation, so does the managerial style that is appropriate to the situation. When speed is of the essence, and critical information and expertise are vested in one person, authoritarian leadership may be appropriate and acceptable. When the conditions are reversed, a more democratic style of leadership is likely to prove more effective. It may be that a particular situation can be effectively handled in more than one way – what matters ultimately is whether or not a style is effective. However, there can be mismatches between the style and the situation. Hopefully, managers can judge what style is appropriate and operate accordingly. To some extent this is done intuitively, but there are limits to the extent to which this matching is done or indeed can be done. The matching issue may not always be recognised or the wrong style may be chosen. Even when the problems are recognised, there are limits to the extent to which anybody can switch from one mode of behaviour to another. It may be that people tend to gravitate to jobs and organisations that suit their natural style. Problems may occur when a situation changes, even if only temporarily, and a person needs to act in what for them is an unnatural style. Managers also need to take the personalities of their subordinates into account: the style that works with one person may not work with another.

Theories X and Y

A particularly useful classification is that given by Douglas McGregor[3] with his distinction between the Theory X and Theory Y managerial styles. The implicit assumptions behind the Theory X style is that employees need, and will respond to, close direction and control. This in turn is based on the assumptions that people would prefer to avoid work if they can, do not want to accept responsibility and effectively have to be coerced if organisational objectives are to be achieved. The Theory Y approach is based on the assumption that individual and organisational goals can be integrated. This in turn is based on the assumptions that work is a natural activity, that people will respond positively to objectives to which they are committed, that emotional satisfaction can be achieved and that employees will, under the right working conditions, accept responsibility. One can use McGregor's classification to examine one's own style and underlying assumptions as well as those of colleagues. Consideration of what style is being used is necessary, primarily to see if it fits the situation. People can adopt a particular style in all situations without pausing to examine when it is appropriate and when it is not. They may also undertake tasks or jobs when they may be better left to someone with a more appropriate style for that situation.

Organisation and social developments have made Theory Y an increasingly important style in recent decades. However, to suggest that Theory Y is always appropriate would be to miss McGregor's basic point that styles need to match situations and the situations will vary. Theories X and Y represent different ends of a continuum rather than completely separate alternatives. There tends to be much more emotional appeal to the Theory Y approach but the reality has to be faced that the right conditions cannot always be created for it to work effectively. It may not be possible to integrate individual goals with organisational goals. In a car factory, for example, whilst work remains thoroughly boring, managers are going to be forced to adopt a more coercive style than in jobs where there is much more opportunity for self-fulfilment.

It also needs to be clearly recognised that the current economic climate has precipitated a change in style in some organisations – with less emphasis being placed on Theory Y and more on Theory X. This has been because of increased divergence in the goals of employers and employees. Consequently, changes such as staff reduction have often had to be imposed, Theory-X-style, because the opportunity for Theory-Y-type agreement was not possible. Thus, managers need to be aware that, even if a particular style has worked well in the past, changed circumstances can necessitate an adjustment in managerial style. Despite chronic unemployment, though, it is interesting to note the deliberate changes that some organisations have tried to make in their style. Deming's approach to TQM, explained in the previous chapter, was firmly based on Theory Y assumptions, which does mean that one has to be sure that such assumptions are appropriate if TQM is to be introduced in an organisation. Japanese and other initiatives for involving the work-force represent at least an element of the Theory Y approach and are in stark contrast to the historic Taylorist approach. Critics of Japanese-style involvement would claim, though, that the aim is a manipulated and coerced consensus.[4]

Other 'style' theories

Besides Douglas McGregor, Tannenbaum and Schmidt have also written about leadership styles[5] and built up a model based on the idea of a continuum of styles ranging from authoritarian behaviour at one end to democratic at the other, as illustrated in Figure 4.1. The model aims to make managers aware of the range of different styles that are available, the idea being that they choose the most appropriate style to fit the situation, even though it may not be their preferred way of operating.

Further leadership studies have emphasised different situational variables that managers should take into account when adopting a particular managerial style. Blake and Mouton's Managerial Grid[6] is based on the notion of employee-orientated and production-

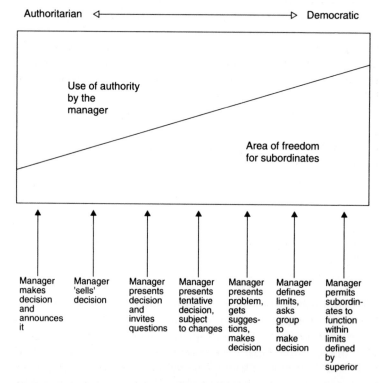

Authoritarian ⟵————————————————————⟶ Democratic

Use of authority by the manager

Area of freedom for subordinates

| Manager makes decision and announces it | Manager 'sells' decision | Manager presents decision and invites questions | Manager presents tentative decision, subject to changes | Manager presents problem, gets suggestions, makes decision | Manager defines limits, asks group to make decision | Manager permits subordinates to function within limits defined by superior |

Figure 4.1 A continuum of leadership styles
Source: Adapted from Tannenbaum and Schmidt, 'How to Choose a Leadership Pattern', *Harvard Business Review*, 1957, vol. 36, p. 96

orientated management styles. The grid is a matrix showing possible management styles based on two major variables: concern for people and concern for production. Blake and Mouton designed a management questionnaire so that individuals could identify where they fell on the grid in terms of management style. Whether this exercise has any scientific validity or not, the grid does help to identify the twin emphases that managers will need to put on both task and employee needs. The thrust of this and related research is that the more effective managers try to reconcile these two sets of needs rather than acting on just one or the other. This finding is of especial importance to those who believe that chronic unemployment is an opportunity to engage in 'macho-management'. The reality is more likely to be that this provides an opportunity for self-indulgence rather than a way of getting the best out of the available resources.

A further perspective is provided by the work of Belbin.[7] He became interested in how groups worked or failed to work. A prime conclusion was that much depended on the mix of the group. Unless the appropriate permutation of roles was present, a group, however apparently talented, might be ineffective. The roles that were needed for a group to be successful were identified by Belbin as being:

- the chair
- the shaper (dominant, passionate extroverted)
- the plant (creative, intelligent introverted)
- the monitor/evaluator
- the resource investigator (source of new contacts but not originator)
- the company worker (the practical organiser)
- the team worker (concerned with facilitating the work of the group)
- the finisher

The implications for managerial style are that it may be necessary to consider the mix of a team and to be prepared to play whatever role or roles are missing. It may be that not all groups require the exact permutation identified by Belbin, and members of the group may be able to switch from one role to another as the need dictates. This is particularly important if one has little control over membership. However, there are enough everyday examples of talented but ineffective groups to underline the importance of

Belbin's work in considering how to make groups more effective. Another important attribute may be that of creativity – sometimes this is crucial for the very survival of organisations. Some senior managers make the mistake of believing that they must be the ones who come up with the creative ideas and ignore what can be a great fund of creativity within their team. There can be actual dangers in having the lead manager as the creative thinker, as the very fact that a person is full of ideas may mean that they are not very good at organising. A dramatic example of the potential importance of this issue is provided by the disaster in 1995 when six climbers (including the British mountaineer Alison Hargreaves, who had recently climbed Mount Everest solo without oxygen) were blown to their deaths whilst descending from the summit of the second highest peak in the world, K2, in the Himalayas (a seventh who did not reach the top died from pneumonia). The lack of a person playing the evaluator/monitor role with regard to the feasibility of the attempt, given the deteriorating weather conditions, may have been tragically crucial. According to fellow mountaineer Peter Hillary (son of Sir Edmund Hillary, the first man to climb Everest) who abandoned his simultaneous attempt to climb K2:

> Summit fever had developed in that group. There was a chemistry in there that meant that they were going for the summit no matter what. They were all driving each other on . . . These people came together and, because of the place and the atmosphere and their personalities, they became blinkered and simply focused on the top . . . There was no careful awareness in the group and the most dangerous thing about groups is that people hand over responsibility for themselves to someone else . . . It means that no one is taking responsibility. There can be a false sense of security in numbers.[8]

The related issues of meetings and chairing are the subject matter of the final chapter of this book.

CONTINGENCY THEORIES

Several theorists have attempted to link together the variables that will determine the leadership style that is appropriate in a particular situation. One such 'contingency style' was developed by John Adair and called 'action-centred leadership'.[9] His idea is that a manager should take three variables into account when deciding what would be appropriate behaviour at a particular time. These variables are task needs, group needs and individual needs, as shown in Figure 4.2.

Adair felt that the successful manager would be one who was aware of the priority attached to each area of needs in a particular situation and was prepared to subsume the other variables as the situation demanded, e.g., if the situation was urgent the task needs would predominate. The manager would therefore be adopting a flexible style depending on the circumstances.

Fiedler also developed a 'leadership contingency model' which involved identifying three important variables:[10]

1 Leader-member relations
2 Degree of structure in the task
3 Power and authority of the manager's position

He concluded that the most effective style when the situation was either very favourable or very unfavourable to the manager would be a structured style. This could be used when the power of the leader was very high or very low, when the leader was either very well-liked or intensely disliked and when the task was very clearly structured or extremely loose and ill-defined. However, in a situation where the variables were only moderately favourable, then a supportive style was best. This theory has been built upon by

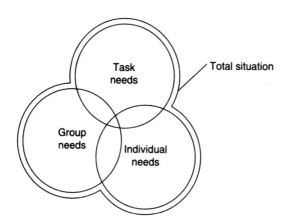

Figure 4.2 John Adair's action-centred model of leadership

Charles Handy who describes a 'best fit' approach in his book *Understanding Organisations.*[11]

ENVIRONMENTAL FACTORS

So far we have discussed the impact of task/goals, the manager's subordinates and the attributes of an individual manager. A manager's style will also be influenced by the environment in which they work. Key features in the environment will be the style of senior managers, particularly the immediate boss, and regional and national culture. When managers move to other organisations they need to pay particular attention to the traditions of the organisation they have joined.

The immediate superior

The person in charge of a manager is likely to have an important say in the selection of a subordinate manager. They will also have their own style of management, which they will often see as being appropriate and perhaps a model for the subordinate manager. Even if the subordinate manager does not accept that the model is appropriate, they are likely to be wary of managing in a style which is not favoured by their boss. If the boss's style is in tune with that of other senior managers, a manager may take a somewhat pessimistic view of their promotion chances if they develop what is seen, rightly or wrongly, as a wayward style. Many subordinates may accept that their boss's behaviour is the received wisdom of how managers should behave in that environment. Sometimes there will be a need for the styles to be complementary rather than similar. This point was made to me by a former Royal Air Force officer with regard to the relationship between the commanding officer of a unit and their adjutant. In his view it was necessary for the one to take a hard disciplinary line, and for the other to take a much softer line and be psychologically available so that they could find out what people really felt as well as smooth any ruffled feathers. This is somewhat reminiscent of police methods of interrogation when one police officer takes the hard line and the other the soft line. In the view expressed to me about the Air Force it was maintained that it did not matter who took the hard line and who the soft line as long as each took one and that they worked as a team. That way, effective control, based on reliable information and reasonable morale, could be exercised. If both the command-ing officer and the adjutant adopted the same style it was argued that either there would be an excess of control and lack of reliable information or the reverse.

Another example of the dovetailing of styles is the relationship between a fee-charging doctor or dentist and the receptionist. The doctor or dentist will usually leave the potentially embarrassing business of payment to the receptionist, so that it does not interfere with the relationship between the professional and their client.

There is one other way in which the influence of the boss on the subordinate manager should be examined. This concerns the extent to which the boss enables the subordinate manager to develop as a manager. One of the problems of authoritarian styles is that the subordinate manager will be expected constantly to refer matters upwards and not encouraged to make their own decisions and stand on their own feet. People tend to learn either by being told or by being allowed to find out for themselves. The latter approach, whilst perhaps taking more time, may lead to a greater understanding and commitment as well as to a greater amount of self-reliance by the individual concerned. In practice, there has to be a mix, but the balance can differ radically from one situation to another. One of the harsh realities that managers may have to face is that at some stage they may find that they are working for a boss who is thoroughly incompetent or unreason-able. There can, however, be some capital in such an experience, provided the experience is not too devastating or too long-lived. This may paradoxically develop the self-reliance of the subordinate manager. They may realise quite clearly that they cannot get help from above and consequently look more to their own abilities and judgement for handling their job, even if their prime objective is to work for someone else as soon as possible.

Culture

As well as having to fit with the style of other managers, it is also necessary for managers to take account of the expectations and constraints of a range of cultures. This can include cultures specific to an organisation, social class or work group as well as to a geographical area. Managers may find that they have to take account of a move from one part of a country to another. It may even be that there are quite false expectations and prejudices about the way a manager is likely to behave because, for example, they speak with a home counties' accent and have gone to work in Merseyside. In working with various regional companies within the Bass group, I found that there were significant variations in managerial style, particularly with regard to employee relations, which seemed to be largely connected with the regional culture. This variation was found to be particularly important when a large new brewery was constructed in Merseyside at Runcorn. Many of the managers who ran the brewery were transferred from Burton-on-Trent and they tended to concentrate on just the technical aspects of their work. They soon found that a rather different style, involving more attention to employee relations, was needed *vis-à-vis* the local labour force, compared with the style that was appropriate in the very different and more compliant culture of Burton.

The need to understand the differing cultures of others that you have to work with is of increasing importance as markets are increasingly globalised. This may be for a variety of reasons, including a wider spread of markets and the greater possibility of working for a multi-national or trans-national organisation. Additionally, countries such as the UK are more cosmopolitan than they were. The differences in value systems between cultures are important but may not be easy to recognise. The importance of age, gender, social position, family connections, rank and merit may vary critically. Attitudes to authority, secrecy and the concept of time can vary widely too. In the West the importance paid to cause and effect in explaining, or seeking to influence events, can be more rigidly applied than in some other cultures. A crucial variable is often religion and this can be a key issue within Western cultures as well as between Western and Eastern cultures. It is possible that many of the differences between the UK and the founder members of the European Union are based on Britain's Protestant ethic and emphasis on the rights and responsibilities of the individual, particularly when there has been a Conservative government in the UK. This in contrast to the Catholic traditions and emphasis on social welfare in France, Italy, Belgium and West Germany (about half of which was Catholic prior to reunification). This may also partly explain the UK's historic dilemma as to whether or not to align itself with Europe or with the USA, which has a closer religious heritage as well as a common language.

The issue of the importance of the individual is a key variable in comparing the UK with Japan and it is full of practical implications for managing work-forces. Unfortunately, the importance of these differences is often not appreciated either by individuals or organisations operating abroad. There are many examples of companies seeking to rigidly impose their home culture in other countries and failing to do so because of the entrenched nature of cultural values. A way of organisations seeking to constructively adapt is to ensure that they have at least one locally appointed executive who is allowed to interpret the local culture to the 'guest organisation'. It is also necessary, though, to avoid stereotyping people because of their ethnic or cultural background and this includes failing to recognise the impact of a person's personality on their behaviour.

Working in other countries

The problems of adjusting to local cultures can be magnified enormously when working in another country. I have found on my various assignments in other countries, mainly in the Far East, that the first key task is to develop some understanding of the local culture. This you ignore at your peril. On one occasion I met an engineering manager who had just started a three-year contract and had flown out from the UK on the same plane as I had. He plunged straight into the technical aspects of the job and gave no attention as to how he might adjust to the habits, beliefs and expectations of his local colleagues. Sadly, we were both on the same flight home, his contract having been terminated after only three weeks!

The temptation in any strange environment, whether it be in a new organisation, a new part of or a new country, or both, is to use one's previous experience as a model. The problem is that in a different country there will be many new factors to take into account. Tradition, religion, climate, language, economic and political constraints, social habits, history, the skills of the population and the very nature of the problems experienced are all likely to be different. With the benefit of historical hindsight one realises that, whilst British colonial rule brought many advantages as well as disadvantages to her former colonies, many of the institutions that were imposed were quite inappropriate in the very different social circumstances. I have in mind particularly such institutions as large hospitals, universities and political structures. Just as institutions need to fit the local situation, so managers must be prepared to adapt their behaviour. Unfortunately, managers may be unused to thinking in these terms; they assume that their home experience represents the best practice rather than the practice that may have been the most appropriate to the home situation. Many of the cultural differences may be all the more difficult to take into account because they are so much part of one's normal behaviour that it is difficult to comprehend that other people think or act in a different way. Consequently, expatriate managers may not even realise there is a difference and local colleagues may not see the need to warn them about a particular convention until it is too late. The commercial importance of the Islamic world, for example, is such that it is vital for managers who work in Islamic countries, or simply with people from those countries, to develop some appreciation of Islam. Offence can unwittingly be caused by ignorance of basic customs. An example of this can be the indelicacy of discussing interest repayments without an appreciation of the theological objections to usury.

One of the critical conventions that I found it necessary to understand in the Far East was the reluctance of people to express open criticism, particularly to a visitor in a position of authority. Unfortunately, this could lead to visitors assuming that their behaviour, in the absence of adverse comment, was entirely acceptable and then plough on, committing blunder after blunder. In the UK hints would be dropped far more quickly but, as far as I can judge, many of the nationalities in the Far East find it far more difficult to suggest that a person is behaving inappropriately. This means that visitors may be deprived of the necessary feedback about the effects of their behaviour, feedback they need more than ever in a different country. This may be reinforced by the tendency of many expatriate managers to spend most of their social time in the company of other expatriates. In some cases this may degenerate into a collective condemnation of the local environment and the assertion that the home country which they voluntarily left holds no equal.

In case the number of new factors that the recently arrived manager has to cope with seems daunting, it should be emphasised that in the process of adjustment one is likely to earn some credit for simply trying. There is also the compensation that eccentricity and mistakes can be put down to a person being new in a country – even if that is not really the case. Another issue which I encountered was the much greater need to save face compared with in the UK. On one occasion I was at a meeting of Indonesian managers, when one of the managers made a suggestion which soon turned out to be quite inappropriate. It seemed to take about three times as long as it would have done in the UK for the manager to retreat from his suggestion with dignity, although even he quickly realised that the suggestion was inappropriate. However, so that his standing was not damaged for future occasions, it seemed entirely necessary in the local situation to spend much time handling the issue. Lest one should appear smug about adapting to local conditions, I should also relate the time I told a Canadian about the problems of adjusting to conditions in the Far East. The response I got was unexpected but fair comment – I sounded like a North American explaining how to come to terms with working in the UK!

Further points are worth mentioning about working abroad, because they indicate rather different problem areas. The first is the possibility for managers, particularly on their first overseas assignment, to behave in an exaggerated fashion. This is likely to be because of their release from social constraints and conventions that would operate more in their home country. Part of the culture-shock problem in working overseas is not just the new environment but the absence of the old familiar environment in which the person knows much more readily what to do in a given situation. Another problem, which can ironically be far more difficult, is that of readjustment when the expatriate returns home. The more successfully a manager has adapted to working overseas, the greater may be the extent of the readjustment on returning to their home country. Because this is a much less expected and less recognisable problem, it may be quite off-putting. Sadly, employers often think out the arrangements for sending a person abroad much more carefully than for their return home.[12] Managers working abroad may occupy positions of much greater responsibility than it is possible for them to occupy in their home country. They may return to find that the employer has not thought out how to reintegrate them and that the organisation in the home country has moved on without them, even though they have valuable experience to offer. One of the morals of this, in considering whether or not to take an overseas appointment, is to pay particular attention to the arrangements for reintegration on completion of an overseas tour.[13] Other issues are the need to prepare people for their usually greater responsibilities and to consider the impact on any other family members. The impact on a partner's career and children's education are especially important. Further, and important, aspects of cultural variation will be considered in Chapter 8, when the topic of communication, including the specific aspect of 'body language', is examined.[14]

Starting in a new managerial job

Some of the problems of working abroad are similar to those experienced by a manager facing a new job. A manager can try and stamp their personality on a new job from the start or size up the situation before they try to change it. A dilemma can be that if a manager waits before establishing their own style they may be seen to condone a pattern they want to alter. It is important for a new manager to get their decisions right in a technical and a political sense. All too often managers may feel insecure in a new job and try to impose patterns of behaviour that were appropriate in their previous and different circumstances. There is much to be said for judging the situation before making any radical changes. It does, in any case, often take time to diagnose what the problems really are. It is only when the diagnosis has been effectively undertaken that it is appropriate for managers to try to implement such solutions as may be appropriate. What can be fatal is for managers to rush in with prescriptions culled from previous experience without checking whether these are appropriate in the new situation. Colleagues tend to be wary of new appointees and it may be that the first thing that a new manager has to do is to make themselves acceptable. One way of doing this is to make sure that initially, in particular, they look for improvements that have a high probability of success, so that they gradually establish their credibility.

A convention that is sometimes adopted with the appointment of new managers, which is in keeping with practice in the armed services, is that they are not appointed to be in charge of work groups from which they themselves have come. The reasoning behind this is that, amongst other things, the new manager will be able to impose decisions on the subordinates without being constrained by social ties. Separate catering and recreational facilities are provided in the services, and sometimes in industry, to prevent social contact. This may be appropriate in situations where the manager or person in charge may have to impose unpalatable decisions on the group. It is only likely to work, though, if the person in authority also has the coercive power, through control of rewards and punishments, to impose their will. In other organisations the practice of not appointing a manager from within the work group may unduly restrict the choice of manager, or it may not prove viable or even necessary. It has already been explained that expertise and information is often widely distributed within organisations. This and other factors may enable the work group to exercise considerable control over the manager if they want to. If the manager, however, is able to operate in an environment where by and large they do not have to impose unpalatable decisions, and where they are able to be much more of a facilitator than order-giver, the convention of not appointing a manager from the work group may be inappropriate.

ASSERTIVENESS AT WORK

One of the concepts which managers may find useful in establishing an effective managerial style is that of assertiveness. Recently, assertiveness training has been associated with training for women who wish to take a more active and effective part in the working environment. However, the ideas that assertiveness training promote are equally useful for men and women and can be employed to good effect in a variety of situations. Basically, the idea is that all our behaviour can be divided into three models: aggressive, assertive and non-assertive. Behind these three types of behaviour lies an assumption about the perceived rights of the parties in the situation. If a manager behaves aggressively they may be standing up for their own rights but be behaving in such a way that the rights of others are violated. They are implying that their own needs are more important than those of others and that whilst they have something to contribute, others do not. The advantages of this in the short term may be that the manager gets their own way and at the same time is able to give vent to their feelings. However, they may be creating hostility in others and also developing a situation in which tension is increased and in which ultimately their health suffers.

Non-assertiveness implies behaving in such a way that other

people's needs and rights are more important than your own. If a manager behaves non-assertively there is an implication that they feel they have little or nothing to contribute. In the short term the non-assertive manager may feel pleased that they have avoided conflict and appear as 'Mr or Ms Nice' to the other party. In the long term, the non-assertive manager may lose self-esteem and become angry. These feelings may increase internal tension in the manager and eventually could lead to a deterioration in health in the same way as too much aggression could. Sometimes, if a manager feels they have behaved non-assertively there may be a tendency to overreact on a future occasion, leading to aggressive behaviour in the manager's effort to compensate for former shortcomings.

Behaving assertively involves the manager stating their rights in a way that also allows other people to express their needs, wants and opinions in a direct, honest and open way. This type of behaviour should enable both parties to feel that their rights are not being ignored. It should ensure that the manager actually increases the chances that their needs are met whilst ensuring that their subordinates behave more assertively. The manager should feel more confident, as should their staff, who will feel encouraged to take more initiatives themselves. Assertive behaviour should result in a saving of energy, both because everybody feels more at ease in the situation and because this style of behaviour leads to more effective activity.

Assertive behaviour involves behaving openly. Such statements which begin 'I think . . . ', 'I would like to . . . ' and 'My idea is . . . ' lead to the manager speaking for themselves. The skills of being assertive include distinguishing between fact and feeling, e.g., 'My experience is that . . . ' and asking questions to find out the thoughts and opinions of others. A simple situation which could easily occur in the workplace serves to illustrate this. The manager wants some work doing urgently. They approach one of their members of staff whom they know is hard-working and who does not argue if they are asked to do extra work. Unbeknown to the manager, this employee is feeling rather frustrated because they have too much work to do. If the manager behaves aggressively towards the employee, the employee may simply respond non-assertively and agree to take on the extra work. In the short term this may seem the ideal solution. However, in the long run the work may suffer. The manager may not realise how overloaded the employee has become and may therefore miss the opportunity to reallocate the work in the light of the available information, thus resulting in an inefficient use of staff. Had the manager behaved more assertively they could have asked for the extra work to be done in such a way that the employee felt able to be equally open and honest and thus brought the true situation out into the open. In the face of an aggressive response from an employee who feels aggrieved about overloading, the manager could use their skills of being assertive to clarify the situation. This should enable the employee to behave in a more reasonable way without further antagonising the employee, nor making them feel that they can 'walk over' the manager. Open questions, asked in a neutral tone, would be the appropriate approach in such a situation.

In their book, *Assertiveness at Work*,[15] Ken and Kate Back give some helpful advice on the non-verbal aspects of behaving assertively. These include a steady and firm voice, which is neither over-loud nor quiet, an open facial expression, eye contact which is firm but not a 'stare-down', and an upright and relaxed posture. The book proves a very useful and comprehensive account of assertiveness in general and in particular of the ways in which other awkward situations, such as giving and receiving criticism, contributing assertively to meetings and resolving conflict, can be handled. A practical illustration of the benefits of this type of behaviour is given by Virginia Bottomley who, when Secretary of State for Health, often had to deal with representations about changes in the National Health service. In commenting on the way representations were made about proposed changes to St Bartholomew's Hospital she said 'she had paid no special attention to "noisy" lobbies and had listened at least as much to those who had made cases calmly and quietly.'[16]

Behaving assertively will not necessarily lead to immediate rewards, especially since colleagues may have a vested interest in the management not being more assertive. However, the development of this approach can bring significant long-term benefits, both in terms of increased effectiveness and with regard to the personal development of the manager concerned.

EVALUATING MANAGERIAL STYLE

Having established the importance of matching managerial style to the requirements of the situation, I would like to offer some guidance on how style can be evaluated. Ultimately, managers should be judged by results, but to some extent this begs the question of which style is likely to give the best results in a given situation. A useful method I have found has been to take the six points that George Homans[17] has found to be relevant in suggesting who will emerge as leader in informal groups. Homans suggests that, in a wide variety of informal groups situations, the behaviour of the leader tends to conform to a certain pattern. The pattern is, needless to say, one in which the leader's ability to adjust to particular situations is incorporated. This may well be a pattern for appropriate behaviour by many managers, as you can judge for yourself. The admittedly rough and ready method of evaluation is to see if managers who conform to this pattern are judged to be effective or not. I have repeatedly asked groups to carry out this evaluation exercise and been surprised at the high level of correlation between conformity to this pattern and judgements about managerial effectiveness. To do this for oneself it is necessary to identify one or more managers in terms of effectiveness or ineffectiveness on the following six-point scale:

1 Excellent
2 Very good
3 Good
4 Meets the minimum standards
5 Does not meet the minimum standards
6 Should be dismissed

It is next necessary to compare the behaviour of the manager or managers already rated against the six points identified by Homans as being characteristic of the behaviour of informal group leaders.

1 Do they represent what the group finds to be
   most important in a person at that time?   Yes/No
2 Do they make decisions which turn out, by and
   large, to be correct?   Yes/No
3 Do they keep their word?   Yes/No
4 Do they settle differences between members in
   a way the group believes to be fair?   Yes/No
5 Do they allow followers to go to them for
   advice and keep them informed about what is
   going on in the group?   Yes/No

6   Do they give information to the group in the
    form of advice, orders, etc., and maintain
    two-way communication?   Yes/No

When this second part of the assessment is completed, one then
compares the number of 'Nos' with the initial rating of managerial
effectiveness. This usually correlates so that the higher the numerical
rating the higher the number of 'No' responses, and vice versa. Not
only can this be a useful guide, but it can indicate specific areas of
weakness and possible improvement. If nothing else, it can make
one feel justified in confirming one's views about a bad manager.
If one is particularly brave it may also be worth using this method
to undertake some self-assessment.

CONCLUSION

The point that has been stressed with regard to managerial style is
that it is a means to an end and not an end in itself. The ultimate
test is how effective it is. Effectiveness may depend on sapiential
authority as much as formal authority. In adopting an appropriate
style managers will also need to take account of their boss's
style and the cultural and geographical setting in which they
work. Much thought may also be needed as to what behaviour is
appropriate when starting in a new job. The point about matching
style to the situation is that this is what is likely to produce results.
However, it is always possible that more than one approach can
work, and if different individuals handle things differently, but still
get results, it may not matter that they use alternative routes to the
same goal. The concept of assertiveness is potentially very useful
for managers. Managers also need to pay special attention to their
working relationships with their immediate colleagues, as this way
they are much more likely to gain their co-operation. This may
help them avoid being unpopular. However, popularity, just as
style, should not be an end in itself. The manager who always
puts their need for popularity above organisational objectives,
where the two are in conflict, can scarcely be effective from the
standpoint of the organisation.

NOTES

1   Charles Handy, *The Age of Unreason*, Business Books, 2nd edn, 1991,
    p. 132.

2 Local Government Management Board, *Managing Tomorrow*, Panel of Inquiry report, Local Government Management Board, 1993, p. 15.

3 Douglas McGregor, *The Human Side of Enterprise*, McGraw-Hill, 1969.

4 Philip Garrahan and Paul Stewart, *The Nissan Enigma – Flexibility at Work in a Local Economy*, Mansell, 1992.

5 Robert Tannenbaum and Warren H. Schmidt, 'How to Choose a Leadership Pattern', *Harvard Business Review*, 1957, vol. 36, no. 2, p. 95.

6 R. R. Blake and J. S. Mouton, *The New Management Grid*, Gulf Publishing, 1978.

7 R. Meredith Belbin, *Management Teams: Why They Succeed or Fail*, Butterworth Heinemann, 1981.

8 Comments reported in (London) *Evening Standard*, 23 August 1995.

9 John Adair, *Action-centred Leadership*, Gower, 1982.

10 F. E. Fiedler, *A Theory of Leadership Effectiveness*, McGraw Hill, 1967.

11 Charles Handy, *Understanding Organisations*, Penguin, 1976.

12 William Holmes and Fred Piker, 'Expatriate Failure – Prevention Rather than Cure', *Journal of the Institute of Personnel Management*, December 1980.

13 For a wealth of information on the practical issues concerning working overseas see Godfrey Golzan, *The Daily Telegraph's Guide to Working and Living Overseas*, Kogan Page, 18th edn, 1995.

14 For further useful accounts of the impact of culture on management see Fons Trompenaars, *Riding the Waves of Culture: Understanding Cultural Diversity in Business*, Nicholas Brealey, 1993; Theodore D. Weinshall, (ed.), *Culture and Management*, Penguin, 1977.

15 Ken Back and Kate Back, *Assertiveness at Work: A Practical Guide to Handling Awkward Situations*, McGraw-Hill, 1990.

16 'Bart's Seeks Merger and Drops Fight', *Guardian*, 18 February 1993.

17 George Homans, *The Human Group*, Routledge & Kegan Paul, 1975, Ch. 8.

Chapter 5

Delegation

INTRODUCTION

Management has already been described as 'getting work done through others'. It therefore follows that delegation is a facet of every manager's job. Unfortunately, however, understanding and effective practice in this area can all too easily be taken for granted. Despite the critical importance of delegation, it tends to receive relatively little attention in management literature and training. I have repeatedly found that the competence that is assumed in this area is often not justified by people's conceptual understanding or behaviour in practice.

Some of the problem areas related to delegation have already been considered in previous chapters. One of the main implications of Chapter 1 was that managers may spend too much time on their historical specialism instead of delegating more in that area. In Chapter 4, on managerial style, it was explained that managers may make incorrect assumptions about the attitudes of their subordinates to their jobs. As a result, it is quite possible for managers to fail to realise that subordinates might be only too willing to help them, if only they were allowed to do so. Good practice with regard to delegation may be difficult to achieve because of factors such as these. Such problems may be compounded by misunderstandings about the very nature of delegation. Consequently, the concept of delegation is explained in this chapter, followed by an examination of the need for delegation. The skills of delegation are then considered as well as the potential obstacles to effective delegation. Finally, the overlapping concept of empowerment, which often focuses on groups, not just individuals, is considered.

WHAT IS DELEGATION?

Delegation may be defined as 'a person conferring authority on a subordinate to act on their behalf'. It should not be confused with the issuing of orders or giving of instructions to subordinates. Although the manager remains accountable for the actions of the subordinate, the essence of delegation is the conferring of authority on the subordinate. Thus, delegation is much more than just passing a task over to be executed.

The accountability of the person who does the delegating was illustrated in a British insurance fraud trial in the 1960s. The owner of the bankrupt Fire, Auto and Marine Insurance, the late Dr Emile Savundra, was cross-examined about the contrast between his personal wealth and the state of his former company. He responded by saying that he had practised modern management techniques – including delegation – and that such questions should be addressed instead to his former financial controller. The judge understood management better than that, and when sentencing Dr Savundra to a lengthy term of imprisonment, commented that whilst authority can be delegated, accountability remains!

Some further amplification of the concept of accountability is necessary. At one stage in the UK it was the practice for government Ministers to accept responsibility and resign if there was a serious enough error by one of their subordinates – regardless of whether the Minister even knew of the action beforehand. This is what happened in the Crichel Down case in 1954 when it was found that land which had been compulsorily purchased by the Government for military use during the Second World War had been used later for agricultural purposes and then sold to a private buyer. This was despite an earlier assurance to offer it for sale back to the original owner. The Minister was obliged to resign, even though he had not been personally involved in the decision and had had no reason to believe that his officials had acted in other than good faith. This convention of resignation, regardless of personal blame, was modified, however, at the time of the Aberfan disaster in 1966. This was when a slag heap slipped down a hill during a rainstorm and engulfed a school and adjacent houses in South Wales. There were 147 deaths, of which 116 were children. The owner of the slag heap was the National Coal Board, and its chairman, Lord Robens, offered his resignation. This was not accepted, however, on the basis that the disaster was not reasonably foreseeable. This modified concept of accountability was applied, one assumes, during the government crisis in the UK in 1982 when the Falkland Islands were occupied by the Argentinean army. Both the British Foreign Secretary, Lord Carrington, and the Defence Secretary, John Nott (later Sir), offered their resignations. In the event, the Foreign Secretary's resignation was accepted, despite his illustrious record, but not the Defence Secretary's. Presumably this was because it was judged that the Argentinean invasion should have been anticipated and preventive action initiated. It was also possible that it was politically necessary for someone to resign. A later example of resignation on this basis concerned the London Underground disaster at King's Cross in 1987 when 31 people died in a fire. Both the Chairman of the London Regional Transport (LRT), Sir Keith Bright, and Dr Tony Ridley, Chairman and Chief Executive of London Underground, resigned. This was on the eve of the publication of the Fennell Report in 1988 which was very critical of LRT's fire precautions and safety policy. Again, if one accepts the Fennell criticisms, the issue was that the potential for disaster was 'reasonably foreseeable'.

The strict application of the concept of accountability as explained above has perhaps sometimes been more honoured in the breach than in the observance in the 1990s. There have been a number of occasions in the public sector when resignations have *not* occurred despite clamouring in some sections of the media for resignations. The circumstances surrounding these suggestions include the effectiveness of the regulatory role of the Bank of England in relation to the collapse of the Bank of Commerce and Credit International in 1991, the admission in 1992 that the Director General of the BBC had been engaged by the Chairman of the Governors on a freelance basis as a means of avoiding tax, and the huge foreign exchange losses suffered by the UK when it was forced out of the European Exchange Rate Mechanism in 1993. A further development affecting the accountability of government Ministers has been the creation of executive agencies. When three prisoners serving life sentences escaped from Parkhurst prison in 1995 the Home Secretary, Michael Howard, maintained that, as this was an operational issue and not a policy matter, responsibility lay with the Prison Service Agency. He reaffirmed this distinction when, later in the year, he dismissed the Director-General of the Agency, Derek Lewis, following publication of the highly critical Learmont Report.[1]

THE NEED FOR DELEGATION

One of the main reasons for delegation is that it is a means whereby a manager can, having decided their priorities, concentrate on the work of greatest importance, leaving the work of lesser importance to be done by others. Usually the manager concerned will need to see that some jobs at least are routed direct to their subordinates rather than having every task sent to them for re-routing as appropriate.

Time constraints

The time of managers is limited and it is important for them to tackle their work in some order of priority so that the most important tasks get the appropriate attention. Thus, if at the end of the day some work has not been completed or has had to be passed on to others, this should be the work of lowest priority. Even if the work of lesser importance is not done, or is not done so well, this is appropriate behaviour for the person in charge. It would not be sensible for a manager to do their own clerical work because they thought they could do it better than their secretary or clerk. Running the risk of a slightly lower level of performance by a subordinate is a small price to pay for free time to concentrate on the more important aspects of a job. The lower the level at which a task is performed, the lower the cost of performing that task is therefore likely to be. Cost needs to be considered not just in terms of the salary of the person undertaking a particular task but also in terms of opportunity cost, i.e., the opportunity that is denied or created for the manager to do other work.

The effective use of subordinates

A further development of the case for effective delegation is that in many cases the delegated work can be performed more competently by the subordinate. It is quite possible that, given time, a subordinate would, for example, do clerical work more effectively than their manager. In some cases there would be a blatant disregard of the specialist expertise of a subordinate if the boss tried to do the subordinate's job. What would be the point, and the results, if, for example, a managing director tried to run the accounts department if they had a finance manager?

Arising out of this is the need for managers to seek to dovetail their activity with that of their subordinates. Everybody has relative strengths and weaknesses in their work. If a subordinate has particular strengths it may be appropriate to make use of those strengths rather than compete in that area or simply ignore those strengths. What matters is the effectiveness of the team as a whole rather than the direct performance of just the manager.

Further possible advantages of delegation are that the subordinate often has more time and readier access to the appropriate information than the boss. Also, what is routine work to the boss may be challenging to the subordinate, as well as carrying prestige. The more that subordinates are developed, the more they are likely to be able to undertake in the future. This can be especially valuable in times of emergency, for example, when the boss is away or when there is the sudden need for a promotion. In one organisation the systematic development of operational managers was accompanied by *increasingly* centralised control, which generated enormous frustration. The point was missed that if the subordinate managers were being successfully developed this should have been accompanied by *reduced* control. Managers have to think carefully about the balance between managing by systems and through people. Detailed control procedures tend to be statements of lack of trust and can be unnecessary as well as demotivating if there are capable subordinates. Such systems may also inhibit healthy evolution and act as an organisational strait-jacket. In any case, systems tend to be as good or bad as the people who operate them. A director of one Civil Service agency commented that the best legacy he could leave his job was to see that the six key jobs under him were manned by capable people.

A further advantage of effective delegation may be that a manager is setting the pattern for their subordinates to delegate in turn down the line. One adage about managerial assessment is that you judge a manager by the quality of their subordinates. Presumably, Philip II of Spain would not have rated highly on this basis, since it is alleged that he governed Spain in a manner which created 'apoplexy at the nucleus and paralysis at the periphery'.

THE SKILLS OF DELEGATION

The case for delegation is easy to make. Consequently, people may rush into delegating without effective planning. The delegated work may then be mishandled, causing the boss to withdraw the delegated authority without realising that the problem lay in the lack of planning rather than the basic idea. The factors critical to effective planning of delegation need identification and explanation.

The first critical factor is the need for clarity about just what has been delegated. A useful concept in this respect is Wilfred (later Lord) Brown's distinction between the prescribed and discretionary content of a manager's job.[2] Prescribed work is that which must be performed in a predetermined manner. This discretionary element of a manager's job is where they are expected to use their own judgement. For example, a personnel officer could be told that they had authority to determine at what point on a given salary scale a recruit to an organisation would start. The salary range to be used would be prescribed, the point along the salary rage would be discretionary. Time and care need to be taken in defining a person's job in this way, particularly, for example, when a person has just started in a job. The use of discretion by subordinates must be tolerated, within reasonable limits. A subordinate cannot always be expected to perform in exactly the same way as their manager would. If that is the expectation, then the work concerned is prescribed content not discretionary content. If there is discretion, and it is used sensibly, it can be very demoralising for a subordinate to be told 'I wouldn't have done it quite that way'. If the discretion had been used unwisely, this may well reveal a weakness in the way the delegation was set up originally. A further critical factor is the need for a manager to set up a control procedure so that they get feedback on the performance of the subordinate. On some occasions, random or periodic feedback may be sufficient; on other occasions much closer control may be needed. The manager, being accountable, has to monitor progress.

The control of specialists and professional staff may pose particular difficulties, especially as some may be antipathetic to any form of supervision. However, the dangers of specialists indulging in meeting their objectives, which may not necessarily be the same as the organisation's, are clearly explained in Chapter 1. The dilemma was explained to me by a BBC executive once 'as how to reconcile creativity with control'. A useful convention is for managers generally to concentrate on what needs to be done and why it needs to be done, then leaving the specialist to determine how best the work is undertaken.

Delegating authority to others may well be accompanied by a need to train them in the way in which that authority is to be used. It is no good delegating authority to a subordinate unless they know what to do. All too often this stage is omitted and managers exclaim that people won't assume authority. There may be a need to start training well in advance of the delegation. Training needs to combine the substantive knowledge and skills required by the subordinate in their job with a careful definition of just what constitutes their job.

The appropriate use of discretionary powers may well involve considerable discussion between manager and subordinate. The access of the subordinate to the manager needs determining. If people are unsure of how to use their delegated powers, they may well act inappropriately or pass things back up to the manager. When items are passed up to the manager, they need to consider whether they should do them or whether they should be passed back to the subordinate with a reminder about the subordinate's discretionary area. When an appropriate discretionary area has been established, it is up to the manager to see that the subordinate gets on with their job and does not seek to over-involve their boss. It is important to clarify what the boss does and does not need to know.

Care also has to be taken with work that is routed to the manager that should be done by subordinates. In some cases colleagues will need to have it explained to them that they should go to the subordinates direct. On other occasions it will be entirely appropriate that the work should come direct to a manager, so that the chain of command is not bypassed. If a manager's boss, for example, routes something to them it does not automatically follow that the manager must do the job themselves. The decision as to who does it is one for the manager. The real pattern of delegation is likely to be set by the way a manager handles routing decisions such as these. The critical question to be asked, before any work is undertaken, is 'whose job is this?' Obviously, authority can only be delegated to people who, in the long run, are going to be able to cope with the delegated powers. This may in turn become a criterion in selection, so that one chooses staff who will be able to integrate effectively with the work pattern of their boss.

OBSTACLES TO EFFECTIVE DELEGATION

Even when people recognise the advantages of delegation and are aware of the skills involved in planning it effectively, they still may not delegate to the extent to which they should. There are a number of barriers to effective delegation – usually these are a lot easier to recognise in others than in oneself. Also, these barriers are sometimes not so much barriers as genuine constraints – it can be very difficult to disentangle the two on occasions.

Finding the time to plan delegation

Paradoxically, delegation may initially be time-consuming. It may require careful thought about just what the discretionary content of subordinate's work should be. When that has been established, time may be needed to train subordinates in the exercise of their delegated authority. Time may also be needed for the establishment of appropriate control procedures. Delegation is like a capital investment: time spent setting it up may achieve substantial dividends – but only in the future. If the manager does not carefully think through the pattern of delegation, it may backfire and discourage them from further attempts.

Factors outside the manager's control

There can be factors over which the managers may have little or no control, which prevent them delegating. They may have so little authority delegated to them that there is very little for them to pass on down the line. Managers may also just not have sufficient subordinates, or subordinates of sufficient competence, to delegate as much as they would wish. In some cases, political factors, such as excessive ambition on the part of a subordinate or rivalry between subordinates, may mean that it is prudent for a manager to retain some aspects of their job that on the face of it could be delegated. These constraints may reasonably be classified as legitimate reasons for lack of effective delegation. There are, however, various less obvious or less legitimate reasons which need examination.

The indispensable employee

One particularly interesting case history was brought to my attention by a postgraduate student whom I was supervising on a study of redundancy at an electronics company. A whole division had been closed and it transpired that this particular division had been managed by no less than seven different divisional heads in the seven years prior to its closure. Before that it had been managed very competently by the same person for 27 years. The problem which emerged was that the one person had managed the division so well that no-one could follow in his footsteps. Ironically, had that divisional head been less capable, he might have left behind a management structure which would have been more able to cope with his retirement. It was his very competence that had prevented the necessary delegation!

A variation of the above theme was encountered by my brother when he was a councillor in South Wales. This case concerned a borough engineer who deliberately set out to make himself indispensable, as opposed to the electronics division head who seemed accidentally to achieve this effect. Some of the maps of the local underground drainage system had been destroyed and the borough engineer was the only person who knew the exact locations of the drains in the relevant areas. He consistently refused to commit his knowledge to paper on the basis that as long as only he knew the complete layout the council would not dismiss him. When it was put to him that if he suddenly fell ill or died the lack of any record of the complete drainage system would cause obvious problems, he responded by saying that they would not be his problems!

The desire to feel indispensable can represent a psychological need as well as an attempt to improve job security. This was apparently the case in a further case history concerning a college principal who had all the college mail addressed to him person-ally. He would open the envelopes and, when rerouting mail to subordinate staff, instruct them on what action to take. This enabled him to complain that no-one else in the college worked as hard as he did or was prepared to assume responsibility. The fact was, of course, that he would not permit anyone else to take responsibility. One of the psychological pay-offs in his game was that, if one starts with the assumption that one's subordinates are no good, this can then become a self-fulfilling prophecy – as good staff will be driven away. There was, I am told, some progress in this particular case. Eventually, the principal's secretary was allowed to open the envelopes before the principal himself took out the enclosures! Lest this case seems too fanciful I should add that when I related it on a course for managers one of the course members confessed to me afterwards that he really would have to get his secretary to open his mail for him!

The connection between delegation and promotion

There are disadvantages for managers, as well as their employers, if they refrain from effective and necessary delegation. This is illustrated by the final case that I shall quote, which I was able to examine when conducting a research investigation into the management structure of a group of hospitals. Two small hospital groups had been merged, partly because of the ineffective management style of the chief executive of one of the groups, who was prematurely retired. He had operated on the classic Theory X assumptions about his subordinates, explained in the previous chapter. The chief executive of the other group now had to administer both groups. He was much more prepared to delegate and, interestingly, had attracted around him a much more capable group of managers than had his retired colleague, despite a common salary structure. Initially, he tried to cope with his own increased workload by increasing the delegated authority of the managers in the group which he had taken over. I was able to observe the effect of this on one of the unit managers in particular. He tried to cope by doing all the extra work as well as the work he had traditionally undertaken. The total workload was too much for him and sadly the work he left undone was most of the extra work which had been delegated to him. He was quite unable to identify his new priorities and to delegate down the line, as his new boss had delegated to him. Consequently, the chief executive had to take back most of the delegated authority, recognising that this particular person had apparently reached his limit as far as his capacity to assume responsibility was concerned. Ironically, he was then able to delegate even more authority to the managers in the other part of the group, as they were used to coping with increased responsibility. The unit manager who had been relieved of part of his authority had imposed his own limit. By demonstrating his inability to cope with increased authority and responsibility, he had not only restricted his own job but ruled himself out of consideration for future promotion. In ways such as this people can set limits on their career without necessarily realising it.

It may seem that promotion decisions are taken by the manager responsible for making the appointments. In reality, though, it may be much more the case that it is the managers being considered for promotion who decide for themselves whether or not they get it. Managers responsible for appointments do not make decisions in a vacuum. The existing pattern of behaviour of a manager is likely to influence any decision about their promotion. If a manager has got their pattern of delegation right, and because of that gets promotion, the onus may then be upon them to establish a new pattern so that they prepare themselves for even further promotion. The same reasoning can apply to people running small businesses. The expansion or non-expansion of a small business may depend less on external factors than is often imagined. Much may depend on the ability of the person running a small business to identify and concentrate on the key tasks, leaving the less critical, even if more enjoyable, tasks to others.

EMPOWERMENT

Much has been written in recent years about the concept of empowerment. Whilst the concept overlaps with that of delegation, it appears to be particularly associated with initiatives such as TQM, de-layering, and often has a focus on the group as well as or instead of the individual. Sometimes it is associated with the appointment of a team leader as a group facilitator. Michael Armstrong defines it as:

> ensuring that people are able to use and develop their skills and knowledge in ways which help to achieve both their own goals and those of the organisation. Empowerment is achieved by organisation and job design approaches which place responsibility fairly on individuals and teams, by recognising the contribution people can make, by providing mechanisms such as improvement groups to enable them to make this contribution and by training and development programmes which increase both competence and confidence.[3]

The general organisational developments explained in Chapter 3 have reinforced the trend towards more emphasis on empowerment. These include economic pressures, developments in information technology and changes in management philosophy. As with so many concepts that become 'fashionable', there is the danger that it may be applied regardless of the logic of particular situations. In many situations, particularly where management is well-organised, competent and with adequate resources, it may be entirely the right development. However, the issues of matching style to the situation, covered in the previous chapter, and clarity of goals need careful examination. Empowerment generally involves showing more trust in the work-force, and the related concepts of accountability and control need considering in this context.

In many organisations that have introduced greater empowerment there is a strong internal social and cultural control to ensure that, for example, semi-autonomous work groups perform in a way that is congruent with organisational goals. Empowering people without thinking through the implications could be disastrous. The lack of control of the Singapore-based derivatives-market trader, Nick Leeson, provides a dramatic example. The trading losses he incurred or caused of £860 million, lead to the collase of Barings Bank in 1995. The tendency of specialists with managerial responsibility to 'go their own way' has been documented in Chapter 1. It is perhaps worth also making an analogy about the dangers of 'self-regulation' by referring to groups such as doctors, lawyers, newspapers and the Stock Exchange, where it is arguable that the interests of the members have had a higher priority than that of other interest groups, including the public. Lloyds of London is an example of a self-regulatory body where many less influential members felt that their heavy financial losses had been caused by a 'rigging' of the insurance risks. A further aspect of empowerment is that of the remuneration of those who are 'empowered' so that they do not see it as a way of them being asked to do a lot more without any corresponding benefit. The motivational implications of empowerment are considered in the next chapter, including the problems that might arise if people are empowered as a consequence of what may be euphemistically called 'downsizing' or 'rightsizing'.

CONCLUSION

Delegation is a critical aspect of management. All managers need to work out the appropriate balance of activities between themselves and their subordinates. Unfortunately, good practice with regard to delegation is often more honoured in the breach than in the observance. The subject is amazingly neglected in management literature and on training courses. The basic concepts are relatively easily explained. Delegation involves conferring authority to subordinates, but those who delegate still remain accountable. Managers, by definition, should not do everything themselves. Thought has to be given to just what is delegated and what is not. Time also has to be spent developing control systems and training subordinates. Consequently, and paradoxically, delegation is initially time-consuming. However, the benefits of good practice are enormous if managers are secure enough as individuals to let their subordinates get on with it within an appropriate framework. A manager's behaviour has a considerable impact – for good or ill – on the motivation of subordinates. Consequently, it is appropriate that motivation is the subject to be covered in the next chapter.

NOTES

1 General Sir John Learmont, KCB, CBE, *Review of Prison Service Security in England and Wales and the Escape from Parkhurst Prison on Tuesday 3rd January 1995*, HMSO, 1995.
2 Wilfred Brown, *Exploration in Management*, Pelican, 1965, p. 123.
3 Michael Armstrong, *A Handbook of Personnel Management Practice*, 4th edn, Kogan Page, 1991, pp. 102–3.

Chapter 6

Motivation

INTRODUCTION

In this chapter we examine the variety of reasons why people work.
It is important to consider the range of reasons because it is all too
easy for incorrect assumptions to be made about why people do or
do not work. If the diagnosis is incorrect, corrective action may
be entirely inappropriate. We then turn to behavioural theories
concerning motivation and the practical use that can be made of
them. The motivational implications of job design are examined
as is the concept of job distortion. Consideration is given to the
ways in which job content and the individual's abilities can be
matched. The impact of philosophies of employee involvement,
including initiatives such as TQM, is considered as are the problems
of trying to motivate employees in the context of job insecurity.
The dangers of over-involvement in the job and managerial stress
are also covered.

WORK PERFORMANCE

An appropriate starting point for this chapter is to suggest that, if
people are not working effectively, or in some cases not working at
all, it is the match between job and person that needs examining,
and not just the person. It may be that some people will never
work effectively under any circumstances; it may also be the case
that some jobs will always pose motivational problems – whoever is
supposed to be doing them. However, it is also likely that there are
circumstances in which most people will work effectively, just as
there are circumstances under which the same people will not
work effectively. Similarly, with most or many jobs there are likely

to be many people who will perform them effectively and other people who will perform them ineffectively. If there is a problem of ineffective work performance, the basic question is whether it is the fault of the person, the job or the matching of the two. Remedial action will depend on the diagnosis. In some cases it may be that in the short term neither can be changed, in which case attention needs to be paid to either the type of person selected in the future, or the job structure or both, according to the diagnosis of the reasons for poor work performance.

Diagnosis of reasons for poor performance

The need for accurate diagnosis has been stressed because it is all too easy for the diagnosis of reasons for poor work performance to be wrong. It is at best a subjective area. The very criteria for judging effective work performance may be difficult to establish, as the section on the definition of objectives in Chapter 2 demonstrated. The essence of good diagnosis in this area is to analyse the situation in role terms and not personality terms. Here, the explanation of role behaviour given in Chapter 3 is relevant. One of the problems of analysing work performance in role terms is that the conclusions may be uncomfortable for the person carrying out the analysis. If the blame is put on the person working ineffectively, that absolves the boss, who may then fail to see the connection when the next person in the job also performs ineffectively. In some cases the fault will be with the person in the job; the point to realise is that this will not automatically be the case. When the fault is not with the person in the job, then uncomfortable implications for the boss may emerge. The onus may then be on them to examine the structure of the job or the support given to the person in the job. It may be that the boss may need to change their behaviour rather than the job holder. It may require considerable insight and intellectual honesty to explore these implications. Such a line of thought may or may not run counter to the implicit assumptions that the manager has about why people work.

Assumptions about why people work

Alternative sets of assumptions that managers may have about why people work were identified in Chapter 4 in the explanation of

Douglas McGregor's Theory X and Theory Y approaches. People's implicit assumptions may or may not be appropriate in relation to particular situations. One of the dangers of assumptions is that one is guessing about people's motivation. In assessing one's own reasons for working, one has self-knowledge to go on, and this is likely to lead to a more charitable set of assumptions than those made in respect of other people. An exercise which demonstrates this, that colleagues and I have frequently used with managerial groups, is to ask them to complete the questionnaire shown below. Managers are asked to rank the factors listed in order of importance in so far as they affect the manager's motivation in their current jobs. The managers are then asked to repeat the ranking in respect of their current subordinates.

Reasons for working:
- Chance to use initiative at work
- Good working conditions
- Good working companions
- Good boss
- Steady, safe employment
- Money
- Good hours
- Interest in the work itself
- Opportunity for advancement
- Getting credit and recognition

Invariably a comparison of the rankings shows that the managers see themselves as giving more importance to factors such as 'interest in the work itself' and 'chance to use initiative at work'. Conversely, the subordinates are invariably seen as paying more attention to factors such as 'money' and 'steady, safe employment' than their bosses. It may be that the difference in rankings achieved is, as far as anyone can judge, justified. It may also be that managers are too ready to assume the worst as far as their subordinates' motivation is concerned. This makes the results of a survey commissioned by the Royal Commission on Trade Unions and Employers' Associations[1] a little worrying. The survey asked 500 foremen and 300 works managers whether their subordinate workers 'could reasonably be expected to put more effort into their job than they did'. Forty-three per cent replied in the affirmative and, when asked why more effort was not forthcoming gave as the three principal reasons 'a lack of financial incentive, laziness and lack of interest'. The exact pattern of responses might differ if this 1968 survey were repeated today, but one wonders if the tendency to jump to hasty conclusions about the motivation of one's subordinates has changed.

Other variables

The motivation of subordinates is just one variable affecting work performance. A number of organisational factors have to be considered as well. These include work flow, supply of materials, the quality of work design, work programming, the availability of appropriate equipment and, above all, the quality of management. Factors such as technology also have to be considered. If, for example, the pace of production is determined by an automatic process rather than by human effort, then it may be more rewarding to spend one's money on efficient maintenance of the process rather than production bonuses for employees for a process over which they may have relatively little control. Contact with colleagues may be another important feature – both for the humanising impact it may have and, as explained in Chapter 3, because of the benefits it may bring in terms of effective liaison.

THEORIES OF MOTIVATION

In order to understand the concept of work motivation it is necessary to have an appreciation of some of the relevant and basic psychological theories. Although the theories that will be examined are not particularly new nor are they beyond methodo-logical criticism, they are important and do have relevance to current problems and initiatives. A. H. Maslow provided a useful frame-work for examining individual motivation.[2] He argued that people's behaviour is centred on a series of needs arranged in a hierarchy. Satisfaction of needs at one level leads to attempts to satisfy needs at the next level up the hierarchy, as shown in Figure 6.1.

The hierarchy is like a ladder – people need to start at the bottom rung and satisfy their basic needs, such as hunger, before moving up to the next rung to achieve safety. The third rung consists of social needs, such as friendship, followed by status needs, and finally at the top of the pyramid the opportunity for self-development. The theory is that people proceed up the ladder rather like a donkey with a carrot in front of it. What is likely to motivate a person at a

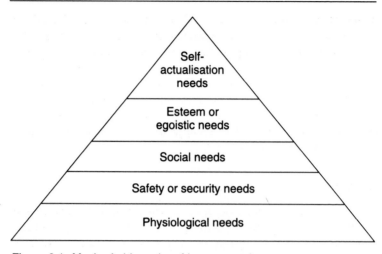

Figure 6.1 Maslow's hierarchy of human needs

given time is the factor that is just within reach. If lower level needs are threatened, people will redirect themselves to securing those needs before resuming any pursuit of higher level needs. There are in practice overlaps between the levels – the precise pattern will vary from one individual to another. Some people will be more prepared to trade off satisfaction at one level for satisfaction at another – for example, security for self-development. Others may have greater status needs than others. People find themselves at different points along the hierarchy at different times. For example, a parent with considerable domestic commitments might be more concerned with the efficient discharge of those domestic commitments than with self-development at work. Increased responsibility at work might become attractive if and when the domestic commitments are reduced. There are also class, cultural, regional and national differences. Not only will values vary from one part of the world to another, but so will the level of attainable needs. Self-development may be a meaningless concept for much of the population of South America, but a potent motivating factor for professional-level employees in the developed Western countries.

If one accepts Maslow's line of argument, the next question is 'What is the practical value of this model of human needs?' The answer to this is that it may help in the recurring problem of matching people to situations. One can examine what motivational factors exist in a particular job, or the factors that can be built into it, and then consider what sort of person should be selected for the job. This may mean in Western society that one should strive to see that there are opportunities for self-development in work situations. However, that will not help if a person is more concerned with lower-level needs. The extent to which individuals wish to self-actualise may depend on their 'need to achieve', according to McClelland.[3] He suggests that this can be a very powerful motivating force which appears to be derived from social conditioning during childhood.

Job motivators and job dissatisfiers

Further research which complements the work of Maslow is that undertaken by Frederick Herzberg.[4] He conducted an investigation into the reasons given by engineers and accountants in America for what satisfied them and what dissatisfied them in their jobs. What emerged was that the survey group identified two different sets of factors – one which could cause positive feelings about the job and one which could cause negative feelings. Care obviously needs to be taken not to overgeneralise from the subjective responses of a group of professional workers in America, but Herzberg's work does throw up some very useful concepts concerning the practical application of motivational theory. One of these concepts is the distinction between job context and job content. The American survey group, when identifying factors which had caused them to feel dissatisfied about their jobs, mainly referred to matters that were external to the basic job structure. The main items in this set of 'dissatisfiers' were: company policy and administration, supervision, interpersonal relations, status, salary, security and the impact of the job on personal life. The absence of dissatisfaction on these counts was not enough to cause positive feelings about the job. Consequently, Herzberg referred to the set of factors likely to cause dissatisfaction in jobs as 'hygiene factors'. They operate in rather the same way as having the wrong room temperature. If it is very hot or very cold in a room that can cause profound dissatisfaction. If the temperature is ideal that does not particularly induce positive feelings about anything. For that to happen in a job people need to find an outlet for their creative energies and, in Maslow's terminology, to be able to achieve 'self-actualisation'. Six main motivating factors were identified: achievement, recognition of achievement, responsibility, advancement,

interesting work and the possibility of growth. Thus, positive feelings about the job could only be accomplished if the job content
was appropriate for the individual concerned.

The people in the survey group appeared to prefer to be a little
'stretched' in their work, and through being 'stretched' found that
they developed as individuals. The hygiene factors needed to be
right so that people were not distracted from getting on with the
job. If people had insufficient salary that could expose a need that
was not being met lower down Maslow's hierarchy. A low salary
could prevent a person from taking or staying in a job, but a high
salary appeared to do relatively little in the way of creating
long-term positive feelings about a job. Similarly, company policies
needed to be such as to facilitate people getting on with the
job and not to frustrate them from doing so. The issue of 'fairness'
also emerged amongst the set of dissatisfiers. Employees could
have strong feelings of injustice if they felt, for example, that
company policy was unfair. Equitable treatment did not, however,
cause strong positive feelings about the job.

The practical implications of Herzberg's work are considerable.
The basic message is: don't ignore the hygiene factors but don't
stop there. People may want considerable involvement in their
jobs for their own self-development. Employers may find that this
is a considerable source of energy that is available. Bored workers
may not only be poor workers but may engage in destructive
activity. One example concerns a group of traffic police allegedly
'booking' vehicles for traffic offences in the same colour sequence
as though they were playing a frame of snooker! I have often taken
the opportunity to check out Herzberg's basic approach with
managerial groups in the UK and Indonesia. The use of a crude
survey using this basic approach has, I have found, invariably
produced similar responses. For example, the Indonesian captain
of an oil tanker said that his most positive feelings about his job
were after he had successfully, and very skilfully, navigated his
ship through a typhoon off Hong Kong in which many ships had
sunk. His most negative feelings about the job occurred shortly
afterwards when the ship's agent carefully checked all the damage
to the ship and neglected to enquire or comment about the risks
that had been experienced by the captain and crew! This particular
example illustrates that the dividing line between situations which
can lead to strong negative and strong positive feelings about the
job can in some cases be very fine. If a person has a job they can just

accomplish that may be fine – but if it is just that little bit too hard for the individual concerned, they may experience failure and the feelings or consequences that go with it. Also, credit and recognition need to be based on real achievement. Positive feelings are likely to stem from the reality of achievement, with the credit of achievement being rather like the icing on a cake. The withholding of credit can lead to negative feelings and the giving of credit and recognition where there has been no real achievement can be rather meaningless.

Perhaps more care has to be taken in generalising from one social group to another than in applying Herzberg's research to professional groups in different countries. There has also been some criticism of Herzberg's research because of his heavy reliance on the 'critical incident technique'. Nevertheless, one can see that the most important thing for managers to do with their subordinates may be to set up their work, if possible, so that it provides a challenge and then help to see that the challenge is met. Excessive help may be counter-productive. The human relations skills of the manager may be relatively unimportant compared with the challenge of a job – at least as far as positive motivation is concerned. Perhaps the main pay-off with human relations skills is the avoidance of upsetting employees rather than the achievement of positive motivation. The control of the manager over job content will vary, but that is an area that obviously merits the closest attention as far as the motivation of subordinates is concerned. In some cases it will be one of the few areas that managers can actually control. They may find that many of the 'hygiene factors', such as salary level, working conditions and company policy, are not within their control. To some extent, however, their pattern of delegation will be. There are obviously selection implications – it is possible to engage a person who is too good for a job, just as it is possible to choose a person who does not have the necessary capability. This mistake is often made, for example, by organisations who recruit overqualified people for status reasons. Another way in which this type of mistake can be made is to pay high wages as a means of attracting and retaining people in boring jobs. The problem is that the higher the wage, the greater may be the ability of the people who are attracted to a job and consequently the greater their frustration if the work is boring. One of the problems for the prospective employee is that it is often much easier to judge the job context – for example, the salary, fringe benefits and working conditions – than the often more elusive factors such as independence within the job. Consequently, the recruits may only find out after they have started in a job that it lacks positive motivational features.

Expectancy theories

Another perspective that needs to be integrated with the previously explained theories is that provided by the expectancy school of motivational theorists. The expectancy approach attempts to overcome one of the criticisms of other motivational theories by accounting for individual differences. The expectancy model of Nadler and Lawler[5] has three major components. The first component (*performance–outcome*) concerns the outcome that individual employees expect from certain behaviour. The second concerns the value (*valence*) that the employee puts on the outcome which they are expecting from particular behaviour – this will determine the motivating strength of a particular reward. The third concerns people's expectations (*effort–performance expectancy*) of how difficult it will be to perform successfully and will affect their decision on whether or not to proceed. The logic is that people will select the level of performance that seems to have the best chance of achieving an outcome they value.

It follows that it is necessary to check to see that the reward system in an organisation actually works in the way that is intended. It is no good, for example, expecting to motivate people by offering incremental salary increases or promotion for meritorious performance, if the reality is that such rewards are based on seniority. Even if reward is based significantly on merit, it is necessary to convince people of this, as motivation is likely to depend on what people perceive happens. It is also necessary to review how equitably rewards are distributed as, even if people are inclined to respond to a particular incentive, they may be discouraged from doing so by perceived unfairness in the way in which rewards are allocated. The gap between intended and actual reward systems can be alarmingly high in the case of incentive payments schemes. As is explained in the section on these schemes in the next chapter, some can degenerate into arrangements where output is carefully restricted.

JOB DESIGN

One of the major implications of the theoretical perspectives that have been explained, particularly Herzberg's, is that considerable attention needs to be given to job design. Consequently, the relationship between job design and motivation will now be examined in some detail – first in general terms and then in terms of trying to match individual needs with job demands.

One of the recurring and basic failings in job design is that jobs are arranged with little or no thought to the needs of the people who are likely to have to perform them. Exponents of classical management theory (as explained in Chapter 2), believed in structuring jobs so that they were as simple as possible and were oblivious of such obvious psychological implications as boredom and social isolation. In conditions of chronic unemployment it may be possible to recruit and retain people in boring, or otherwise badly structured, jobs but the people occupying those jobs may not be motivated, or enabled, to perform well in such jobs. Too often the Procrustean approach is taken to job design. Procrustes was a legendary figure in Greek mythology who had a special bed. He was obsessive about guests fitting his bed exactly. If they were too long for the bed he cut off their feet; if they were too small he stretched them on a rack until they fitted! The moral is that jobs can be designed with little or no thought to the matching with the individual – the assumption being that people can always be found who can be made to fit the job, however badly they are designed.

A concept that can usefully be integrated with the moral provided by the Procrustean approach is that of marketing. Few companies would seek to make products unless they had checked that a market existed. In the same way, it is appropriate to check that a job can reasonably be done by the sort of people who are likely to be available. In the case, for example, of high-performance military equipment, it is essential to have a marriage of equipment and person, based on careful ergonomic design, so that optimum performance is achieved. Failure to achieve optimum performance may mean the difference between accomplishment or non-accomplishment of the military purpose and life or death for the individual operating the equipment in combat or even in training.

A further dimension of job design is to look at the collection of tasks that constitute a job and see if it presents a coherent whole.

Alternatively, as explained in Chapter 9, the job may be expressed as a collection of required competences. One danger is that the span of tasks, or required competences, may be too great in terms of the level of skill needed. The two apparently quite different jobs of skilled manual worker and general (medical) practitioner both tend to suffer from this problem. The tendency is for both of these jobs to contain a relatively small amount of work requiring considerable skill and knowledge and a large amount of work that is relatively routine and undemanding in terms of skill and knowledge requirements. The structure of both jobs may follow the pattern shown in Figure 6.2.

The problem about filling such jobs as shown in the diagram is that the person who is particularly capable may be bored and underutilised with the more routine aspects of the work. People with that conflict may tend to concentrate too much on the work they find interesting at the expense of the work they find boring. They may even try to build up the most interesting parts of their job, even though it may be more appropriate for them to refer that work to others. This may lead to job distortion – a concept that is explained in more detail later in this section. The problem may be compounded by the fact that, particularly with general practitioners, for example, there may be no obvious opportunity for promotion. The problems at the other end of the scale may be that the person who copes well with the routine aspects of the job may not have the skill and knowledge to cope with the more complicated aspects of the work. Unless the work can be restructured, the problem may be like that of a person with a small blanket – either the feet or the shoulders are cold.

The answer is to restructure the job – but that is often easier said than done. Some progress has, however, been made in the particular examples given. More use is now made of auxiliary staff such as social workers and nurses to assist doctors in general practice. There are indications that there may be some much-needed revision of the boundaries between medical and nursing work and the move to have fewer operations done in hospitals may also help build up the job of GPs. There has also been some progress in reducing the length of training for skilled manual trades and sometimes also in increasing the range of skills that are taught. The examples, though, are meant to be illustrative. They underline the need for jobs and people to be looked at in relation to one another at the time the jobs are designed, with reviews as

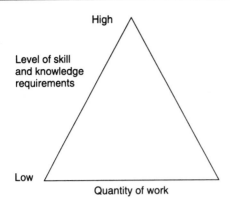

High

Level of skill
and knowledge
requirements

Low

Quantity of work

Figure 6.2 The skill pyramid

and when job demands change, for example. Unfortunately, the human element of job design is all too often ignored and sometimes the requirements are plain contradictory. I was regularly asked by one engineering manager to recruit engineers with 20 years' varied experience in the age range 25–30! Another trap can be to create dead-end jobs with no prospects of progression to anything else. This can't always be avoided, but the best time to consider the issue is when the job is first established and people are being asked to apply. The related problems of role contradictions in jobs have previously been explained in the section on role set analysis in Chapter 2.

Job distortion

A further aspect of job design that has already been referred to is job distortion. This occurs when a job is restructured by the employee in a way that satisfies their own, but not organisational, needs. This is particularly likely during periods of chronic unemployment. Employees may be frustrated in their jobs because of lack of promotion opportunities, lack of jobs elsewhere and 'overselection'. This can lead to employees building their jobs up, both as a relief from boredom and as a means of obtaining an upgrading. If you take the case of a graduate recruited to do a routine clerical job, the graduate, although perhaps glad to have got employment, may rapidly get bored because of the lack of intellectual stimulation. Consequently, the most interesting parts of the job may be expanded and as many as possible of the routine aspects ignored. This can lead to 'job distortion' as shown in Figure 6.3. The continuous lines represent the boundaries of the job that the organisation requires to be performed, whilst the broken lines represent the boundaries of the job as it actually is performed.

The problems that such distortion can create for the organisation were vividly illustrated to me by the behaviour of an office junior working in the postroom of a local authority. Although the young man in the job had been doing it for five years, and although there was not a significant increase in the volume of mail, the post kept on being distributed later and later in the day. As the officers in the directorate had meetings to attend and visits to make, it became an increasingly common occurrence for them to have to wait a full day before being able to read their mail. An investigation revealed that the cause of the problem was the boredom of the office junior. As a counter to this, and the fact that he didn't have enough to do anyway, he had taken to actually reading the mail before distributing it! This, coupled with excessively long refreshment breaks and much social chatter, was a way of him spinning out the day – even though the effect on the directorate was to create a fair amount of chaos. An obvious solution was to move him into a more demanding job, but unfortunately his reputation had become such that no-one else in the directorate wanted him. However, it was clear that it was quite wrong to let the job holder rot in a dead-end job and that somehow he had to be moved to another. It was also clear that the job should be filled in future by a person for whom there was planned progression or by a person who would be content with such routine work – and even then thought had to be given as to what to do about the long periods of inactivity. An alternative approach would have been to get units to collect their own mail and simply eliminate the job.

Other pressures which can lead to job distortion may arise because of the frustrated desire of job holders to obtain jobs they consider to be in line with their ability. This can clearly arise in the previously quoted example of the graduate doing routine clerical work. It can also happen with people who have 'outgrown' their existing job and find that they cannot easily progress. This can happen all too easily in the current economic climate, as opportunities elsewhere may be limited and the person or people above a particular job holder may be similarly blocked from

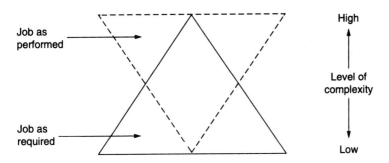

Figure 6.3 Job distortion

moving on. The solution for the individual caught in this trap may be to build the job up and, particularly if there is a formal job evaluation scheme, to claim an upgrading. My own experience, as an arbitrator who often has to judge such grading issues, and that of colleagues – especially in the public sector – indicates that many job evaluation schemes are coming under severe pressure by claims for such upgradings. It is only sensible for employers to exploit any opportunities for job enrichment – especially if job holders are frustrated by the limitations of their current job. However, there is also the danger that poor supervisory control may lead to subordinates undertaking a wrong balance of work in order to engineer an upgrading that is not in line with organisational requirements.

Matching individual needs and job demands

Consideration of the motivation match between individual and job is obviously something that needs to be carefully considered because of the potential gains to both individual and employer if the matching is optimised. However, just as it is important that this area be investigated so it is necessary to recognise that, in some cases anyway, there will be constraints. First, some of the potential constraints will be examined and then some of the strategies for getting a better or optimum match when circumstances permit.

Basic operational requirements and technology may place major constraints on job design. One of the problems in vehicle production has been that there have been overwhelming technological and economic advantages in a high degree of division of labour. This problem has been reduced as more and more production-line jobs have been eliminated by robotics and other developments, but the problem still remains for those production jobs that are left. In jobs such as that of an airline pilot the required safety standards may necessitate that people are employed whose capabilities are well in excess of what they will require for their normal duties. The objectives of employer and employee do not always coincide. Employees may see many opportunities for self-development but the employer is hardly going to welcome them if they do not coincide with organisational objectives. To complicate matters, there may be important differences of perception about what is good for the organisation as a whole. It can be very tempting to assume that work which you find particularly interesting and developmental is bound to be of benefit to the employer. In some cases employees may even find that the organisation of activities that are quite obviously against the employer's interests provide both psychological and material rewards. The adrenalin can run for a person perpetrating a fraud just as it can for honest employees who develop themselves in their employer's interests instead of attempting to outwit the employer.

Added to these problems can be perceptual blockages. Managers may assume that the ego-satisfactions that they get in their job are also experienced by their employees. This is particularly likely in small businesses, where the proprietor may almost completely identify with the business and assume that the employees do, or should do, the same. The point that is missed is that whilst the proprietor may be prepared to make many sacrifices for the business it is also the proprietor who will reap most of the financial and psychological rewards if the business prospers.

Traditional ways of trying to improve the match between individual needs and job demands include job enlargement, job rotation and job enrichment. Job enlargement is a generic term used to indicate a widening of the job, either by increasing the range of activities or the level of responsibility, or both. Job rotation occurs when just the range of activities is increased, which will give individuals concerned the opportunity to have increased work variety but without any increase in the level of responsibility. This may involve changing one boring task for another but it may provide some relief. An example is rotating staff at leisure centres so that they supervise a number of different sporting activities over the course of a day. Job enrichment involves increasing the responsibility level of a job, either by altering the balance of responsibility within the job or by adding a new level of responsibility, or both. This may involve a sophisticated amount of design effort or it may prove to be a relatively simple affair. One easy way to check on whether jobs can be restructured is ask the people doing them for their suggestions.

Managerial style can have an important effect – in some cases enrichment can be achieved by managers showing more trust in their subordinates and simply delegating more. It may also be necessary, as has previously been explained, for managers to examine the assumptions they have made about how their subordinates work, as it may be people are prepared to and able to contribute more and are just not given the opportunity as the manager thought all was well. One useful approach used in the nursing profession is that of 'acting up' so that subordinates assume the responsibilities of the immediate superior when the superior is away. This may bring training as well as motivational advantages. A policy of 'acting down' could bring de-motivation instead. Job enrichment does not always have to be at the expense of another job, however. Often there are tasks which could be undertaken or opportunities that could be exploited that would enrich a number of jobs simultaneously. Selection can also be crucial. As is explained in Chapter 9, selection should involve choosing the person who is the best match for a job. Simply choosing the most able person may result in 'overselection' and the boredom and frustration that can go with it.

Corporate involvement and corporate loyalty

Increasing emphasis has been placed by some organisations and writers on the work-force as a valuable asset, whose potential should be fully exploited, rather than simply as a cost. This is at the heart of initiatives such as TQM, quality circles and Japanese approaches generally. The impact of such initiatives can be reinforced by the social pressures that may be deliberately engineered in so as to obtain compliance with organisational goals. The concept of the 'quality of working life' represents a related philosophy. 'It has the broad aim of bringing together and satisfying both the goals and development of organisations and the needs and development of all their people.'[6] As previously explained, Peters and Waterman emphasised the need to release human potential – potential which is all the more important given the economic pressures on organisations and rising educational standards amongst work-forces.

There seems little doubt that some organisations have consciously changed their policies, and not before time, to try and make much better use of their human resources. However, for this to happen there needs to be realistic planning about how this is to be achieved. Mere sloganising and exhortation won't produce much in the way of results. A major complication is that expectations of increased psychological commitment by the work-force may be held at quite inappropriate times. In an article entitled *The Death of Corporate Loyalty* in *The Economist* it was commented in relation to the trend towards semi-autonomous business units that:

> This trend draws on the work of innumerable management thinkers who champion the idea of cutting corporate flab and 'empowering' teams of employees, which can then be judged by their performance. Some like America's Tom Peters and Britain's Charles Handy, sketch a future in which big firms will become little more than 'networks' of independent businesses. Most such assume that employees will respond to their new responsibility with enthusiasm, even if their firm has just sacked thousands of workers and declared that no-one's job is safe.
>
> This seems naive. Even if many big companies sorely needed a shake-up, scrapping corporate cultures which evolved over decades is likely to be far more costly than many firms, or management theorists, imagine . . . Job cuts at Eastman Kodak, IBM and Philips have shattered morale and embittered many of those who remain, despite lavish redundancy payments.[7]

Comment is also made in the article about the exodus of talent that can occur in such restructuring and the more instrumental attitudes that employees may develop about issues such as geographic moves within a group and selling their skills elsewhere. This is particularly important if one accepts the argument that the most important corporate asset is the intellectual creativity of its employees. Handy himself argues that this is crucial in his concept of the organisation based on intelligence, ideas and information, explained in Chapter 4. Larry Black has referred to the emerging concepts of 'just-in-time employment' and 'the disposable work-force' in the USA and the impact this has on corporate morale.[8] Consequently, one needs to examine the impact of the flexible work-force on motivation and, in particular, on developments such as the increasing use of fixed-term contracts, especially for senior employees. A further complication can arise because of the actual generosity with which employers treat those who are being made redundant:

> British Telecom spent some £1 billion this financial year [1992/3] shedding 33,000 workers. To tempt enough to go voluntarily, employees were baited with counselling, training and pay-offs as high as £100,000. Managers were miffed when 45,000 applied to leave. Morale crumbled, not because workers were forced out, but because 15,000 were forced to stay.[9]

The re-appraisals of commitment to the organisation caused by restructuring may be in tune with a general trend. Scase and Goffee comment that:

> If, in earlier decades, managers were committed to their jobs to the extent that all other interests were subordinated to their work-related goals, they may now be developing more *instrumental* and *calculative* attitudes towards their employing organizations (Hearn 1977). Indeed, by deliberately cultivating personal identities that are separate and removed from organizational demands, they could be better equipped to cope with work-related stresses and to withstand the psychological challenges that can be posed by threats of redundancy and unexpected career changes. Accordingly, managers may cease to be *psychologically immersed* in their work roles and become less committed to their employing organizations. To do otherwise, in the light of increasing uncertainties, would be to make themselves more emotionally and psychologically vulnerable.[10]

Social trends, including changes in the role of women in the family and in society also have an impact on the work relationship. The custom of family commitments needing to be subordinated to the primary aim of promoting the career of the 'man in the home' is breaking down. Almost half of the work-force is now female. The pattern of female careers is also changing – women are tending to have children later and to have shorter 'baby breaks'. The growing number of dual-career couples also imposes constraints upon both partners and lessens the dependency on the primary income. Also, a significant number of employees are single parents.[11]

This issue about the danger of over-involvement in the job is developed further in the next section. Having explained the constraints that may exist with regard to attempts to improve employee involvement and develop corporate loyalty, it would be foolish to suggest that attempts are doomed to failure. It is more logical to argue that, given the organisational turbulence that is often inevitable, it is even more important to consider how to try and get the best out of the work-force in spite of the difficulties. This is more likely to be done effectively if the nature of the difficulties is clearly recognised. It is necessary to consider the human dimension at the time that organisations are being restructured and build in the direct and intangible costs of change before decisions are finalised. It is also important to have positive and integrated human resource strategies, and the nature of these are considered in Chapters 10 (in relation to training) and generally in Chapter 12.

Over-involvement and managerial stress

The general point has been made that organisations tend to under-utilise and under-involve the human resources available to them but that there is an increasing recognition of the need to correct this. The point has also been made, though, that a variety of factors are causing an increasing number of employees to try and set limits to their work involvement. Consequently, it is probably appropriate for both organisations and employees to consider what is the optimum level of involvement. This may be particularly necessary given the increasing potential intrusion of work into the home because of developments in information technology. Individuals may need to look carefully at their work in relation to their general lifestyle and periodically conduct an audit on their 'total quality of life'. Whilst the emphasis in the literature on motivation is on under-involvement, over-involvement may present risks for the employer as well as the employee. The dangers of 'workaholism' may include problems of replacement, damage to health and the loss of a sense of perspective and good judgement that comes from having other interests as a counterbalance. Workaholics may also seek to establish themselves as role models when they are really self-indulging or engaging in compensatory behaviour.

At this point it is as well to distinguish between pressure and stress. Some managers enjoy high levels of pressure and may perform more effectively when they are put under a certain amount of pressure. The pressure may relate to the volume or responsibility level of work, or both. Other managers may react in a different way and their inability to cope with pressure may result in stress. One could therefore define managerial stress as a symptom of being unable to cope with the workload. Unfortunately, this can precipitate a counter-productive chain reaction with those managers experiencing stress amplifying that stress and transmitting it to those in their immediate orbit. Stress may be caused by the problems inherent in a particular job, or the mismatch between the abilities of an individual and the requirements of a job, or a combination of the two.[12] It is important to diagnose the causes of stress in particular situations because it is only when that is done that one can work out whether the appropriate remedy is to change an individual's behaviour or the pressures they are put under, or both.

It is also important to recognise that work-related stress is probably on the increase. This is because of the increasing impact of key factors which generate stress. These factors include the rate of change, pressures for cost-effective performance, downsizing, job insecurity and diminished prospects of alternative employment. It is also important to recognise the manager's responsibility for monitoring the stress that subordinates are placed under. In 1994 John Walker, a senior social worker, won a High Court action against Northumberland County Council because of their negligence in not doing enough to prevent him having a further nervous breakdown because of work overload. He then sought damages of £200,000 as a consequence of his employer's breach of their duty of care to him.[13]

Whether managers are being submitted or submitting themselves to too much pressure, or experiencing stress, the resultant work style may generate an excessive flow of adrenalin within the body, may increase dependence on physical stimulants such as nicotine and alcohol and thus prevent an individual from having an appropriate diet and sufficient physical exercise and rest. Individuals can hardly be expected to change their personalities so that their basic responses to situations are altered, but they can at least try to move out of or change a situation if that is the source of unacceptable levels of stress. If the stress is self-induced it is perhaps just as well to face up to the medical implications in case there is any scope for personal adjustment. There is also the potential benefit that if stress is reduced for oneself it may also be reduced for those around you.

Doctors and stress consultants may be able to measure stress and advise on how the symptoms are treated, e.g., by relaxation techniques. However, managerial skills are likely to be needed to deal with the basic causes of managerial stress. The aim of this book is to do just that, by improving the effectiveness of individual managers. If people persist in doing their former, instead of their current job, as explained in Chapter 1, the consequences in terms of effectiveness and stress can be quite alarming. Other key issues include the need for careful prioritisation, as explained in Chapter 2, and sensible delegation, as explained in Chapter 5. The importance of managerial expertise in containing stress is all the more vital because of the general increase in the amount and complexity of the managerial element in many jobs, as explained in Chapter 3.

CONCLUSION

All managers need to think carefully about how to get the best out of their subordinates. If there are problems of motivation and performance it is all too easy to blame this on the laziness or incompetence of others. Diagnosis of the real reasons may be painful for a manager if it emerges that problems arise because of the way they have organised (or failed to organise) work. If motivation is to be positive it is necessary to try and match the aspirations of individuals to the available work. To do this it is necessary to have some understanding of the basic theories regarding motivation as well as plain common sense. However, over-involvement in the job can also be a problem and can itself be one of the factors that can cause managerial stress. In dealing with managerial stress the development of managerial skills may attack root causes whilst relaxation techniques can only address the symptoms.

Having sounded a cautionary note about the dangers of over-involvement in the job, it is necessary to restate that often the problem is that of under-involvement. It is as well, too, to remember that people tend to live up to, or down to, the expectations that are made of them. In matching people to jobs, managers also need to bear in mind that both sides of this equation can and do change. People can, for example, develop so that the work that stretched them historically has now become boring. Jobs too can change, for example, because of technological innovations. The attempt to match people and jobs is a continuous process that also needs to be linked to remuneration policies. Sometimes pay can be used as a direct financial incentive as well as a means of attracting and retaining people in jobs. The use of financial incentives to increase performance may be used as well as, or instead of, the more psychological approaches that have been explained so far. Financial incentive schemes can be an appropriate way of motivating people, a regrettable necessity or a downright menace, and these issues will be examined in the next chapter in the context of remuneration generally.

NOTES

1 W. E. J. McCarthy and S. R. Parker, 'Shop Stewards and Workshop Relations', Royal Commission Research Paper No. 10, 1968, paras 175–8.
2 A. H. Maslow, *Motivation and Personality*, Harper & Row, 2nd edn, 1970.
3 D. C. McClelland, *The Achieving Society*, Van Nostrand, 1961.
4 F. Herzberg, B. Mausner and B. Synderman, *The Motivation to Work*, Wiley, 1960.
5 David A. Nadler and Edward E. Lawler III, 'Motivation: A Diagnostic Approach', in J. Richard Hackman and Edward E. Lawler III (eds), *Perspectives on Behaviour in Organisations*, McGraw-Hill, 1977, p. 27.
6 Advisory, Conciliation and Arbitration Service, *Effective Organisations: The People Factor*, Advisory Booklet no. 16, ACAS, 1991.
7 'Death of Corporate Loyalty', *The Economist*, 3 April 1993, p. 81.
8 Larry Black, 'Down-sizing Towards a Disposable Workforce – a view from New York', *Independent*, 22 March 1993.
9 'Redundancies, Friendly Firing', *The Economist*, 13 March 1993.
10 Richard Scase and Robert Goffee, *Reluctant Managers*, Unwin Hyman, 1989, p. 13; emphasis in original.
11 See Joanne Foster, 'Balancing Work and the Family', *Personnel Management*, September 1988, pp. 38–41.
12 For a detailed consideration of this topic see Stephen Williams, *Managing Pressure for Peak Performance (The Positive Approach to Stress)*, Kogan Page, 1994.
13 *Walker v Northumberland County Council*, 1994, *IRLR* 35, QBD.

Chapter 7

Payment systems

INTRODUCTION

Having considered the relevance of various behaviourial theories
to motivation, it is now necessary to look more explicitly at the
role of money as a motivator. The advantages and disadvantages
of financial incentive schemes and profit sharing arrangements
are therefore considered in this chapter. The issue of internal
relativities is also examined, as is the way in which job evaluation may
assist in establishing and maintaining a rational pay structure. The
various types of scheme are explained and the ways in which schemes
need to be chosen, operated and maintained if they are to be effective. Consideration is given to the equal value regulations which
stipulate that employees do not suffer pay discrimination on the
basis of sex. The pressures for change in the way job evaluation
operates and its changing role are examined. These include trends
towards smaller and more flexible organisations and a greater
emphasis on rewarding on the basis of individual performance.
General trends are examined including re-examination of incremental salary scales and cafeteria-style fringe benefits. The issue
of individual merit payment, especially performance-related pay
is deferred until Chapter 10, so that it can be considered in the
context of appraisal.

FINANCIAL INCENTIVES

Probably the ideal arrangement for most jobs is that people have
an interesting job, good supervision and an appropriate basic
wage or salary. If the theories of people such as Maslow and
Herzberg mean anything at all, such arrangements should lead to

effective work performance and satisfied employees. However, the achievement of such a happy state of affairs is, needless to say, not always possible. It is particularly when this cannot be achieved that financial incentives may be appropriate, but it is most important for managers to ensure that their diagnosis is correct before they try to improve work performance by the use of financial incentives.

Diagnosis of need

As has previously been explained, problems of work performance may be due to factors outside the control of the employee. Even when it would seem that employees could increase output by reasonable increases in effort, it is necessary to ask why the effort is not forthcoming. The structure of jobs and the matching of individuals to jobs should be examined. If poor performance is because of poor supervision, it may be that it is the supervision that should be changed and not the arrangements for payment. It is particularly necessary to check this, as the long-term effect of incentive schemes can be to diminish the role of the supervisor. Employees operating under incentive schemes may see themselves as akin to independent subcontractors, with the supervisor as an external figure who is likely to come into conflict with them over a host of issues concerning the operation of the incentive scheme. This can lead to the exclusion of the supervisor from the work group, because of attempts by them to monitor schemes in the interest of the employer rather than of the employee. Alternatively, the supervisor may be 'captured' by the work group so that, for example, they do not report on manipulations to the incentive scheme or show excessive concern about safety and quality standards. Unfortunately, either of these developments can lead to the continued erosion of first-line supervisors to a point, sometimes, where they act as little more than a conduit for messages between management and work-force.

Appropriate conditions

There are jobs in which the ideal arrangements identified above will simply not always be attainable. There will, for example, be situations when the structure of jobs is such that they are inherently boring and that, in the short term at least, output will be best achieved by the use of financial incentive schemes. When I was employed at a factory making diesel engines, I had to recognise that in the large machine shop the withdrawal of the incentive scheme would have had a catastrophic effect on production, despite all the problems that it created.

The circumstances under which payment by results schemes might be appropriate are identified in a checklist drawn up by the National Board for Prices and Incomes as part of one of their investigations.[1] The four necessary conditions for the introduction of payment by results were stated to be where:

1 The work can be measured and directly attributed to the individual or group; in practice this generally means highly repetitive manual work – as found in mass-production manufacturing.
2 The pace of work is substantially controlled by the worker rather than by the machine or process they are tending.
3 Management is capable of maintaining a steady flow of work.
4 The tasks are not subjected to frequent changes in method, materials or equipment.

Even under these conditions and with proper monitoring the NBPI commented on the inevitable slackening that occurs in schemes because of factors such as technological change. They found that, even under ideal conditions, there is likely to be an unavoidable wholly unproductive wage drift of at least 1 per cent a year.[2] It is to be regretted that there are so few independent studies on the effects of incentive schemes to warn employers of the ways in which they can be counter-productive. Much of the literature is either in textbooks explaining how schemes are supposed to operate or in literature provided by consultants who make their money in selling and installing incentive packages.

Long-term effects

Proposals for introducing incentive schemes and their short-term benefits can seem very convincing. However, managers need to review carefully their diagnosis of the real reasons for poor performance and the possible long-term effects of incentive schemes before committing themselves to this route to higher output. Figure 7.1 shows what can happen in the short and long term if, for example, a payment by results scheme is introduced.

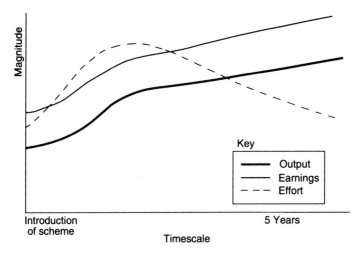

Figure 7.1 The long-term pattern of incentive schemes

Output may well increase by about one-third after the intro-duction of a scheme, with earnings going up in relation to output. However, as time goes on, even in relatively static production situations, there are likely to be improvements in work methods that are not entirely clawed back by the employer in terms of consequential reductions in time allowances. There may also be errors in initial time allowances and employees can be remarkably ingenious in manipulating schemes to their advantage. The most sophisticated manipulations involve 'capturing' the supervisor and other potential 'enemies' so that the higher levels of management are not aware that ultimately effort may decline whilst output and earnings increase. Schemes can degenerate to such an extent that they actually become arrangements for restricting production – for fear that, if normal effort is resumed, the output achieved would give the whole game away. The erosion of the position of the supervisor that may accompany these developments may facilitate, or be because of, the rise of shop steward influence.

Another problem can be the distorting effect that incentive schemes can have on pay structures. If, for whatever reason, the incentive earnings of one group rise this can create stresses with regard to pay relativities. Sometimes these can be acute and lead to the 'negative' differential of those, for example, who are supposed to supervise them. The introduction of new working methods may be accompanied by fear about the impact of this on earnings and may lead to resistance to the changes or haggling about any consequential adjustments to the incentive scheme. Another problem can be resistance to moving from jobs with 'slack' times to those with 'tight' times. The impact on quality of production or service also has to be examined. One of the innumerable examples of incentive schemes adversely affecting quality was the introduction of quotas and financial penalties by the contractors operating Westminster Council's street car parking arrangements. This led to some traffic wardens issuing tickets in breach of the regulations so as to avoid penalties for themselves.[3] The impact on safety also needs to be examined in case employees are actually rewarded for working dangerously. One of the many ways in which this can and does happen concerns some of the 'job and finish' arrangements for truck drivers. Such schemes may enable drivers to be paid at premium rates for trips done over and above their daily standard. As well as encouraging unsafe driving this may also lead to excessive vehicle wear and fuel consumption.

The point that it is necessary to stress is that all the potential disadvantages of incentive schemes need to be taken into account before they are adopted. The trouble is that the short-term tangible benefits may be much more obvious than many of the long-term intangible, but nevertheless important, consequences. A policy of choosing 'horses for courses' is appropriate rather than any dogmatic assertion that one should always use incentive schemes or never use them. The matching of pay arrangements to situations can, however, be ill-conceived or the circumstances in which schemes operate can alter and make them invalid. A common example is when automatic production processes are introduced which predetermine the rate of production, which had previously been determined by operators. If the speed at which, now reactive, operators work consequently becomes an effect and not a cause of some other variable, it becomes pointless to reward them for something over which they no longer have control. The achievement of high levels of production may be related instead, for example, to ensuring that automatic process equipment is properly maintained and does not break down or operate in such a way that there are quality defects.

The importance of careful thought about the appropriate arrangements for paying employees is not confined to groups of manual employees. The method of paying dentists in the UK provides an apt example of some of the dangers. Initially, dentists, working under the National Health Service, were paid primarily on the physical services they provided. This may have discouraged advice being given about dental hygiene. This has led to financial incentives now being offered for dentists to employ dental hygienists. The ramifications of incentive schemes are such that considerable thought has to be given, not only as to whether they should be used or not, but also as to how they should be managed if they are used. Another lesson from the collapse of Barings Bank in 1995 (see Chapter 5) was that the reckless and uncontrolled pursuit of profits and bonuses can destroy an organisation. The fact is that, if incentive schemes are used, they may require just as much, or even more, managerial effort, to see that performance targets are met, compared with the managerial effort involved when people are paid just a basic wage or salary.

Group schemes

Most of the comments made about financial incentive schemes already also apply to group schemes. However, there are some specific aspects relating to group schemes that also need to be considered. Group schemes seem to work best when the group is no bigger than 8 to 12 and the task is inherently a group rather than an individual task. If a plant-wide scheme is used, the relationship between individual effort and reward may be too small for there to be any significant causal relationship between the effort of the individual and overall output. Individual earnings may move in parallel with total output but that does not prove that people are working harder because of a group incentive scheme. Employees may perceive that their earnings will be very much the same, however hard or however little they work. They may also perceive that many factors other than their effort, or even the effort of them and their fellow workers, may affect total output, for example workflow and technological change.

Profit sharing

There are two main types of profit sharing arrangements – profit-related pay and employee share option plans. Both types of scheme may enable participants to gain some tax advantages.

Whilst the tax advantages are popular, the same issues concerning the weakness of the link between reward and individual performance emerge as with group bonus schemes. A fallacy about distributing profits in the form of shares is the assumption that once employees have a shareholder role, they will forget about the far more important wage-earner role and simply behave in the best interests of the shareholders. It is when 'weights' are attached to these two roles that it becomes apparent that any link between group performance and group profits may not actually be caused by a profit sharing incentive. If the roles come into conflict employees may behave in such a way that they protect their wage-earner role and subordinate any shareholder interests to this much greater primary role. Admittedly, often the roles will not be in conflict and there may be a general value in exposing employees to the shareholder perspective. However, variations in profits may in fact have little to do with the supposed motivating effect of a profit sharing scheme regardless of whether the rewards are in the form of direct payments or shares. The conclusion of two commentators is that the popularity of such schemes is primarily related to their tax avoidance potential and that there is little evidence that they have a positive impact on profits.[4] Firms may not have even tried to incorporate such financial benefits as part of a wider strategy of employee involvement.[5]

JOB EVALUATION

Another aspect of remuneration that needs careful consideration is that of internal relativities: Even if employees are paid well in comparison with similar work in other organisations, there can often be acute discontent about perceived internal inequities. Every organisation needs to have some sort of policy with regard to its own wage and salary structure. One way of establishing a pay structure is by use of the techniques of job evaluation. This is very often the way in which the salaries for white-collar employees are established. Pay for manual employees has usually been determined by traditional methods of negotiation, as explained in Chapter 12. However, occupational changes and the impact of the law relating to equal value are increasing the use of job evaluation with manual employees. An outline is given in this section of the different types of job evaluation schemes and of their advantages and disadvantages. Particular attention is given to some of the practical snags that are often overlooked in expositions of how such schemes are supposed to work as opposed to the way they may work in practice. The issue of equal value, which is intended to prevent sex discrimination with regard to pay, is examined in this section because of the role of job evaluation in seeking to either establish a claim or to prevent one being made. The pressures for change in the way job evaluation operates are considered. These include changing organisational structures, the greater emphasis on organisational and individual flexibility, and the increased emphasis on rewarding on an individual basis.

Objectives

The overall objective of job evaluation schemes can be described as assisting in providing a cost-effective pay structure. Sometimes pay structures seem to have a life and direction all of their own but they should be synchronised with other organisational processes such as human resource planning and budgetary control. Such integration is necessary if overall organisational objectives are to be achieved. Few people would argue that the process of job evaluation is scientific – it is essentially a systematic way of making a series of judgements about relativities. The use of scientific method is in making those subjective judgements not replacing that judgemental process. The elimination of all discontent about pay being an impossible target, the value of job evaluation is that it may enable pay relativities to be established in such a way that discontent is less than if job evaluation were not used. The determination of wage and salary levels is a process that takes place after relativities have been established. However, job evaluation provides the basis for the allocation of money to different grades. It may also help with the process of salary surveys.

Types of schemes

A basic distinction between the various types of schemes is between the analytical and the non-analytical ones. Examples of the latter are the job classification, job ranking and paired comparisons. With job classification, jobs are looked at as a whole and then grouped into families to which a grade is allocated (as in the Civil Service). Definitions are sometimes given of the basic characteristics of a classification or grade to judge where particular jobs should go. With job ranking, jobs are arranged in a hierarchy and the vertical rank order can be split up into various job grades. The technique of paired comparisons is a more sophisticated way of arriving at a rank order. It involves comparing each job with every other job to identify the correct rank order. The basic feature of all three of these non-analytical approaches is that the ultimate grading is achieved by comparison with other jobs rather than by systematically identifying the component elements in each job.

The main analytical schemes are points rating and many of the proprietary schemes offered by consultancy organisations. Points rating involves identifying the common factors in jobs and then allocating points to these factors according to the specific demands in each job. The points allocation, or weight, for each factor is established after systematic internal discussion about the relative importance of the factor to the organisation. Each factor in a job is then assessed and a total points score for the job obtained. The total points score indicates what job grade is appropriate. The proprietary schemes are often sophisticated versions of this points rating approach.

Choices of scheme

The dilemma for the individual employers is what, if any, scheme to adopt. No one scheme, or approach, is superior to all others: it is basically a question of choosing 'horses for courses' and then operating whatever scheme is chosen in a sensible manner. However refined and sophisticated schemes may appear to be, it must always be remembered that any statistical calculation is erected on a basis of subjective judgements of, for example, what factors should be chosen and what weights they should be given. Consequently, one should beware of spurious accuracy and of claims that everything is near perfect because ratings are very consistent. Ratings may be consistent in applying a scheme but as schemes rest on subjective judgements this can lead to consistent error. One ingenious personnel officer, bewildered by the rival claims of competing consultants, found the easiest way of finding out the weaknesses of proprietary schemes was to invite comment from rival consultants![6]

The costs of installing and maintaining a scheme also need to be considered. The more sophisticated the scheme the greater such costs are likely to be. Another critical cost is the uplift in pay that usually results from the introduction of a scheme. Job evaluation is unlikely to leave the existing pay structure undisturbed and the holders of jobs that are downgraded normally have their own salary protected. Consequently, an immediate effect of job evaluation is that as no-one has less pay and some will get more pay, the total wage and salary bill will increase. A rule of thumb for major restructuring exercises is that such an uplift will be in the order of 3 per cent of the total pay bill.

Another factor is the size of the organisation or sector of it that is to be studied. The investment in a costly scheme for a small group of employees may simply be too expensive. The ranking and paired comparison methods, however, may prove difficult to apply in large organisations because of the number of jobs that need ordering and comparing. A factor that should not be, but often is, ignored is the expected rate of change in an organisation. A cautionary tale in this respect was given to me by a personnel officer who had been at an engineering company where a scheme had been installed at great expense only to become obsolete within four months because of the rapidity of technical and organisational change. Job evaluation schemes are usually introduced on the assumption that the organisational arrangements are fixed. However, the pace of change is such now that one has to ask of all schemes how well they would cope with projected change. There is not much point in having an expensive sophisticated scheme that is soon going to be out of date. This question also needs asking in a slightly modified form of existing schemes. It may be that existing schemes, which may historically have been sound, have fallen into decay through not being adjusted, or not being capable of adjustment, in line with organisational change.

Implementation and operation

Basic issues which need consideration involve whether a scheme should cover the whole of an organisation or just part of it, and trade union involvement. Whilst it may seem convenient and fair to have one scheme for the whole of an organisation this is not always practicable. There can be so little in common between, for example, manual, technical and managerial grades that one may have to develop different schemes so that the jobs being compared and evaluated have a reasonable amount in common. There is not much point in having an overall scheme that seeks to assess a managing director's job in terms of factors such as physical strength and monotony and boredom! However, a counter-argument that has emerged in favour of schemes covering all employees is that it may help in defending cases brought under the equal value regulations where comparisons are made between different parts of an employer's pay structure (the regulations are explained later in this chapter).

Trade unions are likely to take more than a passing interest in job evaluation and their involvement in schemes has to be considered. They are likely to see job evaluation as a framework for bargaining. In any case, regardless of whether there is a trade union or not, one needs to consider the issue of employee involvement. If schemes are supposed to incorporate internal views about equity and fairness there needs to be some mechanism for taking employees' views into account with regard to the design and operation of schemes. The need to do this has been reinforced by developments in European law. An almost inevitable consequence of job evaluation is that some jobs will be down-graded. Even if a person's salary is protected it is arguable that such a change necessitates consultation with union representatives as statutory redundancy consultation has been widened to cover changes in contract terms. This requirement was incorporated in the Trade Union Reform and Employment Rights Act of 1993 bringing the UK into line with European law. Additionally, even if there is no union there is a requirement to consult with employee representatives in the public sector as a consequence of a case successfully brought by the European Commission against the UK government in 1994. There is also a requirement to extend this right, under domestic legislation, to the private sector.[7]

If anyone ever did design a perfect system, representatives would still feel obliged to bargain about the matter, as what trade union could countenance being told it had no bargaining role? The state of the art, though, is such that unions rightly query the basis on which schemes are based and the results they give. Unions may have to distance themselves a little from schemes, however, as otherwise they may be seen as implementing managerial pay policies. Once a scheme has been established they tend to acknowledge it and to retain and use the right to represent any-one who feels that they have a case for upgrading. Irrespective of whether or not there is union involvement in a scheme, or even union recognition, some sort of appeals mechanism is necessary.

Appeals criteria need to be specified, such as a change in duties, and appeals bodies established. These may be managerial panels, joint management–union panels or involve the use of an outside arbitrator – either sitting alone or chairing a joint panel.

There is a range of other operational issues that need careful attention. One of the basic issues is to remember that it is the job that is being evaluated and not the person. If a job holder has 'outgrown' a job the real answer is for them to be encouraged to seek promotion rather than to distort the pay structure by giving an upgrading that temporarily meets their needs but not the organisation's. One must also beware of the danger, explained in the previous chapter, that employees may distort a job to justify an upgrading. In contrast, if a person is not up to a job, it can sometimes be that this is because the job is not graded highly enough to attract people of the right calibre.

Factors have to be chosen carefully so that they don't overlap. Otherwise a job holder can benefit twice under such factors as 'job complexity' and 'education required', which may be different ways of measuring the same requirement. Another complication can arise from the establishment of 'weights' for factors. Apart from the judgemental problems of doing this anyway, there is the statistical problem that the real 'weights' depend not just on, for example, the points allocated for a particular factor, but also on the extent to which those making judgements use the full extent of the scale. There was once an attempt to introduce a new scheme for nursing officers in the Health Service. It rapidly became apparent that for some jobs the only factors on which the scores differed were those related to the size of the unit in which a person was employed. The reality was that in practice the scheme for some jobs was based on a single factor – the one that was easiest to measure! A further explanation of these statistical problems is given in the section on recording and rating in Chapter 10.

There can be misconceptions about the extent to which employees can be expected to change their duties without receiving any extra remuneration. Changes in the range of work at a given level do not normally constitute a case for upgrading. Work at a higher level of responsibility may provide a valid basis for upgrading, but even in this case it has to be remembered that job grades normally embrace a range of jobs and a person's increase in, for example, responsibility level may not be sufficient to lift them into the next grade. There is a common law requirement for employees to accept reasonable changes in job content and the prudent employer will reinforce this by the use of generic job titles and a flexibility clause in any job description.

Claims for upgrading can also be made on what may turn out to be basic job requirements rather than additional demands. Schemes need to be operated on the basis that there are minimum performance requirements which justify retention in a given job as opposed to justifying an upgrading. However, one cannot but admire the ingenuity with which some cases are argued. One fork-lift truck driver applied for an upgrading at an oil refinery. His case rested on his responsibility for expensive plant and equipment as evidenced by the fact that he had recently fractured a fuel line and caused a fire costing over a million pounds worth of damage! Another such case involved a telephonist/receptionist who was asked to elaborate on the decision-making elements in her job – which consisted mainly of routing telephone calls and visitors. She beamed and said she had to decide whether to come in each day or not! The argument advanced was that she had to decide if she was fit enough for work or not as if she was not it would be bad for the external image of the firm if she came in and was 'grumpy'.

A crucial issue in establishing the grading of any job is its effect on the overall equilibrium of the pay structure. Serious inequities obviously should be corrected but not insubstantial cases for locating jobs in a higher grade. The key issue is not the extra direct costs this would involve but the 'knock-on' effect. The danger is that by solving one person's perceived grievance you can create a host of repercussive claims. Another key issue concerns the relationship of pay to the external job market. It is no good having a scheme that is out of line with the market. However, markets do not always operate so clearly and systematically that you can dispense with job evaluation. In making comparisons with pay in other organisations care has to be taken to ensure that you are comparing like with like. The use of job titles alone may be dangerous as a term such as 'fitter' can cover a wide range of different jobs in terms of actual duties and responsibility level. Sometimes there can be a marked conflict between internal relativities and the market rate for particular groups, for whom there is a strong demand. The realistic answer in cases like this is not to have a spurious re-evaluation of the staff concerned but to openly recognise and deal with the problem. It may be necessary to pay a market supplement for such staff or even take them out of the evaluation scheme altogether. This way at least the rest of the pay structure can remain consistent.

A further issue concerns the transferability of evaluation schemes to different organisations, countries and cultures. It can be tempting to do this as it may seem a short cut to copy someone else's scheme or use one's own in an overseas subsidiary. The usual rationale for job evaluation schemes is that they reflect the attitudes within an organisation about what is a fair set of relativities. However, the attitudes towards what is fair may be quite different in an organisation or country in which there is a different set of values. Consequently, such transfer of schemes may be an extremely hit and miss affair.

Equal value

A further dimension of pay structures and job evaluation is the law regarding equal value. Employees have a broad right not to be discriminated against in terms of pay and conditions of employment on grounds of sex if their work is of equal value to someone of the opposite sex in the same organisation. This is a consequence of the UK Government being obliged to comply with the requirements of the Treaty of Rome. Previously, under the Equal Pay Act of 1970, there was a limited right to equal pay but just for like work or broadly similar work, or for work rated as equivalent under a job evaluation scheme. This was not enough to prevent the European Commission successfully bringing an action against the UK Government in 1982, requiring it to comply with the relevant requirements of the Treaty of Rome and, in particular, with the Equal Pay Directive of 1975. Consequently, the Equal Pay Act of 1970 was amended to also enable claims for work of equal value to be made. The industrial tribunal regulations were amended to establish a special procedure for processing such claims. The right to claim pay of equal value, like the right to claim equal pay, excludes comparisons with employees of the same sex.

The right to equal pay for work of equal value exists where the job demands are the same in categories such as 'effort, skill and decision-making'. This implies a need for some sort of analytical job evaluation if the employer is to try and defend their position. Unless the tribunal decides that there are no reasonable grounds for the claim, and if the parties fail to reach an agreement, an independent expert is called in. The expert reports on whether or not the jobs that the claimant claims are of equal value are so. The tribunal subsequently decides in the light of the expert's report. (However, at the time of writing there is a government Green Paper proposal to remove the statutory obligation to have an independent expert.) All this may sound rather convoluted but the crunch comes if an individual claim succeeds. This may reveal that there is the basis for further claims and if any of these succeed the process may continue. The 'knock-on' effect can lead to the undermining of the whole of an existing pay structure.

The impact that a successful equal value claim can have means that employers must give some thought to this whole area. They may also feel that they should be doing this anyway to avoid sex discrimination. To do that it is necessary to review not just a pay structure but the processes by which pay rates and differentials are established. Implications for the operation of job evaluation schemes include ensuring that there is a fair cross-representation of any benchmark jobs and that there is adequate representation of both sexes on panels. If a points rating scheme is used it is necessary to ensure that the factors and weights used are not discriminatory. This may be all against a background where the internal 'felt-fair' values represent, for example, dominant male values which may be in conflict with the legal requirement to avoid discrimination. Analytical job evaluation fairly applied will help avoid discrimination but not necessarily put a stop to argument. People sometimes think that the use of, for example, sophisticated statistical techniques enables *objective* decisions to be made about pay grades. However, what such techniques do is to provide elaborate means of establishing *opinions* about job relationships. The judgements about how dissimilar factors or whole jobs should relate to one another can be carried out systematically but the judgements are subjective. Consequently, an independent expert may well have a different view about job relationships from those who established a particular pay structure. The judgements of independent experts are also likely to vary from one tribunal case to another.

The case law arising out of equal value claims is proving a guide as to how the law operates in practice. Claims have to involve comparisons with another job where employees are predominantly of the other sex.[8] The existence of a separate collective bargaining structure is not an acceptable defence.[9] The practice of 'slotting-in' jobs to outline structures without analysis of the jobs slotted-in seems to be inadequate.[10] Equal value law may be a powerful pressure for the harmonisation of the conditions of employment of manual and white-collar employees. Otherwise applicants may be able to point to just one element of the remuneration package where they think there is an unjustified difference and argue the case for parity.[11] The defence of a 'genuine material factor' difference may include market rates, but only if that accounts for the whole difference.[12] Employers have strong financial reasons for appealing against adverse judgements (as do unions). Consequently, it can be years before a case is decided. According to a 1993 report in the *Independent* 'there have been only 23 successful cases, many of which took years to complete.'[13] The government does not seem very interested in simplifying procedures by, for example, allowing class (group) actions and had to be forced into introducing the concept of equal value in the first place. The lessons for employers include taking the basic steps already suggested to avoid obvious discrimination and hoping that they are not targeted for an important test case. If the pay structure is adjusted to take account of possible sex discrimination the extra pay costs need to be taken into account when any general increase is considered.[14]

Pressures for change

The major changes that so many organisations have experienced, and which have been previously described particularly in Chapter 3, are having a major impact on the way job evaluation is operated. The trend to less labour-intensive, more flexible organisations has been particularly important. Also, changes in job evaluation have been necessary in some cases to help bring about such organisational changes. Generally there has been a move to fewer job grades, with less-detailed job descriptions and an emphasis on flexible working. In the case of Nissan this has involved the compression of manual jobs into just two different job titles with no job descriptions. The trend to multi-skilling, as an aid to greater flexibility, also puts more emphasis on the personal attributes of the job holder. This may include payment for additional 'competences' that the job holder has acquired. These developments in turn reduce the distinctiveness of individual jobs and encourage the concept of job families. Simpler schemes are more adaptive, more easily controlled in terms of 'pay drift', and less expensive in terms of administrative costs including the use of managerial time. Such costs savings are a particularly important pressure for change given the ongoing pressure to reduce costs in the private and public sectors. Computer-assisted schemes help reduce the costs of operating schemes further, provided the managerial politics are such that the results are viable.

The decline in union power has tended to give management more freedom with regard to job evaluation and this has often been reinforced by more devolved patterns of organisational decision-making. The decline in union power has also facilitated more of an individual and less of a 'collectivist' approach. This trend has tended to emphasise the link between pay and individual performance and to reduce the importance of grade levels. The traditional approach to job evaluation was that individual perform-ance was discounted but there is more acceptance now that the nature of the job may be shaped by the individual performing it. The concept of added value is important in this respect. All this has tended to reduce the need for complex schemes and high levels of 'accuracy', particularly as grade level is a less dominant factor in determining overall pay. The one contrary pressure arises from the equal value regulation which may cause organisations to consider retaining or introducing analytical schemes. Although few claims have been successfully established, organisations may also have to respond to claims during pay bargaining that their job evaluation schemes are sex-discriminatory. Other trends include less emphasis on hierarchies and more use of overlapping pay scales. All this means that the demand for complex and expensive proprietary schemes is likely to fall. One further development is the application of the concept of job competences to job evalua-tion. Constructive use may be made about the information obtained about competences for selection and training purposes. This may also enable evaluators to avoid making what may be spurious judgements about the personal attributes, training and qualifications required by job holders. However, to base job evaluation entirely on competences could lead to as much complexity as with conventional analytical schemes.

OTHER DEVELOPMENTS RELATING TO PAY

The developments regarding the flexible organisation explained in Chapter 3 have had a considerable impact on pay. One of these developments is the greater use of fixed-term contracts but, as also explained in Chapter 3, that is increasingly applied to senior core employees as well. The reduction in the rate of inflation, general economic conditions and the reduced power of unions has caused many organisations to review the practice of giving annual staff increments *and* annual general increases. In some cases organisations have corrected for historically generous pay scales by giving new recruits 'negative' increments, i.e. extending the pay scale downwards. Individual increases are more likely to be related to performance, whether under a performance-related scheme or on the basis of general merit or new competences that have been acquired. This issue is examined in detail in Chapter 10. Another development has been that of cafeteria-style fringe benefits so that employees have some choice in arranging a permutation of fringe benefits. However, the administrative problems that this can generate is a problem, particularly as a change in the level of one benefit affects the relative worth of all the other benefits.

CONCLUSION

Just as in other areas of managerial activity, the effective motivation of employees is likely to depend on patient intellectual effort on the part of the manager. It can be very tempting to pretend that poor performance is all the fault of employees. Saying that does not automatically make it true. The use of financial incentive schemes may help in motivating employees, but that also requires patient diagnostic work. Incentive schemes are not always appropriate and, even when they are, the right one has to be chosen. Schemes also have to be monitored very carefully if they are to remain effective. Even if employees are well paid in relation to the external market they may bitterly resent perceived internal injustices. Job evaluation can help reduce the level of discontent – but schemes have to be carefully chosen, operated and monitored. Despite the equal value regulations there are strong cost and organisational pressures for schemes to be simpler. Even if individuals do not always agree with the results of job evaluation schemes they may at least see that the employer has tried to resolve pay issues in a fair and systematic way.

NOTES

1 National Board for Prices and Incomes, *Payment by Results Systems*, Report No. 65, Cmnd. 3627, HMSO, 1968, p. 11 of pamphlet summarising the above report.

2 Statistical supplement to Payment by Results report (see note 1), p. 50, para. 22.

3 Ian Morton, 'Cheating Traffic Wardens Curbed', *Evening Standard*, London, 8 September 1993.

4 Robert Chote, 'Profit-related Pay Proves no Panacea, *Independent*, 24 May 1991; Hazel McLean, *Fair Shares: The Future of Employee Financial Participation in the U.K.*, Institute of Employment Rights, 1994.

5 McLean, ibid.

6 For an excellent account of the strengths and weaknesses of the various schemes, including proprietary ones, see *Job Evaluation Review*, Incomes Data Services, Top Pay Unit, 2nd edn, 1986. See also: Michael Armstrong and Angela Barron, *The Job Evaluation Handbook*, Institute of Personnel and Development, 1995.

7 For an account of these developments see Olga Aiken and Cherry Mill et al., 'No Escape From Consultation', *Personnel Management*, October 1994, pp. 54–7; *Commission of the European Communities v U.K.* [1994], IRLR, 1994, p. 421.

8 *Pickstone v Freemans plc* [1988] IRLR 267, HL.

9 *Enderby v Frenchay Health Authority*, TLR, 12 November 1993, ECJ.

10 See the Court of Appeal Judgment in *Bromley v H.J. Quick Ltd.*, IRLR, no. 249, 1988.

11 *Hayward v Cammell Laird Shipbuilders Ltd.* [1988] ICR 464, (1988) IRLR 257.

12 *Enderbey v Frenchay Health Authority*, 1993, op. cit.

13 Barnie Clement and Patricia Wyn Davies 'Equal Pay for Women Curbed by Ministers', *Independent*, 11 October 1993.

14 For further accounts of the general area indicating preventive strategies see Dierdre Gill and Bernard Ungerson, *Equal Pay: The Challenge of Equal Value*, Institute of Personnel Management, 1984; *Equal Opportunities: Job Evaluation Schemes Free of Sex Bias*, revised edn, 1985; *Equal Pay for Work of Equal Value*, 1984, both published by the Equal Opportunities Commission.

Chapter 8

Communication

INTRODUCTION

This chapter is probably the most important in the whole book. The topic, as well as needing to be covered in its own right, serves as a foundation for much of the rest of the book. It also links back with material covered in previous chapters. This includes the link between organisational structure and the effectiveness of communication and the growing importance of electronic communication – both covered in Chapter 3. Other phenomena that interrelate with communication are managerial style and culture – topics which are covered in Chapter 4.

The chapter starts with an explanation of why communication is such an important topic. The barriers to communication are examined. This is followed by a detailed consideration of the skills that the manager requires, particularly that of effective listening. The emphasis in the earlier part of the chapter is on oral communication, but attention is given later to the need for, and skills involved in, effective written communication. There is also a section on the media. This covers the evaluation of information and views communicated by the media and basic skills of media presentation.

THE IMPORTANCE OF COMMUNICATION

Managers are likely to spend most of their time engaged directly in some form of communication process. Even when they are working alone – for example, studying or preparing reports – they are relying on other people's attempts to communicate with them or they are preparing to communicate with others. Accuracy in decision-making depends, in particular, on effective communication. If the communication process is faulty then everything else can be affected.

Experiments, research and sheer personal observation show that most people are far too optimistic about the accuracy of the communication process. This applies not just to communication processes within employing organisations but to life in general. Even when errors are identified this may be too late, or the inherent faults in the process that will lead to further errors may not be recognised. The barriers to effective communication are far greater than most people realise. The effective communication of factual information can be difficult enough, but often attitudes and feelings need to be communicated and that can be far more complicated. The number and nature of the barriers are such that there is a strong case for communication skills training being given as part of the standard school curriculum. This is not yet the case, and in this chapter the attempt is made to give managers practical guidance on how to identify the communication processes in their organisations with a view first of all to evaluating their effectiveness. This evaluation can then provide the basis for the development of the manager's own practical skills of communication.

In Rosemary Stewart's previously quoted study of how managers spend their time,[1] it was established that on average the 160 managers in her sample spent two-thirds of their time working with other people. It seems reasonable to assume that most managers spend the bulk of their working day in some type of communication activity. Even the 33 managers in the sample in 'backroom'-type jobs spent about half of their time working with other people. This may be through attendance at meetings, the giving and receiving of instructions, discussions with colleagues and contact with customers or suppliers. Such contact may be face to face or over the telephone, or a combination of both. Much of the remainder of the time is likely to be concerned with the assimilation or preparation of written information. If managers are to make the correct substantive decisions in their jobs, it follows that they need to be able to handle the communication process effectively.

My own experience, and I would suggest that of most people, is that managers differ markedly in their ability to communicate effectively. It follows that the need to develop skills for effective communication may be a critical priority for many managers. Regrettably, this need is often not perceived and managers may neglect the importance of, and the opportunity for, development in this critical area. Communication skills tend to be taken for granted and lack of skill far more easily recognised in others than in oneself. The process of communication is often far more complex than people realise, and this is a further reason why skills development in this area tends to be neglected. It is only when people realise the subtleties concerning effective communication that they may become communication conscious and start to develop their own skills. The complexities are such that those who are good at communication are likely to become even better if they systematically evaluate and consider their own effectiveness in this area.

PROBLEMS AND REMEDIES

Having stressed the importance of the communication process, it is appropriate to develop further the hypothesis that communication in organisations is a great deal worse than most people realise. This will be done by explaining the nature of communication processes, and the potential for breakdown. Case examples are given to illustrate some of the major points.

Listening problems

It is appropriate to explain one major misconception about communication at this stage. This point is not only important in its own right but develops the argument that the approach of many managers to communication may not be sufficiently sophisticated. Communication is usually seen as the need to brief other people. The reality is that most of a manager's time needs to be concerned with the receiving rather than the imparting of information and views. The reason for this is simple – in any conversation between two people there is a need to alternate between talking and listening. There is not much point in anyone talking if the intended recipient is not prepared to listen. If the two people involved in a discussion take equal turns talking and listening, they will obviously spend half of their time in the listening role. As much of the communication in organisations involves face-to-face discussion between more than two people, it follows as a mathematical fact that most managers will need to spend more time listening than talking. There will, be exceptions to this, but the very existence of exceptions reduces the time available for others to do the talking. Admittedly, managers may often need to take the lead in explaining things to their subordinates, but a statistically unequal share of talk in this direction may easily be counterbalanced by the time they have to spend in discussions and meetings involving a number of people when they talk only for a minority of the time. The basic point of this argument is that managers may fail to see that they will normally need to spend more time listening than talking.

Effective listening does not come naturally to all managers, particularly if they do not recognise the importance of it. The mistake of assuming that 'good communication' is synonymous with the imparting of information and views is often made by people who set out to improve the quality of communication in organisations. House magazines, letters from the chief executive, briefing meetings and training in public speaking are based mainly on the assumption that the problem is in disseminating information. The reality may be that it is more important to unblock the obstructions to information and views flowing in to the decision-makers. The problem may be that, until such time as communication is effective, managers may not realise that the obstructions are there. In any case, if everyone concentrates on imparting information and views, just who will be left to receive all these messages?

One case which illustrates this point concerns a nursing officer who attended a review meeting three months after he had attended a middle management training course. When asked what had happened as a result of his training, he explained that the area on which he had been able to concentrate was the development of his communication skills. He had worked on his listening skills and had put a chair by the side of his desk, on which people were invited to sit when they came into his office. He explained that he was amazed at the extra amount of information that he obtained this way compared with his previous pattern of letting people stand up or sit on a chair the other side of the desk. He then realised the limited nature of the information he had been obtaining before and on which basis he had been taking decisions. Before, being unaware of the information that was available, he had not tried to get it. It was only after he had discovered his 'blind spot' that he realised that it existed.

Lack of feedback

The problem of effective communication is unfortunately greater than just the recognition of its scale and importance and the comprehension that one needs to receive information as well as disseminate it. It is all too easy for people to assume that they have effectively communicated and be blissfully unaware that their attempts at communication have only been partially successful or, in some cases, totally unsuccessful. I have often used a simple exercise to demonstrate the undue optimism concerning the effectiveness of communication with groups of managers on training courses. This particular exercise involves asking one of the group to tell the rest, without any questions by them, how to draw a diagram consisting of six rectangles. The instructor is asked to sit facing the wall and convert a diagram such as that shown in Figure 8.1 into words so that the group can reproduce the diagram from their oral instructions. This exercise is described in detail in Leavitt and Bahrani's *Managerial Psychology*.[2] In practice, one would not try to explain how to reproduce a diagram by oral instruction, but there are advantages in using this artificial example. It is easy to check the accuracy with which it is reproduced and it is no more complicated than some of the instructions that people do try to explain orally.

All the rectangles are of equal size and the angles either of 45° or 90°. The rectangles touch one another either at the corner or the mid-point. Invariably, there is considerable error in the attempts of the groups to convert the oral instructions back into the original diagram. Sometimes the results are devastating. On one occasion a zero score was achieved by a group of 16 managers because their instructor had unwittingly described the rectangles as triangles. Invariably the instructor significantly underestimates the amount of error made by the group.

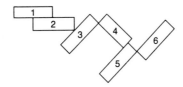

Figure 8.1 Communication exercise

After the results of the attempt to explain the diagram using one-way communication have been recorded, the same instructor is asked to repeat the exercise but the second time facing the group and with unlimited opportunity for questioning. A similar type of diagram is converted into words and back into a diagram again by the rest of the group. There is a standard pattern to this second stage of the experiment. It takes longer, the accuracy is usually much higher, it is rare for there to be no error, and again the instructor overestimates the level of accuracy. The assumption is usually made that, if people have queries, they will raise them. The reality though, is, that, even in the relatively placid context of a training course, people may have inhibitions about asking questions. They may feel embarrassed about their inability to draw the diagram, be confused by the instruction, have wrongly thought that their reconstruction was correct, have failed to catch the eye of the instructor at the right time or simply lost interest. The instructor may fail to appreciate that there can be this variety of reasons for people not raising queries and make the common error of assuming that silence means that everyone has accurately reproduced the diagram.

Bogus feedback

One of the crucial points that emerges from the rectangles exercise is that people responsible for initiating communication need to consider both what the evidence is for them assuming that communication has been effective and the consequences of communication being defective. You can be very aware of situations when you are on the receiving end of an instruction that you do not understand. It can be very tempting, for the sort of reasons outlined above, to create the impression by silence that you have understood something when you in fact know that you have not. The problem is that the initiator may be left with quite a false impression of their effectiveness. If a message is particularly important it is up to them to search for a more positive corroboration than mere silence that communication has been effective. They will need to consider other forms of feedback and to distinguish between accurate and bogus feedback.

Silence is not the only way in which people give false impressions about having understood explanations. There are occasions when people actually say they have understood when they have not.

A common situation when this arises is when you ask the way and are so baffled by the instructions on how to get to a particular place that you may meekly say that you have understood when you have not. This type of breakdown can happen within organisations and for a variety of reasons. These reasons may be the same as those previously given for people remaining silent when they have the opportunity to ask necessary questions during the rectangles exercise. Another reason can be the fear of admitting ignorance, to authority figures in particular.

In discussing this issue with nursing groups I have been deluged with examples of when this has happened. One example concerned the student nurse who was asked to give a patient an air ring. She apparently was not quite sure what to do but guessed that the appropriate interpretation was to move the patient's bed on to the verandah and remove the bedclothes! She had in fact been expected to get an air ring so that the patient could sit on it and receive a blanket bath. Another student nurse was given the same instruction but with slightly different phraseology – she was told to go and get an air ring. Allegedly she returned three-quarters of an hour later saying how much she had enjoyed her walk! Pride of place of the many examples I have been given goes to the case of the student nurse who was expected to give a patient a warm drink of potassium citrate. As is so often the case, an abbreviation was used and she was asked to give the patient a 'hot pot cit'. Unfortunately her interpretation of this instruction led to the patient being sat upon a bedpan of boiling water! In these cases the students' guesswork fortunately just led to comic results. That will not always be the case and such errors in the communication process may be picked up too late or not at all. The errors in the previous examples may be seen as stupidity or feebleness on the part of the student nurses, but such an interpretation is to miss the point. The fault really lies with the person who gave the instruction not ensuring that they had made themselves properly understood. Either they needed to make a positive check that the instruction was understood or, to have had a working relationship with the student nurse such that queries would be raised if necessary. The objective with communication needs to be to see that it is effective rather than being able to lay the blame at someone else's door if things go wrong.

Nursing examples have been given to illustrate the need to get accurate feedback. This is not to suggest that nursing is more prone to this type of problem than other occupations; it is simply that examples come easily to mind from my experience with nursing groups. The culpability of the authority figure can be even worse than I have so far suggested. Some people may contrive to go through the motions of obtaining feedback when in fact what they want is simply the pretence and alibi that people have had a fair opportunity to raise queries. Rhetorical questions may be used, such as 'is that clear?', which do not really invite responses. The technique can be observed with lecturers, or after-dinner speakers, who leave the opportunity for questions until an impossibly late stage in the proceedings. I also recollect it being used in the services, when orderly officers had to go through the routine of asking if there were complaints about the food. Some mastered the technique of asking if there were any queries in such a way that anyone who did complain deserved a medal. This enabled the orderly officer to maintain the fiction that people had been given an opportunity to complain about the food if they were dissatisfied. Should subordinates nevertheless voice criticisms in situations like this they may have the blame put back on them, however unjustly, to discourage further criticism. However, subordinates can also misperceive the response to their comments or questions. Sometimes it may be necessary and possible for them to raise sensitive issues. In doing this it may be as well to remember the skills of assertiveness explained in Chapter 4.

Resistance to criticism

There may be occasions when feedback is sought but resisted if it turns out to be unfavourable. I vividly remember one occasion when I explained to a subordinate personnel officer that I would always welcome suggestions if she thought there were ways in which the running of the department could be improved. She took me at my word and one day somewhat hesitantly started to explain how a change I was planning was, in her view, ill-judged. My immediate response was one of irritation, but fortunately I was just able to hide this and found to my chagrin that she was right and I was wrong. I was relatively new in the job and realised in retrospect that in the moments when I was seeking to control my irritation the future working relationship was being determined. I was able to show, at least with this person, that I would not bite her head off if she expressed views that were contrary to mine. After this incident the personnel officer concerned came to me when she thought that there was a likelihood of my committing other errors. This meant the occasional swallowing of pride when she picked up points that I had missed. There is a strong temptation in situations like this to block off criticism for fear of losing respect amongst subordinates. The conclusion I came to was that one was likely to lose much more respect if one simply hid from criticism. The route I chose did at least enable me to get advice before decisions were finalised. There is a much greater danger of losing respect if one cannot accept critical but helpful advice, especially if that is then compounded by decisions that are incorrect.

It is important to recognise that any manager is going to prefer to hear good news than bad news, and the temptation for colleagues and subordinates is to tell people what they want to hear. In the long term this can be disastrous, and managers and political leaders alike need consciously to recognise the distortion that can occur in channels of communication and beware of succumbing to it. An illustration of the folly of not doing this concerns President Saddam Hussein's invasion of Kuwait in 1990. It was difficult and dangerous for his advisers to warn him of the risk of a Western military response. Consequently, although his advisers are likely to have had a more realistic assessment of the consequences of invasion they were unable or unwilling to try and dissuade him from such action. This communication failure may or may not have been compounded by the lack of a clear warning by the American Ambassador, Avril Glaspie. Eight days before the invasion, she told Saddam Hussein that the US government had 'no opinion on the Arab-Arab conflicts, like your border disagreement with Kuwait.'[3] However, Avril Glaspie maintained that the part of the conversation containing the assurance that there would be no invasion was not included in the tape that was released by the Iraqis when they subsequently claimed they had been misled by the Americans.[4] When Saddam Hussein initiated major military manoeuvres on the Kuwait border in 1994 the allied reaction, particularly that of the Americans, was so strong diplomatically and in terms of military deployments that it meant there could be no possibility of their intentions being misunderstood again.

The chances of blocking out critical or unfavourable news can be greatly reduced if the temptation to do this is consciously recognised and if the ancient Greek tradition of slaying the messenger who brings news of defeat in battle is avoided. It may also be necessary to take independent checks to evaluate the information that is received. It was comprehension of this point which led some generals, at the time of the First World War, to say that 'if you want to know what's going on you have to go to the trenches'. Having said this, it is necessary also to make the point that there are few people, if any, who can cope with the whole truth all the time. Total exposure could be destructive to the individual concerned. What is needed is a realisation that the information fed to one in organisations needs careful evaluation and that other information may be needed but not passed on. Managers may need to seek out the bad news to the extent that it is necessary and to the extent that they can cope with it. An adage concerning delegation is that 'managers get the subordinates they deserve'. The same adage can be used with regard to communication; 'managers get the communication they deserve'.

Selective perception and bias

In considering barriers to communication, it is also necessary to deal specifically with the problems caused by selective perception and bias. The sheer volume of data that is available means that one has to have some basis for deciding what to look for and what to react to. However, careful judgement is needed in making these decisions. A totally open mind can simply mean that a person is swamped with data but a closed mind can mean that a person doesn't respond to what is under their nose. Particular dangers are seeing only what you want to see, making the 'facts' fit what has already been decided, and suppressing unpleasant facts. Norman Dixon, a former Army psychiatrist, explains a number of Western military disasters in terms of such selective perception on the part of the military leaders concerned, in his book, *On the Psychology of Military Incompetence*.[5] Three of the many examples he documents concern the Japanese attack on Pearl Harbor, the fall of Singapore and the failure of the Arnhem offensive in Holland. The pattern according to Dixon is clear and recurrent – the warning signs were there but, because they did not fit into the established thinking, they were ignored until too late.

The extent to which people can be misled or even coerced into believing things which are untrue can be alarming. In one experiment conducted with American students it was found that a quarter of student groups could be coerced into stating that straight lines were of identical length when one was 25 per cent shorter than the other.[6] This effect was achieved by priming the seven other student in the experimental group to say that the lines were identical in length. One must be careful not to over-generalise about the amount of social coercion possible from the results of a series of experiments in America with a particular group and at a particular time. However, if social pressure can have this effect on such obvious matters of fact, what is the scope for social pressure on matters that are more subjective or where people's self-interest is involved?

As well as having to cope with one's own subjectivity, it must also be recognised that much of the data which is available within organisations is subjective or actually misleading. In Chapter 3 some of the reasons were given as to why department managers might be more concerned with protecting their reputations than with supplying objective data about their performance. Most people working in organisations are likely to be concerned with the pursuit of truth, but people in organisations, as in life gener-ally, are under a variety of pressures to highlight some things and not others. There are also pressures to view events in a particular way. This means that a manager, as well as being aware of the pressures on them to see things in a particular way, and to report selectively, needs to evaluate carefully the information that is being fed to them. One of the themes of the TV comedy series *Yes Minister* (later *Yes Prime Minister*) was that information was fed to the Cabinet Minister by his Permanent Secretary in such a way that the Minister thought that he was taking the decisions himself. One stratagem was that the options were put so that the Minister was bound to choose the one preferred by his Permanent Secretary. This is why politicians at both national and local government level sometimes have political advisers and support staff to provide them with alternative viewpoints and other information.

It is also necessary to be careful in evaluating information that is fed down the line. Selective reporting and misunderstanding are not phenomena confined to upward reporting. Error and modifi-cation can also occur in downward communication. Corroboration of the existence and nature of these problems is given by a former civil servant, John Carswell, in a *Sunday Times* article.[7] He explained that, when he was working on the administration of retirement pensions, an experienced superior said to him that there were three National Insurance schemes, not one: 'The scheme we put in the instructions, the scheme the Permanent Secretary talks to the Minister about, and the scheme they administer in the local offices.'

Much of the skill in effective communication lies in recognising the problem areas I have just identified. Effective communication is achieved as much as anything by avoiding these traps. One also has to beware of relying on information that is not in the form of original evidence. Groups such as research scientists, historians, medical doctors and lawyers are amongst those who are particularly aware of the danger of distortion – whether deliberate, subconscious or accidental – through relying on evidence that is not received first hand. It won't always be possible as a manager to rely on direct evidence, but at least the dangers of relying on secondary sources can be recognised. Also, the quality of original or secondary source material can be improved by the positive approaches explained in the rest of this section.

Coaxing information

It may be necessary for managers to work hard at this, particularly if people feel inhibited about discussing a particular issue. The lament 'why didn't someone tell me?' can be as much a condemnation of a manager's lack of skill in developing effective channels of communication as a condemnation of others for keeping them in the dark. It can be very hard for those in authority roles to realise the difficulty that others may have in communicating with them. The authority figure may feel totally relaxed and un-inhibited and not appreciate that perhaps the very factors which create their security create difficulties for others. The proprietor of a business may feel totally self-confident and secure and be amazed to find out, if they ever do, that people who are very dependent on them are reluctant to tell them anything unpleasant. The same problem can be encountered by parents with their children. They may forget what it was like to be a child and be blissfully unaware of many of the thoughts and anxieties that their own children have and see any suggestion to the contrary as quite preposterous.

Listening effectively

Adopting a listening role can be harder than taking the lead by talking. The problem with this can be that the more the authority figure talks, the less the other person may be inclined to talk. There can be a critical moment when people in the subordinate role might just start saying what they really feel, if only the authority figure stays quiet long enough. Once the 'subordinate' has started talking, things may come out with a rush and to the amazement of the authority figure. I have often found that such a critical moment can occur when I am leading classroom discussions. One useful technique in any such situation can be to count silently to 10 before breaking the silence after a particularly important question has been asked. Time after time I have found that such a delay has resulted in someone making a contribution that I had not thought possible. Once a person has started to talk it can be relatively easy to get them to continue and for any others to join in. The problem is likely to be how to get them started. The authority figure needs to be aware of letting their ignorance, impatience or even their own nervousness prevent such a process starting. Care has to be taken with the timing of invitations for people to open up – it is not only the time and the place that can be important but also the stage in a discussion. It may be necessary to build up rapport gently before the invitation is given. Thought also needs to be given to the way in which questions are put. They can be 'leading' in nature, giving the impression that all that is required is confirmation of the questioner's obvious views, such as 'don't you think this is a good idea?'. Alternatively they can be probing and phrased in such a way as to encourage the respondents to state their own views. One useful distinction, that is especially important in selection interviewing, is between 'open' questions, which encourage people to talk, and 'closed' questions which limit responses to, for example, 'yes or 'no'.

The choice of time and place

The choice of time and place to invite people to talk can be critical. Just as one knows oneself that there are times when one is prepared to open up and times when one is not, so this can obviously be the case with other people. One of the skills of communication is picking up the cues as to whether a person is or is not prepared about a sensitive matter. Even if the place cannot always be chosen, sometimes the geography of a room can be arranged to encourage, or for that matter to discourage, a person from talking. The more status symbols surrounding the authority figure, the less likely a subordinate is to feel free to talk. I remember one personnel officer, who was over 6 ft tall, always made a point of seeing that he and an able but peppery works superintendent, who was short, were both seated if anything of consequence was to be discussed. The personnel officer had learned from experience that the superintendent was self-conscious about his lack of height and so he did his best not to emphasise it.

Choice of language

Language difficulties can obviously hamper communication between people who have different national languages. Regional dialects can also, and predictably, complicate matters. However, there can be many other and more subtle language problems even between people who are from the same country, region and class. Technical language may be used in discussion which is beyond the comprehension of some of the participants. In any organisation there are likely to be abbreviations, words with special connotations, and 'in-terms' whose meaning is taken for granted by those inside the organisation. A colleague of mine gave an example of two nurses trying to communicate about sterilisation policies in their respective parts of the Health Service. One was a midwife and the other a community nurse. It took a quarter of an hour before they realised that one was talking about sterilisation as a means of birth control and the other about sterilisation as a means of protecting babies from infection! Problems of language invariably get exposed in the rectangles drawing exercise explained earlier in this chapter. The diagram may be explained by the use of geometric language, points of the compass, the hands of a clock or the use of symbols such as 'L-shaped' and 'an inverted V'. The language chosen by the instructor is likely to be more convenient to some people than others and a person's ability to understand the instructor will in part depend on whether the instructor chooses a language convenient to them or not.

The recurring problem with language in communication is that the person who is trying to explain something may understandably use the language that is most convenient to them without perhaps realising that there is a choice of language. The person receiving the explanation may also, understandably, be reluctant to admit that they cannot understand the language that is used. The skill is in recognising that, even when ordinary language is used, there may be problems of comprehension. The initiator of any communication needs to get positive confirmation that the 'language' they are using is one that can be understood.

In identifying the appropriate 'language' for communication, attention needs to be given to the possibility of ambiguity. The more important the consequences of error, the more attention needs to be devoted to avoiding ambiguity. If stress is needed on this point, it can be provided by the ambiguous use of words which contributed to the world's worst air disaster at Tenerife in the Canary Islands in 1977. The pilot of a KLM Jumbo Jet, who was ironically also the head of their Flight Training Department, was preparing to take off at Tenerife. He explained that he was ready to the air traffic controllers and in response was told 'Okay. (pause) Stand by for take-off. I will call you.'[8] In the pause after the word 'Okay' there was radio interference because of a radio query by the Captain of a Pan-Am Jumbo about the intentions of the KLM captain. It seems likely that this caused the KLM captain to assume that the word 'Okay' was the complete message. In any event, the KLM captain then took off and collided with the Pan-Am Jumbo killing a total of 573 people. The investigators commissioned by the American Airline Pilots Association concluded that this was the most likely explanation of events. They also commented on the ambiguous use of the term 'take-off'. Their comments on the use of the term 'Okay' were as follows:

> The word (or letters) 'OK' can be ambiguous also; to the controller it was either a word of acknowledgement or a delaying term to allow a moment to think. It can also mean a host of other things, such as a state of well-being, a check-off of a task accomplished, or a statement of approval. It could have had the latter meaning for the KLM crew.[9]

Recognising cultural barriers

The impact of national culture on organisations as a whole has already been examined in Chapter 3. However, the topic needs further consideration because of the potential impact on interpersonal communication. Some of the cultural barriers – such as language – are obvious, but there may be more hidden obstacles. An example given to me which illustrates this point concerned the communication between the male Asian workers and the female canteen workers in a London factory. There was a certain amount of friction when food was being served, part of which was said by the canteen workers to be because of the surly response by the Asians when they received their food. In particular, it was commented that the Asians never smiled. Their response to this was initially one of bewilderment as, in their culture, it was seen as being altogether too familiar for a man to smile at a woman he did not know. Far from trying to create offence, they had been trying to avoid it by their impassive expression. When I related this incident to a college receptionist she said that she could now understand why she received so few smiles from Asian callers compared with the broad smiles she received from many other people. A related phenomenon in some Asian cultures is the unwillingness of people to look straight at authority figures. This is often misinterpreted as evasiveness without it being understood that it is a customary sign of respect and deference.

Another example was offered by an Arab colleague who maintained that a problem of communicating in Britain was the British tendency for understatement. In his experience this was aggravated by a tendency in Middle Eastern cultures to overstate the case. Another general issue can be the cultural norms about displays of emotion. These again can vary from histrionic outbursts that don't necessarily have to be taken seriously to a lack of overt reaction that can conceal a deep underlying menace. Negotiations involving an international organisation in India were hampered at one stage by the habit of the people they were trying to do business with shaking their heads from side to side as if in disagreement. It then emerged that in this particular part of the country that gesture meant agreement and not disagreement. Evidence about such issues is perhaps inevitably anecdotal and one must be very careful about making generalisations. However, one should at least be aware of such potential obstacles to effective communication and take them into account.

Body language

The expressions, gestures and other body language that people may use, without necessarily realising it, can be important cues as to what they really think. Communication is not just imparting information; it often involves, or needs to involve, understanding people's attitudes and feelings which are not always clearly expressed in words. In some cases people may even feel obliged to say the opposite of what they really think. It is not uncommon, for example for people to say 'how interesting' but in a tone of voice which indicates that they are in fact bored. An adage which makes the point that people sometimes accidentally misrepresent themselves is 'listen to what I mean not what I say'. As words can be an inadequate, or even a misleading, guide as to what people really think, it can be important to look for other cues as to people's thoughts. A catalogue could be prepared of what particular physical cues could mean – fidgeting, that a person has other things on their mind; a glazed expression, that a person doesn't understand, and so on. Given that such a list could be very long and only be a guide anyway, the point that needs stressing is simply to watch for physical cues as to a person's real thoughts, especially when it is likely that a person is not able to be, or does not want to be, frank about a particular topic. It can be very tempting to rely just on the words that a person uses, particularly if they give the answer that one wants to hear. To rely on words alone can be quite insufficient.

Interesting examples of how people can unwittingly reveal their true intentions are given by the American agent Mark McCormack, who negotiates on behalf of many international, particularly sports, celebrities. In his book he explains how:

> When I am meeting at someone else's office I have often noticed that people will sort of 'lean in' to the situation when they are ready to get serious, even unconsciously using their hands to push everything on their desk a couple of inches forward. Yet almost as often I have seen people at this same point lean back in their chairs and feign a totally relaxed position.[10]

McCormack also explained in a British radio interview how one negotiator would unwittingly reveal his intentions by moving his chair back before making his final offer. The advantage of recognising such a cue is obviously to keep asking for more until the person moves their chair back!

An intriguing example of what might be learnt by studying a person's bodily behaviour concerns an allegation about Nikita Khrushchev's conduct during the famous debate at the General Assembly of the United Nations when he interrupted proceedings by banging on the table with his shoe. This was part of his protest about American reconnaissance flights over the USSR in their

U2 spy planes, which came to light when the American pilot Gary Powers was captured in 1960. The allegation is that TV cameras revealed Khrushchev had shoes on both feet and that the one he banged on the table must have been brought into the conference chamber expressly for that purpose! If the allegation is true, it reveals that the demonstration was a calculated piece of histrionics and not a spontaneous burst of anger.

Another dimension that may be important is the physical distance that people may find comfortable between themselves and whoever they are speaking to. Cross-cultural studies suggest this can vary significantly from one culture to another. 'Arabs and Latin Americans stand very close, Swedes and Scots are the most distant.'[11] 'Americans and Europeans have been seen retreating backwards gyrating in circles at international conferences, pursued by Latin Americans trying to establish their habitual degree of proximity.'[12] This has led to the story, apocryphal or otherwise, of the Latin American diplomat saying that, 'these British diplomats are very good – if only you can catch them!'[13]

DOWNWARD COMMUNICATION AND PRESENTATIONAL SKILLS

Having emphasised the obstacles to effective communication and in particular the importance of upward communication, it is appropriate to say something about the presentational skills involved in downward communication. This interrelates with some of the earlier material in this chapter, the material in Chapter 4 on managerial style and some of that in Chapter 13 on meetings and chairing. At the risk of being repetitious, it is first of all necessary to be aware of the limitations of downward communication, particularly in terms of volume, accuracy and commitment to that which is being communicated. There can be a role for devices such as mission statements and team briefings, but only in the context of the appropriate organisational culture and structure, and only if such devices are carefully thought out and competently implemented. It is as well, too, to remember that Deming's approach to Total Quality Management (explained in Chapter 3) deliberately avoided the use of slogans, exhortations and targets for the work-force.

The issue of written communication is dealt with later in this chapter. The most helpful way of giving advice about presentational skills seems to be to provide the following check list of points that should be borne in mind before making a presentation:

- Objectives
- Identification of the target audience
- Prior publicity
- Geographical and acoustic arrangements
- Structure
- Involvement of colleagues and audience
- Motivation and comprehension of the audience
- Timing, pace and duration
- Time control
- Beware of reading from notes as this reduces spontaneity and eye contact – prompt cards or an *aide-mémoire* may be much better
- Visual aids
- Clarity of expression and choice of language
- Eye contact and body language
- Volume of information (not too little, but beware of presenting too much and losing the audience in the detail)
- Use of humour and dramatic pauses
- Pitch and variety of voice
- Use of examples
- Rehearsal
- Opportunity for feedback
- Back-up notes and sources of further information
- Evaluation of presentation
- Modifications for the future

WRITTEN COMMUNICATION

The emphasis in this chapter so far has been on oral and visual communication. But much communication is written, and some consideration of the special features of written communication is necessary. The main point that needs stressing is that written communication is one-way and the recipient or recipients have, for the time being at least, to rely on the writer's accuracy of expression. The rectangles experiment, described earlier in the chapter, indicated some of the problems with one-way communication. The type of language chosen may not be convenient to the reader, and errors, ambiguities and complicated explanations cannot be questioned until later, if at all. This means that the writer needs to give considerable thought as to how best to express themselves. An explanation that seems clear to them may be far from clear to a reader. The French writer Blaise Pascal wrote to a friend 'I have made this letter longer than usual, only because I have not had the time to make it shorter.'[14] The point is that it may require considerable effort and concentration to write in a clear and simple manner. It also involves the writer being prepared to state what they mean, instead of concealing their real thoughts, or lack of them, behind a smoke screen of words. Unfortunately, people can easily be taken in by verbose or complex explanations, believing that their failure to understand is because of their own limitations rather than those of the writer. It may often be a more appropriate and accurate assumption that, if a person has not explained something clearly, the fault is with their thinking rather than with the reader's comprehension.

Sometimes matters have to be expressed in a precise technical way and the use of particular language is unavoidable. This can be the case with legal documents, where the only way of achieving the necessary clarity is to use precise legal expressions. However, even when technical language is used, there are differences between good and bad expression. Whether technical language is used or not, there would seem to be no virtue in explaining matters in a more complicated way than is necessary. All too often, sophisti-cated terms can be dragged in unnecessarily because of a desire to impress or because of clumsy expression or lack of clarity in the actual thinking. The use of many sociological terms, in particular, can be for these reasons. Unfortunately, this is all too prevalent in the academic world, where a desire to impress often overrides the basic function of education, which is to explain issues in a user-friendly way. As was explained in the Introduction, the writing style adopted in this book has had this latter objective in mind, with theoretical concepts and technical language only being used when necessary and then in a relevant way.

One of the ironies concerning many government forms is that those who have to complete them may need a graduate-level ability to do so. Persons with that level of ability, though, would not often be applying for many of the services in question. Much of the underclaiming of social security benefit may be because of the difficulty people have in understanding the benefit application forms. This is illustrated by the following example published in the

'Diary' column of the *Guardian* newspaper. It quotes the reply sent by the Department of Social Security to a mentally ill 19-year-old living on invalidity benefit who managed to get a job for two days, washing dishes at Olympia:

> The claimant is disqualified for [sic] receiving non-contributory invalidity benefit for 17.5.82 because he failed without good cause to observe the rule that he should do no work other than work which he had good cause for doing and from which his earnings were ordinarily not more than £16.50 a week. S. S. (Unemployment Sickness and Invalidity Benefit) Regulations reg 12(i) (a) (iii).
>
> As a result, an overpayment of non-contributory invalidity benefit has been made amounting to £2.95* as detailed below. Repayment of this sum is required because it has not been shown that the claimant has throughout used due care and diligence in the obtaining and receipt of benefit to avoid over-payment (Social Security Act 1975 sec 119(1) and (2)). * £17.75 ÷ 6 = £2.95.

The *Guardian* diarist went on to add that the reply could, have been worded: 'Please pay back one day's benefit because you worked.'[15]

Organisations, such as the manufacturers of electronic goods, have a strong commercial reason for seeing that the instruction manuals accompanying their products are properly understood. This has led to some of them establishing 'help lines' so that customers can easily get further assistance. This practice has been adopted by some service organisations in an attempt to make their services more readily available and more effectively used.

THE ROLE OF THE MEDIA

The amount of time that people spend watching television and video cassettes and listening to the radio justifies a section on the media. Whilst this fits with a general consideration of communication, there may well be specific issues presented on the media that involve people in their role as managers. The material presented often needs to be carefully evaluated. Managers may also need to use the media to present information, so consideration is also given to basic skills of media presentation.

The impact of television can be extremely powerful and pervasive. Strong visual images of dramatic events and human suffering can be brought quickly into the living room and in turn can have an interactive effect on those events. The coincidence of President Gorbachev being in Beijing at the outbreak of student demonstrations in April 1989 meant that there was a mass of sophisticated television equipment available to film the violent suppression of the Tiananmen Square student occupation. The satellite reporting of the Gulf War in 1990 enabled viewers to watch events as though they were direct spectators. The effectiveness of the reporting meant that Presidents Bush and Saddam watched events on networked television as this gave speedier coverage than their own intelligence agencies.

Technological media developments mean that it is generally much more likely that important issues are handled in public view than in an unobserved or unrecorded manner. There can be great benefit in this but there are also certain dangers. Those involved in publicly conducted events have to bear in mind the simultaneous impact of their statements and actions on those with whom they may be negotiating, those they represent and the general public. This may limit their room for manoeuvre and make it much more difficult for them to retrieve mistakes and misjudgments. There is also the problem of evaluating the information that is presented on the media. Issues of bias or misrepresentation are usually easy to spot in advertisements. However, there are other causes of distortion that may be much more difficult to recognise. These include the balance of a presentation, the advantages gained by a skilled presenter with a good acoustic background and the juxtaposition of items that are reported. A trade union official may, rightly or wrongly, have a hard time explaining the causes of industrial action just after film showing dramatic examples of the inconvenience that the action may be having.[16] There is an inherent conflict between the responsibility of media producers to present a fair and balanced programme and the pressure on them to catch the attention of their audience and attain high viewing or listening figures. This can lead to sensationalised reporting, emphasis on the unusual rather than the usual and 'camera bias', because of the visual impact of anything dramatic. Such problems led John Birt and Peter Jay to refer to the 'bias against understanding' with regard to the reporting of news and current affairs.

Presentation on the radio can be more balanced because it

does not suffer from 'camera bias'. Newspapers often have clear political affiliations but do offer readers the choice of which sections to read and the pace at which they read them. Although one can decide what programmes you watch on television, or listen to on the radio, the content has to be heavily filtered because the material has to be compressed and contained within a standard format. There cannot be the flexible use by the consumer that there is with a newspaper.

The implication of the complexities of media presentation and the opportunity for distortion, deliberate or accidental, means that it is important to evaluate critically what is being presented rather than passively accept it. This is particularly important for the managers if information they receive from the media is likely to influence their decisions as managers. It is well to remember also that a whole range of interest groups are concerned in providing information to the media in order to put over a particular point of view.

It follows from the above that one may also be involved in using the media to present a case or in a reactive way to defend a position that your organisation has taken which has attracted media attention. There are potential advantages and dangers in co-operating with the media. Media coverage can provide a very effective and rapid means of communicating with other members of your own organisation, e.g., in the circumstances of industrial action and of trying to influence public opinion if that is a factor. The proliferation of local radio also gives more opportunities for air time. However, sometimes there are dangers of being 'set up' by reporters. Examples of how this can happen are the agenda being suddenly changed, the tone changing from friendly to hostile, unfair editing of a presentation or placing a contribution in an unhelpful context. One way of reducing these risks is to insist on doing a 'live' presentation. It is also important to understand that you are as much entitled to set the ground rules as anyone. A media interview is not an exam or a court of law where you are obliged to follow the rules decided unilaterally, and sometimes suddenly, by the interviewer or producer. It is important to recognise the potential conflict of interests between yourself and the media reporter, who may suggest that your role is just to behave as you are told. One useful technique, whatever question or questions are asked, is to insist on saying what you want to say, before you decide whether or not to answer the questions that have been put to you. Another technique is to issue a prepared statement, that is either read out on the television or radio or issued as a press release.[17]

CONCLUSION

The obstacles to, and skills involved in, effective communication are formidable. The main aim of this chapter has been to make the reader aware of some of the major pitfalls and basic skills. The increasingly important dimension of electronic communication has been covered in Chapter 3 – that material clearly has a direct bearing though on the content of this chapter. It is probably most constructive for readers to assess their level of skill in communication rather than aspire always to be an effective communicator. The volume of communication and problems involved means that one can only hope to develop one's level of skill rather than overcome all the problems. Effort in communication needs time, and time is invariably at a premium. However, it is important that people recognise that accuracy in communication is usually much lower than is assumed. Decisions need to be based on realistic assessments of what has been effectively communicated rather than on naively optimistic assessments. There also needs to be recognition of matters that it is critical to communicate accurately. Not just managers but everyone needs to have a range of communication skills that they can use when appropriate. The lack of attention in schools and organisations in this critical area means that people generally need sensitising to the problems and skills involved. The sad fact is that feedback is often not obtained when it is required and that, even when it is obtained, it is not evaluated. People tend also to see the main need in this area as communicating with others rather than the, quantitatively at least, more important task of letting others communicate with them. The volume and problems are such that experiments in this area are likely to lead to the relatively easy development of one's existing skills, which may in turn encourage more experiments and a further development in skill. The bonus here can be reflected in a more accurate basis for decision-making for oneself and for those one has to deal with, not just within organisations, but in other aspects of life as well.

NOTES

1 Rosemary Stewart, *Managers and Their Jobs*, Macmillan, 2nd edn, 1988, p. 50.
2 Harold J. Leavitt and Homa Bahrani, *Managerial Psychology*, University of Chicago Press, 5th edn, 1988, Ch. 8, pp. 103–12.
3 Jeremy Campbell, 'Why Bush Needs Saddam', *Evening Standard*, London, 2 October 1991.
4 John Simpson, 'Why Saddam Went to War', *Observer*, Review section, 21 July, 1991, pp. 41–2.
5 Norman F. Dixon, *On the Psychology of Military Incompetence*, Cape, 1976.
6 For a summary of S. E. Asch's experiments see P. F. Secord and C. W. Backman, *Social Psychology*, International Student Edition, 1964, McGraw-Hill Kogakusha Ltd, pp. 304–7.
7 John Carswell, 'The Slave of the Lamp', *Sunday Times*, 29 March 1981, p. 39.
8 Air Line Pilots Association (American) *Aircraft Accident Report: Engineering and Air Safety – Human Factors Report on the Tenerife Accident* (1978), pp. 22–4.
9 Ibid.
10 Mark H. McCormack, *What They Don't Teach You at Harvard Business School*, Collins, 1984, pp. 23–4.
11 R. E. Lett, W. Clark and I. Altman, quoted in Michael Argyle *The Psychology of Interpersonal Behaviour*, Penguin Books, 4th edn, 1990, p. 39.
12 E. T. Hall quoted in Argyle, ibid., 5th edn, 1994, p. 195.
13 For a further account of this topic area, including a report of E. T. Hall's study, see Michael Argyle, ibid., 5th edn, 1994.
14 Blaise Pascal, *Lettres provinciales*, 1657.
15 The seminal work on clarity of written expression is Sir Ernest Gowers, *Plain Words*, revised by Sidney Greenbaum and Janet Whinart, HMSO, 1986, also Penguin, 1987.
16 Nicholas Jones, *Strikes and the Media, Communication and Conflict*, Blackwell, 1986.
17 For a more comprehensive treatment of this topic see Sarah Dickinson, *How to take on the Media*, Weidenfeld Paperbacks, 1990.

Chapter 9

Selection

INTRODUCTION

One of the most critical decisions that managers may have to make is the appointment of subordinate staff. Managers may also be involved in the appointment of subordinate staff for other managers – for example, by membership of interview boards. New staff may be appointed from within the organisation or by external recruitment. It is easier to exercise discretion at the appointment stage than later – it is much more difficult to remove staff once they have joined you. Considerable effort may be needed to train and develop staff, especially if they have inappropriate experience, aptitude or qualifications. The abilities of subordinate staff can have a critical effect on the performance of the manager concerned. Even though managers may only be involved in appointment decisions relatively infrequently, it is important that they make the right ones. It is for this reason that a chapter has been devoted to selection. Many managers may have the advantage of a specialist personnel service but, even if that is the case, they need to know the nature of that service and how to make best use of it. Managers also need to be able to recognise when specialist advice in this area is inadequate and, if appropriate, to press for a better level of service.

Topics covered in this chapter include the need to identify carefully the nature of a job that has to be filled. The long-term nature of the job has to be considered as well as the immediate requirements. The next step is to identify appropriate selection criteria. The ways in which information can be collected about candidates are explained. So too are the actual skills involved in selection interviewing, including the skills that may be required at panel interviews. The rather different skills that may be required if one is the person being interviewed for a job are also considered. A self-assessment form is included as an appendix to help readers see how they might develop their, or other people's, selection interviewing skills.

The policies, procedures and norms relating to selection vary considerably between organisations. This is often very marked when comparing the private and public sectors. Key differences are the generally greater formality of proceedings and the detailed ways in which equal opportunities policies have been developed in much of the public sector compared with much of the private sector. Different philosophies about how far one needs to go to limit subjective judgements and to have open access to jobs are often at the heart of these contrasting approaches. However, whatever the organisational culture, there is a need for validity in selection, i.e., ensuring that those selected are appropriate for the job. There is also a statutory obligation not to discriminate on grounds of sex, marital status, race and trade union membership. Such protection is to be extended to cover disabled people, but without a supervisory commission. At present there is no statutory protection against age discrimination but employers need to be aware that in some circumstances they can be guilty of indirect sex discrimination by specifying an upper age limit.

DEFINING THE JOB

Whether a job is new or old, considerable care needs to be taken in defining its exact objective and scope. The material in Chapter 2 concerning the identification of objectives and key tasks may be relevant in this context. Even when jobs are well-established it is important to remember that the requirements may have changed. The actual tasks that have historically been performed may not be appropriate in changed circumstances. A manager may be unaware of some of the adjustments that have taken place in a job since they perhaps occupied that position. A starting point for identifying the requirements of a job may be to get the existing incumbent to prepare an updated job description. Other information may, however, also be necessary. A job may have been tailored to take account of an individual's strengths and weaknesses. It may be necessary, therefore, to consider the extent to which such 'tailoring' should remain if a new person is being appointed. An account given by a person of their job may be inaccurate or may reflect what is done rather than what needs doing. The manager concerned may need to consider what changes they and others think are necessary in a particular job. It may even be that the job does not need filling – either because there is no longer any purpose to it or because the individual tasks can more effectively be redistributed amongst other staff. Peter Drucker gives such an example in his book *The Practice of Management*:

> For 20 years a large shipping company had difficulty filling one of its top jobs. It never had anyone really qualified for the position. And whoever filled it soon found himself in trouble and conflict. But for 20 years the job was filled whenever it became vacant. In the twenty-first year a new president asked: 'What would happen if we did not fill it?' The answer was: 'Nothing.' It then turned out that the position had been created to perform a job that had long since become unnecessary.[1]

I have witnessed more than one case where the clear identification of the purpose and content of a job was only completed after the candidates were interviewed. The original reasoning about the job in question was inadequate and the questions asked during the selection interviews led to a more accurate assessment of what was really required. On one occasion this led to a redefined job being advertised and the whole process of selection being started again. On another occasion it was decided, as in Drucker's example, that no appointment was necessary. The consolation in these examples was that at least the initial error of inadequate assessment of the real job requirements was not compounded by an appointment based on inadequate job definition.

Short-term and long-term needs

A potential problem area, which is often overlooked, is the distinction between the short-term and long-term needs in a job. A person may be recruited to fill a pressing but temporary need. The problem that may then arise is what to do with them when the need has passed. The pace of technological and organisational change, in particular, means that this is likely to be an increasing problem. Traditionally, jobs have often been seen as positions which will remain substantially the same during the working life of the job holders. This can cause people to try and 'freeze' the activity of an organisation so that the demand for their existing skills is perpetuated. Once people join an organisation they become part of the political power structure. They are likely to take a lively interest in the prospects for security and promotion of people with their particular range of skills. I have found that academic staff, for example, can take a ferocious interest in seeing that college departments run courses that provide the maximum prospects for advancing their particular specialism. This can lead to a conflict of interests between the short-term interests of the individual and the long-term interests of the organisation. This means that it is necessary to anticipate the pressures that potential employees will put on the organisation to develop in a particular way or remain in a particular mould.

An example of how this problem has been tackled concerns the training of skilled workers in the engineering industry. The length of apprenticeships has been gradually reduced and opportunities for apprentices and skilled workers to increase their range of skills improved. The concept of the multi-craft worker has also made some headway. The advantages that these developments can bring include the possibility of reduced resistance to technological and organisational change because the employees are more able to adapt to changed circumstances.

The same type of problem should be anticipated with professional-level employees. I found that there was a clear recognition of this problem with one large petrochemical firm with which I was once involved on a consultancy assignment. They recognised the dilemma of acquiring people with specialist skills for immediate problems and of nevertheless needing people who would be prepared to adapt to the rapidly changing circumstances of their industry. The solution adopted was to recruit some graduate chemical engineers with specialised training to cope with immediate specialist needs. Other graduate chemical engineers, with a more general training, were also recruited and were given either technical or managerial jobs. They were recruited with a view to being moved around the organisation so that they developed a range of technical and/or managerial skills. The reasoning was that, as the organisation needed to adapt, so this latter group would be able to fill the emergent new jobs. Had only narrowly trained specialists been recruited, it seemed much less likely that the organisation would have been able to adapt to the rapidly changing circumstances of the petrochemical industry. This point has also been made in the context of local government. Recognition of the greater fluidity of organisational structures and job content 'could mean building into recruitment and assessment procedures a much more open and more generous estimation of capacity'.[2] This is in contrast to the often very narrow and mechanistic methods by which employees are sometimes recruited and selected, with the criteria only relating to current needs.

The distinction between short-term and long-term needs has to be considered whenever appointments are made. The pace of technological change, in particular, is such that one has to ask whether a person will be prepared and able to adapt to the radical changes in job content that are increasingly likely. Admittedly, in some cases one may say that the short-term problems are those that have to take priority and that, if necessary, future inability to cope may have to be dealt with by redundancy. It seems prudent, however, at least to consider taking on a person with a temperament and range of skills that would make adjustment an easier process compared with applicants who may be overspecialised. Alternative approaches for dealing with short-term problems are to use short-term contracts or buy in consultancy expertise.

SELECTION CRITERIA

Having defined a job and balanced the short- and long-term needs, the next stage is to identify appropriate selection criteria. One of the dilemmas in identifying criteria is that what is relevant is not always easily assessable. Two approaches for identifying criteria are explained – establishing a person specification and identifying the required job competences. One way of creating a specification is to use the seven-point plan described by the late Professor Alec Rodger in a pamphlet published under the auspices of the former National Institute of Industrial Psychology.[3] The headings he identified were:

1 Physique, manner and bearing
2 Attainments
   (a) educational
   (b) experience
3 General intelligence
4 Special aptitudes

5 Interests
6 Disposition
7 Circumstances

One may consider adding an eighth factor – the motivation to do a particular job. Care obviously needs to be taken in itemising the various requirements. Even though a job may have been carefully defined, the specification can be completed so that it gives a spurious impression of accuracy and certainty. It may also be best to focus on the specific achievements and skills of candidates.

The alternative competences approach side-steps the issue of personal characteristics and identifies instead the job competences that a person needs to have in order to adequately do a job. Advantages of this approach are that it concentrates on establishing relevant job criteria, identifies training needs clearly and avoids the screening out of applicants by irrelevant criteria contained by an 'overtight' person specification. Sometimes personnel specifications have age criteria that may unnecessarily screen out the young or the old in particular. Upper age limits may also unnecessarily penalise women who have had 'baby breaks'. This point is developed further in the section on equal opportunities. Sometimes upper age limits can be a coded way of saying that the organisation does not want to pay for a fully experienced person.

If possible, it may be appropriate to consider the extent to which people, satisfactorily performing the same or a similar job, fit the specification or competences that have been identified. One soft drinks company used this approach and identified the main factors that were linked to good performance in service engineers who maintained and repaired drink dispensers. They found that the key factors were social skills and organising ability. Customers liked service engineers who were polite and who kept them informed about when they were coming and of any changes in appointments. The company had previously recruited people mainly on the basis of their engineering skills. It found it had overspecified in that direction, particularly as the relevant technical skills could fairly easily be taught in-house. As a result of this investigation, the selection criteria for the job were radically altered. I conducted a similar survey of university lecturing staff and found that for some years different criteria had been subconsciously applied regarding applicants who had not had previous contact with the department surveyed and those who had (e.g., as visiting lecturers or researchers).

The former group had been primarily judged on their academic excellence. Different criteria had, however, been applied to those applicants who were known to panel members. This was because of the knowledge about the relative strengths and weaknesses of these applicants. The key attributes which emerged with this group were commitment, organising ability and teaching skills. It also emerged that the good performers in the department were mainly from those in this group and not in the group chosen primarily on the basis of academic excellence.

Another aspect of selection may be to look at the totality of a job and of an applicant so that one sees the applicant as a whole person and does not get lost in the detail. Practice may vary, though, as to whether this approach is considered too judgemental or not. Consideration has to be given as to what constitutes a good 'match' between a person and a job, as explained in Chapter 6. A person with high intelligence may make a poor 'match' for a routine job. The likelihood of problems arising because of people being appointed who are too good for a job is sadly increasing because of the continuing high levels of unemployment. An intelligent person who gets bored with a job may perform less well than a less intelligent person who does not get bored with a routine job. The practice of discriminating against people because they are too able may vary according to the organisational philosophy of 'open access' to jobs. Japanese companies operating in the UK often pay particular attention to attitude and try and ensure that those appointed 'fit' with the overall culture of the organisation. For example, Sony have said 'if it's a choice we'll go for 90 per cent skill and 100 per cent attitude and never the other way round.' This in turn raises the issue of how attitude is judged.[4]

Particular care has to be taken in identifying the differences between a person's previous work experience and the job for which they are applying. A person who has performed admirably in one job will not necessarily perform well in a different job, particularly if that different job necessitates work at a higher level of responsibility. There is more than a grain of truth in Lawrence Peter's concept of people passing through their threshold of competence (previously explained in Chapter 1).[5] His theory is that people are promoted on the basis of having done their last job well until they find themselves a job which they cannot do, which is when the basis for promotion ceases. He was not the first person to note this phenomenon, however. In reflecting on when he was Minister of Munitions in 1915 during the First World War, David Lloyd George wrote:

> I cannot claim that my first choices were always the best. They were, I think, the best available at the time. I found that some were admirable workers provided they were under the control and direction of others, but not equal to the responsibility of a supreme position. It was then that I realised thoroughly for the first time that men ought to be marked like army lorries with their carrying capacity: 'Not to carry more than three tons.' The three-tonners are perfect so long as you do not overload them with burdens for which they are not constructed by Providence. I have seen that happen in Law and Politics. The barrister who acquired a great practice as a junior and failed completely when he took silk; the politician who showed great promise as an Under-Secretary and achieved nothing when promoted to the headship of a department.[6]

Further advantages about establishing appropriate selection criteria is that it can help with the recruitment and shortlisting stages of the selection process. Clear and valid selection criteria encourage those who potentially fit those criteria to apply and may discourage those who don't. It also facilitates any shortlisting process and provides a documentary base against any subsequent claim of illegal discrimination.

THE COLLECTION OF INFORMATION ABOUT CANDIDATES

Information about candidates can be collected from a variety of sources. The identification of realistic and clear selection criteria can be of great value in determining what information is relevant to selection decisions. Scrutiny of job advertisements indicates which employers have worked out the sort of person they want and the information they require, and which employers have not. A well-designed application form can present the relevant information to an employer in a way that they will find easy to follow. Examples of a person's work may help, as may references and testimonials from current or previous employers.

There is often confusion between the terms reference and testimonial. A testimonial is an open letter given by an employer to an employee to show to future prospective employers. As it is given to the person who is the subject of the testimonial, the writer may be reluctant to say anything detrimental about the person concerned. On the other hand, the fact that a person is prepared to praise a former employee in an open letter may be because the person deserves it. References are communications direct with a prospective employer which are given in confidence and not normally revealed to the person who is the subject of the reference. This means that the current or past employer may be more prepared to be frank about the person concerned. However, care has to be taken in the interpretation of written references. A person writing a reference may feel reluctant to state the shortcomings of a person and mention just their good points. It is often the omissions that are the most important feature of a reference. Oral references may be the most accurate, but it is important to beware of the employer who praises an employee in order to get them off their hands. It may be appropriate to approach an employer that a candidate has worked for previously, rather than a current employer, so that the candidate's relationship with their existing employer is not compromised. In evaluating a reference, whether it be good or bad, it needs to be remembered that the information received is about a person's performance in a job which may be significantly different from the job for which they have applied. The past record, although often useful, should only be seen as a guide in making selection decisions.

If a candidate is applying for a transfer or promotion from within an organisation, there may be a wealth of information available about them. Care needs to be taken in evaluating the information, but the quantity and quality of the information may mean that any interview is much less important than may be the case with external appointments. It can have a devastating effect on an organisation to promote people who are recognised by colleagues as being incompetent. However, practice varies about the extent to which internal reports are admissible. Sometimes the view is taken that it is necessary to rely primarily on performance at selection panel interviews. This issue is considered further in the section on selection panels.

The development of the flexible organisation, as explained in Chapter 3, can bring distinct advantages as regards the effectiveness of selection. This is particularly so if there are peripheral and core work-forces. Experience of employees in the peripheral work-force, and by them of the organisation, can provide invaluable information for both parties if there is ever the prospect of transfer to the core work-force. Another way in which such information may be obtained about internal candidates for promotion is to give them periods 'acting-up' at a more senior level to see how they handle the increased responsibility.

Assessment centres

A way of increasing the available information about internal and external applicants is the use of assessment centres. These have become increasingly popular in recent years. They were initially established primarily to assist with selection but, according to the results of a survey of 900 organisations published in 1994, the relative lack of job movement means that they are now more concerned with staff development, particularly in the management area.[7] It was also reported that 70 per cent of public sector organisations in the survey had started to use centres since 1990. The process of assessment often includes group exercises, job-related exercises and psychometric tests. The potential of centres for development purposes can be limited by the lack of development opportunities.

Dulewicz claims that small increases in the validity of selections can generate a handsome return on the investment in assessment centres. He also claims that the following factors are key to the design of effective assessment centres:[8]

1 Adequate specification of target competences
2 The design of relevant and valid exercises
3 Adequate integration of results of competence exercises and of any psychometric tests that are used
4 Assessor training
5 Careful selection and briefing of candidates
6 Efficient programming and management of the process
7 Adequate feedback to participants and follow up of recommendations
8 Monitoring of the validity and benefits of the process

I have found just the addition of a standard case study to conventional selection methods can generate much useful information from candidates applying for managerial jobs. Psychometric tests have also become increasingly popular over recent years, both within the context of assessment centres and independently of them. Whilst they can provide useful information to facilitate effective selection and development like any technique they can be mis-applied. Dangers include irrelevant tests, incompetent administration, cultural bias, a belief that the tests can give the decision instead of facilitating decisions made in conjunction with other relevant information, and overzealous sales promotion.[9]

THE SELECTION INTERVIEW

Various studies have shown that the selection interview can be much more subjective and unreliable than people realise.[10] However, it is often the only or an important element in the process. Even if an employer were to dispense with the interview, they would need to consider how they were going to provide the candidates with information and answer their queries so that they could make their decisions as to whether or not they should apply for, or accept, a job. The existence of clear selection criteria does enable an interview to be conducted systematically with the interviewer at least knowing what they are looking for. All too often the information collected at interviews is relatively worthless because the interviewer has not identified clearly enough what they wanted to know. Even when this has been done, a significant amount of skill may be needed to obtain the relevant information. The interviewer may have identified what they want to know, but a candidate may quite understandably be concerned with emphasising their strong points and with concealing their weaknesses. There is a considerable amount of technique involved in obtaining information from a candidate.[11] Readers are likely to have noticed the variation in skill demonstrated by people who have interviewed them for jobs. Appropriate training can improve the performance of interviewers both with regard to one-to-one interviews and selection panels.

Planning

The first stage in the interview is fairly obviously the prior preparation. Interviewers need not only to have established the selection criteria but also to have studied any relevant information before the interview starts, including organisational policies and procedures regarding selection. They also need to consider what information should be given to a candidate before the interview. The location of an interview needs to be considered, so that it takes place in surroundings that are as congenial as possible for interviewer and candidate. It is also necessary to arrange for the interview to be free from interruptions.

If more than one person is to interview candidates it is necessary to decide whether the interviewing is sequential or joint. Generally, it is easier to coax information on a one-to-one basis. This may not involve any more organisational time as those involved in single interviewing do not have to sit through the questioning of other people. If more time is needed after the interviews to reconcile a variety of views about candidates this may be well worth the effort because the volume of data may be very valuable. However, the information so obtained may be selectively interpreted and reported and this needs to be borne in mind if this approach is used. The issues involved in joint interviewing, are dealt with further in the section on Selection panels.

Interviewers should have a good idea of what they want to find out during an interview. They may also want to identify the basic information that they will need to convey to a candidate. Checklists of information to be obtained and imparted can be very useful. It is also prudent to bear in mind that candidates are often understandably nervous and may not absorb much of what they are told. It is necessary to consider the structure and sequence of an interview so that the dialogue can be as effective as possible. If candidates are nervous it may be best to get them speaking as early as possible. It may be only when they have settled down that they are capable of absorbing important information.

One way of providing a clear and useful structure is to undertake a biographical interview. This involves the candidate being asked to explain their educational background and employment history in a chronological sequence. Having done this in a demonstration with John Munro Fraser,[12] I can testify that it immediately sets the agenda for the candidate in a way that puts them at their ease and enables them to explain their record in a systematic way. The interviewer can then concentrate on asking the supplementary questions that are needed to fill in any gaps. Such supplementary questioning may also need to focus on what the interviewee's actual achievements and skills are. Even if the biographical approach is not used, thought needs to be given to the structure of an interview and the agenda explained to the candidate. All too often interviews are conducted in a grasshopper style, with questions being asked at random with little if any thought being given as to how to lead up to sensitive issues. This can be caused not just by lack of skill on the part of the interviewer but also by their nervousness. The development of selection interviewing skills can have the advantage of giving the interviewer sufficient confidence to conduct an interview in a relaxed and effective manner.

Interviewing skills

Two other critical and related skills in selection interviewing are questioning and listening techniques. The interviewer will want to find out if there are any reasons why they should not appoint a particular person. They may need to ask questions in such a way that they do not reveal what will be regarded as an acceptable or unacceptable answer. To do this they will need to frame their questions in a neutral manner. Even if one were to convert a leading question such as 'do you work hard?' into a neutral one, it would be fairly obvious what the interviewer was after. It may be more appropriate to ask what were the tasks in a previous job that most interested a candidate and which were the ones which least interested them, and why. It may also be appropriate to ask questions in an open-ended way so that the candidate may open up and talk freely. The more a candidate talks, the more the interviewer is likely to learn. The role of the interviewer may be to guide the interview gently, to look for leads that need following up and to be on the watch for inconsistencies in the candidate's answers. Nervousness or lack of skill of the interviewer may prevent this. One of the most common errors in interviews is for the interviewer to do most of the talking. This reduces the information that can be obtained from the candidate on which the decision needs to be based. A useful rule of thumb is for the interviewer to spend no more than a quarter of the time talking, and to allow in any such estimate for the tendency to underestimate the amount of time that one speaks oneself. Listening carefully can require much more self-discipline and concentration than talking. If answers are unclear to the interviewer, it may be important to clarify just what an interviewee has meant. It may require considerable tact and patience to establish whether one has properly understood the point that a candidate is trying to make. These points are dealt with further in the section on counselling in the next chapter.

A hidden agenda in interviews may be that the interviewer, in particular, is frightened of losing control and suffering one of the greatest punishments of all in the British culture – embarrassment.

This may be a reason why interviews are often played far too cautiously, with important issues remaining unexplored. The development of selection interviewing skills may be the most effective way of overcoming this obstacle. This may particularly affect the close of the interview and the explanation to the candidate of just what the position is with regard to their application.

Many selection decisions turn out to be fairly straightforward. This is most likely to be the case with people who are clearly unsuitable. Much more time may be needed to eliminate the possibility of weaknesses with a candidate who turns out to be suitable. The greatest time may need to be taken with those candidates who are genuinely marginal and where extra relevant information may justifiably tilt the balance one way or the other.

The development of one's interviewing technique may not just depend on practice but on getting feedback on one's performance and adjusting future performance in the light of such feedback. It may be possible for readers to do this themselves and for this reason a selection interviewing self-assessment questionnaire is included as an appendix to this chapter. Readers can complete the questionnaire and identify any weaknesses with a view to seeing if these have been eliminated or reduced when they do their next interview.

Other common problems

One of the major problems in selection interviews is that both the interviewer and the candidate may 'freeze' into a set pattern of question and answer, with the candidate feeling fairly restricted about the information that they can volunteer. I used to find, when interviewing in the engineering industry, that candidates could relax considerably when invited around the plant. A dialogue could then develop under much more relaxed circumstances. I have also noticed that, when managers are being taught how to interview, they can relax and talk far more casually and usefully to candidates when the interview is apparently over. I often contrived to let managers and people playing the part of candidates stay together when a practice interview was apparently over. I was repeatedly amazed at the way in which the exchange of information, which should have taken place but did not, then occurred.

There are further pitfalls that need to be avoided. One is the danger of overreacting to a particular selection failure. A current or former employee may have a particular failing which blinds those responsible for choosing a successor to the other ways in which a person can fail in a job. There is also the danger of choosing in one's own image. Particularly with senior positions, what may be needed is a person who complements, rather than replicates, the skills of the other team members. This fits with the findings of Belbin, explained in Chapter 4, on how effective teamwork is achieved. One of the frequently voiced criticisms of Civil Service selection is the high degree to which those who enter at the administrative grade level replicate the backgrounds of those appointing them.

Ironically, it may well be that the higher up an organisation selection decisions are taken, the less appropriate they may be. The peer group may often be in the best position to judge what is really required in a candidate because of their close knowledge of the demands of the job. Consequently, it may be appropriate to consider whether the observations of the peer group should be sought, including their views on internal candidates. Factors such as seniority and length of experience tend to weigh heavily with selection panels in particular. This may be because they do not have the detailed knowledge of candidates and jobs that those closer to the situation have. Consequently, their decisions may be based on very superficial reasoning. One is reminded in this context of the tart observation that one particular candidate did not have 20 years' experience in a job but rather one year's experience 20 times. It may be that senior managers see requirements in a job that are not perceived by the peer group. It is also possible, though, that they do not have as much understanding of the job's demands as they think they have. Also they may not have to suffer the direct consequences of an inappropriate appointment.

Care also has to be taken to avoid the 'halo' effect, where a particular strength in a candidate leads to overgenerous assessments of their other attributes. A reverse 'halo' can also develop where a particular weakness leads to a candidate being unnecessarily marked down in other areas. Obviously employers also need to be aware of their own subjective views and biases and to allow for such factors in making decisions. A basic point is to beware of placing too much emphasis on interview performance, whether before a single interviewer or a panel. This can unduly favour the fluent performer, whose actions may not live up to their interview 'performance'. This can be an important issue regarding selection panels. Their role and operation is considered next.

SELECTION PANELS

Selection panels are such a prominent feature of public sector appointments that they need examination and explanation. The presence of several people on a panel may be necessary because of the various interests that need to be represented at the selection stage. One of the historical reasons for the establishment of selection panels in the public sector was the need to see that jobs were not allocated on the basis of patronage. Subsequently, their structure and operation have often become key features of equal opportunities policies especially in local government. Even when there is no formal requirement for selection panels, there may be a preference by the representatives of an employer to see a candidate together rather than separately. Thus, a line manager and personnel officer may conduct a joint interview.

If there are clear policies and procedures about how selection panels are to operate, it is incumbent on panel members to understand and respect those policies and procedures. As was stated in the Introduction to this chapter, organisational policies vary about the balance to be struck between asking candidates what may be deemed relevant and that which is relatively easily assessed. Basic issues concerning panel interviewing will now be explored. This is done to enable readers to understand the dynamics and to assist them with regard to any scope they have for interpreting or designing selection policies and procedures.

In some organisations there is a strong belief that selection panels should be set up and operated in such a way that they provide a 'level playing field'. In these circumstances the selection decision may be based primarily on interview performance. An alternative approach to providing a 'level playing field' is to rely on the established selection criteria and to allow information from a variety of sources to be tested against those criteria. This will involve making subjective judgements on a wider base of relevant data.

A basic issue is that, however much effort is put into attempting to create a 'level playing field', selection decisions in the end are subjective. The difference in approaches may be how far subjective decisions can be justified rather than by replacing a subjective with an objective approach. If, for example, standard questions are asked of each candidate at a panel, subjective, if systematic, judgements have to be made about what questions are asked, their relevance and the quality and the weighting given to individual responses.

Judgements can be influenced by a variety of factors including hidden interdepartmental rivalries. Questions may rightly or wrongly favour some candidates more than others. If questions are too rigidly standardised it may prevent members from following up leads about strengths and weaknesses that may be relevant to a candidate's application. There is also the danger that standardised questions may be anticipated, particularly by internal candidates, or even that pre-arranged questions are 'leaked' to a favoured candidate.

The problems of coaxing information out of candidates and probing for their strengths and weaknesses are likely to be much greater at panels compared with single interviewing. The amount of time available to each interviewer is much more restricted and the formality of the situation may inhibit candidates from making fluent responses. Sometimes it is argued that the ability to cope with panel-type situations is a critical aspect of the job. However, this is often not the case and this argument may be used as a rationalisation for a selection procedure which has been adopted for quite different reasons. Whatever method of selection is used it is necessary to remember that the prime purpose is to discriminate

"Right, Mr Smith, just relax"

Source: *Private Eye*, 8 May 1992, no. 793, p. 12

in favour of those most capable of performing particular work. Inappropriate or unlawful discrimination occurs when invalid criteria are used. Follow-up studies may be necessary to determine the validity of the process. If those involved with selection decisions then work with those appointed they will get regular feedback on the appropriateness of their decisions. Problems can arise if panel members make inappropriate decisions and fail to recognise what modifications in selection processes may be needed because of their ignorance of the consequences of past decisions.

Something may be done to improve the chances of effective decision-making at panels by careful chairing. Panel members may also benefit from formal training. If this is not possible, the person chairing may be gently able to coach members in the skills of interviewing and selection – bearing in mind that often the worse interviewers are, the less they are likely to recognise their deficiencies. Where the information obtained by panel interviews is of little value, at least it is best to recognise that, and use what other valid information is available to panel members as a basis for decision-making.

EQUAL OPPORTUNITIES

It is also necessary to consider the impact of selection processes in terms of equality of opportunity and the legislative rights that prospective employees, and those applying for promotion, have to protect them against discriminatory employment practices. Key rights are embodied in the Sex Discrimination Act, 1975 and the Race Relations Act, 1976. The rights do not extend to religious discrimination within the UK, apart from in Northern Ireland. The provisions of the Sex Discrimination Act also include protection against discrimination on grounds of marital status. Applicants who feel they have been the victims of discrimination can pursue their case at an industrial tribunal, claiming damages. Anti-discrimination orders about future selection practices by the organisation concerned can be issued by the relevant agencies and enforced in the courts. The relevant agencies are the Equal Opportunities Commission and the Commission for Racial Equality. The Commissions may also assist applicants in pursuing claims at a tribunal. Protection was extended to cover disabled people by the Disability Discrimination Act of 1995. This affects employers with more than 20 employees. The rights and means of enforcement proposed are similar to those with regard to race and sex discrimination but without an agency to monitor process and assist with enforcement.

Under the terms of the 1990 Employment Act it is illegal to discriminate at the selection stage on the basis of membership or non-membership of a trade union. Protection against discrimination for promotion of employees because of their trade union is covered under the terms of the Employment Protection (Consolidation) Act of 1978. The issue of discrimination needs to be viewed not just in the light of the minimum standards set by the law, but what it is sensible for employers to do anyway.

The Equal Opportunities Commission and the Commission for Racial Equality have both published codes of practice advising employers on how to avoid discriminatory practices.[13] A key method of doing this is by monitoring the composition of the work-force. Other important issues are the need to examine recruitment practices, including the pattern of applications and rejections, and promotion procedures. It is perhaps easier for employers to fall into the trap of indirect discrimination than direct discrimination. Indirect discrimination occurs when an unnecessary selection criterion is used which has an adverse effect on applicants from a particular sex or ethnic group. One such established example was the use of an upper age limit of 28 for people applying for positions as executive officers with the Civil Service. This was held to be discriminatory against women – because of the likelihood that family commitments would disproportionately reduce women's chances of applying for such positions.[14] Another example, this time concerning racial equality, was the requirement that un-necessary standards of English were demanded of applicants for manual work. The Commission for Racial Equality helped seven Bangladeshis pursue such a case against the British Steel Corporation. The seven were deemed to have failed a language test when they reapplied for work after an extended holiday in Bangladesh. The Corporation argued that the tests, for production workers, were necessary for safety reasons. The applicants argued that 'the test had an adverse impact on ethnic minorities whose language was not English and was not justifiable having regard to the job in question'. Under the terms of the agreed settlement the Bangladeshis were compensated and re-engaged, and the Corporation also agreed to obtain professional help in reviewing its test procedures.[15]

A related phenomenon which can occur is that of subconscious bias. Those responsible for making selection decisions may genuinely believe that they do not practise discrimination but may do so by, for example, their preference for the candidate who has, as far as they are concerned, a conventional background.

Employers are increasingly obliged to demonstrate the fairness of their employment practices when challenged at tribunals. This may include providing a statistical analysis of their labour force and a reason for a particular mix. However, whilst employers may adopt equality targets and positive action programmes to reduce imbalance, positive discrimination, such as recruitment quotas, with very limited exceptions, is illegal. One emerging issue is the need to examine job structure, including terms and conditions of employment. Some jobs may easily be altered to increase their accessibility to particular groups. One example is the option of part-time work, especially to mothers returning from maternity leave. Some employers, particularly in the local authority area, have developed their own comprehensive equal opportunities policies which cover other groups as well. Obviously, if one is employed in such an organisation it is necessary to know the details of such policies. It may also be important, and necessary in terms of the law, to review any services that an organisation offers to the public to ensure that they also are offered on a non-discriminatory basis.

BEING INTERVIEWED

This chapter has so far been written from the perspective of the employer selecting candidates for a job. As readers will also inevitably be in the position of applying for jobs, it is appropriate to devote some time to considering the process from the perspective of the job applicant. As ever, one needs to be clear about the objectives of the process. The obvious objective is to secure a job, but there may need to be other objectives as well. It may be counter-productive to concentrate only on how to persuade an employer to offer you a job if it leads to you being offered a job that you cannot do, starting a job you find you do not want or accepting an offer on unfavourable terms. Consequently, the interviewee, as well as planning how to present themselves, also needs to plan to extract the information that they need, to see if a job is worth having or to find out if there are any areas where bargaining can be conducted. It may be useful to bear in mind that you can at least ask for time to make your mind up if you are unsure whether or not to accept an offer. Also, the time when your bargaining position will be strongest is when the employer has made an offer and you have not given your decision.

Having clarified the range of objectives at an interview, it is now appropriate to concentrate on the skills relating to the prime objective – that of getting the employer to make you a job offer. One of the most important skills will be the ability to understand the selection process and get 'inside the mind' of the interviewer in order to see things from their perspective. In order to do that it will help to be aware of the formal stages in the systematic selection process. In preparing for interview, the candidate should go through the same process as the interviewer, so that they can work out what the interviewer is likely to be looking for. In this the most important tool will be the job description which will be sent, more often than not, with the application form. As explained previously, the job description lists the main tasks and responsibilities that the candidate will be expected to perform. Some organisations, notably those with an equal opportunities policy, will also state their selection criteria. If the employer does not send selection criteria, then it is advisable for a prospective employee to try and identify them. Background research about the organisation will also help in getting a good approximation of this. When completing the application form and answering questions in the job interview the candidate should ensure that the information they volunteer is as relevant as possible to the potential employer's selection criteria. If the applicant feels any important aspects have been missed out, they can always volunteer more information at the end of the interview when they may be asked if there is anything else they need to say. This preparation technique has two advantages. First, the applicant will be presenting the most useful information to show that they are a very likely candidate for the job. Second, the interviewer, or interviewers, will feel gratified because their questions actually seem to be eliciting the information they need to make a decision. In connection with this, it is likely that interviewers will feel better disposed towards those candidates with whom they feel they have conducted a good interview.

In presenting oneself at interview it is more important to concentrate on the content of what is being said than on peripheral issues like the positioning of one's hands or elimination of gestures. Having said that, pre-prepared responses will sound too mechanistic, so it may be better to make notes on background information and leave them at home on the day rather than have a scripted response. The questions probably will not come up exactly as envisaged, anyway. As first impressions tend to be disproportionately important, dress should be on the conservative side. Bearing in mind that the prime objective of the interview is to secure an offer, it may be best to appear assertive rather than aggressive under any testing questions. Giving the interviewer, or panel, 'a run for their money' may not increase your chances of an offer!

In seeking to demonstrate how well you fit the selection criteria it is as well to be clear that your purpose will be to demonstrate the strengths in your case whilst the employer should be probing for weaknesses. In demonstrating your strengths, clear and interesting responses are to be preferred to convoluted statements which may be boring. Samples of work or other relevant evidence may help in presenting your case. Many people undersell themselves by being too deferential to the interviewer(s) or volunteer weaknesses in their case that may have been better left unsaid. Account also needs to be taken of the stress that can be present in job interviews. The stress inherent in such situations can be aggravated by problems involved in finding the location, being left waiting, changes in the arrangements and errors by the employer. The ability to cope with such stress before and during the interview can have a critical effect on the outcome. Particular reactions to avoid are talking too quickly and being aggressive.

If you are unsuccessful it may be appropriate to reflect on whether or not it was because you did not match the criteria as well as someone else. In the last analysis, all you can hope to do is to present yourself as well as possible. If one application fails there are likely to be other opportunities where one can successfully demonstrate that you provide the best fit to an employer's selection criteria. If you have a run of rejections it is important to try not to let it lead to you going into an interview with a defeatist attitude and thus underselling yourself. If you are perplexed as to why you have not got jobs you feel you should have, one further piece of preparation may be to get a friend to give you a simulated interview and feedback on your performance. If this can be done with the aid of close-circuit television so that you can see how you perform, so much the better.

CONCLUSION

To some extent the evaluation of selection procedures will always be speculative. Whatever follow-up investigations may reveal about the level of performance of people who join an organisation, one cannot really make judgements about how the people would have performed who were not selected. However, it would seem prudent to review selection procedures in the light of the performance of the people who are chosen, to test the validity of those procedures. Even then, care has to be taken in coming to conclusions. A person whose performance is poor may still have been the best of a bad bunch. There can also be other explanations for poor performance such as ineffective work arrangements. There is also the problem of whether you judge people by their contribution to short-term needs or by their long-term contribution to an organisation.

If selection procedures are lengthy, they may lead to the best candidates taking jobs elsewhere. Consideration also needs to be given to the public relations aspects involved. Quite apart from the considerations of natural justice, it would seem sensible for employers to leave unsuccessful candidates at least with the impression that their application has been considered fairly. It is also necessary to bear in mind the legislation concerning discrimination.

The systematic review of selection methods, whilst not leading to any magic answers, may reveal weaknesses which can be corrected in the future. One of the advantages of exit interviews is that personnel officers, in particular, can consider whether the pattern of people leaving indicates weaknesses in the selection procedure. The criteria for evaluating appraisal systems are also relevant to the selection process. These criteria are itemised in the next chapter in the section on rating and recording.

NOTES

1 Peter F. Drucker, *The Practice of Management*, Heinemann, 1955, p. 320.
2 Local Government Management Board, *Managing Tomorrow*, Local Government Management Board, 1993, p. 16.
3 Alec Rodger, *The Seven Point Plan*, National Institute of Industrial Psychology, London, 3rd edn, 1970.
4 M. Kirosingh, *Changed Working Practices*, Allen & Unwin, 1984.
5 Lawrence Peter and Raymond Hull, *The Peter Principle*, Pan, 1970. Alternatively, see the Souvenir Press Edition, 1969, reisssued in 1992.

6 David Lloyd George, *War Memoirs of David Lloyd George*, Odhams Press, 1938, Vol. 1, p. 149.

7 See the report of a study by Pearn Kandonla and Robert Wood, 'Assessment Centres See their Popularity Soar', *Personnel Today*, 9–29 August 1994, p. 1.

8 Victor Dulewicz, 'Improving Assessment Centres', *Personnel Management*, June 1991, p. 50.

9 For a general account of assessment centres see Charles Woodruffe, *Assessment Centres: Identifying and Developing Competence*, Institute of Personnel Management, 1990.

10 P. E. Vernon, *Personality Tests and Assessments*, Methuen, 1953. See also H. J. Eysenck, *Uses and Abuses of Psychology*, Pelican, 1953, Ch. 5 ('From Each According to his Ability').

11 Harold F. Lock, *Interviewing for Selection, Paper No. 3*, National Institute of Industrial Psychology, 3rd edn, 1970.

12 John Munro Fraser, *Employment Interviewing*, MacDonald and Evans, 5th edn, 1978.

13 Equal Opportunities Commission, *Code of Practice for the Elimination of Discrimination on the Grounds of Sex and Marriage and the Promotion of Equality of Opportunity in Employment*, HMSO, 1985; Commission for Racial Equality, *Code of Practice for the Elimination of Racial Discrimination and the Promotion of Equality in Employment*, HMSO, 1984.

14 *Price vs the Civil Service Commission*, IRLR. Industrial Relations Services, 1977, p. 291.

15 *Industrial Relations Legal Information Bulletin No. 131*, 21.2, 1979 (Industrial Relations Services), p. 12.

APPENDIX TO CHAPTER 9: INTERVIEW ASSESSMENT FORM

When making your judgements try to relate these to specific acts or omissions on your part. Be sure *why* you rate each item as you do.

++ Very good	0 Not so bad, could have been better
+ Largely satisfactory	− Not so good

	++	+	0	−
1 *Preparation* Were you well prepared? Did you have clear and appropriate selection criteria. Were you aware of relevant organisational procedures and policies? Did you have a plan?				
2 *The opening* How successful were you in opening the interview?				
3 *Putting the subject at ease* Was the subject very nervous? Could they talk freely?				
4 *Facts* Did you collect the relevant facts? Did you find out why and how as well as what?				
5 *Attitudes/feelings* Did you manage to discover these as well as the facts (if appropriate)?				
6 *Questions* Did you ask open-ended questions, probe where necessary? Did you ask leading questions or answer your own questions?				
7 *Listening* Did you listen enough? Did you talk too much?				
8 *Giving information* Did you give all the information the candidate needed in a way that they could understand?				
9 *Manner* Were you courteous, factual, tactful? Were you tense, abrupt, argumentative? Were you given to making value judgements?				
10 *Discrimination* Was there any invalid or illegal discrimination?				
11 *Closing* In what frame of mind did the interviewee leave?				

Chapter 10

Appraisal, training and counselling

INTRODUCTION

In this chapter attention is paid to three interrelated areas – appraisal, training and counselling. The various objectives of appraisal are identified, and the point made that this is an area that can be fraught with difficulties. One of the difficulties is that if schemes are not thought out properly they may contain conflicting objectives. Particular attention is paid to performance management, performance-related pay and to the skills that are required in appraisal situations generally as well as in relation to performance. Changes in the way appraisal is being handled are also considered. The ways of identifying training needs are covered as is the manager's responsibility for acting as coach as well as working out how to make good use of an organisation's training department. New developments in the training and development area, such as the assessment and development of competences, modularisation, the concept of the learning organisation and institutional changes and initiatives are also examined.

The need for the manager to have counselling skills is explained and the nature of these skills is analysed. These skills may be needed in appraisal, training and a variety of other situations. The techniques of counselling will not solve all the problems in these areas, but a mastery of the techniques can lead to the avoidance or resolution of a great deal of aggravation with the bonus that often potentially destructive situations can, with proper handling, have thoroughly constructive outcomes. A complication is that there is often very little advance warning of when counselling is required, so that managers need to have the skills at their fingertips.

APPRAISAL

Objectives

There are a variety of reasons why managers may need to appraise their subordinates. The main reasons are likely to be:

- Performance appraisal
- Identification of training needs
- Merit payment
- Upgrading
- Promotion
- Probationary review
- Review of duties

The distinction between upgrading and promotion is that upgrading normally means that a person is paid more because it is recognised that most of their work is, or will be, at the higher levels of responsibility within the existing job. Promotion, on the other hand, normally involves transfer to a different job that is at a higher level of responsibility.

In many organisations managers are required to undertake appraisal of their subordinates as part of a formal scheme. However, whether or not there is a formal scheme, managers need to have an ongoing dialogue with their subordinates. A formal scheme should supplement and not replace this. The absence of a formal appraisal scheme does not remove the need for the manager to consider systematically, for example, the performance, training, payment or suitability for promotion of subordinates. A formal appraisal between the manager and subordinate should not contain many surprises, rather the interview should review the ongoing dialogue that has taken place since the last formal meeting. Discussion is crucial, not only to check that any formal assessment is accurate but to enable any need for change to be talked through and hopefully agreed between the two parties. For this to be productive a manager needs to have clear ideas of what they are trying to assess and why, especially as this is an area where managerial thinking is often very muddled.

The first point that needs stressing about formal appraisal schemes is that the objective or objectives need(s) to be clearly defined. There is little point in appraising just for the sake of it. This may not only be a waste of time but may actually be counter-productive. If judgements are made and communicated for no apparent purpose, the people who are judged may rightly feel resentful. Unfortunately, there is a great temptation for people in organisations, as in life in general, to make judgements about other people simply because they like doing it. This may be compounded by superficiality in the judgements and tactlessness in the way any views are communicated.

The compatibility of appraising with different but simultaneous objectives also needs to be considered. Often this point is overlooked and organisations adopt formal multi-purpose appraisal schemes not realising that some of the objectives may be contradictory. Some employers even carry this to the extreme of formally including the maintenance of discipline as one of the objectives of a multi-purpose scheme. If a person being appraised sees their level of pay or future promotion as being influenced by the outcome of the exercise, they may be eager to demonstrate how good they are and to play down any shortcomings in their performance or training requirements. If the objectives of appraisal conflict in this way, it is much better to pursue the various objectives at different times rather than have the subordinate push in a single interview to achieve the objective they have singled out as being the most important.

Potential problems with appraisal schemes

Lack of thought about the objectives of appraisal, or of the managerial skills required for it to be successful, means that many of the formal schemes adopted by organisations are of little use and may actually do more harm than good. Explanations in textbooks about appraisal tend to suggest by implication that formal schemes can be relatively easily implemented. What is lacking in the literature is an appraisal of appraisal schemes. I have had the opportunity to see a number of investigations by mature personnel management students into the appraisal scheme in their own organisations. The overwhelming pattern in practice that has been presented to me is that the formal schemes are badly thought out and badly implemented. I do not pretend that this evidence is totally representative, but I have found corroboration when discussing the actual effectiveness of such schemes with a wider audience of personnel specialists and personnel management students, who have not actually conducted investigations into their appraisal schemes but who have been in a position to comment about the schemes they have experienced. This is also the experience of the author of an article about appraisal schemes which appeared in the journal *Personnel Management*. He reported:

> One thing that is common to most [appraisal schemes] is a marked lack of evidence that they work, or have any clear impact on the day-to-day management of the company. Increased productivity, improved profit, a more effective organisation, still elude precise links to any appraisal process.[1]

There may be some schemes that operate in the recommended textbook manner, but on the evidence that I have been able to accumulate they must be rather atypical. Fletcher (1993) also refers to a study where 80 per cent of respondents were dissatisfied with their appraisal schemes – mainly because of the multiplicity of objectives.[2] It is necessary to show the potential problems of formal appraisal schemes, to caution people against overoptimism about such schemes, and to explain how to try to make a formal appraisal scheme work, or at least minimise the possible damage if one has to operate such a scheme. Regardless of whether there is a formal scheme or not, appraisal may need to be handled informally either to supplement a formal scheme or to provide an alternative. The skills of effective appraisal can be explained in part by identifying the potential difficulties. An explanation of these also establishes the considerable time investment that is necessary by those involved for appraisal to have any chance of being worthwhile.

Considerable conflict can be built into appraisal situations, particularly performance appraisal. A subordinate will not automatically accept that the criteria by which they are being judged are appropriate, or that the judgements made about their level of performance are accurate. This may be because of misperception by the subordinate of what is appropriate or because, in some cases, the subordinate has the best appreciation of what is required. The deployment of people in organisations cannot reach that level of perfection where the manager is always more competent than the subordinate. There is the additional problem that the subordinate may appreciate what is required, as far as the organisation is concerned, but recognise that this is not necessarily in their own best interests. This was a point that was raised in Chapter 2, when considering 'management by objectives', and is sufficiently important to need reinforcing here. Organisational and personal objectives do not always neatly coincide. This can mean that at an appraisal interview a person finds themselves under pressure to do what they do not want to do. This could involve developing the job in a way they find inappropriate, or making cost savings that could affect their status, promotion prospects or even job security. The delicacy of these and the other issues that have been identified, which can arise during appraisal, is such that the manager may require considerable skill and sensitivity to handle the situation.

Another danger of formal appraisal schemes is that managers may be precipitated into confrontations with their subordinates that they cannot handle. The 'pat' answer to this is to train the managers in appraisal interviewing, but the reality is that many managers, however good they may be in other aspects of their job, will never have the inter-personal skills to handle delicate appraisal interviews effectively. Many, perhaps wisely, just pay 'lip-service' to formal appraisal and simply complete any necessary forms with as little embarrassment as possible. Others may simply upset their subordinates, often without realising it. Silence by the subordinate may be taken to mean agreement when the reality may be that the subordinate may just be managing to avoid losing their temper. A recognition of these problems does at least give the manager a chance of handling performance appraisal constructively, or of seeing when it is best to leave the issue alone.

Strategies for handling appraisal effectively

The rest of this section on appraisal is meant to show how schemes might be made to work effectively. The subsequent sections on training and counselling are also relevant. Effective training necessitates accurate diagnosis of training needs and appraisal may play a critical part in the identification of these needs. Whatever purpose appraisal is used for and whether it be formal or informal, or both, counselling skills are required by the managers handling the process. Consequently, the section on counselling is a key part of this chapter.

The need for clear and compatible objectives for appraisal schemes has already been stressed. What also needs stressing is that it is not enough to select one objective and to assume that the logic of having a scheme geared around that is self-evident. Care has to be taken to ensure that the objective is realistically attainable and that the actual scheme devised will facilitate the achievement of that objective. It will be no good, for example, deciding to have a performance appraisal scheme that is based on unreliable, inconsistent and irrelevant judgements. Whatever the scheme, a considerable amount of intellectual effort is likely to be needed in identifying its precise objectives and the operational detail that is required if the objectives are to be accomplished. Because precise objectives, and the circumstances in which schemes have to operate, are likely to vary widely from one organisation to another, it is unlikely that one can simply buy an 'off the shelf' scheme or copy someone else's. This may not stop people doing just that, which is no doubt one of the reasons why evidence of schemes actually working is so scarce. If schemes are to have a chance of success, much patient effort is needed in developing appropriate 'in-house' arrangements. The stages in the process include identifying and agreeing objectives with appropriate managers, the preparation of appropriate forms and briefing notes, and pilot runs to test the system. It is only then that the next essential step of training line managers in how to operate a system can be undertaken.

Rating and recording

A basic aspect of appraisal that needs to be explained is the way in which ratings are made and these and other material recorded. The first step at this stage is to ensure that the criteria that are used to judge the employees are the appropriate ones. Ratings also need to meet the following criteria:

1 Validity: ratings must relate to observable behaviour.
2 Reliability: ratings made by different raters should be comparable (i.e., produce closely similar results), as should ratings made by the same individual at different times.
3 Relevance: the behaviour or qualities rated should be important to success in the particular job concerned.
4 Discrimination: the ratings should genuinely discriminate between above average, average and below average individuals.
5 Comprehensiveness: ratings should cover all main aspects of behaviour relevant to the purpose of the scheme.
6 Assessability: loyalty, sense of humour and such mean different things to different people.

Particular care is needed to ensure that ratings really are reliable. The dangers of inconsistency are considerable and can easily bring a scheme into disrepute. The hazards include the 'halo' effect where there is a spin-off from one desirable quality in an employee which causes overgenerous ratings on other factors. The 'reverse halo' effect occurs when an undesirable quality causes other factors to be marked too harshly. Another phenomenon can be the 'blue-eyed boy' (or girl) syndrome. This occurs when people are favoured for characteristics or behaviour unrelated to the job. It is concern over issues such as these that can arouse considerable union hostility to appraisal schemes. Another problem that can arise concerns the need to reconcile the ratings of managers who rate the employees either consistently highly or consistently badly. Other managers may create another problem – that of rating nearly everyone as 'average'. Care has to be taken to ensure that any weighting of the various factors has the effect that the designers of a system intended. One illuminating example where this proved not to be the case concerned a merit-rating scheme in which the most important factor was 'punctuality'.[3] This was not the intention of the designers of the scheme but was a consequence of the way the raters operated. It was much easier to assess punctuality than other more important but less tangible factors. As the dispersion of ratings for punctuality was therefore much wider than was the case with the other factors, the result in practice was that the differences in the total scores for individuals were accounted for more by the punctuality rating than by any other single rating.

Various methods of recording ratings and other relevant information can be used – some of which are aimed at producing statistical reliability and consistency. The methods include:

- Comparison with established standards
- Rating on a graded scale
- Comparative rating of employees
- Paired comparisons of employees
- Forced choice questions
- Forced distribution of marks or grades
- Critical incident recording
- Written reports

Combinations of the above methods are likely to be used, the exact choice depending on the specific appraisal scheme. Another issue that has to be resolved is whether or not appraisal reports are shown to the employees who have been appraised. One consequence of having 'open' systems is that, not surprisingly, they are likely to lead to only mild criticisms being made by the manager. If any information is kept in a computer system the subject will have the right to see it. This is as a consequence of the Data Protection Act, 1984, and the Subject Access provisions, operative from 1987.

Appraisal interview preparation

One of the critical contributions that line managers need to make in operating an appraisal scheme is spending an adequate amount of time in both preparing for and conducting interviews. Their 'homework' needs to include thoroughly understanding a scheme and also being clear what it is they want to get out of an interview. This commitment is required by all the managers involved. The boss's boss (the organisational grandparent), may also need to be involved and there may need to be inputs from other people with whom the appraisee interacts.

Preparation prior to an interview is likely to involve rather more than understanding the paperwork associated with a scheme. All relevant data should be assembled prior to an interview. There is no point in making judgements about, for example, levels of output or attendance patterns if objective data is available giving exact details. Judgement may be appropriate about the reason for a particular level of output or attendance pattern – but not to establish what the figures actually are. Care will be needed in deciding what judgements are relevant. Criteria also need to be established to ensure that the judgements are made systematically. The ways in which judgements may be rated and recorded are explained in a later section. Other relevant documentation that will need to be assembled includes details of any previous relevant appraisals – and particularly of any follow-up action that was planned. The job description and selection criteria are also likely to be needed.

Both the appraiser and the appraisee need time to prepare for the interview. The process should be seen as a two-way discussion and both parties need to think beforehand about how the interview can be constructively handled. It is hardly satisfactory if the appraisee is not given notice or, perhaps worse still, is told they have an interview but not told what it is to be about! A certain amount of tension and anxiety should also be anticipated which may affect both appraiser and appraisee. Appraisal interviews may reveal conflicts between the parties. This may well happen in performance appraisal interviews – as is explained later – but can happen in any type of appraisal situation. One implication of this is that the appraiser may need to consider what adjustments they need to make, either in their own behaviour, or in organisational support, to help the appraisee accomplish their legitimate objectives. It is all too easy to see appraisal interviews as situations, where adjustment just has to be made by the subordinate but such a view is profoundly misconceived. A further way of endeavouring to secure a constructive outcome is to ensure that recent achievements by the appraisee are clearly acknowledged. All this means that a manager should not try and conduct too many appraisal interviews in one day. The interviews, as well as being likely to be time-consuming, may also be emotionally demanding. Time also has to be allowed for writing up and planning any appropriate action.

Performance appraisal

One of the most common reasons for appraising the work of subordinates is to review their level of performance with a view to improving it. If that is the objective, it then follows that what needs to be assessed is the performance of subordinates and not their personalities. There is no point in making judgements about the people themselves unless such judgements are a necessary part of the assessment of performance. Considerable thought and care may be needed to identify just what the appropriate criteria are for assessing performance. A way of establishing appropriate criteria has already been suggested in Chapter 2 when 'management by objectives' was considered. It is also necessary for managers to think carefully about what they plan to discuss with subordinates.

Giving feedback

An extremely dangerous fallacy is that employees always want to know exactly where they stand and will always welcome feedback about their performance. The reality is that most people make a sharp distinction between receiving praise and receiving adverse criticism. Praise is invariably acceptable but the extent to which people are prepared to accept criticism is limited. One principal nursing officer I know of failed to make this distinction and conducted a frank appraisal interview with a senior nursing officer, since when they have apparently not spoken to one another! However, skilled appraisers should be able to handle interviews rather more productively. The technique of self-appraisal and the skills of counselling, both explained later in this chapter, can be of considerable assistance in this respect. Other constructive strategies involve presenting data rather than judgements, being specific, considering the needs of the person being appraised, praising strengths and achievements, offering appropriate support and recognising the need for appropriate adjustment by yourself as well as the appraisee. It is also necessary to bear in mind that there is generally only merit in giving feedback to people about issues, including their own personality, they can do something about.

Having identified ways in which feedback may be handled constructively it is also appropriate to spell out more of the potential problem areas. Effective appraisal interviews are achieved not just by doing the right things but also by avoiding doing the wrong things.

Self-appraisal

If one is to embark on the performance appraisal of subordinates, whether formally or informally, it is likely that the best results will be achieved by encouraging the subordinate, as far as possible, to engage in self-appraisal. This can be done by asking the subordinate to identify the appropriate criteria, the extent to which criteria have been met and areas of possible improvement. Employees may welcome the involvement this offers and may be more prepared to criticise themselves than have it done by others. People often tend to be their own harshest critics. Subordinates may also tend to overcriticise themselves for fear of seeming immodest. If this approach is taken, the manager may ironically find that they are in the position of telling the subordinates that they are being too harsh on themselves and explaining that their assessment is more favourable. There may though be aspects of a subordinate's performance where the subordinate does not appreciate the need to improve. The manager is in a far stronger position, psychologically, to try to draw such aspects tactfully to the attention of the subordinate if they have previously been building them up, than if they had made such observations 'cold'. Careful judgement has to be made, however, as to the extent to which a subordinate is able to benefit from criticism. If a person is simply going to reject it, there may be little point in pursuing discussion. Often, however, a person may be able to take a certain amount of adverse comment – the skill lies in recognising how much a person can take. If someone has volunteered three ways in which they will try to improve their performance, and is able to accept directive comment about one out of three other areas in which they need to improve, it may be best simply to forget about the other two areas. If their attention is drawn to these other areas, they may become so defensive and demoralised that they refuse to accept the case for any improvement whatsoever.

Informal guidance

The general philosophy of self-appraisal can be used in giving people informal guidance about how to improve their performance. It may be best to help people see for themselves how they can improve, but only to do this when it seems likely that the person will be able to benefit from such 'steering'. The timing of discussion can be critical as well, with the manager needing to distinguish between when the time is ripe to help people improve and when such advice will be resisted. Often this will be best handled as problems actually occur. One of the further dangers of formal schemes is that they may be seen as a mechanism for raking up old scores which are best forgotten. When problems do arise, a counselling technique may still be appropriate. If a subordinate has a problem, it may be best to start by asking how they think it should be handled. This may not only give the required result, but may develop in the subordinate the capacity to work things out for themselves.

Handling other appraisal situations

Many of the points already made concerning appraisal generally and performance appraisal in particular are relevant to other appraisal situations. Material relevant to these other situations is also included elsewhere in the book: the appraisal of training needs is covered later in this chapter; promotion is covered in Chapter 9.

It is appropriate here to comment about the process of handling upgradings. A particular issue that will need careful thought in this respect is the choice of the criteria by which upgradings are given or withheld. These need to fit with organisational objectives and to enable consistent and defensible decisions to be made. Upgrading arrangements should also motivate employees to acquire any extra knowledge and skills that are needed so that they can cope with their new pattern of work. Sometimes this is now done by rewarding people for the acquisition of new and relevant job competences. However, care also has to be taken to ensure that there is an appropriate balance of employees at the higher and lower grades, otherwise there may be a mismatch between people in a grade and the work available at that level. It would be somewhat counter-productive, for example, to upgrade everyone in a section leaving no-one to do the routine work.

A particular point about probation appraisal is that arrangements for handling this often seem to be more honoured in the breach than the observance. Employees are frequently left to infer that their probation has been completed successfully by the absence of any comment whatsoever. It may even be that their performance has not been satisfactory but the manager concerned has indicated otherwise by default, i.e., by not saying anything at the end of the stipulated period. Apart from anything else this may create difficulties in terminating the employment of an unsatisfactory employee. Even if a person does not have sufficient service to take an action for unfair dismissal to an industrial tribunal, organisational procedures for dismissal are usually much more comprehensive for the person who has completed their probation. One useful device that can be used in the case of marginal performers is to extend their probationary period. This can give the probationer more time to improve whilst retaining the relative freedom of the employer to terminate if the required improvement does not materialise.

The other appraisal situation that requires specific comment at this stage is where the duties of an employee are reviewed. This may be as a consequence of another aspect of appraisal or because the primary objective of an appraisal is to review the duties of an employee. Regular reviews of job content may be needed for a variety of reasons. Misunderstandings can easily arise about what actually is required. Additionally, job demands change and the capacity of employees to undertake particular tasks can also change. The motivational needs of employees also need to be considered, as was explained in Chapter 6, as does the danger of employees wanting to do, or actually doing, work that is not in the best interests of the organisation. It is necessary to remember the propensity of people to neglect managerial work in favour of specialist activity, as explained in Chapter 1, and the pressures for job distortion, as explained in Chapter 6.

Performance-related pay

The increasing use of performance-related pay schemes necessitates some specific comment. This topic was held over from Chapter 7, on payment systems, because of the need for performance-related pay to be grounded in an effective appraisal scheme. The distinction between performance appraisal generally and performance-related pay is that with the latter there is a formal link between performance and pay. Merit payment can be viewed as a generic term that subsumes performance-related pay. Merit payment has become increasingly popular in recent years. It has been introduced also into the public sector – particularly in parts of the Civil Service, the National Health Service and local government. This is perhaps not surprising in view of the greater pressures for a 'performance culture' in the public sector, as explained in Chapter 3. Also, the option of profit-related pay is not usually possible in the public sector. The schemes are normally, but not exclusively, used with white-collar and managerial grades. Further factors have been the harsher economic climate and relatively low rates of inflation. This has caused some employers to question whether they should give annual pay awards *and* annual pay increases. One solution has been to substitute performance-related pay for automatic incremental scales.

It will be instructive to see what long-term success the increased use of performance-related pay has. The general aim of helping develop a performance culture in this way is laudable, but it is unlikely to be achieved unless patient thought is given to the general problems already explained with regard to appraisal. There are also specific issues relevant to performance-related pay. One is whether or not performance payments should be given to the minority or the majority. If only the minority receives them, the rest of the work-force, theoretically eligible, may feel punished and demotivated by not receiving such payments. Conversely, if the payments are too readily available they may be seen as too automatic. Care has to be taken in identifying defensible criteria which in the end will rely on subjective judgements about appropriate performance standards and/or success in making targeted improvements.

The decision as to whether or not a person is to receive an increase, and if so how much, needs to be taken in private after an informed discussion between the manager and subordinate. The discussion itself, or the subsequent communication of the decision, should not be allowed to degenerate into a bargaining session about payment. Decisions also have to be taken about whether payments are lump sum or consolidated and the extent to which they can be forfeited at the next review. Unions tend to be unhappy about performance-related pay because of its emphasis on the individual employment contract – as opposed to collective negotiations and the potential for divisiveness within a work-force – though they may not take their opposition to the extent of wanting to prevent their members from having an opportunity to receive more money.

The use of performance-related pay involves risks as well as opportunities. It is likely to sharpen the interest in discussions about performance and there are further ways in which the dangers can at least be reduced, if not overcome. These include running pilot schemes and not viewing performance-related pay as a substitute for effective management, but as an aid to it. Appeal procedures need working out, but one needs to beware of removing ultimate pay decisions from the immediate manager(s). The judgement of others, remote from the situation, could easily be less accurate. Consequently, appeals are best restricted to procedural issues with decisions referred back for review if the immediate manager(s) has/have not handled the process adequately. Any linkages with mechanisms for identifying training needs and promotion also need consideration. If there are particular skills shortages, these are better handled by the pay scheme to retain people simply because their skills are in short supply. The impact of schemes, both short- and long-term, needs careful monitoring. If the forced distribution method is used to control the number of performance-related payments it needs to be remembered that this method has its limitations. This is because of the small numbers that may be employed in individual departments. Also, if the objective of raising the general level of performance succeeds, then it could be somewhat harsh to limit performance increases to just those who increase their performance the most. A further complication is that such arrangements may be interpreted as rewarding a few but 'punishing' the majority who have not had increases.

The increasing volume of evidence is that recent initiatives to introduce performance-related pay, especially in the public sector, have generally not been a great success.[4] This has been partly because of the inherent difficulties already explained. Another problem has been that the performance-related pay element has been often such a small part of total pay that it has not had much motivational impact. Consequently, any benefits have not justified the time and effort in setting up such schemes. Employers also have not always been careful to ensure that their schemes have operated in such a way that they are not biased on a gender or ethnic basis. In 1993 London Underground made a £60,000 settlement in a case taken by the Commission for Racial Equality on behalf of 20 black station managers who had claimed that they had suffered indirect racial discrimination under a performance-related pay scheme between 1989 and 1992.[5]

The continuing pressure to keep or introduce schemes, in the public sector especially, seems more an act of faith than based on the evidence of their effectiveness. Some of the public sector employers who have had discretion in this matter have abandoned their schemes, or at least the pay aspect. It seems likely that many employers have concentrated either exclusively or too much on the pay element regarding performance and have not identified the other variables, nor have they often even worked out which are the critical ones. Performance related pay can be a very limited and prescriptive approach to performance improvement. It is logical now to consider the wider concept of performance management.

Performance management

The term 'performance management', imported from the USA, has become increasingly fashionable and it is important to identify its meaning. Organisations may use the term differently but key elements are objective setting, formal appraisal and the linking of organisational and individual goals. Practice varies regarding linking performance to pay. There is much similarity with management by objectives – explained in Chapter 2. Performance management also overlaps with human resource management (covered in Chapter 12) and Total Quality Management (covered in Chapter 3). Despite the many similarities with management by objectives there are some differences, if only of emphasis between the two concepts. Performance management is a looser term – it is not a brand name associated with one particular consultancy. Also, it generally involves more emphasis on the definition of organisational mission statements aims and objectives, places less on quantification of performance and more ownership by line management, particularly by the senior management team.[6]

Having explained the concept of performance management and, by implication, its potential benefits, it is as well to remember the rapid demise of management by objectives. The causes of that demise included the mechanistic approach, the lack of genuine involvement by managers, the ritualistic way in which it was often introduced and the failure to recognise the conflicts of interest that change can precipitate. The same problems confront performance management. However, performance is the essence of management and it is to be hoped that organisations apply the concept of performance management in a constructive way. The emphasis on aspects such as organisational objectives, integration of activities and employee development are vital ingredients for success under whatever banner they feature.

Recent developments

Recent developments relating to appraisal include a hiving off of some areas and a rejection of the concept of individual appraisal. The development of the competences approach can affect appraisal with regard to performance, training, upgrading and payment. It may provide a new framework within an existing appraisal scheme or lead to the separate handling of these areas. The increasing use of assessment centres, and their greater concern with development issues, explained in the previous chapter, implies the separate handling of development potential. The concept of performance management may also lead to the separate handling of this area. It may even not focus on the individual. As explained in Chapter 3, Deming, in advocating TQM, fervently believed that the focus for improvement should be the group and not the individual. Changes, which partly reflect growing organisational complexity and sophistication, involve employee assessment by internal and external clients and peer group review. Finally de-layering and the reorganisation into business units often reduce the role of centralised personnel departments and of centrally administered appraisal schemes.[7]

TRAINING

Introduction

Appraisal is one way of identifying training needs, and this process will be considered as will the various ways in which training needs may be met. There are other ways in which training needs may be identified which also merit consideration.

There have been a number of relatively recent developments in the training area which it is also important to explain. These include the concept of 'the learning organisation', the competences approach to identifying needs and organising learning, the modular approach to course design and open access, and changes in views and approaches to management development. Consideration of these issues involves examination of related institutional developments such as National Vocational Qualifications (NVQs) and the Management Charter Initiative (MCI).

Identification of training needs

The identification of training needs may overlap with performance appraisal e.g., shortfalls between required and actual performance. In identifying the training needs of subordinates, managers need to consider any impending changes in the job which could necessitate training, even though a person may currently be performing perfectly adequately. As was explained in Chapter 9, assessment centres have increasingly been geared to the identification of training needs. Changes in organisational policies, structure or activities invariably have training implications. Training can be at the heart of initiatives such as TQM, explained in Chapter 3, and the development of genuine Human Resource Management strategies, explained in Chapter 12. These focus training on the strategic needs of the organisation rather than the needs of the individual. The impact of changing technology, particularly in the area of electronic data processing, is likely to generate ongoing training needs as explained in the section on technological developments in Chapter 3. Thought also has to be given to training employees for promotion, as well as with regard to the existing job. The willingness, and the ability, of employees to co-operate in implementing change may be considerably influenced by the extent to which they have been equipped to handle any such change.

Great care has to be taken to ensure that training needs are realistically identified. The need for training can all too easily be used as a spurious alibi for explaining all shortcomings in performance. Furthermore, performance problems are not always the fault of the individual concerned. What at first sight may seem to be a training requirement may, on closer examination, prove to be a case for changing work arrangements, amending policy or even 'buying in' particular skills. Realism has to be used in judging whether a particular person will benefit from training – some individuals have a remarkable talent for emerging unscathed after the most rigorous of training. Some areas though are easily ignored. The development of the flexible organisation means that it is increasingly important to consider the training needs of the 'peripheral' work-force. Cost issues that need to be worked out include the marginal costs of releasing an employee, the other things the employee could be doing in that time and the time it will take for there to be a return on the training investment. Training needs to be geared to the major problems and issues facing an organisation. That way it is more likely to be seen as a necessary investment rather than an expendable cost. It also needs to be recognised that some needs can disappear, for example, when skills are transferred from operators to the production process.

The emphasis so far has been on the identification of training needs by the organisation. Increasingly, though, individuals may need to take responsibility for identifying their own needs. The rate of technological change and the reduced predictability of career paths make it increasingly difficult to judge what the needs are and individual employees may increasingly be the ones best placed to make an informed guess about the nature of their training needs. This may involve them in identifying how they retain or develop their marketability in case they lose their jobs, for example, in a restructuring exercise.

Meeting training needs

Training can all too often be seen as something to be handled entirely by external agencies, including an organisation's training department. However, there is only so much that can be handled externally, and even that may not be appropriate. People sometimes offer themselves for training that is not related to their needs. This can be for a variety of reasons, including an inflated view of the level at which they require training. A person may opt for a seminar on corporate strategy when their needs may be much more basic, such as the need to develop supervisory skills. External training may also be sought because of its prestige, enjoyment or the prospects it offers for getting a job with a competitor. Not all external training is well handled anyway.

Whilst it would be a dangerously parochial view to ignore what external training agencies can offer, one must also be clear about the potential conflict of interests between an organisation selling training services and one considering buying those services. Standardised packages may be inappropriate for particular buyers, as can be consultancy services generally. Also one has to beware of entering into dependency relationships with outside organisations that discourage client organisations from working out their own strategies for salvation. Other problems can be the lack of responsibility of consultants for implementation and the lack of ownership of their recommendations by the client organisation. Care has to be taken too about buying in programmes that are related to the latest fashion and not the needs of an organisation. One sales technique can be to 'bounce' a senior manager into a commitment before those with the internal expertise to judge the appropriateness of what is on offer have had an opportunity to comment. This is not to suggest that one should not use external agencies – their services can be very useful or even essential, provided what they have to offer matches the real needs of an organisation.[8]

One way of checking the relevance of what courses are on offer is to examine the objectives, or intended outcomes, and to compare these with the actual, as opposed to imagined, needs of subordinates. If the objectives or outcomes of courses are not clearly stated, that in itself may tell you something about the care, or lack of care, with which the course has been designed. The statement of clear objectives or outcomes can also help to check if a person has benefited from a course. It is this, rather than just asking a person what they thought about a particular course, that is the acid test. When external training is appropriate the manager needs to help the subordinate to apply any relevant lessons, rather than let them suffer the frustration of seeing what needs to be done but being unable to do anything about it.

Developments in electronics are significantly increasing the range of ways in which training can be delivered. This includes more opportunity for computer-assisted learning, interactive training videos and the possible development of a national electronic 'superhighway' by the use of fibre-optic cabling that will make educational and training packages widely available.

An issue that managers may need to carefully consider is the competence of their own training department, if they have one. Effective training is literally disturbing, as the whole point of it is to alter existing patterns of behaviour. Some training departments help identify and facilitate such change, whilst others either opt out of mainstream activity or are never allowed near it. This can result in the activity of a training department being anaesthetised. An indication of this phenomenon is the preoccupation of a training department with soft options that do not contain a workshop element. Other indications are whether the training department is working in relative isolation from line management and engaging in training that is merely fashionable, random or token, or perhaps all three. Hopefully, managers who want a genuine contribution from their training department will encourage them to become involved with real issues that are relevant to the needs of the organisation and not connive in their relegation to dealing only with peripheral issues.

Whatever formal training can achieve outside the line manager's department, the crucial issue remains of the extent to which managers see themselves as coaches. If they systematically identify opportunities to help subordinates improve themselves, managers may find that, when performance of those subordinates is assessed, there is relatively little need for further improvement.

The learning organisation

A number of developments have led to the concept of 'the learning organisation'. This has been defined as 'an organisation which facilitates the learning of all its members and continuously transforms itself'.[9] It overlaps with the concept of individual continuous development. However, as Rothwell has observed, it can be 'difficult to distinguish between good intentions and good practice'.[10] Some of the factors that have contributed to the practical and theoretical development of the concept have already been examined independently. These include the increasing rate of change, the greater need for flexible organisational structures, the concept of continuous improvement and the need to structure the pattern of interactions within an organisation so that there can be optimum interaction between its members – all covered in Chapter 3. The need to consider recruiting people who are prepared to adapt their roles and career patterns in line with organisational needs was considered in Chapter 8, and the problems generated by specialist as opposed to organisational cultures in Chapter 1. The importance of the manager as coach is covered elsewhere in this chapter and empowerment is dealt with in Chapter 5.

The objective of the concept of the learning organisation is to enable those involved in an organisation to learn and thereby adapt in line with external changes and internal developments. This is meant to involve structuring the whole organisation so that such learning is facilitated, particularly in an experiential manner. This makes the approach qualitatively different from discrete 'bolted-on' training activities. The process ideally involves all key stakeholders, including customers and suppliers. The successful creation of a learning organisation is seen as the key to organisational survival and development. Other aspects are the importance of learning from those engaged in other functions so that a 'holistic' approach can be developed. Human resources are seen as 'elastic' and in need of effective motivation and development. The learning organisation also creates a learning climate that in turn creates and is reinforced by a social system that values and encourages learning.

The objectives of the learning organisation are praiseworthy However, it is important that its practical implementation is thought out rather than have a climate where 'anything goes'. Not all development opportunities can or should be followed up – otherwise organisational activity may lack coherence. There is the danger too that individuals may assume that personal developmental opportunities are automatically beneficial for the organisation. In stable situations, or ones where risks need to be carefully controlled, strong central direction may be entirely appropriate. It may be very difficult too to create an experiential learning climate when an organisation is restructuring or 'downsizing'.

The concept of continuous learning is being gradually but unevenly applied to the membership and training arrangements by professional bodies. More emphasis is being placed on the need for professional updating. Much of this needs to be work-based and there is a need for members of professional bodies to plan their own arrangements for continuous professional development. Some professions now make such arrangements a condition of continuing membership. There is a need too for educational institutions to place an increasing emphasis on teaching people to 'learn how to learn' and to help them manage such ongoing development. Judgements about learning priorities and access to reference material are increasingly important because of the ongoing explosion in the quantity of information.[11]

NVQs and related developments

There have been radical and comprehensive developments regarding the organisation of much of the vocational training in the UK, particularly, but not exclusively, with regard to manual skills. The General National Council for Vocational Qualifications has been created. This body is responsible for establishing occupational standards over a very wide area. It has taken this role from the City and Guilds, the Business and Technology Education Council and the Royal Society of Arts. Those bodies still operate, but devise and validate courses to the criteria set by the GNCVQ. The certificates that are now awarded are National Vocational Qualifications (NVQs, or SNVQs in Scotland) and General National Vocational Qualifications (GNVQs) for vocational A-levels. NVQs are not 'courses' in the traditional sense. They are national standards against which employees (or prospective employees) must measure themselves and then seek ways of acquiring the necessary knowledge and skill to ensure that they reach the required standard. Training is only needed in those units where individuals are not able to demonstrate that they can meet the established standards. Those standards are expressed as occupational competences. When training is arranged it is usually a combination of on-the-job and off-the-job. The Government's target is that by the year 2000 50 per cent of the work-force will be qualified to at least level 3. (5 being the highest).

A further impetus to these developments has been given by the establishment of 82 Training and Enterprise Councils (TECS). They had a budget in 1993/4 of £1.7 billion. They are particularly concerned with economic regeneration and the development of a skilled work-force. They give advice to employers on business and training issues and administer training grants, particularly to young unemployed people. A further incentive to employers is the possibility of obtaining the 'kitemark' of an Investors in People Award (IIP). This scheme is run by the TECs.

The training developments outlined above represent a major break with tradition. Training needs are expressed in terms of required behaviour rather than in terms of knowledge. This facilitates speedier progression by providing for recognition of existing competences, however acquired, and by excluding irrelevant knowledge. The arrangements have the potential for greater flexibility of training portfolios and multi-skilling. A further incentive to acquire NVQs is given by the possibility of being able to claim them as a tax deductible expense. Some of this thinking is being adopted in higher and university education. Important developments include learning development contracts, modular course design, accreditation for prior learning (APL), and accreditation for prior experiential learning (APEL). Historically, in both craft trades and in the professions, the length and complexity of training was sometimes used as a means of restricting entry to an occupation. This new approach challenges such restrictive approaches. Even in those professions where there has been no covert policy of restricting entry, some may be ripe for a fundamental appraisal of their arrangements for training and membership. If these ideas are taken seriously they could have a major impact on job design, occupational standards, syllabus structure and content, methods of training delivery and entry routes to most of or possibly all the established professions.

Inevitably, there have been problems in introducing sweeping changes in the training field. Employers can find that NVQ standards are broader than they require for their organisational needs. This is likely given that the qualifications are awarded for the ability to meet national occupational standards. The balance between knowledge and competence can be skewed too much towards physical performance; it is often necessary for people to have a theoretical underpinning to a competence if they are to have versatility. The higher the level of the competence the more this can be a problem, especially with management competences, as will be explained later. The volume and validity of assessment can also present major problems, particularly pressures to generate a throughput of 'qualified' students. Other issues are the complexity of the related bureaucracy and the need for more co-operation from employers. Hopefully, though, progress can be made in resolving, or reducing the scale of such problems as the new approach has much to commend it.

Management training and development

The development of occupational standards and the facility for NVQs has also been applied to management. As was explained in Chapter 1, the Management Charter Initiative body is the leading body in this respect. Consideration of some of the problems in identifying, developing and assessing national occupational standards were also considered in Chapter 1 and again in Chapter 4 when the topic of situational leadership was examined.

The case for reviewing the quantity and quality of management training in the UK is overwhelming. However, for the quality to be improved, some of the problems relating to the area need to be clearly recognised. Apart from the variety of managerial situations, there are considerable problems in establishing valid methods of assessment. The difficulties of doing this are of a completely different order compared with, for example, assessing manual skills. The skills (or competences) of accurate problem diagnosis, decision-making and soundness of judgement may be crucial to effective management performance but be very difficult to assess. Observation of a person's behaviour during an assessment simulation or written evidence about their skills may not give an accurate indication of how they really behave in practice. There is also the danger of designing training on too compartmentalised a basis, and with too little theoretical underpinning, when a key attribute of managers may be the ability to synthesise knowledge and skills relating to a range of areas. Assessment and learning can also conflict, because of the volume of assessment that may be required and the inhibiting effect that assessment can have on experimentation and enquiry. The assessment of competences is also resource-intensive, and training resources are often being reduced rather than increased.

Whatever qualifications a person obtains, it is particularly necessary in the management area to use the selection process to check that people have the appropriate personal qualities to be able to perform adequately. If qualitative improvement is to be achieved in management training proper account needs to be taken of these issues. Change will not be for the better if a rigid approach is imposed, more suitable for the development of relatively easily identified and assessed manual skills.

Management development in Japan has some potentially useful lessons. A competitive advantage they have is that, as managers often spend their entire careers with a single organisation, any benefits accrue to the employer who has made the investment. This also facilitates and justifies a long-term approach to management development. Much of the development explained in Chapter 1 is arranged by planned job rotation and career development, with individual commitment being to the organisation rather than the specialism. Extensive use is made of appointing in-house mentors to supplement the activity of the boss as coach. The concept of mentoring has begun to develop in the UK. Sometimes there is a case for appointing an external mentor.[12]

Another approach that needs covering is that of 'action learning'. This can combine problem solving with management development so that organisations gain a double benefit. It also ensures that development is focused around an organisation's real problems. A further advantage is that if done on an in-house group basis it overcomes the problem of managers being sent on external programmes and returning to a working environment that may be unsympathetic or unsupportive to any new ideas they have developed.[13]

Evaluation and follow-up

Whatever pattern of training and development is adopted in an organisation, it is important that it be monitored to ensure that it is meeting the appropriate needs and giving value for money. As has already been stated, the identification of training needs in terms of objectives and/or expected outcomes makes it easier to judge whether training has been worthwhile. Follow-up studies may be needed, though, to judge the long-term impact of training, particularly in areas such as management development. Such studies may need to consider alternative ways of achieving required results. The nation's economy can only develop on a high value added basis if that value is added to the goods and services it offers by a skilled work-force.[14]

COUNSELLING

Introduction

The techniques of counselling have already been covered to some extent in this chapter in considering appraisal. It is now appropriate, however, to deal with the subject in greater detail. The best point at which to start is to explain just what is meant by the term. 'Counselling' can be defined as a purposeful relationship in which one person helps another to help themselves. It is a way of relating and responding to another person so that that person is helped to explore their thoughts, feelings and behaviour with the aim of reaching a clearer understanding. The clearer understanding may be of themselves or of a problem, or of the one in relation to the other. The point of all this is to enable people to work out how they will handle for themselves issues, problems or decisions that have to be made. The technique is necessary because it may be that it is only by this process that an issue can be understood and/or the commitment created that will lead to an appropriate course of action being taken by the person concerned.

The need for counselling can arise in a wide range of situations. Appraisal has already been mentioned, and the requirement for these skills in grievance and disciplinary situations is explained later in this chapter. The need for counselling skills can arise whenever a subordinate or colleague has a work or work-related problem. Sometimes it may be necessary to use these skills with clients as well. As well as managers needing counselling skills themselves, they also have to consider the extent to which their subordinates need these skills. It may be particularly important that any employee who has direct contact with clients or the public is trained in how to handle such contacts.

Usually, counselling discussions are initiated by the person who needs the help. However, there will be occasions when managers need to take the initiative and encourage employees to face up to issues that are having an adverse effect on their work. Whoever initiates discussion, some interpretation of an employee's responses will be necessary. Care needs to be taken about the level of discussion and analysis that is attempted. In depth 'Freudian' probing and analysis (for example) is better handled by those qualified to do it than by amateur psychiatrists. The requirement for counselling in work situations is usually for work-related rather than personal problems anyway. Obviously, personal problems can affect behaviour at work and counselling may be given by one person to another in the capacity of personal friend. There may well be situations, though, where it is not appropriate for a manager to get involved or where the best help that can be given is to refer a person to an appropriate agency or service.

The value of counselling

The need to develop the techniques of counselling became rapidly apparent to me when I first started work as a personnel officer. I had not been trained in advance how to counsel, but was fortunate to have friends in the social work field who counselled me on how to deal with the flood of callers I received wanting help with a bewildering variety of problems, many of which I did not even understand, far less have answers for. In my enthusiasm I had previously offered directive advice which often simply revealed my ignorance and increased the frustration of the colleague concerned. Eventually I was able to learn how to talk people through their problems so that often they came up with their own 'solution' or came to terms with the fact that there was no 'solution' and that they just had to put up with something. Once I had acquired this skill, I found that all manner of people, instead of viewing me as remarkably ignorant, thanked me for helping them resolve issues which I had still often barely understood. I realised in retrospect that previously I had all too often fallen into the trap of giving directive advice when I did not know all the facts or, if I did, had recommended the course of action that I would have followed, which did not of course allow for the different personality of the person who had come to see me. The non-directive style that I subsequently came to use enabled people to take account of facts that they had not explained to me, and also to take account of their own personal reaction to the problem. The further advantage of this non-directive approach was that the individual concerned was far more likely to be committed to a solution that they had worked out for themselves than to one that someone had sought to impose on them. The need that people had in these situations was not so much to be told what to do, but rather to have someone to calm them down and help them navigate their own way through the maze. In doing this they may have made their first systematic attempt to deal with the problem and, with luck, found that they could see the appropriate course of action for themselves.

Specific skills

Having explained the general nature and purpose of counselling, it is now appropriate to explain the skills in more detail. The pressure that people are often under before they speak needs to be borne in mind. An apocryphal story that makes this point concerns the person who had moved into a new house and knocked at a neighbour's door to ask if they could borrow their lawn mower. The newcomer had worked himself up into such a state about the legitimacy of his request to someone he hadn't yet met that when the neighbour opened the door he shouted 'you can keep your lawn-mower – I know you won't lend it to me!'

The choice of who counsels, and when, is much more in the hands of the person wanting this type of help than with the potential counsellor. A person may not choose to speak about their problems to some people and may refuse offers of help that are made. So, the opportunity for counselling is likely to be determined by the person wanting help, but it is up to the manager whether they have the inclination and skill to respond. The counselling that is required may be easily dealt with in a few moments or may involve several lengthy discussions. Those who have the opportunity to provide this type of help have to judge whether it is appropriate for them to give it and to assess if they are really likely to help, if they have the time to spare and whether there are other more appropriate ways of helping. A complication is that decisions on whether or not to counsel may have to be taken very quickly. If a person is rebuffed they may not ask again or, if counselling-type help is offered, it may be very difficult to stop once it has started.

The amount of direction given by the counsellor will vary according to the situation and the personalities involved. It is the essence of counselling, though, that the person is helped to work the problem out for themselves. Not only may value judgements be inappropriate if made by the counsellor but, if they vary from the value judgements of the person requiring help, that person may see the counsellor as unsympathetic and consequently terminate any discussion. Nevertheless, even given all this, there can be a range of counselling styles. At the one extreme a person may be totally non-directive and just give sufficient response, perhaps by ways of grunts, to let the other person know that they are actually listening. In other cases it may be appropriate for the counsellor to be rather more interventionist, whilst at the same time avoiding imposing their own views. This can be done in a neutral but friendly manner by positively encouraging a person to elaborate on an issue. Further interventions can be to clarify what has been said and to ask questions that are designed to get the person to talk more. It may be necessary for a person to add information in such a way that the person being counselled feels free to make use of the information or ignore it. This represents a further stage in counselling intervention without sacrificing the neutrality of the counsellor. Another stage is to help the person concerned identify the options available to them – the critical point being that the choice has to be made by the person being counselled and not by the counsellor. This can involve a person taking a decision that is not necessarily in the interests of the organisation – for example, to leave (or in some cases not to leave!). There is little point, however, in the counsellor seeking to impose the decision that is in the organisation's interests as the person would undoubtedly ignore it. If a person is going to decide to leave, for example, it may be just as well to help them come to that decision relatively quickly rather than to let the issue drag on.

Throughout a counselling interview the counsellor needs to be aware of the need for eye contact when appropriate. That is not to say that they should spend all their time staring at the subject, but such contact can be helpful in showing that the counsellor is actively listening. It is also necessary to be aware of signals that are being given by a person's 'body language'. This concept has already been explained in Chapter 8. Premature intervention by the counsellor can prevent further disclosure by the subject. A problem or issue may be the lead into another and perhaps much bigger area and the counsellor needs to be aware that the closing of discussion on a particular topic is by no means necessarily the end of a counselling interview.

The problem that a person raises may just be a lead-in or a pre-text for going on to discuss much more serious issues. Often the stated problem is rather like the tip of an iceberg. The subject may want to test that they are going to get a sympathetic response before being prepared to reveal the next part of a problem. Sometimes a person may not even be aware that the problem is much deeper than that indicated by them initially. This shows the danger of trying to deal with just the 'tip'. The help that a person may need is to reason through the whole of a problem in such a way that they can cope with it, allowing for their own personality. It may be that there are also issues of which they are aware but which they deliberately keep secret. This is yet another reason for the counsellor to beware of seeking to impose a solution, as it may be based on an incomplete knowledge of the facts.

In order to discover the rest of the iceberg and to get the person to speak freely, the counsellor will find it useful to pay attention to their questioning technique. 'Open' questions (i.e., those which start with an interrogative such as 'how', 'what', 'why', 'where') are more likely to help widen the conversation and explore the issues involved in a particular problem than 'closed' questions. 'Closed' questions are often phrased in such a way that they start with a verb: for example, 'Do you enjoy your work?'. If the interviewee is reluctant to talk, the 'yes' or 'no' given in answer to such a question may only help in a marginal way. (It ought to be added that there will also be situations when a straight 'yes' or 'no' answer is what is needed.) Other skills which may be useful in building up rapport and encouraging the employee to talk include the processes of summarising, clarifying and reflecting back: saying, for example, 'So that made you feel rather annoyed?'.

'Active' listening skills, which are also necessary in a counselling situation, involve two aspects. The first is being aware of appearing to be listening as well as actually hearing what is being said. Non-verbal skills in this situation include eye contact, leaning forward, not shuffling papers or making notes. The second aspect of listening skills, which is important, includes being aware of the source of barriers to hearing exactly what is being said. These barriers include some obvious ones like language differences, daydreaming and environmental noise, but also selective perception (or hearing what we want to hear), self-consciousness, where the counsellor is more aware of the impression they are making, and behaviour rehearsal, where the counsellor is busy working out what they are going to say next. There may also be a barrier when the counsellor has problems of their own which occupy their thoughts or where the content of what the employee is saying arouses anger or hostility in the counsellor. In many instances, simply being aware of the likely barriers can help the counsellor to make a conscious effort to eradicate them. These points on listening skills will also be relevant in other types of interview, as will the idea of 'open' and 'closed' questions. Some further points on questioning technique are made in Chapter 9 on selection.

Normally, the whole basis on which counselling takes place is one of complete confidence. Sometimes, however, the counsellor will need to warn the subject that information that may emerge, or already has, cannot be treated confidentially. If, for example, an accountant is told that their cashier has been systematically embezzling money it is hardly likely that they can, or should want to, keep this a private matter between the parties.

Reference has been made in this section to the various stages that there are likely to be in a counselling interview. Part of the skill of counselling effectively is to identify the pattern an interview may take. The main stages are likely to be as follows:

1 Identification of the problem
2 Collection and exchange of information
3 Checking that all the necessary statements have been made
4 Establishing the criteria for a satisfactory 'solution'
5 Deciding on the appropriate 'solution'
6 Subsequently checking whether or not the 'solution' has worked

The issue of the different stages in a counselling interview is not quite the same as the different styles of counselling. Each person who counsels may have their own style, which may vary from that of other people at the level of intervention (or non-intervention) and the specific skills that are used. However, whatever basic style is used it will need to be varied according to the personality of the subject, the issue under discussion and the stage of the counselling process.

Given that managers spend most of their time in some form of communication and that much of it is oral communication – as explained in Chapter 8, the need for counselling techniques can arise very frequently. The skills may not have the glamour of more high-status management activities but can nevertheless be one of the most critical of all management skills. The skills may also be constructively applied in one's personal life. Two of the situations where counselling techniques can be particularly necessary are next examined – grievance and disciplinary handling. These, however, are but two of the many situations in which the skills may be appropriate.[15]

Grievance handling

Grievance interviews are situations where counselling skills are particularly likely to be necessary. There is a statutory requirement for employers to give written details to employees of the grievance procedure if 20 or more people are employed. This must include the name, or title, of the person to whom an individual employee can complain and also the details of any appeal procedure. It may also, as explained in the next chapter, be appropriate to use a grievance procedure as an appeals mechanism against minor disciplinary warnings. Unfortunately, grievance procedures tend to be little used, as the immediate boss is usually designated for the task of hearing the grievance but is normally also the cause of it! I once worked for a company where employees were given a standard letter informing them of their right to take a grievance up with the managing director if necessary. On the one occasion that this right was invoked it turned out the managing director was quite ignorant of this arrangement – the undertaking have been given by one of his predecessors! However, managers may handle many grievances quite informally, and the range of situations will be much wider than just that of dealing with dissatisfied subordinates. Working relationships with colleagues may generate grievances as may contact with client groups, particularly the public.

There can be a variety of ways of handling grievances, including having a first-class row, ignoring it, referring it to someone else, or giving the person what they want. Often, however, grievances cannot, and should not, be ignored, yet there may be nothing that the manager concerned can do to resolve the grievance. It may be that a person has a perfectly justifiable grievance, but nothing concrete can be done about it. It is in situations like this that counselling may be not only desirable but the only course of action that can be taken.

Grievance handling skills may be needed by many levels of people within an organisation. Employees who have customer contact may need it in their handling of customers, though managers may also need it in this context as well as in handling dissatisfied employees.

I have often marvelled at the way some airline staff cope with irate passengers who seek to hold them personally responsible for the weather, strikes or technical failures. This presumably is often because of the training they have received. In some of these situations the answer is simply to let people talk themselves out of their fury. Their frustration may require an outlet, and counselling techniques may enable them gradually to dissipate their anger. At the end of it, an aggrieved person may actually thank the person at whom they have directed their anger for their help and go away reconciled to the situation. The dilemma for the person who has to handle the grievance is that, if they openly agree with the complaints, they may compromise their employer and, if they rebut the complaints, they may infuriate the complainant. Neutral, but sympathetic, listening in many cases is not merely the only option but may be a complete answer. It may even be appropriate for the person at the receiving end of the grievance to take the initiative as the anger subsides and probe to see if there is any more anger that needs ventilation – like poking a balloon with an open neck with a stick to see if any more air comes out.

In some cases the counselling of a person with a grievance will simply mark the end of the first stage of the 'discussion'. It may then be necessary to see what, if anything, can be done about the person's complaint. It may be that a decision has to be deferred or the answer given that, whilst you are sympathetic, nothing can be done. It is crucial, however, that, where feelings run high, this is only attempted after the counselling stage has been completed. It may be only then that a person can participate in a rational discussion of what can or cannot be done. Even if they still expect some action, a hearing of their case may have gone some way, if not the whole way, to providing psychological restitution. It may also emerge that their anger has prevented them from properly explaining their grievance and that the cause of their dissatisfaction is rather different from that which first seemed to be the case. Clarification of the nature of the grievance may be crucial, as otherwise decisions cannot be sensibly taken about what action should, or should not, follow – yet sometimes it may only be at a relatively late stage in the proceedings that this is possible. When customers complain organisations can sometimes seize the initiative by empowering front-line staff to make routine decisions regarding compensation and thus convert dissatisfied customers into people who praise the organisation instead.

The processes I have just described can be very necessary in confrontations between managers and union representatives, or with other special interest groups for that matter. It may be impossible to communicate effectively with representatives until they have ventilated their feelings about a particular issue. It may be only then that representatives are able to listen to the management side of a case. The problem for whoever is chairing such joint meetings is to prevent anyone on the employer's side from retaliating and so inflaming a situation. This may be particularly necessary as the opposing interest group may have actually moderated their position after saying their piece.

A common failing is for managers to ignore grievances. Sometimes this can work but it can also lead to issues festering. I knew of one case where a person asked for two years about not being paid an 'acting-up' allowance. After receiving no reply during that period he resorted to using the formal grievance procedure. Unfortunately, by the time the grievance was heard, relationships had deteriorated so much that he ended up being sacked and instituted proceedings against the organisation for unfair dismissal. Even if the employer felt justified in not paying the allowance, a patient explanation of the reasons at the outset may have prevented this breakdown in working relationships. Another common failing is for grievances to be heard and then the aggrieved person be told nothing about the outcome. Again it would seem better, even if the answer is negative from the employee's or customer's point of view, to have the courtesy to at least tell them that.

There can be a legal dimension to grievances. Failure to respond to issues regarding sex or racial discrimination or harassment can mean that employers are in breach of their statutory obligations and can result in proceedings at industrial tribunals. As explained in Chapter 7, employees can also complain of sex discrimination with regard to pay under the equal pay regulations. Aggrieved customers may also resort to the use of consumer protection legislation and/or report issues to their local trading standards department. Organisations are generally taking the issue of customer complaints more seriously. Procedures in this area are increasingly seen as an essential part of quality control and good customer relations. An example of this development is the requirement that solicitors who are franchised to provide legal aid must provide clients with a written complaints procedure as a condition of being franchised.

Counselling in disciplinary situations

Counselling may also be applicable in disciplinary situations. As with grievance handling, it can be a necessary first, and even only, stage in resolving disciplinary problems. The best form of discipline is usually self-discipline, and the attempt to impose a pattern of behaviour on an employee should normally only be considered if the employee is unable to show the appropriate self-discipline. If it is appropriate to 'bring an employee into line', one should normally seek to do this with the minimum amount of pressure consistent with that objective. If an employee's performance or conduct is inappropriate, it would generally seem sensible to encourage the employee to see this and work out for themselves the required change in their behaviour. As was stated during the section on performance appraisal, people can often be their own harshest critics. It would seem far better, therefore, to give an employee the opportunity to mend their ways voluntarily rather than to try to impose one's authority. Apart from the greater commitment that this may create, it may also save the employee's face if they are allowed to work out their own salvation. Again, as with grievance handling, even if counselling does not prove to be a complete answer, it may clear the way for appropriate action on any residual disagreement. The counselling stage may also be necessary to clarify the exact nature of the shortcomings, if indeed there are any. One of the problems of disciplinary handling is that there may need to be a considerable amount of discussion before it can be clarified whether there is a disciplinary problem or not. Counselling may, however, be just the first stage in the disciplinary process. The handling of further stages in that process is the subject of the next chapter.

CONCLUSION

A theme of this chapter has been the need to systematically identify the needs of employees by the interrelated methods of appraisal, training needs analysis and counselling. Once the needs have been established they need to be synthesised with organisational needs. The ability to identify these needs and reconcile them with organisational needs can require considerable interpersonal skills. The topics can have a vital bearing on the central issue of performance management, which is why this area has been included in this chapter. Other aspects of performance management have previously been covered in Chapter 2. The chapter also links particularly with Chapter 12, which includes the topic of human resource management. In that chapter further attention is given to the often increasingly strategic role of training and performance management and how these issues can flow out of strategic organisational plans.

NOTES

1 A. Savage, 'Reconciling your Appraisal System with Company Reality', *Personnel Management*, May 1982, p. 131.
2 Clive Fletcher, 'An Idea Whose Time Has Gone?', *Personnel Management*, September 1993, p. 34.
3 Deirdre Gill and Bernard Ungerson, *Equal Pay: The Challenge of Equal Value*, Institute of Personnel Management, 1984, p. 47.
4 Institute of Employment Studies, *Pay and Performance: The Employee Experience*, Institute of Employment Studies, 1993.
5 'Merit Pay Scheme was "Discriminatory"', *Personnel Management*, News Section, May 1993, p. 3.
6 Alan Fowler, 'Performance Management, The MBO of the 90's?', *Personnel Management*, July 1990.
7 Ibid., pp. 34–7. See also, by the same author, *Appraisal: Routes to Improved Performance*, Institute of Personnel Management, 1993.
8 Roger Bennett, *Choosing and Using Management Consultants*, Kogan Page, 1990.
9 Mike Pedler, John Burgoyne and Tom Boydell, *The Learning Company: A Strategy for Sustainable Development*, McGraw Book Company, 1991.
10 Sheila Rothwell, 'Annual Review Article 1992', *British Journal of Industrial Relations*, March 1993, p. 151.
11 Institute of Personnel and Development, *Code of Practice, Continuous Development: People and Work*, Institute of Personnel and Development, 1993.
12 W. David Rees, 'Someone to Watch Over Me – An Experiment in Mentoring in Hackney', *Local Government Management*, Autumn 1992, pp. 20, 21.
13 W. David Rees, 'A System for Assessing Work Priorities', *Personnel Management*, December 1989, pp. 46–9; Reg Revans, *The ABC of Action Learning*, Chartwell Brett, UK, 1987.
14 For a further coverage of the training area see Frances and Roland Bee, *Training: Needs Analysis and Evaluation*, Institute of Personnel and Development, 1994.
15 A particularly useful handbook on counselling is Michael Reddy, *Counselling at Work*, British Psychological Society and Methuen, 1987.

Chapter 11

Disciplinary handling and dismissal

INTRODUCTION

The need to discipline subordinates can be unpleasant and embarrassing, but it is a necessary aspect of a manager's job. Often the term 'discipline' is seen as synonymous with dismissal, but discipline is a generic term and dismissal simply the severest in the range of penalties the employer can enforce. If everyone behaves in an appropriate way then the manager does not need to be concerned with disciplinary action, but sadly that is not always the case. When managers are confronted with disciplinary problems they may handle them effectively, but often the problems are ignored or dealt with unskilfully, too harshly or too leniently. Many managers would prefer to have nothing to do with discipline but, if they opt out of this area, they are in reality opting out of what is an integral part of their job. The embarrassment that managers can feel can affect the skill with which they handle disciplinary issues. This is an area, however, where some skills at least can be developed relatively easily. Effective action can contain problems and prevent them getting out of hand. The effectiveness of managers in this area can have a considerable impact on their relationships, not just with those who may have to be disciplined but with the other subordinates who may see particular incidents very much as test cases.

In considering the topic of discipline it is important to stress that there can be many causes of poor performance, and wilfully inappropriate behaviour by employees is just one potential cause. Many of the potential causes are firmly management's responsibility and include competent management, sound organisational structure, appropriate policies and adequate training. An illustration of this basic point concerns the organisation where it emerged that a key factor in creating 'disciplinary' problems was the lack of validity in selection procedures. Also, some dismissals may be quite unrelated to discipline, because of ill-health or redundancy for example. Because these are important areas and there is considerable overlap in the related law and procedures these issues are also included in this chapter.

In this chapter attention is paid to the objectives of disciplinary policies which are often not clearly thought out. The legal position in the UK is explained, partly because this is one aspect of discipline, but more importantly because of the impact that it can have on disciplinary action other than dismissal. The responsibility of the individual manager is considered, as are the procedures and procedural skills necessary for appropriate action. Counselling skills may be particularly important in dealing with issues at an early stage and preventing them escalating. The general topic of counselling was covered in the previous chapter and an explanation also given as to how it could be applied in disciplinary situations.

THE OBJECTIVES OF DISCIPLINE

The primary objective of discipline is to prevent or, failing that, to deal with inappropriate behaviour by employees which has an adverse effect on their work or the work of colleagues. The preventive aspect involves educating employees about the behaviour that is expected of them and reinforcing that with effective management control. Unless a person is dismissed, the aim needs to be to change a person's behaviour so that it becomes acceptable. Another important objective is to demonstrate that discipline is administered fairly. It is necessary to try to demonstrate this, not only to the person who may be the subject of disciplinary action, but also to their colleagues, whose attitudes can be considerably influenced by the action taken.

Just as with appraisal, so with disciplinary situations, managers need to work out quite carefully just what they are trying to achieve. Too often consideration of this topic simply consists of a discussion of an employer's track record at industrial tribunals. It may be that an employer has never lost a case at an industrial tribunal, or has never had to defend a case at a tribunal, but that may prove very little. There is not much point in an employer always winning legal cases if, in the meantime, their line managers have opted out of their disciplinary role, possibly with a marked adverse effect on standards of performance. Dismissal may be a necessary step to take and, when taken, it is undoubtedly best for an employer to be able to defend their actions successfully. However, it is no good just looking at the dismissal end of the disciplinary process. Dismissal is necessary only if other, more appropriate, means of dealing with a disciplinary problem, including attempts to alter a person's behaviour, have failed or clearly are pointless. Any formal intervention can, to some extent, be regarded as a sign of failure in that the more satisfactory approach of self-discipline may have failed.

Disciplinary action may only be appropriate if a person's behaviour is having a detrimental effect on their or other people's work. It follows from this that the objective is normally to try to get a person to mend their ways so that their behaviour is improved. If this is likely to prove impossible, then a manager has to make a judgement about whether to put up with it or to consider following the avenue that could lead to dismissal. Judgements about when to intervene, and over what issues, may need considerable thought. People may have many irritating habits that they cannot or will not change, and it may be pointless trying to make them. Conversely, if managers are too lenient, they may find that events get seriously out of hand: the analogy of a stitch in time saving nine can be highly appropriate with regard to discipline. A small issue discreetly checked at the right time can prevent escalation into something far more difficult to contain.

Often employees prefer a tighter discipline than actually exists and may resent seeing colleagues being able to behave in an unconscientious way. This tends to devalue their own job and may lead to them leaving or deciding that they may as well follow the lead that is given. Inconsistencies in treatment, especially within a department, can also create considerable resentment. Standards of attendance and punctuality can vary widely from department to department, even within the same organisation, according to the lead given by the managers concerned. Employees can also object to too harsh a regime, which is why managers need to think carefully what standards are appropriate and how they should be achieved, rather than avoid thinking about the issue at all.

The political judgements that managers have to make may be particularly difficult when dealing with professional-level employees. Some of them may find any concept of external control unacceptable, yet develop their work in a way that does not fit with the needs of the organisation. It is useful to distinguish between the professional's technical competence and their accountability for achieving objectives. It may be more effective, and acceptable, to make the point that discussion about the latter topic does not necessarily reflect on the professional employee's specialist competence.

There is a tendency for some managers to overestimate the extent to which standards in the disciplinary area are decided externally. It can be very convenient to assume that the responsibility for establishing and maintaining disciplinary standards lies elsewhere – either within the organisation or outside it. Organisations invariably have overall policies and procedures concerning discipline, but these provide a framework within which a manager should operate, rather than devices for passing the buck. It is only the manager in an individual department who can monitor and interpret the policies and procedures. If a person is not doing their job properly, it would seem to be a fundamental part of the manager's job to consider bringing the matter to the person's attention. The definition of standards within a department has to be undertaken, communicated and, when appropriate, enforced by the manager concerned. The existence of overall policies and procedures does not take away the individual manager's responsibility in this area, however much some managers would like to pretend that it does. The legal rights of an ex-employee to pursue a case for unfair dismissal are likely to have an impact on the disciplinary policies and procedures, so it is appropriate to explain the legal position in Britain before considering the skills involved in disciplinary handling.

THE LAW RELATING TO DISMISSAL

Since 1972 people who have been dismissed have had the right to claim before an industrial tribunal that they have been unfairly dismissed. This legal right was part of the Industrial Relations Act, 1971 with the unfair dismissal provisions being implemented the following year. The current legal framework is contained in the Employment Protection (Consolidation) Act, 1978. Before 1972 the only significant right of employees who had been dismissed was to take an action in the civil courts under common law if they had not received their proper entitlement to notice. Such actions alleging 'wrongful dismissal' were restricted to considering the amount of notice, or money in lieu of notice, to which the ex-employee was entitled. Statutory rights to redundancy payments were first introduced in 1965, but the rights under the Redundancy Payments Act were restricted to the amount of compensation to which an employee was entitled, not whether or not they should have been dismissed.

Grounds for dismissal

The grounds on which an employer can establish that a dismissal was fair are quite broad. The three main grounds, in practice, are capacity, conduct and redundancy. Dismissal also has to be reasonable in the circumstances. Dismissal on grounds of lack of capacity may be justified because of a person's poor performance or on medical grounds. Alternatively, medical cases might be dealt with under a further category 'other substantial reasons'. Dismissal on grounds of misconduct may be either because of a single instance of gross misconduct, which can entitle an employer to summarily dismiss (without notice), or because of cumulative misconduct in which case the appropriate notice, or money in lieu, has to be given. Gross misconduct is not easy to define but legally occurs when an employee's (mis)behaviour goes to the root of the contract. It is prudent for an employer to clarify the position by giving predictable written examples of what is considered to be gross misconduct. These might well include theft or fraud perpetrated against the organisation and physical assault in the course of employment. This may have both an educative effect and make it easier to establish that particular behaviour constituted gross misconduct. However, lack of such advance publicity will not automatically prevent employers from treating other behaviour as gross misconduct if it is sufficiently serious.

There is a statutory requirement for disciplinary rules to be notified to employees and these need to cover basic requirements, not just examples of gross misconduct. If 20 or more people are employed these rules need to be in writing. It is increasingly important for rules to refer to the need to refrain from sexual or racial harassment. Quite apart from the inappropriateness of such behaviour the obligations of employers to provide a harassment-free working environment have been underlined by a series of cases where damages have been awarded to applicants where employers have failed in this respect. Hopefully, though, the rules will have a powerful educative effect, so that the required behaviour is achieved without resort to discipline. The basic expectations the employer has of employees should also be an integral part of induction training for newcomers. Also, if new rules are introduced, or if there are other changes in the expectations that employers have of employees, these should be communicated in advance. It is important that employees don't learn of the existence of rules or new expectations by being disciplined! Employers also need to demonstrate that they have systematically and fairly sought to enforce any such rules. Their position at a tribunal would be weak if a former employee were able to demonstrate uneven application of any such rules. Erratic attendance and time keeping are particularly common examples of cumulative misconduct and in cases like this the employer needs to be able to demonstrate to a tribunal that they have tried to operate policies fairly, and in such a way that the pressure on an employee was gradually stepped up, before any consideration of dismissal.

In cases of redundancy, an ex-employee may argue that a redundancy was bogus or, if it was genuine, that they were unfairly selected. A crucial test in establishing whether or not there was a redundancy is whether or not the person was replaced. Selection for redundancy may be in accordance with a previously established policy which may also have been agreed with recognised trade unions. However, under the Deregulation Act, 1994, employers are released from the obligation to follow an established policy if they can produce a good reason for not doing so. Redundancy selection nevertheless has to be 'reasonable'. Length of service is an important criterion in deciding who should be retained and who should be dismissed, but other criteria may need to be considered as well. Redundancies are also affected by collective law. Under the terms of the Trade Union Protection (Consolidation Act) of 1992 employers planning *any* redundancy are required to consult with relevant trade union representatives *at the earliest opportunity* and in any event 30 days before dismissal with redundancies of between 10 and 100 employees, and 90 days if the redundancies are expected to be 100 or over. They are also obliged to give notice to the Department of Employment of redundancies of 10 or more in line with the minimum time scales given above. (At the time of writing the government is considering increasing the figure for collective redundancies from 10 to 20 – the minimum European requirement. Similarly, it is considering replacing the requirement to consult *at the earliest opportunity* with *in good time.*) Under the terms of the Trade Union Reform and Employment Rights Act of 1993 the requirement to consult has been strengthened by the further requirement to consult *with a view to reaching agreement.* An important practical effect of this is that dismissal notices cannot be issued *until* that consultation process has been completed. A further development in 1994 was the decision by the European Court of Justice, in an action brought by the European Commission against the UK government that, in areas where there were no recognised unions, employers were required to consult with 'representatives of the workforce'.[1] This has led the government to actively consider giving the employers the option of consulting with trade unions or other worker representatives. The duty to consult applies when redundancy, or adverse contract changes, are proposed. As was explained in Chapter 3, employers acquiring new businesses, or even sometimes winning contracts for economic entities, will be covered by the above law in handling any consequential redundancies of the 'acquired' or existing employees, as well as the legislation relating to the transfer of undertakings.

Exclusions

Not all dismissed employees can take their case to a tribunal. The main exclusions are:

- Employees who have not completed two years' continuous employment;
- Employees who have reached the normal retiring age;
- Employees engaged under fixed-term contracts who have signed away their rights to take an action for unfair dismissal.

There used to be no general access to tribunals for employees who worked less than 16 hours a week (or eight hours or more if they had worked for five years) with regard to unfair dismissal and/or redundancy claims. However, the Equal Opportunities Commission successfully persuaded the House of Lords in 1994 to make a declaration that this was sex-discriminatory and in contravention of the Treaty of Rome.[2] As the decision was simply a 'declaration' of how the Lords viewed the law, the domestic legislation needs amending to give full effect to their view. The declaration did though have immediate effect with regard to the public sector. Subsequently, the two year service requirement has been challenged on the basis that it is sex-discriminatory. At the time of writing, people dismissed between 1985 and 1991 may be able to bring a claim on that basis, but not those dismissed since 1991. The legal developments in this area need to be monitored in case the two year rule changes further with regard to dismissals.[3]

Applicants have to apply to a tribunal within three months of their dismissal (unless there are exceptional circumstances). The length of service requirement does not apply to applicants who maintain they were dismissed on account of their sex, race or activity as a trade union or health and safety representative, or because they took necessary steps to protect themselves or others from immediate physical danger. Employers are also required to observe the statutory procedures regarding consultation with recognised trade unions in the event of redundancy, regardless of the length of service of employees. Additionally, the two year requirement does not apply in unfair dismissal claims arising out of transfers of undertakings.[4]

Remedies

Employers are still, of course, able to dismiss – the application for unfair dismissal is made only after the employee has been given notice or dismissed. Normally any tribunal hearing will only take place some months after a dismissal has actually taken place. Industrial tribunals are obliged to consider reinstatement (or re-engagement) as a remedy if an application alleging unfair dismissal is upheld, but this can only be recommended and not enforced. Although tribunals can award extra compensation if a recommendation to reinstate is resisted by the employer, the normal remedy is financial compensation and not reinstatement. (In 1993/4 only 1.2 per cent of successful applications resulted in an award of re-instatement or re-engagement.) Financial compensation takes the form of a *basic* award, equivalent to a person's statutory redundancy entitlement and, if appropriate, a *compensatory* award to cover other loss. There is also provision for a *special* award for people unfairly dismissed because of trade union or health and safety activity.

With both the basic and compensatory awards there are upper limits on the earnings for which damages can be awarded. At the time of writing, the earnings limit set is £210 per week with an overall maximum for the compensatory award of £11,000.

Additionally, there is a limit of 30 weeks' earnings for the basic award. The earnings cap and the maximum figure for compensatory awards are reviewed from time to time. However, in cases of sex or race discrimination there is no limit on compensatory awards following successful claims in both the public and private sectors that this was in contravention of European law. The average (median) compensation awarded by tribunals in 1993/4 was £2,773.[5] In redundancy situations there can also be a claim for a protective award, with regard to an employer's failure to consult, for the full salary for the period for which the employer was in breach of the statutory duty to consult.

Employers also have to consider the industrial repercussions of a dismissal. Irrespective of whether a tribunal judges a dismissal to be fair or unfair or, irrespective of whether a tribunal even hears a case, sanctions may be applied by the remaining workers to try to secure the reinstatement of a colleague. Changed economic circumstances and access to tribunals have greatly reduced industrial action about dismissal though.

Defences by the employer and the operation of industrial tribunals

In considering whether or not an employer has acted reasonably, a tribunal has to judge the employer's behaviour on the evidence available at the time. Even if evidence available after the dismissal (and any internal appeal hearing) proves that the employer was wrong, the dismissal may still have been 'reasonable'. However, in some circumstances the employer may have more latitude. An employer who had acquitted an employee for misappropriation of petrol subsequently successfully dismissed him using the evidence of a subsequent prosecution concerning the same incident.[6] Reasonableness is looked at from the *employer's* point of view and not the employee's, although a reasonable employer would be expected to take the employee's interests into account.[7] In some cases, where employer's have suffered losses and been unable to identify the culprit, their action in dismissing those who could have been responsible have been upheld.[8] Much will depend on the circumstances in such cases, but this emphasises the point that it is the *employer's* reasonableness that is the issue. In defining 'reasonable behaviour' it is necessary to consider what a reasonable (not a perfect) employer might have done, the size and administrative resources of the employer, how genuine the belief was, the basis for the belief and the norms in an industry. Tribunals are obliged to accept that there can be a number of different ways of handling a situation, all of which can be regarded as reasonable. An employer's judgement does not necessarily have to coincide with the judgement that the tribunal members would have made in the same situation for it to be regarded as reasonable. The employer's behaviour needs to be 'within the range of reasonable options'.

Regard has to be paid to the procedure that an employer has followed in dismissing an employee. The Code of Practice on Disciplinary and Dismissal Procedures issued by the Advisory, Conciliation and Arbitration Service (ACAS) provides the guidelines that employers are expected to follow. These guidelines are rather like the Highway Code – a breach in itself is not actionable, but in the circumstances of a dismissal a breach of the guidelines can lead to an application for unfair dismissal succeeding. The importance of following an appropriate procedure was heightened by the House of Lords decision in the case of *Polkey v. A. E. Dayton Ltd* (1987).[9] This ended the practice of justifying dismissals by arguing that had the procedure been followed it would have made 'no difference' and emphasised the statutory right of employees to a fair procedure. Consequently, although the specific circumstances of dismissal can be important, procedural failings are more likely to lead to a verdict of unfair dismissal at tribunal hearings. The 'no difference' concept can though be very relevant to the calculation of compensation. Also, as explained later, any compensation awarded to dismissed employees can be scaled down if their contributory behaviour warrants it.

Employers should have their own disciplinary procedures and these should be the subject of consultation, but not necessarily agreement, with any recognised trade unions. They need to follow the pattern recommended in the Code of Practice. The critical recommendations concerning procedures are reproduced as Appendix I of this chapter. The Code has now been incorporated in a general advisory handbook entitled *Discipline at Work* published by ACAS.[10] Though the rest of the handbook does not have the status of the Code, it is full of practical and useful advice that employers would be rash to ignore. Employers have a statutory duty to notify employees of the disciplinary procedure and if they employ twenty or more people the procedure needs to be in writing. However the disciplinary (and grievance) procedure does not have to form part of the contract.[11] A practical effect of making it part of the contract is that employees who have been dismissed can argue that a dismissal that has short-circuited the disciplinary procedure amounts to breach of contract and claim earnings for the period it would have taken for their case to have been heard.[12]

Industrial tribunals have three members – a person drawn from a panel submitted by employers' organisations (mainly the CBI), one from a panel submitted by trade union organisations (mainly the TUC) and a lawyer who acts as chair. In some circumstances, when the issue is essentially a point of law, there is provision for the chair to sit alone. Appeals can be made against tribunal decisions, but only on points of law. The tribunals have proved to be more formal and legalistic than was originally intended. This was almost an inevitable development, given the right of appeal through the legal system against the decisions of industrial tribunals. The rising case load regarding unfair dismissal in particular and the continuing extension of the jurisdiction of tribunals in other areas of employment law has also significantly increased the time before cases are heard. The volume of case law has contributed to the increased use of lawyers. Applicants are not allowed to apply for legal aid at tribunals – although they can apply for aid with regard to case preparation and appeals to the Employment Appeals Tribunal. The complexity of many cases is such that it is conceivable that, at some stage, legal aid will be extended to cover tribunal cases. Costs do not go 'with the action' as in other civil cases, but in some circumstances an award can be made against unsuccessful applicants. In some cases a preliminary hearing is held to determine whether a case is substantial enough or eligible to proceed to a full hearing. The main costs to an employer can be the time spent in defending a case and any fees paid to professional representatives. Former employees can be deterred by the formality and legal complexity, although if they have the services of a union representative they have free representation. A further issue though is the unlikelihood of them getting their job back, even if they win. Although the impact the law has had in improving organisations' disciplinary procedures has been constructive, it is not surprising that there have been some calls for reform of the way tribunals operate. One of the suggestions has been that the parties have the option of using arbitration, *instead* of going to a tribunal. Many employers are reluctant to use the arbitration process as, at present, if an applicant is unsuccessful at arbitration they can still go to a tribunal. The rising costs to the state of operating the tribunals has also been a matter of concern – estimated as being £27 million in 1994.[13]

The freedom of action of the employer to dismiss is often greatly underestimated. This may be because of misunderstandings about the legal position or because it may be a convenient alibi to maintain that the employer has much less discretion than is really the case. One of the common mistakes that is made is for people to confuse the burden of proof in civil actions before a tribunal with the burden in criminal cases. An employer does not have to establish their case 'beyond reasonable doubt', as is the case in criminal prosecutions. It is up to the tribunal to determine whether the onus of proof rests with the employer or former employee. Even so, the case has only to be established on the balance of probabilities. At the risk of oversimplifying the issue, it is useful to liken the burden of proof to being 95 per cent at a criminal case but only 51 per cent at an industrial tribunal. Of the 31.6 per cent of cases in 1993–4 that were not withdrawn, or that resulted in a conciliated cash settlement, 56 per cent were decided in favour of the employer.

Employers are more likely to be defending the defensible rather than the indefensible if they appear before a tribunal. The requirement for them to be 'reasonable' sets a maximum standard for behaviour as well as a minimum – they do not have to have acted perfectly. Any well-organised employer should, almost by definition, be able to have a much better track record at tribunals than the national average. Successful applications against the employer occur particularly in the less well-organised sectors of the economy where managerial resources are limited. A convenient rule of thumb is for an employer to expect to win four out of five cases. A lower success rate may indicate weaknesses that need attention. A very high success rate might raises the possibility that the employer is being too cautious. I am not suggesting that employers should be cavalier in their attitude to dismissal, but rather that it is in the nature of events that there will be occasional genuine differences of opinion between employers and tribunals. Employers can always consider reinstating if they lose a case at a tribunal. It is important to recognise that, if employers are seen to opt out of dismissing employees, unless the reasons are overwhelming, this can create a climate where nobody tries to tell anybody what to do, on the basis that nothing is likely to be done if the person refuses. The impact of decisions concerning dismissal needs to be seen in relation to the signals it is sending within an organisation and not in isolation, or just in terms of the track record at tribunals.

The need for effective procedure

The Achilles' heel of employers at tribunals often turns out to be their failure to follow a systematic procedure, even though there may be a clearly defined procedure within the organisation that the employer should follow. Individual managers may fail to deal with a disciplinary issue and then, when their frustration builds up, dismiss an employee in a moment of anger. The legal requirements are not so much aimed at preventing dismissal but at ensuring that, when it does take place, it is done for appropriate reasons and in a manner which preserves the rights of the individual concerned to natural justice. The guidelines in Appendix I do not seem too difficult to follow but, as with so many areas of management, the problem is one of application of existing knowledge rather than having some magic wand for dealing with problems. One particularly apt quote from a tribunal illustrates this point: 'Mr G did not on that occasion give the applicant a serious reprimand, although he did mention that he would kill him if such a thing occurred again.'[14]

The observance of appropriate procedures is not just a technical matter but one which can affect the actual decision that is taken. The decision to dismiss a person before they have, for example, had the opportunity to state their case is wrong, not just because it is a breach of justice but also because the fact-finding process is incomplete. However, employers also need to beware of over-compensating in this area and having procedures that are unduly elaborate. In some organisations, especially with some public sector employers, this has led to the procedures being too complex for many of their managers to handle. This in turn may lead to managers opting out of discipline and/or the organisation repeatedly losing tribunal cases because they have not kept to their self-imposed elaborate requirements.

Consideration may also need to be given to separate procedures for handling performance, sickness, or attendance problems that do not arise from any misconduct on the part of employees. There are, unfortunately, occasions when people can be trying their best but nevertheless still fail to meet minimum job standards. These, strictly speaking, are not disciplinary issues. In some organisations separate procedures are established to deal with such cases, whilst in others the cases are handled within the disciplinary procedure. Guidance on this and related issues is contained in the ACAS *Advisory Handbook.*

Sometimes employers try to circumvent the whole disciplinary process by putting so much pressure on an employee that they leave. One of the dangers of this approach, apart from its doubtful morality, is that a tribunal could treat a forced resignation as a constructive dismissal. This can happen if the pressure by the employer amounts to a breach of the employment contract. The particular problem that the employer then has is to explain what opportunity the former employee had to state their case before being forced out. Employers may also need to determine whether resignations given in anger are really intended as such. Relevant factors here can be the provocation and the psychological make-up of the employee.[15] Actions for constructive dismissal cannot be taken unless the employee has actually resigned.

It is not sufficient for employers to have good procedures; it is also necessary for their managers to have the skills to operate the procedures appropriately. This is necessary for the handling of all disciplinary cases, not just the small proportion that result in dismissal. Consequently, the skills involved in disciplinary handling are the next issue that needs to be considered.

THE RESPONSIBILITY OF THE INDIVIDUAL MANAGER

The first prerequisite for effective disciplinary handling is that managers accept their responsibility and discretion in this area. It is also important for them to encourage colleagues to do the same. There is a great temptation for subordinate managers to refer disciplinary matters upwards. It may be better to coach managers who do this to handle disciplinary situations for themselves, rather than take away their responsibility in this area.

Any form of action needs to be preceded by careful diagnosis. There can be many reasons for inappropriate behaviour, including an inaccurate definition of what is appropriate. It is only when the facts have been checked out that one can begin to consider if disciplinary action is appropriate. Even if a person has behaved inappropriately, it may be that they see this for themselves and do not need to have salt rubbed in their wounds. This was the judgement made in one chemical works when a technician wrecked a particularly expensive piece of equipment. The manager concerned took the view that that was one mistake the technician would never make again. However, sometimes employees do need to have the error of their ways pointed out to them – either because they do not realise that they are in error or because they think that they can behave in a particular way with impunity.

Having established just who has the proper responsibility for dealing with such situations, it is important to stress that reform might as well be achieved with the minimum amount of pressure that is required to bring about the desired change in behaviour. If a quiet word will do the trick, there is little point in antagonising employees by using more pressure than is necessary. The oral warning may be the most important level in the disciplinary process. It may be convenient for people to argue that the only sanction is dismissal, but the reality is that most people do not like being corrected and that, psychologically, the oral warning is a sanction that managers may find they can use effectively. Only if this does not lead to the required change in behaviour does a manager need to consider more formal measures.

The introduction of the law to protect employees against unfair dismissal has tended to concentrate attention on issues related to dismissal. Discipline, however, as explained in the Introduction to this chapter, is a generic term and dismissal is just one aspect of the disciplinary process. Ideally, policies and practices should be such that disciplinary issues are contained, so that it is rare for a dismissal to be necessary. If there is effective supervisory and managerial control, issues should be so contained. If this is not the case, too many issues may be allowed to spiral upwards before being dealt with. The main volume of activity should be at the lower levels (see Figure 11.1).

A heavy emphasis on severe penalties may be indicative of ineffective control at the lower levels of the pyramid. This can happen all too frequently and what can emerge is that 'disciplinary problems' are a symptom of much deeper organisational problems, such as the lack of effective supervision and management. Contributory factors to this can be a general opting out of the management process and poor selection and training of supervisors

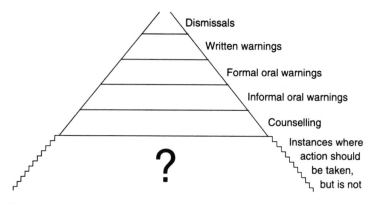

Figure 11.1 The disciplinary pyramid

and managers. Sometimes supervisors see themselves either as not having any disciplinary responsibility at all or are extremely vague about just what those responsibilities are. The area where greatest organisational attention and clarification is often needed is the responsibility for investigation and follow-up of minor issues and the administering, where appropriate, of low-level penalties. This involves not just the drawing up of a clear procedure but also the training of supervisors and managers in how to handle their responsibilities. If these steps are not taken one is likely to have supervisors and managers intervening and getting it wrong or getting away with the potentially disastrous attitude that disciplinary control of their own subordinates is nothing to do with them but is some other mysterious person's responsibility! It may also be necessary for an employer to dispel myths about the operation of the disciplinary process. In one health authority where I was involved it was a generally held belief that there was no point in taking disciplinary action against employees because such action would only be reversed on appeal. On investigation it emerged that in the previous 12 months of the 10 internal appeals against dismissal nine had failed and the one that had been allowed was generally felt to be the correction of an inappropriate previous decision. This simple statistic had not previously been established and the myth was what people believed, not the reality. People may actually want to believe such myths, which is why it may be necessary to communicate what really does happen, as opposed to what people may prefer to think happens.

DISCIPLINARY PROCEDURES AND PROCEDURAL SKILLS

When formal disciplinary proceedings appear to be appropriate, it is necessary for managers to refer to the disciplinary procedures which their organisations should have or, failing that, the guidelines contained in the ACAS Code of Practice. It may also be necessary to refer to any disciplinary rules that exist or the need for such rules.

Disciplinary hearings

Perhaps the most crucial of all the distinctions that need to be made is that between a disciplinary hearing and disciplinary action. A common failing, revealed by a Department of Employment survey, is for managers to assume that the outcome of proceedings is a foregone conclusion, and to 'sentence' the employee early in such proceedings.[16] The word 'hearing' is as important as the word 'disciplinary', and one cannot be sure that disciplinary action is appropriate until the hearing has been completed. A formal 'hearing' may not be necessary if relatively minor action is likely but, whatever the level of formality, it is important that the employee is given the opportunity to state their case before any action is taken. At a formal hearing it is appropriate for whoever is conducting it to recess before communicating any decision. This gives the chair time to consider the position carefully or, if a panel is involved, to consider any differences of view, before any action is determined. Even if an employee's conduct seems quite inexcusable, there will be occasions when it turns out that an issue was not as straightforward as it first appeared. In any case, justice needs to be seen to be done, not just for the benefit of the employee concerned but for their colleagues as well. Although these points are obvious enough, my own experience has often been in line with the evidence revealed in the Department of Employment survey. On one occasion I found that an employee was listened to carefully, only to be handed a letter of dismissal which must have been typed before the hearing started. On another occasion an employee was asked to sit outside the room to await the decision of a disciplinary panel and was then given a letter of dismissal, which could have been typed during the recess apart from the fact that it was dated a week previously!

Suspension

A predicament which employers can face is behaviour by an employee which necessitates them leaving the employer's premises immediately. This could be for a variety of reasons, including fighting, apparent drunkenness or apparent theft. The appropriate course of action in such situations is to suspend the employee on pay pending an investigation. Even if it appears that the employee has committed gross misconduct, which justifies summary dismissal, such a decision should not be taken without there being a disciplinary hearing. If the case against an employee is established at a hearing, then dismissal may be given without notice from that point of time. If there is no such hearing, the employer will have fallen into the trap of pre-judging the issue. Apart from giving an employee time to prepare their case, an interval between an incident and a decision can lead to a cooling of tempers all round and increase the prospects of a rational decision. This type of suspension is quite distinct from suspension without pay, which is sometimes used as a penalty after a hearing has been completed. The distinction may need to be made to employees who are being suspended, together with an explanation that nothing is decided until the hearing is completed and that there is no loss of pay involved. The important point is that managers faced with the problem of needing to get somebody off the premises immediately should do this by paid suspension and not instant dismissal.

Relationship with criminal law

A further source of confusion can arise if a person has apparently committed a criminal action. It is a fallacy to assume that such action can only be handled by the police. If, for example, a person has apparently stolen something, it may be appropriate for the employer to institute disciplinary proceedings about the employee's apparent unauthorised possession of property belonging to the employer. Any decisions about whether or not there should be a prosecution should be handled separately. The option of letting such an issue be handled simply by the police may not be as easy as it seems. As has already been explained, the burden of proof in criminal law is much higher than in civil law. The procedural rules are much tighter in the criminal courts and it may be necessary to establish that a felony was committed or attempted. Added to this is the problem that, if no action is taken pending a court hearing, an employee may have to be suspended on pay for several months. In any case, the employer may find that, if the case is substantiated, the primary remedy they want is to be able to dismiss the person concerned. The point that needs stressing is that apparent criminal activity by an employee against their employer does not remove the employer's rights to handle an issue as a disciplinary matter.

An interesting illustration of the perils for the employer of relying solely on the prosecution route was the case of Clive Ponting, a former senior civil servant in the Ministry of Defence. He admitted having leaked information about British naval operations conducted during the Falklands War of 1982. Ponting was consequently charged under the Official Secrets Act but was able to convince the jury that, as the information was divulged only after the war was over and was, in his view, in the national interest, he should be acquitted. The government could still have initiated disciplinary proceedings after his acquittal in 1985 and pressed for dismissal on the grounds of misconduct – which would have been an easier procedural task. However, because this would probably have been seen as a case of 'sour grapes' on the part of the government, it could have been very counter-productive politically. As it was, Ponting saved the government further embarrassment by resigning.

Provided there is no specific procedural requirement that a prosecution should be resolved before disciplinary proceedings are taken, it is normally better for the employer to resolve the disciplinary issue in advance of a prosecution being resolved. Amongst other things, this avoids the dilemma of what to do if a person has already been acquitted in the criminal courts. Subsequent acquittal does not invalidate disciplinary action previously taken, because the disciplinary action should be based on the rather separate issue of the extent to which the employee, or ex-employee, fulfilled their employment contract. Documentation, including statements by those accused, may need to be prepared separately and to different standards in any subsequent criminal case.[17] People may raise the issue of 'double jeopardy', unaware that this is a concept to do with the criminal law only. Whilst it is not possible for a person to be charged twice with the same offence under criminal law, there is no prohibition on an employer taking the civil action of terminating a person's employment irrespective of whether or not prosecution is initiated based on the circumstances that led to the person's dismissal. Employers though may want to carefully consider the timing of any disciplinary action so that they do not jeopardise any covert police surveillance that is in progress.

The role of the representative

Another critical issue concerning disciplinary procedures is the need for an employee to be accompanied by a representative. Sometimes managers see this as a sign of weakness, but ignoring the right to representation is far more likely to create trouble than prevent it. Unless this facility is offered in formal disciplinary situations, it will be a breach of natural justice, the disciplinary procedure and the guidelines contained in the Code of Practice. The issue may then turn into the possibly larger issue of the right to representation and the role of any trade union that is involved. In any case, a representative's function is to help a person put their case so that any decision is taken only after all the relevant arguments have been considered. The representative may have heard only the employee's version of events. A formal hearing can provide an employer with the opportunity to put over their version. This may influence the representative, whose views may be crucial if an issue is sensitive and likely to lead to industrial action. If an employer has a good case, it is appropriate that it should be explained; if the case is weak, then perhaps it should be dropped. Often managers fail to realise that the really critical audience in disciplinary proceedings can be the employee's colleagues.

The position of the representative has also to be considered. They may well feel that, whatever an employee has done, they have the right to have their case argued strongly, even if privately the representative does not condone the employee's behaviour. At the end of a hearing at least the representative can explain that they have done what they can for the employee concerned. If the representative does not agree with the action that an employer eventually takes, at least any subsequent disagreement need not be compounded by arguments about whether the person had a fair hearing. The crucial distinction is that, whatever an employee has or has not done, this should not affect their right to a fair hearing. Care should be taken to ensure that employees know their procedural rights and it is preferable that they have a copy of any relevant disciplinary rules and procedures. Employers may want to consider restricting the rights of represention to colleagues or trade union officials. If there is no restriction they may find that an employee is accompanied by a lawyer who may introduce a greater level of formality and legalism into the proceedings than they wish to have.

The role of the chair

When formal disciplinary hearings are held, consideration should be given to one of the managers acting as chair. A manager obviously will not be viewed as a totally independent person, but proper chairing can help ensure that proceedings are conducted as impartially as possible. The chair should not have been directly involved in the case beforehand. One of the dangers of the senior manager present putting the case is that they may then be seen as judge, prosecutor, jury, executioner and possibly witness all rolled into one. A further problem is that, if the senior manager gets involved in an argument, which would not be surprising given such a load of conflicting roles, then it is difficult for anyone else to keep the proceedings in order. A more satisfactory procedure is for the senior manager to concentrate on chairing, leaving other people to present any case and evidence. This is not only necessary for form's sake but to see that the proceedings are conducted in a systematic manner, so that no decision is taken until the arguments have all been properly considered. This role of chair should continue during a recess. Consideration also has to be given as to who should participate in the discussions during the recess. Managers who have been involved in presenting the case against an employee are best excluded from any further involvement. This is in order to reduce the possibility of collusion between those playing the roles of 'judge' and 'prosecutor'.

Procedure during a hearing

Perhaps the most awkward part of the whole disciplinary process is handling disagreements either about what happened or about what action should be taken. It is a fallacy that management is impotent unless an employee agrees to be disciplined, or that irrefutable proof has to be produced to substantiate any difference of opinion. The reality is that it is necessary for the managers carefully to hear and consider the relevant points and then to consider what action, if any, is appropriate. As with tribunals, the standard of proof, or the strictness of procedure, does not have to match criminal proceedings. The parties are in fact considering a civil issue – concerning the degree to which an employee has fulfilled their contract of employment – and not a criminal trial. However, for proceedings to be handled effectively, a clear and preferably agreed sequence of events needs to be established. This should include arrangements for the exchange of any written documents and explanations of when each side should state their case, produce witnesses, cross-examine and sum up. The framework is essentially judicial but sometimes the parties can mistakenly adopt a negotiating approach. If that happens, proceedings can degenerate into an unsystematic attempt by each side to browbeat the other, which can aggravate an already delicate situation instead of defusing it. The chair will also need to be aware of one or other party trying to take over the chair's role by, for example, giving procedural rulings (as opposed to raising points for the chair to rule on). Other dangers are the use of leading questions to the party's own witnesses and attempts to intimidate witnesses produced by the other side. An example of a procedural sequence that will help a chair maintain control and facilitate a systematic hearing is given in Appendix II.

When any decision is communicated it is imperative that there should be no argument – if proceedings have been properly conducted all the relevant points should already have been considered anyway. If an employee disagrees with the decision, the appropriate way of handling that is to explain any rights of appeal. Often violent arguments can break out at this stage simply because it is not made clear to an employee that there is an appeals procedure that they are entitled to use.

Preparation and presentation

Managerial representatives presenting a case also need to prepare carefully beforehand. A person's guilt may be self-evident, but the whole point of a quasi-judicial hearing is to enable the person or people sitting in judgement to decide solely on the basis of the evidence and argument that is openly presented. Consequently, patient work has to be undertaken in developing logical arguments and collecting relevant evidence. Consideration also has to be given to the presentational skills involved. All this is particularly important, as the skills of advocacy are often much more part of the 'stock in trade' of union representatives than of managers. This means that if managers fail to do their homework they may needlessly lose cases, and their confidence. Some of the basic issues concerning preparation and presentation are listed below.

Preparation
- Select charge(s) carefully (pick the important one or ones you can sustain and don't use a scatter-gun approach);
- Copy documents to the chair and employee's representative;
- Organise witnesses.

Presentation
- Use an *aide-memoire* if it helps;
- Speak clearly and to the chair or panel (you have to convince them rather than the opposing party);
- Use logical argument and avoid 'purple prose';
- Identify and see if you can destroy the main argument in your opponent's case – if you can do that the rest of the issues may fall into place;
- Be assertive, not aggressive, and show conviction in your case;
- Do not let yourself get riled by the other side;
- Ask one question at a time;
- Beware of asking questions to which you do not know the answer;
- 'Ride the bumps', i.e., keep cool if under pressure.[18]

Communicating the result

Before any decision is taken after a hearing there needs to be a careful review of the options and of the need to communicate accurately what has been decided. The options include stating that the employee has been cleared. In cases of cumulative misconduct it is appropriate to step up the pressure on an employee gradually, so that they either mend their ways or are made perfectly aware that failure to change their ways will result in more serious action next time. Care needs to be taken in deciding just what a person is to be warned about. If the grounds of the warning are narrow, for lateness for example, an employee may be able to maintain that their lateness record cannot be taken into account if they are subsequently disciplined for absence. Thus it may be appropriate to broaden the base of a warning from lateness to general attendance. Warnings about other matters may need to include a proviso that repetition of a particular action or related misconduct can result in further disciplinary action. Too narrow a definition of what the warning is about can lead to the possibility of a person getting a number of 'final' warnings, all for different offences.

Consideration also needs to be given as to whether or not there should be automatic time limits for any penalties imposed. These are recommended in the ACAS *Advisory Handbook*.[19] However, one needs to beware of the rigidities that specific time limits can create. Holidays, sickness, staff changes and other work commitments can cause procedural delays and cause a warning to be 'spent' before it can be used as a platform for further disciplinary action. If fixed time limits are not used, consideration will have to be given when a penalty is imposed as to how long it is reasonable to take into account previous warnings. It is also necessary to consider just what previous warnings can be taken into account. One union representative I discussed this with made the reasonable point that informal oral warnings should not be part of a person's record because that contradicted the concept of informality. The concept of a person receiving a copy of a formal oral warning may also be contentious. The most appropriate step in the early stages of discipline could be from informal oral warning to first written warning, with only the latter going on a person's record. A manager may, however, find it useful to keep a diary noting any informal oral warnings.

It may be necessary to put the first formal warning in writing, not just to create procedural clarity, but also to ensure that a person realises what is happening. It is all too easy for disciplinary interviews to be handled with so light a touch that a person comes away with the impression that they have been commended rather than rebuked. Ambiguities and carelessness in communicating just what has happened, as a consequence of a disciplinary hearing, can result not only in failure to achieve the desired effect but also in confrontation, if a person is disciplined again, about what really was decided the last time. The representative of an employee should be given a copy of any written warning so that it is also clear to them what has happened. This may also help to prevent subsequent argument about whether or not an employee has received their copy. A further way of avoiding argument on that score may be to ask an employee to acknowledge receipt of a warning, making it clear that this is only an acknowledgement, and not meant to commit the employee either to agreeing or to disagreeing with a written warning. The importance and number of points to be considered in drafting written warnings is such that a checklist of the potential issues is necessary. Such a checklist is produced as Appendix III to this chapter.

Appeals

Thought has to be given to the stage at which appeals can be lodged. It may not be necessary to provide for appeals against informal warnings, for example, especially as an employee can always use the grievance procedure if there is no formal procedure for handling appeals against minor penalties. It would seem appropriate, though, to build an appeals procedure into a disciplinary procedure when warnings get to the stage of indicating that dismissal is becoming a possibility. Appeals should be to managers not previously involved in the case. The grounds for an appeal should be clarified – they should not involve a total re-hearing of a case unless that is clearly appropriate. One set of circumstances that may be appropriate for a re-hearing, though, is where procedural defects occurred at the initial hearing.[20] If, however, an appeal is just against the disciplinary action that has been imposed, for example, it is just the level of 'penalty' that needs to be considered. Another important issue concerns the admissibility of fresh evidence by either party. If it is relevant to the original charge it must be taken into account with internal appeals.[21] An employee's right of appeal should always be made clear, regardless of whether or not they argue about the decision when they are told about it. Time limits need to be imposed, so that if an appeal is not lodged within a certain period of time it lapses. This can avoid subsequent disagreement about whether or not the employee accepted the decision. It may also be appropriate to specify the time within which appeals are to be heard. In cases where employees are dismissed, consideration also has to be given as to whether or not they stay on the payroll pending the hearing of their appeal. A danger of keeping people on the payroll pending appeal is that some people may appeal simply as a means of securing further payment.

CONCLUSION

If managers are prepared to accept that they have a responsibility for discipline, much can be done to give them the necessary support to handle this aspect of their jobs effectively. Clear objectives and policies are necessary, as are clear procedures and rules. If appeals are upheld – either internally or at an industrial tribunal – it is important that employers do not engage in 'witch-hunting' exercises. If there are lessons to be learned from appeal decisions, it is best that these be quietly noted and applied rather than being used to castigate the parties concerned. 'Witch-hunting' may cause the rest of the managers to adopt a low profile and to opt out of the disciplinary process.

In giving an appropriate lead to subordinate managers, senior managers may need to dispel the myth that the immediate boss is powerless unless they have complete authority to dismiss subordinates. There are points on the spectrum between no authority and total authority. The right to institute disciplinary proceedings and, if necessary, to recommend dismissal, can be a powerful sanction that also brings with it an element of protection for the immediate boss. If they have the right to recommend, rather than decide, it removes the danger of dismissal being seen as motivated simply by personality factors. It also means that, if a decision is subsequently reversed or criticised, then the immediate boss can point out that the decision was taken or endorsed by their superiors.

Much can be done by way of coaching and formal training to develop the skills of managers in this area. I am much more optimistic about the ability of managers to benefit by training in this area than in the rather more complex area of appraisal interviewing. If managers have the will to accept the disciplinary aspect of their jobs, it is not too difficult to get across the basic concept that, whatever an employee appears to have done, they are entitled to a fair hearing. I have found in running internal company courses that, after about a day and a half using closed-circuit television, managers can develop from a level of farce to one of considerable competence in handling disciplinary issues. There is the further advantage that in this way people can constructively learn from their mistakes instead of making them for real in a sensitive situation. The manager who stays out of this area or who never has the process explained to them is never going to learn. Exposure to the skills involved in handling disciplinary issues, whether for real or in training sessions, or both, gives the manager the chance to develop their skills and to realise that the processes are not that complicated. This, in turn, may give them the confidence to handle issues that they previously chose to ignore. A positive approach to this area will not resolve all problems – there will, for example, always be some behaviour that cannot be changed and some people who master the art of operating always just within the limits of any rules. However, positive action can lead to many problems being contained by timely intervention, so that standards of performance are achieved rather than undermined by managers opting out of their responsibilities.[22]

NOTES

1 *Commission of the European Communities v UK* [1994] IRLR, *Industrial Relations Law Reports*, 421, ECJ.
2 *Equal Opportunities Commission v Secretary of State for Employment* [1994] All ER 910, H of L.
3 *R v Secretary of Employment ex parte Seymour, Smith and Perez, The Times*, 3 August 1995, Court of Appeal Judgment, 31 July 1995.
4 *Milligan and Another v Securicor Cleaning Ltd*; EAT/918/94, *People Management*, 29 June 1995, p. 47.
5 See 'Industrial and Appeal Tribunal Statistics, 1992–93, 1993–94', *Employment Gazette*, HMSO, October 1994, pp. 367–71.
6 *British Gas plc v McGarrick* [1991] IRLR 305, CA.
7 *Chubb Fire Security Ltd. v Harper* [1984] IRLR 311, EAT.
8 *Monie v Coral Racing* [1980] IRLR 464 CA, and *Whitbread and Co plc v Thomas* [1988] IRLR 43, EAT.
9 *Polkey v A. E. Dayton Services Ltd*, 1987, IRL 503, H of L.
10 Advisory, Conciliation and Arbitration Service, *Discipline at Work, The ACAS Advisory Handbook*, ACAS, 1987.
11 See Olga Aikin, 'Particular Requirements', *Personnel Management*, August 1993, p. 57.
12 *Gunton v Richmond-upon-Thames London Borough Council* [1980] ICR 755, IRLR 321, CA.
13 'Ministers Aim to Streamline Workers' Rights', *Independent*, 15 December 1994.
14 Incomes Data Services, *Brief 99*, December 1976, p. 13.
15 See *Kwik-Fit (GB) Ltd. v Lineham* [1992] IRLR 156, EAT.
16 Department of Employment, *Manpower Paper No. 14*, HMSO, 1975, para. 99, pp. 33–4.
17 Chris Hoad, 'Dealing With Dishonesty: The Best Policy', *Personnel Management*, February 1993, pp. 24–7.
18 For an excellent and detailed coverage of this topic see Keith Evans, *Advocacy at the Bar: A Beginner's Guide*, Financial Training Publications Ltd., 1983.

19 Advisory, Conciliation and Arbitration Service, *Discipline at Work*, p. 30.

20 *Whitbread and Company plc v Mills* [1988] ICR 716, EAT.

21 *West Midlands Co-operative Society v Tipton* [1986] ICR 192, H of L.

22 For a further account of this area, including specimen procedures, see Philip James and David Lewis, *Discipline*, Institute of Personnel and Development, 1992.

APPENDIX I TO CHAPTER 11: GUIDELINES ON DISCIPLINARY PROCEDURES CONTAINED IN THE CODE OF PRACTICE

1 Management should ensure that fair and effective arrangements exist for dealing with disciplinary matters. These should be agreed with employee representatives or trade unions concerned and should provide for full and speedy consideration by management of all the relevant facts. There should be a formal procedure except in very small establishments where there is close personal contact between the employer and his employees.

2 Management should make known to each employee:
   i) Its disciplinary rules and the agreed procedure;
   ii) The type of circumstances which can lead to suspension or dismissal.

3 The procedure should be in writing and should:
   i) Specify who has the authority to take various forms of disciplinary action, and ensure that supervisors do not have the power to dismiss without reference to more senior management;
   ii) Give the employee the opportunity to state his case and the right to be accompanied by his employee representative;
   iii) Provide for a right of appeal, wherever applicable, to a level of management not previously involved;
   iv) Provide for independent arbitration if the parties to the procedure wish it.

4 Where there has been misconduct, the disciplinary action to be taken will depend on the circumstances, including the nature of the misconduct. But normally the procedure should operate as follows:
   i) The first step should be an oral warning or, in the case of more serious misconduct, a written warning setting out the circumstances;
   ii) No employee should be dismissed for a first breach of discipline except in the case of gross misconduct;
   iii) Action on any further misconduct, for example final warning, suspension without pay or dismissal, should be recorded in writing;
   iv) Details of any disciplinary action should be given in writing to the employee and, if he so wishes, to his employee representative;
   v) No disciplinary action should be taken against a shop steward until the circumstances of the case have been discussed with a full-time official of the union concerned.

APPENDIX II TO CHAPTER 11: EXAMPLE OF PROCEDURAL SEQUENCE AT A DISCIPLINARY HEARING

1 Introduction by chair
  Explanation of charge
  Explanation of sequence of hearing
2 Presentation of case against the employee by the appropriate line manager
  Management witnesses
  Cross-examination of management witnesses
3 Union presentation and response to management submission
  Union witnesses
  Cross-examination of union witnesses
4 Further points by management
  Further points by union
  Further questions by chair/panel
5 Summing up by line manager
  Summing up by union representative
6 Recess
7 Decision – orally and/or in writing later

APPENDIX III TO CHAPTER 11: CHECKLIST FOR DISCIPLINARY LETTERS

1 Requesting attendance at hearing

Item	*Comments*
Specify charges.	The charges are allegations. They may or may not be proved as a result of the hearing.
Suggest the employee brings a representative if they wish, and witnesses if appropriate.	If a representative comes it gives you the opportunity to put your case over to the representative.
Refer to the disciplinary procedure.	The employee should have a copy. If there is doubt enclose a copy.
Indicate that disciplinary action could be imposed according to the result of the hearing.	

2 Disciplinary letter (given after the hearing)

State what disciplinary action, if any, is to be taken.	
State the nature of the offence(s).	You may wish to incorporate general terms, such as misconduct, in any warning letter. This may make it easier in the future to refer back to earlier offences. Alternatively, you may warn an employee about future conduct and any repetition or related offence may/will render them liable to further action.
Specify any conditions about future conduct. This may include any help you are prepared to give.	
Specify any time limits.	Sometimes procedures provide for warnings to lapse after a certain period of good behaviour. If you do not have to put in time limits it may be best not to – they can be rather rigid.
Specify an appeal procedure. Also the time limit for invoking the appeal procedure.	The more serious the penalty the more important it is to give a person the right of appeal.

APPENDIX III TO CHAPTER 11: CHECKLIST FOR DISCIPLINARY LETTERS *(cont.,)*

State if you want the employee to:

i) Acknowledge receipt of the letter;
ii) Register dissent about any part of the letter they consider to be inaccurate.

If suspension is involved, state if it is with or without pay.

If suspension is without pay, check you have the legal right to do this.

Send a copy of the letter to the person's representative. Also to any managers concerned.

Chapter 12

The manager and employee relations

INTRODUCTION

In the previous chapter consideration was given to the role of the trade union representative in disciplinary situations. Some attention was also given to the issue of employee representation in Chapter 7 in the context of payment systems. The pressures for cost and staff reduction in organisations were examined in Chapter 3. Key factors causing pressures for ever higher levels of performance were identified as being intensified competition, including that caused by globalisation, developments in information technology and restrictions on public sector funding. In this chapter attention is given to further aspects of employee relations. The term 'employee relations' has been used rather than the narrower one of 'industrial relations' which implies just dealing with issues on a collective basis. The term employee relations is generic and covers individual employer–employee relationships as well as collective relationships.

The potentially different perspectives of management and unions (and/or individuals) are examined in this chapter. Key issues for management are the reduction of labour costs, organisational change and the introduction of new technology. The responsibilities and accompanying skills of the individual line manager are examined in the context of what is happening internally within organisations and externally in terms of the labour market and domestic and European law. Changes in the labour market have not only greatly reduced trade union bargaining strength but also the power of individuals to sell their skills. The loss of collective union power has been reinforced by the significant reductions in their legal immunities under domestic law regarding industrial action. The general lack of union bargaining power has encouraged unions and individuals to examine their legal rights as a means of protection. These rights have been given a boost by developments in European law.

Much of the thrust of organisational change in both the private and public sectors has been to increase the responsibility of local management, as budget holders, for pay, working arrangements and levels of performance. The trend has been reinforced when management strategies have led to the greater integration of personnel management and corporate activity. Such developments have also often involved the reduction in the role (or even elimination) of centralised personnel departments. The generally increased responsibility of line managers in the employee relations area has made it imperative that they develop the appropriate skills to handle any new responsibilities.

The sophisticated diagnostic skills that may be required by managers in the employee relations area are examined in this chapter. Often problems can be created as a side-effect of decisions taken elsewhere in an organisation which, on the face of it, have nothing to do with employee relations. Consequently, a 'systems' approach is necessary to consider problems in the context of the organisation as a whole. The likelihood of conflicts of interests between managers and employees is examined, as is the nature of union organisations. Procedural skills are examined in the context of joint agreements and procedures. The issue of supervisory control is also covered because of its potential importance. Special consideration is given to negotiating skills. These skills may be just as relevant in the context of other types of negotiation – for example, in commercial situations. Finally, the issue of the manager as a trade union member is considered, including the case for joining one and the potential role conflicts for the manager if the union also contains subordinate staff.

OBJECTIVES IN EMPLOYEE RELATIONS

The primary aim of managers in the employee relations area is likely to be to obtain the co-operation of their subordinates in achieving organisational objectives. It is just as well to specify what those objectives are likely to be:

- Cost-effective performance (resulting in low unit labour costs)
- Control of change

- The avoidance of stoppages and other sanctions

The pursuit of these objectives needs to be balanced as they may conflict with one another. This can also be the case with the objectives of trade unions (and/or individual employees) which are likely to be:

- The maintenance and if possible improvement of the terms and conditions of employment
- Job security
- Control of change
- The avoidance of stoppages and other sanctions

The terms under which people work are negotiated either individually or between union representatives and the employer. The negotiated agreements represent a balance which provides sufficient incentive for both parties to come together. The parties will, however, take a continuing interest in the extent to which their concerns are being met. This may be done quite amicably – the resolution of areas of conflict through negotiation does not mean that sanctions have to be applied. Often the term 'conflict' is used in an industrial context synonymously with 'strike', ignoring the point that the application of sanctions is a way of trying to resolve conflict only when negotiations have broken down.

It follows from the above analysis that one has to be wary of the term 'good employee relations' as that begs the question 'good from whose point of view?'. Each party will need to assess success according to whether or not they have adequately achieved their objectives. There can be 'win–win' situations when, for example, an organisation is flourishing, wages are generous and there is job security. However, there will be occasions when this is not possible and one needs to beware of adopting an unrealistic unitarist view of organisations which ignores the potential for genuine conflicts of interests. This issue was examined in Chapter 2 and is examined in further detail later in this chapter.

EMPLOYEE RELATIONS IN THE CONTEXT OF THE ORGANISATION

Despite the trend to generally greater devolution of authority for employee relations, responsibility for it is likely to be distributed within an organisation by means of the personnel department, if it exists as a separate function. The involvement of a personnel department is often necessary to ensure that decisions form an integrated pattern and not a set of conflicting precedents. However, the individual manager is bound to have some, and often increasing, responsibility within this framework. Even if all the financial and other formal agreements are determined outside their department, line managers have, as a minimum, to control labour costs and standards of performance.

Despite, or partly because of, the greater devolution of authority to local management, there has been a tendency to integrate employee relations activity more closely with other organisational activity. When union power was strong the role of personnel departments was often to act as 'trouble shooters' and to act in an executive role, leaving line management to concentrate on production and/or service delivery. This could have the effect of detaching policy in this area from policy decisions elsewhere. This tendency was reinforced by national bargaining and membership of employers' associations. Other changes in the role of the personnel department have been a reduced emphasis on recruitment, because of the generally greater retention and availability of staff, and the increased volume of employment law emanating from Europe. The increased involvement of line management in many human resource management strategies has been another reason for a changed pattern of personnel management activity.

The term 'human resource management' (HRM), is subject to a variety of interpretations. It is sometimes sub-divided into hard (quantifiable) and soft (intangible – but often important) areas. The use of the term is often no more than an attempt to sound fashionable by renaming existing but unaltered personnel management activities. However, it can involve a genuine attempt to integrate the various aspects of personnel (or human resource) management with one another as well as with corporate and other policy decision-making. The need to integrate the training and development area with corporate developments was explained in Chapter 10. The need to take account of the human resource dimension in corporate policy and initiatives such as TQM was explained in Chapter 3. The clarification of organisational policy and objectives by devices such as mission statements and performance indicators may be a necessary part of this process of integration. Aspects of strategic human resource management that have clear employee relations implications include the need for cost-effective performance, the reorganisation of work and jobs and attempts to increase organisational commitment. There will also be employee relations implications in attempts to change organisational culture and to increase the amount of direct communication between employers and employees. Strategic human resource management is often part of the management philosophy and practice particularly of Japanese and North American companies who have inwardly invested in the UK. Competition and the increased pace of change are also pressures for such policies. Some critics argue that the concept is 'unitarist' and that it ignores the potential conflict of interests between employers and employees. However, sound strategies take account of such potential conflicts. Inevitably, strategic human resource management requires the close involvement of senior management and it is a process that is essentially driven by line management. How-ever, the important point regarding such initiatives is whether or not they are taken and how effective they are, not whether they are labelled 'personnel management' or 'human resource management'.[1]

Another way of analysing the changed shape of employee relations activity is to consider the greater cost pressures on organisations. When financing was less of a problem in both the private and public sectors increased costs could be more easily passed on to the consumer or central government. However, pressures for cost control and cost reduction are now forcing employers increasingly to examine their labour costs and to search for ways in which they can be reduced. Sometimes this is necessary for organisational survival. Consequently, employers are less likely to respond passively to union wage claims by agreeing to an annual pay rise roughly in line with inflation. They are more likely to come up with suggestions for reorganising work on a more cost-effective basis and the review of existing contractual arrangements. In some cases the search for savings has led to actual wage reductions and also the suspension or elimination of incremental scales for salaried staff. Another development has been that in some organisations newcomers are employed on less favourable rates and/or conditions of employment than existing employees. All this involves a much more pro-active approach by employers with employee relations policies being linked to clear organisational policies for cost reduction. Employers are more able to do this because of the great changes in the labour market which will be examined next.

CHANGES IN THE LABOUR MARKET

Since the 1960s the labour market in many Western countries, including the UK, steadily changed from being a seller's to a buyer's market. Unemployment levels in the UK in the early 1960s were at about half a million people and much of that was 'frictional' unemployment. This steadily rose and in both 1986 and 1987 the level of unemployment was three and a quarter million people (11.8 per cent of the work-force).[2] Since then the figure has fallen and in June 1995 the seasonally adjusted figure was 2.3 million people (8.3 per cent of the work-force).[3] However, whilst most of the fall is genuine, it also has to be taken into account that the method of calculating the figures has been successively altered. According to a study undertaken by the Royal Statistical Society into the jobless in 1994, there were 150,000 more people seeking work than those recorded as being un-employed.[4] Also, many of the new jobs created are in the peripheral labour market and do not equate to the full-time jobs that they have replaced. There are a number of causes of a generally high level of unemployment that have affected economies throughout the West. These include structural economic change, the impact of new technology, excess productive capacity, the drift of jobs to countries where labour costs are cheaper and the relatively high levels of international interest rates. As the ability of individual governments to influence these events is limited, it seems unlikely that unemployment levels will alter significantly in the foreseeable future. The new market conditions have also created both the opportunity and the incentive to experiment with the new forms of employment arrangements outlined in the section on the flexible organisation in Chapter 3.

The labour market in the UK has also been affected by govern-ment policy. Successive Conservative governments have sought to 'free up' the labour market by a series of deregulatory measures. Examples include compulsory competitive tendering in the public sector (examined in Chapter 3), the abolition of Wages Councils in 1993 and the large privatisation programme, all of which have had a deregulatory effect. Devolution of authority within what has remained of the public sector has also enabled the government to distance itself from cuts in services and to attempt to distance itself from pay bargaining. The level of pay settlements in the public sector has, however, been indirectly but strongly affected by the level of funding. When the government has been indirectly involved in disputes such as in mining in 1984/5 or the signal-workers in 1994, employers have been encouraged to take a hard line. An avowed intention of government policy has been to encourage people to price themselves back into work and the above measures have been intended to do that by reducing the price of labour.

Given the scale of the above changes it is not surprising that the ability of individuals to sell their labour and union bargaining power has considerably diminished. '1993 saw the lowest number of work stoppages arising from industrial disputes ever recorded in the UK. And at 0.6 million, the number of working days lost was the second lowest on record.'[5] The threat or reality of redundancy has been a key factor undermining union bargaining power – particularly when employees have wanted to take advantage of generous voluntary severance schemes. It is these market changes, rather than the considerable reductions in trade union immunities which will be examined later in this chapter, that seem to have been the key to reduced individual and union bargaining power. The confrontations in the mining industry in 1984/5 and at Rupert Murdoch's News International were won because of the 'industrial muscle' of the employers and there was little use of the law by the employers in either dispute. Critical factors in the mining dispute were alternative forms of energy, government backing, the failure of the miners in key coalfields to support the strike and the lack of active support by the union movement generally. In the News International dispute the availability of an alternative labour force with more appropriate skills for the new high-technology plant that had been built and who were willing to be bussed into Wapping each day was crucial. The establishment of the company's own distribution service was also an important factor.

Despite the generally greatly reduced bargaining power of individuals and unions in the labour market, there have been limits to this process and some groups and individuals have even done well. Sometimes the proportion of labour costs as a fraction of total costs has shrunk so much that employers can afford to be generous to the remaining employees. Often the real wages of those who have kept their jobs in the private sector has risen, though they may have had to work rather harder for their money. There are always likely to be some geographical and specific skills shortages which will increase the bargaining power of individuals or groups. The incidence of skills shortages is exacerbated by the lack of training investment.

Some senior executives and directors have done particularly well despite the general state of the labour market. This can be because of the shortage of people with specific managerial skills and the value added to an organisation by having the best available talent. Sometimes, though, it may reflect the weakness of control by the owners of an organisation over its senior management. The size of the golden handshakes some directors receive, for example, has attracted comment. The Greenbury Committee was set up under the auspices of the CBI to consider the whole issue of directors' pay.[6] Its report, in 1995, concluded that there had been mistakes but that these had been in relation to share options rather than salary levels. It rejected the concept of statutory controls but proposed that a code of practice be established, with the sanction of de-listing from the Stock Exchange for those companies who did not follow the code. Other specific recommendations were that directors' remuneration committees consist only of non-executive directors, that there be full disclosure of remuneration packages to shareholders and that notice periods normally should be for a maximum of one year. How enthusiastically these suggestions are accepted and/or implemented remains to be seen, as does the public reaction to the outcome. This may lead to institutional shareholder pressure for greater control of directors' remuneration. There has been particular press and political comment about the remuneration packages for directors and senior executives in privatised utilities and whether the scale of the remuneration, particularly the size of share options, is always in line with market needs. An issue concerning share options in the utilities is that it creates a conflict for those holding them between their responsibilities to shareholders and consumers as, the higher the declared dividend the greater the gains on share options. A further issue is the monopolistic nature of the markets in which the utilities operate.

Industrial action can sometimes still be costly for the employer. The signalworkers' dispute with Railtrack in 1994 cost Railtrack and the other employers operating under the umbrella of British Rail a combined total of £200–£250 million in lost revenue and inflicted losses on industry estimated as being a further £300 million. Whilst the government was concerned about the impact of this dispute on the general level of settlements, the bargaining difference between the employers and employees was about a relatively small amount of money. Although one has to allow for the fact that the signalworkers had hoped to get a better deal than they achieved, the final settlement cost £10 million and a significant portion of that was for non-recurring 'one-off' payments. £7.6 million of the cost of the settlement was recouped by recurring productivity gains. These figures are crude estimates and different sources give different figures, but it is clear that the net cost of the trade-off of improved pay for changed working arrangements was little, if anything. Unfortunately, the loss in income and future trade is likely to have significant adverse repercussions for both the employers and employees in the whole of the industry.[7] Employers need to consider how they handle their bargaining power. As was explained in Chapter 6, if management are seeking to gain increased commitment from employees to enhance product quality and service delivery, this is not consistent with an abrasive management style. Consideration also has to be given to the way in which members of the peripheral work-force are treated.

Another important development in the labour market has been the growing importance of women. Although they are often concentrated in particular occupations and in low-paid and/or part-time jobs, they now account for nearly half the work-force. Social and legislative trends are such that they are likely to continue to break through 'glass ceilings' and acquire a greater share of senior positions as well as outnumbering employed men. Upward mobility is also likely to happen with members of ethnic minorities, particularly those who make good use of the educational system.

The impact of inward investment

Another aspect of the labour market that merits consideration is the impact of inward investment. The UK has been successful in attracting investment from a number of countries, particularly Japan and the USA. This has been for a number of reasons. One is the low level of wage costs in comparison with other European partners, particularly with regard to fringe benefits. Other reasons include the foreign exchange rate, language – i.e., the universality of English – government grants, the availability of greenfield sites and membership of the European Union. This investment has generated much-needed employment and foreign exchange earnings. The companies that have inwardly invested have mainly been sophisticated multi-national organisations in capital-intensive industries. Given the scale of inward investment and the publicity about new-style employee relations it is appropriate to try and identify the actual impact and to separate fact from media hype.

A stereotype of employee relations in Japanese firms operating in the UK has been of a single union, single status and no-strike deals involving pendulum arbitration. The reality has been that the bargaining strength of employers is such that few are prepared to surrender decision-making about wages to outside arbitrators, regardless of whether the process involves pendulum arbitration or not. A study commissioned by the Department of Employment into Japanese firms operating in Britain published in 1993[8] reported that a distinctively Japanese model was only being used in motor manufacturing. This included total quality approaches and teamworking, 'just-in-time' production and flexible working. Even there it was being used in a modified form, partly because of the strength of local culture and tradition but also because policies such as lifetime employment could not be guaranteed. Also, attempts to introduce new practices at component suppliers had had little effect. Spectacular productivity levels have been reported at Nissan at Sunderland but critics also reported a 'downside' for employees. This included a pattern of imposed consensus and employee dependency based on the marginalisation of unions, local unemployment and the lack of transferable skills.[9] A general conclusion of the study commissioned by the Department of Employment was that when 'new-style' employment practices had been introduced there was no evidence that they had had much impact on productivity or profitability compared with traditional systems. The general pattern, however, appears to be that individual elements of the Japanese model have become more common, particularly total quality initiatives and flexible working, but one has to bear in mind that there were strong pressures for such changes anyway.

THE ROLE OF TRADE UNIONS

The greatly reduced bargaining power of unions caused by the factors already explained has been reinforced by other changes. Membership fell in every year from 1979 to 1992, from 13.3 million to 9 million or more than 30 per cent. The end 1992 level was the lowest since 1946. Union density among people in employment fell to an estimated 31 per cent in 1993.[10] The causes of this are mainly related to structural changes in the economy, particularly the reduced levels of overall employment, the decline of manufacturing and other traditional areas such as coal mining and privatisation. Consequently, unions have had to cope with significantly reduced membership income. This has given a further boost to the pressure for amalgamation. The two health service unions amalgamated with the National Association of Local Government Officers (NALGO) in 1993 to form the largest trade union in the country, UNISON. Previously the engineering and electrical unions had combined to form the Amalgamated Engineering and Electrical Union (AEEU).

The reduction in union membership is not because of any great reduction in the logic of membership. 'Traditional reasons for joining unions, such as "support" should a problem arise at work, remain paramount. And management attitudes are among the most important sources of grievances.'[11] It would also appear that there has been no general trend by employers to derecognise unions. ACAS reported only nine cases of full derecognition in their Annual Report for 1993. However, there is an element of creeping derecognition with some grades being excluded, the range of issues reduced, non-recognition at new organisations and less notice taken of what unions have to say anyway. Another example of this erosion is the increase in the number of personal contracts and performance-related pay. Flexible working and generic job titles also reduce the opportunity of unions to make cases for upgrading. The increased tendency of employers to engage in direct communication with their work-force is also significant.

Despite the general change in the power relationships between managements and unions it is still necessary to take into account the fact that power within trade unions lies at the bottom of the organisation rather than at the top. The fact that unions have an organisational hierarchy can cause people to believe that they either do, or should, behave like organisations where power is much more at the top – as is the case with employers generally. Control in unions is ultimately in the hands of the lay members who pay their subscriptions and who elect their leaders. Elected groups of lay members have the ultimate formal authority in unions but, in any case, unions have to move in line with their members' wishes. This reality has been reinforced by the legislation introduced regarding ballots. The mistake that some people make is to see union officials as being akin to police officers with the responsibility and ability to instruct their members about what they should do. Even if union officials were to accept this debatable view of their role, they have little if anything in the way of sanctions to impose their will on their members.

Clearly, the ability of unions to serve their members and the way in which they serve them has altered. They are much more on the defensive now, often seeking to protect their members against redundancy and changes in working arrangements and employment contracts. The focus of bargaining is more localised which makes groups in weak positions more liable to be 'picked off'. Local bargaining also creates resourcing problems for unions. It is also increasingly difficult for unions to gain access to the real decision-makers, particularly if they are based at headquarters in another country. One of the reactions of unions to these generally unfavourable developments has been to arrange for a range of discounts for members on the products and services provided by a range of commercial organisations. Another has been to pay increasing attention to the legal rights of members and unions, particularly given increases in these rights emanating from Europe. It is therefore appropriate to consider next the main recent developments in individual and collective employment law.

LEGAL DEVELOPMENTS

A number of individual and collective employment law rights have already been explained. These include the rights of employees when the ownership of their business is transferred (Chapter 3), protection against discrimination on grounds of sex, race and trade union membership and activity, (Chapters 3, 9 and 11), equal pay and equal pay for work of equal value (Chapter 7), unfair dismissal and redundancy (Chapter 11). Individual rights were consolidated in the Employment Protection (Consolidation) Act of 1978, but there have been additions since then.

The whole issue of employment law is something of a political football. This is not surprising given the links between employers and the Conservative Party and the trade unions and the Labour Party. Traditional trade union immunities against legal action in the circumstances were re-established by the Labour government during their 1974–9 administration. However, the industrial action in the 'Winter of Discontent' in 1978/9 alienated public opinion and Mrs Thatcher came to power in 1979 with a mandate to curb the power of the unions. Her programme for doing this included a series of Employment Acts between 1980 and 1990 which considerably reduced (again) trade union immunities in the circumstances of industrial action. Secondary action and secondary picketing became unlawful. Secret ballots were required before industrial action. Industrial disputes were redefined in a more restrictive way and union funds made liable in civil actions by employers and those affected by unlawful disputes, e.g., suppliers and customers. The closed shop was made unlawful as was disciplinary action by trade unions against non-strikers. A Commissioner for Trade Unions was appointed to protect individual trade unionists rights. Unions were obliged to rapidly repudiate unofficial action and industrial tribunal access of those taking unofficial action and any others subsequently supporting them, e.g., against dismissal, withdrawn. Unions were also required to ensure that all members of their national governing bodies were elected directly by the membership in postal ballots. Postal ballots were also required every 10 years to approve any political funds. This series of acts were incorporated in the Trade Union and Labour Relations (Consolidation) Act of 1992.

Yet more restrictions were included in the Trade Union Reform and Employment Rights Act of 1993. These included the requirements that all industrial action ballots be postal and that if more than 50 members were involved the ballot be independently scrutinised as well (all costs being borne by the union). Ballots were also required regarding check-off arrangements (the deduction by employers of union subscriptions from pay). These had to take place if subscriptions were increased, and every three years in any case. Individuals, including members of the public, who were affected by unlawful action were given the right to seek an injunction to restrain such action. A further Commissioner, for Protection Against Unlawful Industrial Action, was appointed to facilitate such actions. Additionally, employers were enabled, within reason, to pay more to those on personal, as opposed to collective, contracts of employment if they wished to restructure their pay and bargaining arrangements.

The cumulative scale of the reductions in union collective rights since 1980 is dramatic. However, it is probably prudent to see the actual impact of this legislation as reinforcing the great shift in the balance of power between unions and employers caused by the changes in the labour market previously explained rather than being the main cause of the change in power relationships. Nevertheless, the new legal rights have sometimes been used against trade unions and some of them have found, to their cost, that there is no financial limit to the fines that courts can award if their orders are ignored. Unions, too, have had to cope with the threat of legal action and have had extra administrative and financial burdens placed on them in trying to organise industrial action lawfully. It was reported in 1995 that there were on average 10 actions per year by employers against trade unions regarding alleged unlawful industrial action but none so far by the Commissioner Against Unlawful Industrial Action.[12] If there is a change of government many of the changes introduced since 1980 may be reversed and a national minimum wage introduced. However, in the event of a change of government it is unlikely that all the changes will be reversed, because of deference to public opinion. Also, unions have generally come to accept the need for many of the balloting requirements and even to use affirmative ballots for industrial action as a useful tactical weapon in negotiations with employers.

Having examined the reduction in union collective rights under domestic law, it is next necessary to look at the developments in European law that have been in quite the opposite direction. At the Maastricht Summit in 1991, the UK government secured the right to opt out of the future extension of certain European Union employment legislation. However, it is still bound by European legislation passed before that date and case law judgements about such legislation whenever they are made and in whatever member country. Reference has already been made to some of the changes in domestic law that have been caused by developments in European law. Many of the rights of employees explained in other chapters, and referred to at the start of this section, have been because of developments in European law. The Trade Union Reform and Employment Rights Act of 1993 as well as reducing collective rights under domestic law also contained a series of new rights for individuals and unions because of the obligation of the government to comply with European law. These included the right of *all* employees, regardless of length of service or hours worked a week, to 14 weeks maternity leave on part pay. This supplements previous statutory and contractual requirements. Dismissal on grounds of pregnancy was made illegal. Stricter requirements regarding the provision of written particulars of employment to employees were introduced. As was explained in Chapter 3, under the Act employment rights are now protected in all transfers, not just those involving commercial undertakings. In transfer and redundancy situations employers are now obliged to consult with employee representatives *with a view to reaching agreement* prior to implementation (see Chapter 11). This means that redundancy notices cannot be given until that consultation process has been completed. Developments in case law, also explained in Chapter 11, mean that where there is no union there is an obligation to consult with employees.[13]

Part-time employees have been given equal access to organisational pension schemes which must not discriminate between the sexes, e.g., on the age at which people qualify for their pension. The government has also agreed to the terms of the Working Hours Directive, which includes a commitment to a 48-hour maximum working week. However, this requirement has been extensively watered down, e.g., by allowing working hours to be averaged, exempting some categories of worker and allowing the hours to be exceeded by mutual agreement. There is the further proviso that compliance by the UK to the whole Directive can be delayed until 2003. Additionally, there is a legal dispute, as the UK government has objected to these particular changes being introduced as a health and safety issue and thus by qualified majority voting. Multi-national organisations with 1,000 employees in two or more European Union member states will have to introduce a European works council or European information and consultation procedure by 1999. Under the opt out, the UK is not required to implement this legislation, but many UK organisations will be affected, particularly those with two or more large subsidiaries in other member states. A potential future major issue is that, if there is a change of government, the UK may retrospectively accept whatever other arrangements have been negotiated by the other members under the Social Protocol on the basis of qualified majority voting.

Health and safety

Health and safety is an area that as well as being important in its own right has a important employee relations dimension. The framework legislation covering this area is the Health and Safety at Work Act, 1974. Employers are required to establish safe systems of work not just for their employers but with a view to protecting the public as well. There is also an obligation on manufacturers and suppliers to provide safe products and systems. Management in organisations employing five or more, including those operating on a self-employed basis, apart from private households, are obliged to have a written safety policy, which they must publicise, and clear management arrangements for implementing the policy. Accidents must be recorded and serious ones reported. Employees must be briefed about any particular risks and changes. There is an obligation to consult with any recognised trade union about health and safety issues and the union may appoint safety representatives. If there is a written request from two safety representatives to establish a safety committee, the employer must comply. The obligation to consult with a trade union has now been widened to an obligation to consult with the work-force in the absence of a union.[14] Employers must also provide free protective clothing, eyesight testing and safety training where appropriate. Codes of practice and regulations about substantive safety issues are regularly issued, the latter having the force of law. Breach of the statute law makes organisations liable to criminal prosecution. There are also obligations under common law and organisations may be sued by those who have suffered injury through its negligence. Employers must also comply with European directives which can be approved on a qualified majority voting basis. A relatively recent example of how health and safety practice has evolved is the development of no-smoking policies at many organisations.

Under the Trade Unions and Employment Rights Act of 1993 protection for employees and safety representatives has been increased. Safety representatives cannot be lawfully disciplined for carrying out designated duties. Employees cannot be lawfully disciplined for taking reasonable steps to protect themselves or others from a danger they reasonably believe to be serious and imminent. Special compensation is available for representatives or employees if they are dismissed in these circumstances. Also, employees taken off their job for health and safety reasons have to be transferred to suitable alternative work or suspended on full pay.

Unfortunately, despite the comprehensive nature of the legislative framework for the protection of employees and members of the public, the safety systems employers operate do not always work. Deregulation of the labour market, economies at the Health and Safety Commission, which has a supervisory responsibility in this area, and cost and competitive pressures may have also increased the risks. The dangers were highlighted by a series of disasters, mainly in the late 1980's, which included the capsizing of a P. & O. ferry at Zeebrugge, fires at the Bradford football ground and at Kings Cross underground station, rail crashes at Clapham and Purley, football spectators being suffocated at Sheffield's Hillsborough stadium, the sinking of *Marchioness* pleasure boat on the river Thames and the fire on the *Piper Alpha* oil rig. The sinking of the ferry *Estonia* off the coast of Finland in 1994, with the loss of over 900 lives, emphasises the potential scale of tragedy and its avoidability. Preventive action is needed at all workplaces. Unfortunately, there can all too easily be neglect in this area and a conflict between pressures for production and the delivery of services. The potential conflict between incentive schemes and safety was explained in Chapter 7. In the USA a multi-million-dollar law suit was instigated because of a person being knocked down by an employee trying to meet their employer's guarantee of the delivery of pizzas within 30 minutes of an order being placed. The road behaviour of many courier motor and pedal cyclists is another example of the potential conflict between commercial pressures and safety.

DIAGNOSTIC SKILLS

It has been necessary to spend some time in clarifying the framework within which managers operate in the employee relations area as the context has powerful implications regarding their behaviour. It is also necessary to spend some time examining the diagnostic skills that managers need. The nature of employee relations problems can often be easy enough to recognise – some of the most likely ones being interruptions to work, poor performance, resistance to change and restrictive practices. What can be much more difficult is establishing the actual causes of these problems and working out what, if anything, can be done about them. The emotional nature of the subject can hinder accurate diagnosis – if one has come to hate the sight of a particular representative it can be very tempting to go along with a stereotyped view to the effect that all trouble-makers should be sacked or, according to some, imprisoned or shot! The reality is, of course, that whatever one's feelings one usually has to live with particular representatives, and they with their managers, about whom they may have equally strong views.

Bad personal relationships can exacerbate management–union relationships and in some cases conflicts can be no more than personality clashes. However, even if all the people involved were angels, they would still have to resolve issues where the interests of the parties are in conflict. One of the skills that managers need in this area is the ability to identify the basic conflicts that lie behind any personal issues. It is important, too, for the manager to judge the extent to which a representative is reflecting the views of their colleagues. Getting rid of the representative, even if this was possible, would not do much good if they were then replaced by someone else who behaved in a similar manner.

Recognising conflicts of interest

Perhaps the most critical ability needed by the manager with regard to employee relations is that of being able to recognise when managerial and employee interests come into conflict. Some people adopt a unitary perspective of the organisation and simply do not accept that this can happen. The line of argument can be that what is good for the organisation is automatically good for all its employees. Whilst this approach may present a simple and comforting philosophy for those who hold it, it does not help equip managers to deal with the genuine conflicts of interest that can and do arise about wage levels, working arrangements and job security, for example. Managers may be so preoccupied with the various pressures upon them that they neglect to consider the implications for their employees of particular decisions. If their employees see their interests being threatened by changes, they are hardly likely to be enthusiastic about such changes. It may, for example, be highly inconvenient for an employer to find that employees don't co-operate with the introduction of new processes because they threaten their career opportunities and job security, but decision-making needs to be based on an accurate assessment of the employees' views and not wishful thinking.

Resistance to change can blandly be ascribed to the innate conservatism of the work-force, but such an analysis may miss the point that employees may resist a particular change because it represents a threat to their interests. Other changes, such as pay increases, may be eagerly accepted. It is the nature of the change and its impact on their interests that employees are likely to consider. In a study of restrictive practices carried out for the Donovan Commission, it was concluded that 'there must be few restrictive labour practices which are not genuinely thought by at least one of the parties concerned to be defensible in terms of their own interests'.[15] If diagnosis has been accurately undertaken, it is at least possible for managers to consider what, if anything, can be done. Acceptance that one just has to live with some problems may be much more constructive than time, money and effort being wasted on false solutions that will not work because the diagnosis was faulty. With some problems remedial action can be taken. It may be that effective communication can remove misunderstanding, or that it can pave the way to a negotiated answer which gives sufficient concessions to both parties to make a deal worthwhile. Anticipation of problems can lead to their being avoided or reduced in scale. Much can be achieved simply by managers thinking through the implications of their decisions as far as the employees are concerned. Managers may, for example, make apparently simple technical decisions blissfully unaware of the problems their decisions could create in other parts of the organisation. If production schedules, for example, are to be altered in such a way that people's earnings are affected, it is best to anticipate the likely reaction of employees, and to take that into account at the decision-making stage, rather than to take the decision in ignorance of its likely effects. Diagnosis also needs to take account of the power relationships. If a clash of interests is identified, it is then necessary to calculate the extent to which the respective parties are able to impose their views. It may seem regrettable that conflicts are determined by power relationships as well as by intellectual, technical and moral criteria, but it is hardly prudent for a manager to try to impose a particular decision if it can easily be resisted. Conversely, the mere fact that employees protest about a proposal does not automatically mean that the employer is unable to implement it.

The integration of employee relations with other management activities

The emphasis in this chapter so far has mainly been on looking at employee relations as a subject on its own. However, for there to be any real understanding of the area it is vital to see the way in which employee relations interrelates with other management functions.

This can be a crucial diagnostic skill. This is because often the causes of employee relations problems, and by implication any 'remedies', lie in these other areas. This basic point is often missed because of departmental boundaries. This may be compounded by lack of knowledge of those inside the employee relations area of what goes on outside it and, conversely, lack of knowledge of those outside the area of what goes on within it.

This crucial interactive relationship is best explained by way of relevant examples. A particularly neat one concerns a bag manu-facturing company in a Caribbean country. The company endured a strike of several weeks over a redundancy. The organisation had invested in equipment and labour to meet a large order from a sugar producer. The order was not met on time and was then cancelled. Subsequent investigations revealed that delivery had been promised at the time of peak seasonal demand for bags and there had never been any prospect that the order could be delivered on time. A contrasting example – but which makes the same basic point – concerns the causes of employee relations prob-lems in the National Health Service prior to the reorganisations described in Chapter 3. An ACAS investigation concluded that the prime causes of the problems were deficiencies in basic organisa-tional structure.[16] These included weak links in the chain of command, consensus management, a poorly defined personnel function and poor communications between NHS disciplines. Karen Legge gives an illuminating account of an ill-conceived attempt at a children's clothing firm to switch the product range from long-run 'bread-and-butter' production runs to a wide range of small-batch fashion garments.[17] This came to grief because of the failure to take into account the learning problems for the production employees together with the impact of the change on their bonus earnings.

It is necessary to make this crucial point about the inter-relationship of employee relations with other functions by way of example because of their illustrative value and the lack of systematic study in this area. Unfortunately, there has been a historical tradition of viewing employee relations as a self-contained activity. The Donovan Commission concentrated on the need for improve-ments within the 'industrial relations system'. The main thrust of the Report was that the way forward was the formalisation of procedures at plant level. The 'central defect in British industrial relations' was identified as being disorderly bargaining at factory level.[18] The narrowness of this approach may have been why so little was apparently achieved as a result of the Donovan recommendations.[19] The implications of this analysis for the individual manager is clearly not to look for or expect progress in tackling employee relations problems to come just from initiatives in that area. The argument is not that procedural arrangements and employee relations expertise are not desirable or important, but that one has to look elsewhere as well. Unfortunately, the training and background of those in employee relations is sometimes such that they may not understand that the causes of many of their problems lie outside their sphere. Conversely, those outside the employee relations area may know so little about the area that they do not appreciate the need to work out the employee relations implications of decisions they are taking. One answer to this problem is general management training for all managers. The case for this is all the more powerful when one realises that the way in which employee relations problems can be created by decisions or failures elsewhere is but one example of the way in which problems can be transmitted into any area of management. To take the analysis further it is not just a question of getting managers to see the implications of their decisions in other areas but recognising that plain incompetence in one area can easily precipitate crises elsewhere.

A positive development is that genuine strategic human resource management initiatives, linked to corporate policy, should embrace employee relations issues in the context of an integrated systems approach to organisational issues. However, not all corporate and human resource initiatives are properly integrated and thought out. There are many examples of the human dimension being ignored or it being considered too in a simplistic way without specialist advice at the design stage of policy. This topic was examined in Chapter 2 and relevant examples are given concerning some TQM initiatives (Chapter 3) and the high failure rate of performance-related pay schemes (Chapter 10). This problem of narrowly based or superficially integrated initiatives unfortunately characterises the way many different types of organisational change are often handled.

JOINT AGREEMENTS

Relationships between employers and employees may to some extent be regulated by joint agreements. Collective agreements may be about substantive or procedural issues. Substantive agreements cover matters such as wages and conditions of employment; procedural agreements can be likened to the Queensberry rules for boxing – there can at least be rules regulating the manner in which arguments about substantive issues are conducted! Procedural agreements may be about the resolution of differences over individual or collective issues. Consideration has already been given to the individual procedures that may exist concerning grievances, disciplinary issues and dismissals. Collective differences may be handled by a disputes procedure, which may also be used for handling wage claims. On the other hand, there may be a separate procedure for dealing with such claims. Sometimes there are also substantive agreements about redundancy payments and procedural arrangements for negotiating the implementation of possible redundancies. Obviously, managers need to know the details of any agreements that may affect them. It is necessary for them not only to honour any substantive agreements but also to avoid making concessions that could have embarrassing repercussions in other parts of the organisation.

Procedural arrangements can provide a very useful framework for handling differences when they emerge. Managers and stewards can both be somewhat at a loss as to what to do when discussions end in failure. They can have a common interest in defining the area in dispute and agreeing on the next step and what, if anything, is to happen in the meantime. In this way a dispute can be processed without either party having had to give way, with the issue normally being referred to the next level so that it can be tackled afresh. The definition of the area of disagreement and time thus bought for fresh thought, may help in the subsequent resolution of a dispute. If nothing else, procedures can get the immediate parties to the dispute 'off the hook', at least for a while. Ultimately, if discussion at higher levels does not produce agreement, the thorny issue of what happens next has to be considered. Either side may give way or consider imposing their will, which in a way is the final stage of procedure. Managers will have to weigh up carefully the disadvantages of risking union resistance and the impact on employee morale against the disadvantages of giving way. This needs to be a consciously taken decision.

Although the handling of differences via an agreed disputes procedure will not guarantee a satisfactory resolution, it does at least provide an alternative to an immediate 'shoot-out', and gives the parties the opportunity to explore the possibilities for an agreed solution. Knowledge that, if there is no agreement, there may be resort to 'other means' can in itself have a sobering effect on the parties. Sometimes arbitration is seen as the answer to unresolved differences, but if it is too readily available it may relieve the parties of the responsibility for settlement and lead to exaggerated claims and counter-claims with no movement towards a negotiated settlement. However, employers are now generally reluctant to use arbitration for collective bargaining given the powerful bargaining position they currently hold in the labour market. This point has not been lost on the government which has systematically reduced the importance of outside agencies in wage determination in the public sector. Under these circumstances arbitration is perhaps more appropriate for differences about interpretation of agreements or the resolving of individual differences where there are no great financial implications to the decision.

One of the advantages of agreed procedures is that the parties can at least limit the area of disagreement by agreeing what is in dispute and how the difference should be resolved, even if resolution can ultimately mean one side coerces the other. A further way of limiting the area of dispute can be the use of a '*status quo*' clause in a disputes procedure, which provides for the continuation of work on the basis that existed before a dispute began. This can be a useful device, but there can be occasions when it is difficult to identify just when a dispute arose and therefore what the *status quo* position was. Sometimes, too, managements feel that they are conceding too much opportunity to unions to block changes which are not to the unions' liking, if such a clause is part of a disputes procedure. The solution one engineering company adopted to resolve this dilemma was to introduce a 'ten day rule'. If management felt that discussions about changes in working practices were being unduly protracted they reserved the right to serve notice that in ten days the change would be introduced unless there was some other agreement in the meantime.

SUPERVISORY CONTROL

A crucial aspect of employee relations in any organisation is the extent to which managerial interests are safeguarded at the level of first line supervision. This may involve considerable time and thought being given to the viability of the position of those with direct supervisory responsibility. As was discussed in Chapter 3, considerable attention may have to be given to the identification of the rewards which can be given by those managing at this level, so that supervisors are not in the position of only handing out penalties. Responsibilities need to be clarified and discretion in decision-making given where appropriate. The selection and training of managerial and supervisory staff are also important. When all this has been done, it is important that those who have been given responsibilities are integrated into the management team, listened to and not bypassed. It is no good managers at very senior levels taking tough stands if, in the meantime, they have let managerial influence at shop-floor level be quietly eroded over the years. Although the above points are basic, sadly all too often they are given insufficient attention and organisational performance suffers significantly because of weakness at this crucial level. The importance of the role of the supervisory level is illustrated in the diagram of 'the disciplinary pyramid' in Chapter 11.

In some organisations basic changes are happening in the role of the first line supervisor. The increased sophistication of capital equipment and supporting technical services, flexible working and multi-skilling has tended to increase the demands 'on supervisors, particularly for the management of people and provided a threat to their traditional "telling and directing" role'.[20] Harmonisation of terms and conditions of employment may also have eroded some of their status. A further development, particularly in the context of the Japanese model, has been the appointment of team leaders. Sometimes the role of team leaders include trouble-shooting, acting as a 'floater' in case a key worker is absent and technical instruction. However, great care has to be taken to work out whether team leaders are meant to supplement or replace first line supervisors. A further issue that needs careful consideration is the levels at which union representatives raise issues with management. Team working and de-layering have tended to push this upwards to more senior managers.

NEGOTIATING SKILLS

Contact with trade unions can involve managers in negotiations. These may be informal or routed via an agreed disputes or negotiating procedure or other joint arrangement. The process of negotiation may be very similar to other types of negotiation in which a manager can be involved, for example, commercial negotiations. Negotiation may be seen as a mystic art which is only learned through practice. Whilst perhaps there is no substitute for experience in negotiation, there are basic skills which it is perfectly possible to identify and for people to consciously develop. There are also complexities in the process of negotiation which are not always appreciated but which will be explained in this section.

Defining objectives

As with so many managerial skills, it is essential that people with responsibility for negotiation clarify their objectives. The pattern of reaction and competition in negotiation can be so ingrained that it is possible to lose sight of the exact purpose of negotiations. Usually the objective is to see if a mutually advantageous bargain can be struck. This may involve taking initiatives to ensure that there is something in a proposal which is of benefit to both parties, rather than just trying to outwit the other side. Whilst in some negotiations one side can only gain at the other's expense, this is not always the case. There is no point in failing to agree just because the other side would do better than you if agreement would mean that both parties would have gained. Success needs to be judged against the achievement or non-achievement of overall objectives, not just by relative comparison with how well the other side did.

One of the problems of identifying objectives in negotiations is that there may be considerable differences within a management team as to what the objectives should be. Short-term problems may conflict with long-term aims and the pressures to give concessions in a particular department may have to be balanced against the repercussions this action might have elsewhere in an organisation. Managers may also differ in the risks they are prepared to run. This often means that it is crucial for agreed objectives to be hammered out before there can be any question of meeting the other side. Managers may also need to liaise with their superiors about the parameters within which they must negotiate. They must also avoid being so caught up in considering their personal position on issues that they may fail to realise that colleagues may have a quite different perspective. If negotiations are conducted before any reconciliation of differing managerial views, the results can be disastrous: the wrong points can be conceded, managerial disunity advertised and managers may feel that their colleagues have been disloyal to them. The device of adjournment may be necessary as a means of coping with such problems. This can enable the management group to consider fresh points or to re-examine their position if new differences emerge within the group. It may also sometimes be appropriate to suggest that union negotiators adjourn so that they can properly consider new points. A further advantage of clearly identifying objectives is that it can help managers avoid developing 'tunnel vision' during negotiations. This can happen when, during a complex negotiation, there is obsessive attention to a particular point which may turn out to be of only marginal importance.

The allocation of roles

Preparation for negotiating meetings needs to involve consideration not only of the substantive issues, but also of the roles that managers will assume during negotiations. A common mistake is for one manager to try to negotiate, chair and record what has happened. This can be too much for any one person and is quite unnecessary if there are other managers present who could share these roles. Unless this is done, the lead manager can suffer from *role overload* and *information overload*. A manager who tries to combine the three tasks may all too easily find that the control of the meeting suffers and that there is misunderstanding about what has actually been agreed. The crucial roles to consider giving to different people are those of chairing and negotiating. The chairing process needs to be identified before a meeting begins at, for instance, a management pre-meeting. As has already been explained, there may be a need for considerable discussion amongst managers to try to reach agreement about just what their objectives should be. For this to be done there may need to be a systematic attempt to establish the views of the interested parties which necessitates some type of chaired meeting either formal or informal. When the two sides meet to negotiate, it can be of advantage for one person to chair the management team with the responsibility for co-ordinating the presentation of the management view. Given that there can be conflicting objectives on the management side, it can be appropriate for one person in particular to watch that the team does not depart from its agreed

be conducted with a view to the long-term relationship as well as short-term advantage. If, however, you are dealing with a person or organisation on a 'one-off' basis, it is as well to be beware that if they do not envisage a continuing relationship with you or your organisation they may not be so concerned about issues such as 'good faith'.

It may be just as well to see that any hard-liners are included in negotiations, so that they have a front-seat view of what is really happening. Even if some stewards do not actually participate in negotiations, their presence as observers may help considerably with the report-back process. Managers who receive 'report-backs' need to be prepared to coax an accurate summary out of the negotiators. If they jump down their throat when the first concession is mentioned, negotiators may, whether consciously or subconsciously, refrain from revealing all the concessions which were made. The skills required in meetings, particularly by the chair, are so critical that the whole of the next chapter is devoted to them.

The ritual of negotiation with its claim, offer, counter-proposal and ultimate compromise agreement seems to many people to be a waste of time. Such a judgement ignores the very necessary functions that such a ritual can fulfil. Even if the parties directly involved in a negotiation could come to a quick settlement without such a ritual, it is necessary to remember that they both have audiences to consider. If either side accepts too quickly it may leave the suspicion that a more favourable settlement could have been achieved. A union official is hardly going to enhance their credibility with their members if they develop a reputation, however unjustified, for settling too easily. Apart from the 'show' element in the ritual, however, considerable skills can be needed by the parties in handling the ritual so that an appropriate settlement can be achieved.

The 'pitching' of an initial offer can have a crucial effect on the ultimate outcome. If an offer is too low it may so antagonise the other side that attitudes harden and the prospects of a settlement are reduced. If, on the other hand, too much is offered initially this can create the expectation that the offer can be improved by further negotiation and frustration and resentment if this is not forthcoming. Parties may have particular styles in the way they handle, or mishandle, such rituals and it may be useful to try and establish the past pattern of the style of a person you are negotiating with. One also has to take account of possible changes in style when a new person takes over or joins a team.

Conduct after negotiating meetings

Written reports of negotiating meetings can be subject to conflicting interpretations. There are powerful pressures that can create the illusion rather than the reality of agreement. People may remember only what they built into an agreement and fail to recall – or have never realised – what the other party was building into an agreement. Ambiguous terms can be used which increase the possibility of this happening. One side may interpret an ambiguous term in their own favour, whilst the other side may place a conflicting interpretation on the same term. It is much better to face up to such problems during negotiations rather than have arguments afterwards, with the possibility of accusations of bad faith. Parties may feel that they have been tricked into an agreement when the reality was that the possible conflict in interpretation was simply not clarified at the time. Sometimes, however, ambiguous phrases are necessary – but as an open device for deferring some differences until another day, not as a way of pretending there is agreement when there is not.

The problems of accurate communication during negotiations can be compounded by the pressures and problems that can arise during the report-back process. People who have not been exposed to the pressure and argument of negotiations may be critical of any concessions that have been made, both on the management and the union side. This can lead to the front-line negotiators playing down the concessions they have made, or even neglecting to mention them at all. In some cases it can even change their perception of what really was agreed. If there is such distortion at one or both ends of a negotiating chain, there can be obvious problems when an agreement is implemented contrary to the expectations of the other side. Care then needs to be taken to give any help to stewards to explain just what has been agreed at a negotiation. It may also be useful to arrange to issue joint written details of agreements directly to employees as soon as possible. It may be even more important for management to issue written details whilst employees are considering an offer or if talks have broken down.

THE MANAGER AS A TRADE UNION MEMBER

One of the implications of white-collar unions is that managers may have to give serious thought as to whether or not they join a trade union. If they are in a union, they may find that the possibility of industrial action by their own union leads to their greater involvement in union affairs. The sheer size of an employing organisation may mean that union membership is the only way in which there can be proper discussions about a manager's terms and conditions of employment. Whilst the increase in the use of personal contracts and merit or performance-related pay increases has reduced the emphasis on collective negotiation and the rigid application of job evaluation schemes and incremental salary scales for white-collar staff, managers may still sometimes want the 'cover' of a union to represent their interests. The relative weakness of employees in the labour market, worries about job security and, in some cases, abrasive management styles are further reasons for joining unions. The legal insurance that unions offer and the services they provide at industrial tribunal hearings can also be selling points to the potential managerial recruit.

One of the decisions that a manager may have to make is just which union they should join. A specialist union, because of its specialised appeal, may not have many members and therefore lack comprehensive support services. Larger unions, whilst not perhaps offering the same degree of understanding about the individual manager's problems, may have a comprehensive range of services and specialists and the negotiating strength that can come from having a large membership, particularly if this membership includes large groups of key workers. Whilst some specialist unions thrive, others fail to last and merge with larger unions, often to the relief of the employer, for this reduces the number of different unions with which they have to deal.

Whilst it may be to the advantage of the individual manager to join a trade union, membership can bring with it a fresh set of problems. Managers may find that it is not always easy to reconcile their union and managerial roles. Sometimes the accommodation is fairly easy. The manager may join a managerial union, or the white-collar section of a manual workers' union. On the face of it there may be no problem in negotiating as a representative of the employer with employees who are in other unions, or even the same union but in a different section. However, sections of the same union can be bound by common policies and also some union branches can take in a large vertical section of the white-collar workers with a particular employer. This can lead to role conflict, such as a manager wanting to pursue a grievance against their boss, who may not only be in the same union branch but also one of its officers! In the circumstances of industrial action, members may find that there is a conflict between the need to maintain production or services and a union desire to disrupt those services. Such conflicts have been most common in the public sector. The individual may find that they are damned by their employer if they do not keep services working and damned by their union if they do. There is no easy answer to the conflicts that can arise for managers within unions. However, if the individual manager recognises the problems that can arise, this should help them make careful judgements about whether or not they should join a union, which union it should be, whether they should hold office within that union and the way in which role conflicts that occur for themselves and their colleagues within the union can be resolved.

CONCLUSION

As has been demonstrated, the area of employee relations is potentially both complex and fluid. Even if one works in a non-unionised environment there will still be conflicts of interest that need to be identified and 'managed'. Often problems in the employee relations area are precipitated by decisions in other areas of managerial activity, so remedial strategies may need to embrace those areas as well. Further problems or issues may be generated by changes in the external environment. Consequently, one has to be beware of developing 'tunnel vision' with regard to employee relations problems, as they need to be viewed in their organisational and environmental contexts. A range of skills are needed to handle the emotionally sensitive areas involved, which may be of use in a range of other situations as well. These skills include those of accurate diagnosis and negotiation. Chairing skills may also be necessary in these and many other management situations. The skills involved in chairing meetings are appropriately considered in the next and final chapter.[21]

NOTES

1 For an authoritative and comprehensive coverage of this topic see John Storey (ed.), *Human Resource Management: A Critical Text*, Routledge, 1994.

2 'Unemployment: UK Summary', *Employment Gazette*, S. 20, March 1988.

3 'Claimant Unemployment: UK Summary', *Employment Gazette*, S. 24, August 1995.

4 *Journal of the Royal Statistical Society*, Series A, vol. 158, 1995, part 3, pp. 363–417.

5 *Employment Gazette*, 'Labour Disputes in 1993', June 1994, p. 199.

6 *Directors' Renumeration: Report of a Study Group Chaired by Sir Richard Greenbury*, Gee & Co., 1995.

7 'Railways Count the Long-Term Cost of Strikes', *Independent*, 29 September 1994. See also Robert Taylor, 'Intricate Compromise a Model for the Railways', *Financial Times*, 29 September 1994 and *Sunday Times*, 9 October 1994.

8 Sue Milsome, *The Impact of Japanese Firms on Working and Employment Practices in British Manufacturing Industry*, Industrial Relations Services, 1993.

9 Philip Garrahan and Paul Stewart, *The Nissan Enigma*, Mansell, 1992.

10 'Trade Union Membership and Density 1992–3', *Employment Gazette*, June 1994, p. 189.

11 Interim report of a study by Wadddington and Whitston reported in *People Management*, 26 January 1995, p. 47.

12 Neil Merrick, 'Unofficial Strike Action Proves Costly for Unions', *People Management*, 23 February 1995, p. 12.

13 For an authoritative account of developments in European Employment Law see Michael Gold, *The Social Dimension: Employment Policy in the European Community*, Macmillan, 1993.

14 *Commission of the European Communities v UK* [1994] IRLR, 421 (see also Chapter 11).

15 Royal Commission on Trade Unions and Employers' Associations (the Donovan Commission), *Productivity Bargaining and Restrictive Labour Practices*, Research Paper No. 4, HMSO, 1967, p. 52.

16 Royal Commission on the National Health Service, *ACAS Evidence*, *ACAS Report No. 12*, ACAS, May 1978.

17 Karen Legge, *Power, Innovation and Problem-solving in Personnel Management*, McGraw-Hill, 1978, pp. 45–6.

18 *Royal Commission on Trade Unions and Employers' Associations 1965–8*, Cmnd. 3623, HMSO, 1968, para 1019.

19 Norman Singleton, *Industrial Relations Procedures*, Manpower Paper No. 14, HMSO, 1975, Ch. 8.

20 Advisory, Conciliation and Arbitration Service, *Supervision*, Advisory Booklet, ACAS, 1991, p. 3.

21 For a comprehensive account of developments in employee relations see Sid Kessler and Fred Bayliss, *Contemporary British Industrial Relations*, Macmillan, 2nd edn, 1995.

Chapter 13

Meetings and chairing

INTRODUCTION

Attendance at meetings can occupy a considerable part of a manager's time. There is often much flippant comment about the pointlessness of meetings, such as the description of a camel being 'a racehorse designed by a committee'. However, meetings, whether formal or informal, are increasingly an integral part of organisational activity and it is naive for people to suggest that meetings are unnecessary. What is important is that meetings be conducted effectively and that people distinguish between unnecessary meetings and those which need to be properly organised.

The people who most need to develop skills related to the effective conduct of meetings are those concerned with their organisation – particularly the chair, and secretary if applicable. Ordinary members may also need to develop skills such as working out just what they want to achieve at meetings. An appreciation of what is happening at meetings may also be educative in terms of understanding how organisations work, or do not work. Understanding in this area may also be a useful preparation for the day when an ordinary member has to chair a meeting. Some of the skills have already been considered in the section of Chapter 12 concerned with employee relations negotiations. However, this whole area requires treatment in its own right, which is why it forms a separate chapter. The need for meetings and the consequences of ineffective meetings are considered. The various types of meetings are also identified.

There is a need for considerable preparation prior to meetings and once meetings have started they need to be chaired with skill. The skills required include the need to optimise the contributions by the various members. An underlying theme in many of the sections is the way in which the chair's role in contributing to substantive issues can conflict with their procedural and process control roles. Consequently, advice is offered on how a chair can resolve this dilemma. A section is also included about recording the outcome of meetings. Finally, an Appendix is provided which explains the main rules relating to formal committee procedure.

The term 'chair' is used throughout the chapter rather than the alternative expression 'chairman' to emphasise the point that the chair can be a man or a woman.

THE NEED FOR MEETINGS

Meetings can be an indispensable part of an organisation's structure. In some organisations – for example, in local government – policy decisions must be taken with a committee-type structure with various committees, or sub-committees, reporting to the council as a whole. In commercial organisations the need for meetings below the level of shareholders' and directors' meetings may not be obligatory but may still be very necessary. Meetings may be necessary as an aid to the running of departments. They can also be vital in promoting inter-departmental co-operation which otherwise might not be achieved. The growing complexity of decision-making, caused partly by the diffusion of knowledge within organisations, means that very often decisions can only be taken effectively by groups of people coming together and pooling their knowledge and expertise. Globalisation and developments in information technology mean that some meetings involve simultaneous multilingual translation and/or electronic conferencing. If meetings are ineffective it can mean that a vital aspect of organisational structure is failing.

The consequences of ineffectiveness

There are many reasons why attention needs to be paid to the effective conduct of meetings. The decisions that are taken in meetings can be very important. The quality of decision-making may well correlate with the skill with which meetings are conducted. Small improvements in the effectiveness of meetings can lead to considerable savings in time because of the multiplication of the time saved by the number of people present. Meetings can also have functions other than decision-making, such as providing briefing for those present or ensuring that decisions are taken in an open way. The quality of decision-making and the efficiency with which business is conducted can also affect working relationships outside meetings and the credibility of the role of meetings for future occasions. It is as well too for managers to be aware that they are in the spotlight when chairing meetings and that the effectiveness of their performance is likely to enhance or damage their reputation, often before critical audiences.

TYPES OF MEETINGS AND CLASSIFICATION OF ACTIVITY

Meetings can vary in importance and formality, from the proceedings of the House of Commons to the informal discussion of a temporary problem between colleagues. Whatever the type of meeting, it is necessary for the participants to be aware of the methods by which the business is conducted, as well as the *substantive content* of the meeting. The *procedural arrangements* may be formally embodied in the constitution or terms of reference of a committee, or agreed by the parties present or, in some cases, imposed by one party on another. It is also necessary to identify a third dimension of the activity of meetings and that is the interpersonal interactions between those present. For meetings to be effectively handled there needs to be constructive management of these interactions. The term we shall use to describe this is *process control.* Even in very informal situations there is always a process aspect to the discussions, and the skill with which this is handled can affect the quality and acceptability of any outcome. Behavioural scientists often distinguish between process leadership and task leadership. Sometimes the term 'process control' is used in a broader sense to include formal as well as informal procedural issues.

As well as the level of formality, the purpose and decision-making arrangements can vary. Meetings can be part of a constitutional decision-making process, for briefing purposes only, for negotiation, for consultation or for the mutual exchange of views. In some meetings decisions are taken in accordance with the views of the majority of the members. In other situations the decision-making power may be vested elsewhere – for example, in a management structure with the most senior manager or in the armed services with the most senior officer present. In some cases there may be no decision to make, or if there is it may be by a manager in their own right and not by virtue of their membership of a particular committee. This basic classification is necessary because people may fail to distinguish between the different purposes and decision-making arrangements of meetings. If the members of a meeting fail to see the distinction it can lead to confusion; if the chair does not see the differences it can lead to chaos. This can happen if people have a stereotyped view of meetings and start applying the wrong conventions in a particular situation. Managers may assume that they have to operate by consensus or majority vote, when the reality may be that an organisation has vested them ultimately with the sole decision-making responsibility within a particular area. Management chairs at joint consultative meetings can, and sometimes do, use voting procedures and short-circuit established management structures because the chair has not appreciated that a consultative meeting literally means just that. It is an aid to decision-making via established management procedures – not a substitute for those procedures. During formal negotiations there can be three different centres of decision-making – at the pre-meetings of two separate groups before a joint meeting and during a joint meeting. All three discussions require effective chairing.

THE ROLE OF THE CHAIR

The variety of aims and the differing nature of meetings means that those responsible for arranging meetings have to consider just what their particular aims and procedures should be. A chair needs to understand the substantive issue under discussion, but needs also to devote some time to a consideration of how the meeting is to be handled effectively. A common error is for the chair to be so immersed in the substantive issues that they neglect the procedural arrangements and the issue of process control. This is especially likely to happen if the chair is anxious to achieve particular outcomes with regard to controversial issues. This can lead to a further complication, which is that a chair may seek to manipulate, or cut through, any inconvenient arrangements about decision-making in order to secure a particular result. They may get their way in securing a particular outcome, but this may be at the expense of reducing the quality and/or acceptability of a decision. If the case for a particular decision is that strong, it may be that there is little to fear from open and fair discussion. The danger is, though, that the manager concerned is so involved substantively and emotionally that they fail to consider the procedures and processes adequately.

Poor quality decisions for which there is little commitment may stem not so much from a desire to manipulate decision-making procedures and processes as from a failure to consider the relevance of these issues to the business in hand. If the decision-making process requires the pooling of information and elements of negotiation amongst colleagues, the chair needs to ensure that just that takes place. If conflicts have to be resolved, the chair may also need to ensure that discussion takes place in an atmosphere in which those with opposing views each feel they have at least had a fair opportunity to state their case. Whilst a chair will need to understand the substantive issues, it may be best if they refrain from taking a partisan line as far as possible. There are those people who have the skills to referee, for example, a football match in which they are also playing – but it does require a high degree of ability and it is best for a chair to avoid doing this as far as is practicable. The person with the greatest knowledge of the substantive issues will not automatically have either the time or the aptitude to chair discussions.

It is critical to recognise that there needs to be a division of labour at meetings. Otherwise, for example, a group of people may be invited to a meeting and find that their views are not sought or are ignored. The chair will need to ensure that they obtain the necessary contributions from those present at a meeting, and may want them to concentrate on resolving, as far as possible, the substantive issues at hand. Assisted sometimes by a secretary the chair will have to concentrate on the procedural and process issues so that there is a framework within which the group can operate. It is only when the chair has satisfactorily created the framework for a meeting that they should consider taking time off from their chairing role to get involved in the substantive issues. Even then it may be best to do that to the minimum extent as, if the framework of the meeting is right, the rest of the group may be able to resolve the business themselves, looking to the chair only for procedural and specialist guidance when appropriate. Meetings do not automatically keep on the rails and, if the chair becomes so involved in the discussion that they neglect to consider how the meeting is handled, the discussion may be inadequately guided. A division of labour, whereby the chair spends perhaps most of their time on procedural matters and process control, someone else takes the minutes and the other members concentrate exclusively on the substantive issues, does not seem unreasonable. A meeting where no-one concentrates or even bothers about the procedural and process aspects is the one most likely to be ineffective.

A complication concerning the chairing of meetings is that the chair may be the person with the greatest knowledge of the substantive issues. Even if that is the case, the chair still needs to recognise that they must find time to give adequate attention to procedural and process issues. The chair may find that they are also fiercely committed to a particular outcome. In such cases they need to pay considerable attention to seeing that their commitment to a particular view does not prevent them from giving those people who have a different view a fair opportunity to state their case. Some people have, or can develop, the skill to explain a partisan line yet at the same time chair a discussion fairly. It may be important that they do both, so that the substantive decision is based on a consideration of all relevant views, including the chair's. If, however, the chair finds that they cannot combine these two tasks, then it could be that they should consider letting someone else take the chair, at least for the duration of discussion of a particular topic. The role of the chair is examined later in the chapter with particular regard to resolving conflict during meetings.

PREPARATION BEFORE MEETINGS

The amount of preparation required before meetings will vary according to the type of meeting – its formality, importance, predictability and the role that the individual who is attending the meeting is going to take there. There can be few meetings, however, to which people do not need to give some prior thought. Perhaps the most important issue to consider is what your own objectives are going to be at a meeting. It is only when these have been clarified that it is possible to establish what other prior preparation is required. It is also necessary to consider what is likely to be expected of you at a meeting. This may indicate the preparation you need to make so that other people's needs can be satisfied. At formal meetings it will be necessary to see that the agenda and papers are distributed well in advance. Any procedural rules or constitutional statement about the powers of a meeting needs to be not only to hand but also thoroughly understood, so that such issues can be dealt with immediately and reassuringly if they emerge during a meeting. One would not be reassured by a football referee who had continually to refer to a book on the rules of football whilst a game was being played. The more formal the meeting, the more a chair may rely on the secretary to handle procedural matters before a meeting and to be a source of information during it. It may be expected that the meeting will be run, not just in accordance with its constitution but by the normal conventions of committee procedure. Consequently, a list of these conventions is included as an Appendix to this chapter. The chair will also need to understand the substantive issues and their history sufficiently well to guide the discussion effectively.

THE AGENDA AND ITS MANAGEMENT

Clearly, meetings need a structure for the consideration of substantive items. This is normally provided by an agenda. However, it is necessary to be pro-active in thinking about an agenda and not simply list the items in the order that they are received. The chair and the secretary in particular may have to think carefully about what items need to be considered. If decisions are to be taken at a meeting, the 'degrees of freedom' available need to be identified and explained. The frequency of meetings and their duration need to be related to the volume of business. The volume of business may also need to be managed by combining items. Thought should also be given to logical sequence of items. A further issue is the need to allocate time for discussion of individual items. It is all too easy to spend an inordinate amount of time on easy and relatively minor items with key issues being left to the end when people may be in a hurry, tired and a meeting not even quorate. Approval may be needed from a committee as a whole about issues such as sequence, time allocations and deferment of items. Exceptionally, the order may need to be varied, for example, because a key person has to leave. Other items may be introduced under 'any other business', but not if they are controversial and should have been identified on the original agenda. The chair also needs to beware of the agenda being hijacked by a member or members raising items 'on the back of' other items instead of tabling these issues beforehand with written reports if necessary. Another issue for the chair to beware of is a meeting being used as a dumping ground for issues where responsibilities lie elsewhere or for problems that simply can't be resolved.

Who should attend meetings?

Thought may have to be given to who should be invited to a meeting. This may be totally prescribed by the constitution of a committee but, when the constitution is first established, the matter has to be examined. In any case, constitutions sometimes need amending, people may need to be specially invited to attend meetings and, on occasion, people may need to be excluded from meetings, or for part of the proceedings, because of conflicts of interest. A balance usually has to be struck between having the interested parties present and not involving too many people because of the varying levels of interest and the costs involved, particularly in terms of time. A system of sub-committees can be a way of getting the optimum balance between differing interests and economy of time. Sometimes it will be appropriate to establish *ad hoc* sub-committees that can enable the detail of a particular issue to be examined without holding up the main business of a meeting. It can be particularly dangerous to exclude a person from a meeting primarily because they are likely to take a controversial position, or controversial as far as the chair is concerned. To exclude on this basis may lead to charges of unfair chairing, which may then mean that the chair is under procedural challenge, as well as being challenged on a substantive issue. Controversial issues tend to surface anyway, and it may be best to see that this happens via the established machinery for resolving conflict rather than in another way, particularly if the chair would otherwise lose respect in the process.

Other preparation

Other issues that may require forethought include the exact nature of information that people attending meetings need to have beforehand so that they can contribute effectively and the seating arrangements at a meeting. The type of room and layout can affect discussion, as can seating arrangements. Seating arrangements can be controlled by providing place names, which has the added advantage of identifying those present.

It is only realistic to add that there may be pre-meetings before the main meeting. This may be part of the established procedure – for example, it may be customary for the chair and secretary to go through the items before a meeting so that they are familiar with the issues. Other pre-meetings may be of a political nature, with one or more sub-groups within a committee forming a caucus to try to agree the line that they will take during a meeting. A small minority who prepare in this way can have a powerful influence on the outcome of any discussions. They will be primed and create a certain amount of momentum for the views that they express during a meeting. If they vote together at a meeting, they may find that the natural divisions amongst the other people present make it relatively easy to get a majority in favour of their point of view. This may lead other sub-groups to have pre-meetings as well, in an attempt to counter such tactics. One way of dealing with an attempt to bulldoze a minority point of view through a committee, or other meeting, is simply to alert other members as to what is happening beforehand. The chair, or for that matter any member of a committee, may wish to forestall a particular proposal. It may be a matter not so much of converting others, which is sometimes difficult, but of alerting people as to what is happening, so that they are on guard as far as their own interests are concerned. This may also be necessary when there is an attempt to conceal information.

The importance of preparation before meetings was confirmed for me by a study I was able to undertake into the operation of joint consultative committees within one of the former regional Gas Boards in the UK.[1] Eight out of the 19 consultative committees collapsed, ostensibly because the employees were not prepared to continue sending representatives to the meetings. This was attributed by some to apathy, but raised the question as to whether or not the Gas Board was in breach of its statutory duty to consult with employee representatives. A detailed analysis of the committee proceedings revealed that the key variable was the managerial style of the chair. Some worked out what they wanted from the meetings and also considered what the employee representatives expected. Other managers clearly saw the meetings as an unnecessary chore and went through the motions of holding meetings without thinking of the uses to which the meetings might be put or what the employees wanted. The pattern that emerged was remarkably clear. The managers who prepared carefully for their meetings found their committees survived and made a constructive though not dramatic contribution. Invariably, there were more items initiated by the management side than the employee side. The other committees all collapsed, and it emerged on studying the committee minutes that with the collapsed committees invariably more items were raised for discussion by the employee representatives than by the managers. The last meeting of one committee ended somewhat dramatically when, after repeated requests for clothing lockers had been turned down, the employee representatives commented acidly that it was strange that an employer who could not afford clothing lockers could afford major capital expenditure at the same site. Ironically it also emerged that the consultative meetings tended to operate efficiently where they were least needed – the need for open communication being greatest at the undertakings where the local managers were unwilling or unable to make their joint consultative committees effective.

CONDUCT DURING MEETINGS

The job of chairing a meeting effectively obviously depends a great deal on prior preparation and on the ability of the chair to distinguish between substantive issues and procedural and process issues. Consideration will now be given to some of the potential problems, not already covered, that may arise during a meeting. A key job of the chair is to see that they actually use the knowledge of the people who are present. It is up to the chair to see that the appropriate issues are identified and then ensure that the collective knowledge and skills of the members are used to resolve the issues. If further information would help, the chair needs to consider releasing or obtaining it. The chair may contribute to the substantive discussions, but should only do so when the issues have been properly identified. The position as chair should not be used to exclude members from discussion who may have important contributions to make or who may feel neglected if they are not given the opportunity to contribute. This may seem an obvious enough point to make, but in practice chairs vary considerably in the skill with which they use the abilities of the people present. Good and bad examples are obvious on radio and television programmes, just as there will be good and bad examples of chairing in most organisations. Some chairs are very adept at drawing out the views of those who have been invited to speak and at controlling subsequent discussion. Others, lacking this skill, invite people to contribute to, for example, media programmes and then use their procedural position and studio confidence to grab the limelight – and in so doing wreck any discussion.

The chair's role in resolving conflict

One of the key roles of meetings can be as a way of resolving conflict. Ironically, one of the key roles of a chair can be to identify what the conflict is in the first place. Unless this is done, agreement may be reached before the basic issues have been adequately considered. Another general problem is the need to handle conflict in such a way that the mechanism for resolving it is not destroyed in the process. Sometimes there is little or no conflict and the exchange of specialist information leads to a decision to which all contributors are equally committed. On other occasions the conflicts can be so bitter that the decision-making process collapses. The range of potential conflict within the House of Commons is such that members do not risk having a chair who is not neutral: the Speaker, who chairs the proceedings, has a neutral procedural role. The mayor fulfils the same function in meetings of local government councils. Many trade unions appoint a president who fulfils a similar function.

The conflict between providing leadership on substantive policy issues and in the procedural and process areas is sometimes obvious within the British Cabinet. Prime ministers need to provide leadership in all these areas, but run the risk that, if they fall out of step with the majority of Cabinet members on policy issues, their position will become threatened. The problem of achieving balance may influence the choice of party leader in the first place. Party leaders have to be careful not to be identified with too extreme a position for fear that they are seen to frustrate the democratic process within their party, particularly in countries which pride themselves on their democratic traditions. It is also necessary for party leaders to demonstrate that they can distinguish between their own views and those of the party, particularly as the views of the party which they will have to present will sometimes differ from their personal views. Neglect of these issues may well have contributed to the replacement of Margaret Thatcher by John Major in 1990.

Examples of the problems of reconciling these different types of leadership are particularly easy to give from the world of politics because of the blaze of publicity that surrounds political activity in democratic countries. A balance still has to be kept within less democratic structures, as few leaders have so much power that they can afford to ignore totally the views of their supporters. In any case, a balance is necessary so that decisions are taken after the relevant information has been considered, and not imposed by one person regardless of what information is available from others.

One of the ways in which the chair can retain credibility and acceptability when they are involved in securing a particular outcome is by avoiding getting involved in controversial discussion unless it is as a last resort. They may find that the conflict resolves itself satisfactorily without their involvement, or that the residual conflict between themselves and the majority of those present at a meeting is so small that accommodation between the two views is relatively easy. Even when the residual conflict is large, the chair may then preserve their position by demonstrating that, after providing for fair discussion of a particular point, they will resolve the outstanding conflict by whatever method is agreed. If the decision-making process is democratic, this may mean that the chair is outvoted, but the defeat on the substantive issue need not affect the chair's credibility to lead procedurally if they have shown that their views have not affected the quality of their procedural and process leadership. In a more hierarchical structure, the chair may ultimately say 'I have heard you all but disagree' and impose their own decision. Resolving conflict in that way means at least that the chair is fully aware of the arguments against their particular decision and has demonstrated that colleagues have had a fair opportunity to state their case before the final decision is taken. What is likely to be counter-productive is the chair appearing to be willing to listen or to share decision-making powers when they have decided what to do anyway. What is then likely to emerge is that the members have complete freedom to come to the decision that the chair has already determined!

The need for process leadership may exist even in informal discussions between relatively few people. It may be important to think carefully about how such meetings are handled, as so much business can be conducted in this way. Sometimes the level of informality, the competitive nature of relationships or the sensitivity of the issues being discussed is such that it is inappropriate for a formal chair to be appointed. It may nevertheless be both useful and necessary if one person, perhaps quite informally, deals with the process aspects of discussion. This may involve taking a purely neutral role and asking such questions as 'What is the problem?', 'What are everyone's views?' The other parties may be quite prepared to let one person emerge as the informal chair, particularly if it is seen that they are confining themselves to a neutral role. It may later be possible for that person to enter into the substantive discussions, but only so long as they demonstrate that this is not going to endanger the process control arrangements that have evolved. Otherwise, the person may find that their substantive contributions are not welcome or that process leadership is challenged.

The danger of overinvolvement by the chair

It is very easy for the person chairing a meeting to underestimate the extent to which they get involved in discussion and to overestimate the extent to which other people are involved. This is a problem that can confront lecturers who have responsibility for leading discussions. One system for training lecturers in the technique of discussion-leading is to chart the pattern of contributions during a discussion. The resultant chart or 'sociogram' can reveal a pattern of which the discussion leader was unaware. A typical pattern is shown in Figure 13.1. An examination of the flow of discussion shows that most of it was centred around the chair (or discussion leader). There was little cross-discussion and one person did not contribute at all. If this was appropriate, and the chair was aware of what was really happening, it may have been perfectly satisfactory. However, it is very easy for a chair to assume that, because they are involved and interested, so is everyone else. This is not automatically the case. It is possible for a person to sit through a meeting, seething with frustration, but not contributing. Others may remain passively silent though able to contribute. Meanwhile, the chair may be quite unaware of all this. It can be instructive for a chair to be shown a flow chart (or sociogram) of a meeting they have chaired and mentally try to build up a picture of the actual pattern of discussion during their next meeting. Regular checks on the body language of those present can provide important clues as to their feelings about particular topics and about the conduct of the meeting generally. The possibility of talking more than one realises is illustrated by the following example:

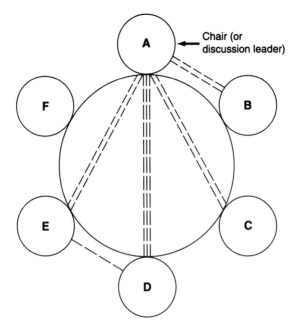

Figure 13.1 Chair-centred discussion

[A] story is told about a brand new judge who took his place on the bench determined to achieve standards of self-restraint. At the end of his first day he thought he had done remarkably well and went round to his old chambers to see a friend who had been appearing in front of him all day. 'How did I do?' asked the new judge confidently. 'Not bad at all dear boy,' said the other. 'But you really must stop talking so much.'[2]

Involving members

Often the flow of discussion that is actually needed is more like that shown in Figure 13.2. In this second chart it is much less obvious who is the chair. Everyone has contributed and there is more cross-discussion than was the case in the previous chart. The flow of discussion may need to be routed more through the chair in large formal meetings, but even in that situation it may be appropriate to allow some cross-discussion provided it is not disruptive. In large formal meetings it may still be necessary for the chair to check out the attitudes of members to the way meetings are handled.

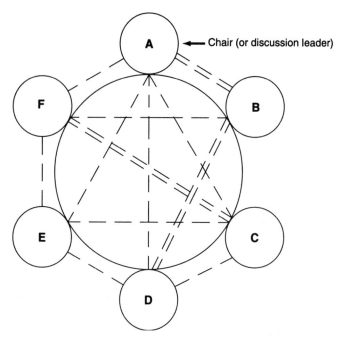

Figure 13.2 Group-centred discussion

I was once able to compare the attitudes of the various members of a hospital management group towards the way in which meetings were handled and found that there were some surprising differences in perception. The chair and secretary appeared convinced that everyone had ample opportunity to contribute, whilst the senior member of the nursing staff who was present at the meetings was clearly of the opinion that she was only permitted to speak when invited to do so. I, as an outsider, seemed to be the only one aware of these differences in perception. In this particular case, open discussion was not helped by the fact that meetings were conducted in a long rectangular room. The seating arrangements conveyed an impression of there being a hierarchy within the meeting, and it was significant that the nursing representative sat at the far end of the table from the chair and secretary. At another hospital within the same group meetings were held in a room which permitted seating arrangements to be in the form of a semi-circle, which seemed to permit more genuinely open discussion. I was left wondering whether this was accident or design in view of the more open managerial style of the hospital manager who convened those latter meetings.

There are other important points to note. These include the need to protect the position of the member who is being ridiculed, particularly if they have a potential contribution to make. Conversely, it is important to see that the authority of the chair is not used against an individual, unless there is very good reason. Members may feel much more keenly about opposition to their views expressed from the chair than from ordinary members of a meeting.

Careful judgements have to be made about the amount of control exercised by the chair. If the chair is seen as being primarily concerned with organising discussion so that the group can resolve its differences and proceed with its business, control by the chair is much more likely to be accepted compared with a situation where there is suspicion that the control is being used to establish particular policy decisions. If exchanges become too heated, that may be the time to insist that all contributions are routed through the chair, even if subsequently that convention is dropped. The routing of all contributions through the chair may only be necessary when the group lacks the self-discipline to evolve a means of taking it in turns to speak. If the chair is ignored, or if people talk whilst the chair is speaking, the pointed silence may be a more appropriate way of re-establishing control than by the raising of one's voice.

Chairs also need to strike the right balance concerning the pace of discussion. People may be very concerned to state their own views but impatient of the right of others to do the same. Too quick a pace may leave many people with the feeling that they have not had adequate opportunity to state their views, whilst too slow a pace may leave many people with the view that their time has been unnecessarily wasted. The ease with which points at issue can simply be misunderstood should never be underestimated. It is important that the chair clarifies and summarises whenever there appears to be any doubt or whenever decisions are taken.

Recording the outcome of meetings

The possibility of confusion about the content and outcome of a meeting is obviously going to be reduced further if there are minutes or whatever other record is appropriate. However, for this to be undertaken effectively, meetings need to have been conducted properly in the first place. One does not, for example, want mis-understandings about what was really decided to be left to surface when the minutes are distributed. The reasons why this all too easily happens have already been explained in the section on the conduct of negotiating meetings in the previous chapter. The comments in that section on written reports are also very relevant to meetings generally. Recording can take a variety of forms but verbatim records are rarely necessary or useful. A circulated minute is the most common type of record but, if this is inappro-priate, as a minimum the chair should make an *aide-mémoire* even in many informal situations. Other parties involved may also find it prudent to record an *aide-mémoire* where there is no formal minute. A record of the outcomes of a meeting is what is crucial. A record of the discussions prior to an outcome may be counter-productive. In the heat of discussion people may say things that it is in no-one's interest to record. Consequently, considerable tact may be needed in writing up minutes so that the outcomes are accurately recorded without rekindling arguments that have been settled. The respon-sibility for action also needs to be carefully identified to help ensure that action that is agreed is actually implemented. Where the scale and importance justifies it, one may need a recorder who is separate from the person advising the chair on procedural matters.

CONCLUSION

The theme that has been continuously developed in this chapter is the need for chairs to recognise that substantive issues cannot be considered properly unless there is an appropriate procedural framework and effective process control. This need is reflected in the procedural convention that points of order take precedence over other issues during meetings. What is crucial is that the load on the chair is clearly recognised, with a view to seeing either how the load can be handled or, if necessary, whether part of it can be redistributed. There is often a dangerous assumption that the procedural and process leadership can be left to look after itself – rather like the quaint notion that in sports teams the choice of captain involves no more than picking the best player.

Emphasis has been placed on the procedural and process control roles, because that is common to all meetings. This chapter should provide a basic understanding of the key issues, but should be seen as a starting point only. Much can be learned by observing the way discussions, meetings and committees operate – both within employing organisations and elsewhere, including within the family. This in turn can be a basis for practising the skills of chairing when the opportunity presents itself. If a person has the ability to learn in this way, they may find that they increasingly assume the chairing role in a variety of situations. This in turn can provide opportunities for further practice and development, and also help ensure that meetings are run more effectively.[3]

NOTES

1 W. David Rees, 'The Practical Functions of Joint Consultation Considered Historically and in the Light of some Recent Experiences in South Wales', M.Sc.(Econ.) thesis, University of London, 1962.

2 Keith Evans, *Advocacy at the Bar: A Beginner's Guide*, Financial Training Publications, 1983, p. 87.

3 For an excellent account of the rules of meetings procedure see Michael Cannell and Norman Citrine (eds), *Citrine's ABC of Chairmanship*, NCLC Publishing Society Ltd, distributed by the Fabian Society, 1982. For further and comprehensive accounts of this subject, see ICSA Study Text, *Meetings*, BPP Publishing, London, 1993; P. Lawton and Eric C. Rigby, *Meetings – Their Law and Practice*, Macdonald and Evans (Handbook series), 1992.

APPENDIX TO CHAPTER 13: DEFINITIONS AND EXPLANATIONS OF SOME TERMS USED IN FORMAL MEETINGS

Ad hoc: this Latin phrase means, literally, 'to this'. Its meaning has been extended to 'set up to serve a particular purpose'. Thus, an *ad hoc* committee is one which has been set up to serve a particular purpose and which will cease to exist as soon as this purpose has been served.

Agenda: this is a Latin word meaning 'things requiring or deserving to be done'. It is really plural in form but is now used as a singular word and means simply 'a list of the items of business to be dealt with at a meeting'.

Amendment: when someone moves that a proposition should be altered in some way, they are moving an amendment. It should be noted that an amendment proposes an alteration of a proposition, not a direct negation of it nor a completely different proposition.

Ballot: this means simply 'a secret vote'. Members register their votes on paper and not by a show of hands.

Casting vote: the chair is allowed an ordinary vote as a member of the meeting. Sometimes, however, the standing orders allow them an extra vote which is called a 'casting vote', because they may, if they so wish, use it to decide on an issue on which the voting is equal.

Co-opt: if a committee feels that it would benefit from the services of some person possessing, for example, special qualifications or experience, it may decide (if it has been given such powers) to co-opt that person, i.e., to make them an additional member of the committee. The committee has exercised power of 'co-option' and the person has been 'co-opted'.

Ex officio: a person may claim to be a member of a committee, not because they have been elected but *ex officio*, that is 'by virtue of their office'.

Minutes: this word means 'a brief but accurate record of what took place at a meeting'.

Motion: this is a general term which means 'anything that is moved or proposed at a meeting'. Thus, a proposition is a motion but also an amendment is a motion.

Nem. con.: this is an abbreviation for the Latin phrase *nemine contradicente* and means 'no-one speaking against'. Thus 'carried *nem. con.*' does not mean the same as 'carried unanimously' which means that every one present voted for the motion.

Next business: when a motion is being debated it may appear to some member or members that it would be unfortunate for the meeting to reach a decision on the matter in question or that it would be a waste of time to continue the debate. One device to stop the debate is for a member who has not already spoken to stand up and say 'Chair, I move next business'. If this motion is seconded it is put to the vote immediately, without discussion and if it is carried the meeting does in fact move on to the next business. If the motion is defeated, the meeting then resumes the debate on which it was already engaged.

Nominate: This means 'to propose someone for election to an office'. Usually a nomination does not need to be seconded.

Any other business: This may appear on the agenda of a meeting to allow members to raise items which have come to light after the agenda has been prepared. However, any items the chair allows under this heading must be agreed by the meeting to be urgent and to have come to notice so recently that there was no time to have them included in the agenda.

Point of information: Sometimes a member who does not wish to take part in a discussion or who is preparing to speak later may wish to ask a question on relevant facts. They may do this by saying 'Chair, on a point of information, can you tell me, etc.'

Point of order: A member may rise at any time and say something 'on a point of order' – but they will soon be told to sit down if what they say is not in fact 'on a point of order'. The member must be able to prove that, or reasonably to question whether, another member has spoken or acted, or something has been done, or is going to be done not in accordance with the rules, standing orders or terms of reference or other regulations which govern the conduct of the meeting. A point of order relates only to procedure: if the point raised is really part of the subject under discussion, it is not a point of order.

Previous question: This really means 'that the question be *not* now put'. If the motion is carried, no more discussion of the main question can occur, and it is shelved. If it is not carried, then the original motion must be put to the vote at once. Previous question can only be moved for an original or substantive motion.

Quorum: This is a Latin word meaning simply 'of whom'. Its meaning in meeting procedure is extended to 'the number of members who must be present before the proceedings can be valid'. The quorum for a meeting is usually laid down on the rules or standing orders which apply, but if it is not laid down it is generally taken to mean a minimum of approximately one-third and never less than three.

Reference: When a task has been delegated by a meeting to a committee or by a committee to a sub-committee, the committee or subcommittee will eventually report to the main body and will probably recommend some action. If a member of the main body does not agree with any action reported or recommendation made, they should 'move the reference back' to the report. This motion is discussed and if it is carried it means that the committee or sub-committee must reconsider the subject in question and report again later.

Resolution: It is wrong to talk of moving or proposing a resolution. One can move or propose a motion or proposition and either of these becomes a resolution if it is passed. In other words, a resolution is something that a meeting has resolved to do.

Right to reply: It is customary to allow the mover of a proposition (but not of an amendment), who will have spoken first in the debate, the right to speak again at the end of the debate. In the second speech, however, they must not introduce any new material but merely reply to points already raised by other speakers.

Standing orders: Organisations which hold regular formal meetings (e.g., trade unions, councils, clubs) often have rules which stipulate the manner in which the business of their meetings shall be conducted. These are called 'standing orders' and they deal with such things as the length of time for which speakers may speak, the order in which speakers shall speak, the manner of conducting elections of officers, the order in which items shall be taken. Standing orders may be in addition to, or may even override, the general rules of meeting procedure. If there are any, the chair and the secretary should be very familiar with them. A member may at any time move 'suspension of standing orders' and have this motion debated. For instance, if standing orders stipulate that a speaker may speak for only five minutes, it may occasionally be desirable to allow someone to exceed this limit in order to complete an important statement. Suspension of standing orders, if carried, will allow them to do this.

Substantive motion: When any amendments to a motion have been passed, the motion has its wording altered accordingly and is then called the substantive motion.

Teller: This means a member who has been appointed to count the number of votes cast on any question.

Terms of reference: These are instructions given, generally to a committee, defining clearly the nature and the limits of the task which it has been set.

That the question be now put: This may be moved at any time during the debate on a motion, but must be moved by someone who has not already spoken. If it is carried, the matter under debate is immediately put to the vote; if it is not carried, the debate is resumed. Clearly this is a useful device to stop unnecessary or useless discussion (see also *next business*).

Conclusion

The aim of this book has been to help those who have, or expect to have, managerial responsibilities. Readers may have found that the content is relevant to the problems they see or face to a surprisingly large extent. The reality is that many other people have had to face similar problems and one may as well profit from their experience. There is little point in rediscovering the wheel on your own if such rediscovery, or rather the managerial equivalent, is unnecessary. The coverage of the book is not intended to be exhaustive. However, anyone with managerial responsibilities must be confronted with many of the problem areas that have been identified and need to have, or to develop, the conceptual understanding and related skills to deal with these issues.

The skills of management are not a mystic art which people either do or do not have. Neither are they a pattern of behaviour which can only be acquired in a mysterious way which defies analysis. As with so many skills, careful study and practice can lead to substantial improvements in performance. Admittedly, some people will have more potential than others, but perhaps the most important requirement for the conscious development of managerial skills is the realisation that this is possible.

Some readers are likely to have had little in the way of formal management training and those who have may have found that not all of it has helped improve their managerial performance. This book is intended to provide a sound base for the development of a range of critical managerial skills. The conceptual understanding that is required is the vital first stage. That needs to be followed by the conscious development of skills and evaluation by the reader of the extent to which they have been able to able to apply them. It may well be that readers are already proficient in some of the areas that have been identified, but there may be other areas where there is the potential for significant development.

A key feature of this book has been stress on the need for managers to develop their diagnostic skills. The book is not intended to provide a set of prescriptive remedies to be applied without thought. It is only after careful analysis has been undertaken to identify the nature and cause or causes of problems that it is appropriate to consider solutions. The range of techniques explained in the book, or any other techniques for that matter, should only be applied after adequate diagnosis. Careful thought may also need to be given as to the sequence in which various problems are tackled.

The self-development of the individual manager and improvements in job performance may hinge on the identification of realistic objectives. This may necessitate not just concentration on one or two key areas but also the setting of attainable standards. It may be quite counter-productive for a person to set out to change the world in managerial terms, either in the range of improvements they attempt or in the level of performance which they set. Setting unrealistic standards of performance may confirm the adage that the 'excellent is the enemy of the good'. It is far better to achieve a good improvement than to fail in attempting the impossible. A gradual approach to development of managerial skills may also help in the assessment of what improvements are politically possible. It is no good a manager identifying improvements in an organisation, however desirable, if they are not politically attainable. It may also be appropriate to identify short-term and long-term objectives for improvement – both in oneself and in organisational performance.

The development of the reader's managerial skills is likely to result in an advance up the 'managerial escalator'. This in turn is likely to lead to a need to pay even more attention to the managerial aspects of the job and to the relevant areas of skill. This also emphasises the constantly changing pattern of work in organisations. Just as the individual is not a static creature, so organisations change and the environments in which they exist. Individuals may also move from one organisation to another. The reader may not only have to cope with a fairly continuous pattern of change but may find that much of their work is concerned with implementing change that affects other people. This is likely to be both the continuous everyday changes and the more spectacular one-off changes caused by, for example, the development of specific new technologies or markets. In short, the manager will find that they have continuously to adapt to changed circumstances and also to help other people adapt. The realisation of this, and the development of appropriate skills, should help the individual not only to handle such change more effectively but also to influence events as well as simply be influenced by them.

One of the particular problems likely to be encountered as a person acquires increasing managerial responsibility is greater exposure to criticism. 'Back seat' advice can be very annoying, particularly if it comes from people who are neither particularly well informed nor competent. It can be all the more annoying if sometimes the advice turns out to be correct. As the importance of the decisions that the manager has to take increases, it is inevitable that those affected will comment on those decisions – either openly or covertly. This is a cross that just has to be borne – hopefully somewhat more easily if it is recognised in advance. It is the price to be paid by almost anyone who accepts responsibility. What is particularly needed is the ability to react sensibly to criticism – neither overreacting to ill informed comment nor ignoring what may be sound advice.

This book is not intended as a substitute for decision-making but as a means of helping managers develop the ability to take appropriate decisions for themselves and to acquire the ability to implement those decisions effectively. The more that managerial problems are consciously identified and tackled and the more that the individual works at their managerial skills development, the more effective they will be. This should generate confidence and create the opportunity for even further development. Ironically, one of the ways in which managers may learn most is when they make mistakes. This can cause them to question their pattern of behaviour with a view to improving their performance. The critical need is for managers to use such incidents as opportunities for learning, instead of letting them affect their self-confidence.

One of the biggest adjustments that a successful manager may have to make is that of continuously outgrowing their job. In coping with that, however, they may not only gain substantial material rewards but develop as a person and make a powerful contribution to the particular organisation in which they work and to society in general.

Index

Note: figures are indicated by bold numbers.

Aberfan disaster (1966) 124
accountability 125; empowerment and 134
accreditation for prior experiential learning (APEL) 249
accreditation for prior learning (APL) 249
'accuracy' in payment systems 174
Acquired Rights Directive 84, 89
'acting down' 9
'acting up' 211
'Action-centred Leadership **109**
'action learning' 251
Adair, John 109
added value, concept of 80, 174
'administration', historic emphasis of 82–3
Advisory Conciliation and Arbitration Service (ACAS) 272, 276, 305
Advisory Handbook 276, 286
ageing population, problem of 91
agency concept 82
Amalgamated Engineering and Electrical Union (AEEU) 305
American Airline Pilots Association 191
American Airlines, computer reservation system (Sabre) 69
American companies, human resource management and 299; quality circles in 61
appraisal 227, 242–3; giving feedback 235–6; handling effectively, strategies for 231–2; and interview preparation 234–5; links with performance management 30; objectives 228–9; performance 235; potential problems with schemes 229–31; rating and recording 232–4; self-appraisal 236–7; various other situations, handling of 237–9
Armstrong, Michael 133
assertiveness 98, 117–19
Assertiveness at Work 119
assessment centres, key factors in effectiveness 211, 242–3
Atkinson, J. 59
Audit Commission, 'value for money' investigations 88

Bahrani, Homa 181
Bank of Commerce and Credit International 125
Belbin, R. Meredith 107–8, 216
Belgium 112
'best fit' 110
'bias against understanding', reporting news and 198
Binney, George 66
Birt, John 198
Black, Larry 152

Blackler, Frank 15
Blake, R.R. 107
body language 116, 192–4, 255
Bottomley, Virginia 119
Boydell, T. 15
Bradford football ground fire 311
Bright, Sir Keith 125
British accreditation (BS 5750) 65
British Aerospace 80
British Medical Research Council 43
British Rail 302
British Steel Corporation 220
British Telecom 153
Brown, Wilfred 128
Burns, T. 55–6
'burnt out' 14
Bush, President George 198
business process re-engineering (BPR) 47–8
Business and Technology Education Council 248
'buying– in' 244

Cabinet Efficiency Unit, review of 'mandarin' system 87
Carrington, Lord 125
Carswell, John 187
causes of imbalance between managerial and specialist activity, managerial selection 11–13; pressure from sub-ordinates 16–17; training of managers 17–19; rewards and work preferences 13–16
chair-centred discussion **341**
'charisma' 97
'chartered manager' 21
chronic unemployment, advantages to employers of 59–60; changes in organisations despite 105; job distortion during 147; 'macho management' and 107; and motivation 145; problems created by 91
'citizens' charters' 83
City and Guilds 248
'civilianisation' of police forces 92

Civil Service, competitive tendering 84; Ibbs Report and 5–6; job classification in 165; 'mandarin' approach in 19; merit payment 239; more commercial approach in 82; radical developments in 53; selection in 216; upper age limit in 220
Civil Service Agency 82, 127
Civil Service Select Committee 87
Classical Management theorists 53, 145
coal mining, decline in 305
coal mining dispute (1984/5) 301, 322
Code of Practice on Disciplinary and Dismissal Procedures 272, 279, 282; guidelines on disciplinary procedures 291
'comfort zone' 9
Commissioner for Protection Against Unlawful Industrial Action 307–8
Commissioner for Trade Unions 307
Commission for Racial Equality 219–20, 241
common law, employees and reasonable job changes 170
communication, body language 192–4 ; bogus feedback 182–4; choice of language 190–1; choice of time and place 189–90; coaxing information 188; downward and presentational skills 194–5; importance of 177–9; lack of feedback 181–2; listening effectively 188–9; listening problems 179–80; recognising cultural barriers 191–2; resistance to criticism 184–6; role of the media in 197–200; selective perception and bias 186–8; written 195–7
communication exercise **181**
community charge (poll tax) 88–9

companies, key attributes of good 57–8
'competence' 21
competences 22, 174, 242, 249; assessment of 250; management 1, 22, 250; occupational 248; required 146; reward for new 173, 175, 238
competition, for design work 80; level of performance and 295, 299
competitive pressures, effect on health and safety 311
competitive tendering 84, 88, 300
computer-assisted learning 246
computer-controlled production, organisational structure and 67
computer technology, impact of 48, 59
conduct during meetings 337–8; chair's role in resolving conflict 338–40; danger of over-involvement by chair 340–1; involving members 341–3
Confederation of British Industry (CBI) 302
conflict between specialist and managerial activity, experience elsewhere 9–11; general consequences of 8–9; nature of problem 4–6; specialist career structures and their limitations 6–8
Conservative Party, labour market 'free up' policy 300; links with employers 306
Constable, Dr John 18
contracting out, local government and 90; in public sector 60
'core' civil servants 86
core work-force 59, 174–5, 210–11
corporate involvement, corporate loyalty and 151–4
'cost-plus' system 91
Council for National Academic Awards 92
council tax (1993) 89
counselling 227, 252–3 ; in disciplinary situations 261; and

grievance handling 258–60; specific skills in 254–8; value of 253–4
counselling interview, stages in 257
'creaming off' of parts of the job 16
Crichel Down case (1954) 124
'critical incident technique' 143
'crowding out' of long-term issues 46

'damage limitation' 36
Data Protection Act (1984) 234
Death of Corporate Loyalty 152
debt repayment, chronic unemployment and 91
decentralisation, Shell UK and 48
decision-making, discretion in 318; effective communication and 178; management and 53
de-layering 69; changes in organisations and 20, 243, 318; in Civil Service 87; empowerment and 133; in local government 90; in provincial police forces 92
delegation 123–5, 134; clarity about what delegated 128; effective use of subordinates 126–7; and factors outside manager's control 130; finding time to plan 130; the indispensable employee and 130–1; initially time-consuming 135; obstacles to effective 129–33; overlap with empowerment 133; promotion and, connection between 132–3; the skills of 127–9; time constraints and 126
Deming, W. Edwards 64, 66, 105, 194, 243
Department of Employment 85, 268, 279
deregulation, bus services and 92; in developing countries 81; in the West 81, 112

Deregulation Act (1994) 268
developing world, deregulation in 81
diagnostic skills, integration of employee relations with management activities 313–15; manager and employee relations and 311–12; recognising conflicts of interest 312–13
Director General of BBC, engaged on freelance basis 125
Disability Discrimination Act (1995) 219–20
disciplinary hearings 279–80; preparation and presentation 284–5; procedural sequence at 292; procedure during 283–4; relationship with criminal law 280–2; the result, communicating 285; role of the chair 283; role of the representative 282–3; suspension and 280
disciplinary letters, checklist for 293–4
disciplinary pyramid **278**, 318
discipline 263–4; appeals against warnings 287; objectives of 264–6; responsibility of individual manager for 276–9, 289
Discipline at Work 272
dismissal, exclusions from tribunals 269–70; grounds for 267–9; law relating to 266–7; remedies for employers 270–1; underestimation of freedom of employer 274
disputes procedure, collective differences and 316–17
Dixon, Norman 186
Donne, John 76
Donovan Commission 313–15
'double jeopardy' 282
'downsizing' 79, 134, 155, 248
Drucker, Peter 29, 204
Dulewicz, Victor 211
Dunkirk evacuation (1940) 43–4

Eastman Kodak 152
economic *activity* 84
economic *entity* 84
Economist, The 152
education, managerials roles in 20
'efficiency unit' 88
effort-performance expectancy 144
Eire, computer programming for America 80
Electronic Data Interchange (EDI) 68
electronic data processing 60
electronic mail (e mail) 68
'emotional hardening', managerial roles and 15
employee relations, the organisation and 297–99
employers, 'industrial muscle' of 301; NVQ standards and 249; obligations for health and safety 310; 'reasonable behaviour' by 268, 272, 274; required to consult with 'representatives of workforce' 269; 'witch-hunting' and 288
Employment Act (1990) 220
Employment Acts 307
Employment Appeals Tribunal 273
employment at the periphery, core employment and 59
Employment Protection (Consolidation) Act (1978) 220, 266, 306
empowerment, delegation and 123, 133–4, 152
'end of line' activities, errors and 62
'enterprise' as opposed to 'dependency' 81
equal opportunities, selection processes and 219–21
Equal Opportunities Commission 219–20, 269
equal opportunities policies, differences in public and private sector 203
Equal Pay Act (1970) 171
Equal Pay Directive (1975) 171

equal value 171–3
Estonia ferry sinking 311
ethical business practices, private
    organisations and 84
European Commission, case
    against UK (1982) 171; (1994)
    168, 269
European Community, Acquired
    Rights Directive 84, 89
European Court of Justice 269;
    part-timers and 61, 309
European Exchange Rate
    Mechanism, UK (1993) 125
European law, employees and 168,
    271, 295–6, 306, 308–9
European standard (ES 2200) 65
European Union 303; culture of
    founders of 112; employment
    legislation 308; local authority
    links with 91
Evening Standard 30

factors that determine structure
    of organisations 66, 92–3;
    identifying the critical function
    72; impact of technology 67–8;
    national culture 73; size 72
Fair Wages Resolutions 84
Falklands War (1982) 125, 281
Fayol, Henri 1, 53
Fennell Report (1988) 125
fibre-optics, information
    superhighways and 71, 246
Fiedler, F.E. 109
Fire, Auto and Marine Insurance
    124
'fire-fighting' activities 40
'fit', job 12, 58, 76
fixed-term contracts, disadvantages
    of 60; payment schemes and
    174
Fletcher, Clive 230
Follett, Mary Parker 1
formal meetings, terms used in
    346–9
Fox, Alan 31
France 112
Fraser, John Munro 213
'frictional' unemployment 300

functional flexibility, organisations
    and 60
further and higher education,
    changes to 92

'gap-analysis' 47
Garrett, John 87
General National Council for
    Vocational Qualifications 248
General National Vocational
    Qualifications (GNVQs) 248
'genuine material factor', payment
    rates and 173
geographic arrangement of work,
    Civil Service agencies and 88;
    impact of 77
George, David Lloyd 209
Germany 19, 80
'get it right first time', TQM and
    62
Glaspie, Ambassador Avril 185
globalisation of markets 80; effect
    on meetings 329; impact on the
    private sector 93; intensified
    competition and 295; planning
    and 48, 59
Goffee, Robert 12, 15, 153
Gorbachev, President 198
government purchasing power,
    business behaviour and 83
Government White Paper (1994),
    Civil Service and 87
Greater London Council 81
Greenbury Committee (1995) 302
Green Paper, equal value,
    independent expert and 172
group-centred discussion **342**
Guardian 85, 197
'guest organisation', local culture
    and 113
Gulf War (1990) 185, 198

'halo' effect 216, 233
Handy, Charles 18, 48, 57, 99,
    110, 152; report by 21
Hanson organisation 48
Hargreaves, Alison 108
Hawthorn experiments 54
Healey, Denis 49

Health and Safety at Work Act (1974) 310
Health and Safety Commission 311
'heroic' medicine, cost of 92
Herzberg, Frederick 141–3, 145, 158
high-cost economies, and relocation of manufacturing 80
Hillary, Peter 108
Hillsborough stadium disaster (Sheffield) 311
'holistic' approach to learning 247
Holland, Arnhem offensive 186
Homans, George 120
Home Office, core and ancillary activities 92
House of Commons, role of the Speaker 338
House of Lords, decision on part-time staff (1994) 61, 269; *Polkey v A.E. Dayton* (1987) 272
Howard, Michael 125
Hull, Raymond 12
Human Relations School 54
human resource management (HRM) 80, 242–3, 298–9, 315
Humble, John 29–30
Hussein, President Saddam 185, 198
'hygiene factors', importance of 142–3

Ibbs Report (1988) 5, 86
IBM 152
identifying the manager's job, role set analysis 32–9
Imperial Chemical Industries, technical career structures 6
incentive payment schemes 144, 159, 175; group schemes 163; long-term effects of 160–3
Independent 173
Indonesia 142
'industrial muscle' of employers 301
Industrial Relations Act (1971) 266
industrial tribunals, composition of 273; defences by employer

and operation of 271–5; fairness of employment practices and 221; need for effective procedure 275–6
information technology 52, 67; advantages of 69–70; 'business scope redefinition' and 68; constraints of 70–1; effect on managers 28; effect on meetings 329; impact on private sector 93; intensified competition and 295; interdepartmental co-operation and 76
Inner London Education Authority 81
In Search of Excellence 57–8
interactive training videos 246
interdepartmental meetings, hidden agenda at 75
international standard (ISO 9000) 65
interview assessment form 226
interviewers, and identification of information 213
Investors in People Award (IIP) 249
Islamic world, usury and 114
Italy 112

Japan 19, 59, 62; attack on Pearl Harbor 186; concept of TQM and 64; management development in 251
Japanese companies, corporate loyalty and 151; human resource management and 299; multi-skilling and 60, 318; quality circles in 61–2; reasons for success 73; TQM and 64–5; in the UK 208
Jay, Peter 198
job classification 165
job demands, matching individual needs and 149–51
job descriptions, generic 60; interpretation of 27; in nursing profession 7
job design 145–7; and job distortion 147–9, 239

job distortion **149**, 239
job evaluation 22, 164–5, 325;
    careful choice of factors in 169;
    choices of scheme 166–7; equal
    value 171–3; implementation
    and operation 167–71; job
    competences and 174; need for
    appeals mechanism 168–9;
    objectives of 165; pressures for
    change 173–4; transferability of
    to other organisations 171; types
    of schemes 165–6
'job and finish', truck drivers and
    162
job insecurity, and motivation of
    employees 136, 155
job ranking 165–7
joint agreements, manager and
    employee relations and 315–17
'just-in-time employment' 152
'just-in-time' production 64, 70,
    304

kaizan 64
Keenan, T. 14–15
key decision-makers, long-term
    planning and 46
Kings Cross fire (1987) 125, 311
'knock-on effect' 170, 172
Krushchev, Nikita 193–4
Kuwait (invasion of 1990) 185

Labour government,
    administration (1974–9) 306–7
labour market, changes in 300–3;
    disputes in 301; effect of
    deregulation on 311; the impact
    of inward investment 303–4;
    legal developments 306–9;
    women and 303
Labour Party, alternative local
    government scenario by 81–2;
    links with trade unions 306
Lawler, Edward E. 144
leadership 58; authoritarian 104;
    charismatic 99; contingency
    theories of 108–10; traditional
    and situational approaches to
    102–3

'leadership contingency model,
    variables of 109
leadership styles, a continuum of
    106
'lean and mean', concept of 79–80
learning development contracts
    249
Leavitt, Harold J. 181
Legge, Karen 314
Lloyds of London, self-regulatory
    body 134
local authorities, employment
    policies of 83–4; Equal
    opportunities policies 221; links
    with the European Union 91
local authority services,
    compulsory competitive
    tendering 88
local government 53, 82, 84,
    88–91; merit payment 239;
    pressure for cost-effectiveness
    90; 'professional' orientation of
    departments and officers 74
Local Government Act (1988)
    88–9
Local Government Audit
    Commission for England and
    Wales (1982) 88
Local Government Management
    Board (1993) 89–90, 99–100
Local Government Planning and
    Land Act (1980) 88
local management of schools 90
London Ambulance Service
    (1992) 70
London Metropolitan Police
    Service 35–6
long-term and corporate planning
    45–9
long-term pattern of incentive
    schemes **161**
long-term planning, key decision-
    makers and 46; 'top-down' or
    'bottom up' 47

Maastricht Summit (1991) 308
McClelland, D.C. 141
McCormack, Mark H. 193
McCormick, Roger 18

McGregor, Douglas 104–6, 138
McKinseys (management
consultants) 57
Mafia, information technology
and 69
Maier, Norman R.F. 43–4
Major, John 338
management 1, 123; delegation
and 134; emphasis on results
and taking calculated risks 82
'management by crisis' 26
'management by objectives' 29–32,
230, 235, 241–2
Management Charter Initiative
(MCI) 21–2, 243, 250
management style, alternatives in
104; culture and 111–13, 121;
environmental factors 110; the
immediate superior and 110–11;
theories, other 'style' 106–8;
theories X and Y 104–6
manager, the organisation and
52–3
manager and employee relations
295–6; employee in context of
the organisation 297–9; health
and safety and 309–11; manager
as trade union member 325–6;
objectives in employee relations
296–7
'managerial cycle' 1–2
managerial escalator 3–4, 20, 351
'managerial gap' 4
Managerial Psychology 181
managerial roles, 'emotional
hardening' and 15
managerial stress, over-
involvement and 136, 154–6;
ways of coping with 39, 156
managerial style 97–8;
effectiveness of 121; evaluating
119–21; mix of team needed to
make a group successful 107;
starting in new job 116–17;
working in other countries
113–16
managers, communication and
177; how people become 2–4;
multi-skilling and 20; need to

develop diagnostic skills 50, 351;
successful, effect of outgrowing
their jobs 352
manager's job, activity versus
effectiveness 25–6; definition of
work 26–7; identification of
27–8; identification of
objectives in 29–30;
identification of short-term
and long-term needs 28–9;
long-term and corporate
planning 45–50
manager, the, authority of 98–100;
as a facilitator 99–100, 102, 117;
relationship with people in
other departments 101–2;
sapiential authority of 100–1
'mandarin' approach to
management 19, 87
Marchioness disaster 311
market changes, information
access and 68
'market testing' 83
market turbulence, organic-type
structures and 57
Maslow, A.H. 139–42, 158 ;
hierarchy of human needs 140
Masso, Angela 44
'match' between person and job
208
Mayo, Elton 54
meetings 328–9; agenda and
its management 334–5; need
for 323; need for, and
consequences of ineffectiveness
329–30; preparation before 45,
333–5, 353; preparation of
other issues in 335–7; recording
outcome of 342–4; role of the
chair at 331–3; terms used in
formal 346–9; types and
classification of activity 330–1;
who should attend 335
merit payment 239, 325
mission statements 31, 194, 242,
298
motivation, expectancy theories
144; financial incentive schemes
and 175; job motivators and job

dissatisfiers 141–4; role of women in workforce 153; theories of 139–41
Mouton, J.S. 107
multi-craft worker 205
multi-national corporations, global basis of 73
multi-skilling 60, 173, 249, 318; managers and 20

Nadler, David A. 144
National Board for Prices and Incomes 160
National Coal Board 124
National Curriculum in schools 90
national economic growth, low rate of 90
National Health Service 20, 53, 69, 74, 82, 91–2; ACAS investigation 314; administration costs 92; merit payments 239
National Institute of Industrial Psychology 206
National Insurance schemes 187–8
national league tables, schools and 90
National Association of Local Government Officers (NALG0) 305
National Vocational Qualifications (NVQs) 21–2, 243; and related developments 248–50
'needs-led' policy-making 88
'negative' differential of supervisor 161
'negative' increments 175
negotiating skills, allocation of roles 320–21; conduct after negotiating meetings 324; conduct during negotiations 322–4; defining objectives and 319–20; identifying power realities 321–2; the manager and employee relations 318–19
negotiators, 'report-backs' and 323–4
'network planning' and 'network analysis' 43
networks, of independent

businesses, big firms as 152; informal 76–7
New Management Grid 106
News International dispute (1986) 301, 322
Nissan 173; at Sunderland 304
Nolan Reports 86
Nott, John 125

O'Brien, R.C. 66
Observer, the 84–6
occupational sociologists, organisations as social entities 54
Official Secrets Act 281
oil companies, management skills in 19
'old-boy' network 86
On the Psychology of Military Incompetence 186
opportunity cost 126
'opted-out' schools 90
'organic' systems, organisational structure and 55–7, 97
organisation, the flexible 59-61; the manager and 52–3; mechanistic and organic structures 55–9; quality circles 61–2; restructuring and 248; theories of 53–5; total quality management (TQM) and 62–6
organisational activity, inter-departmental problems and 75–7; interrelationship of 74–5
organisational effectiveness, conscious prioritisation and 39
organisations, accommodation of people with specialist skills 19; entry is into specialised activity 3; ethical business practices and 84; matrix structure in 57; 'organic' systems 55–7, 97; overcentralisation in 69; role of creativity in 108; systems concept of 54
overcentralisation, organisations and 69
'overselection' 147, 151

paired comparisons, job ranking and 165–7

Parkhurst prison escape (1995) 125

'partnership administrators' 21

part-time employees, European law and 61, 309; mothers as 221

Pascal, B laise 196

'pay drift' 173

payment by results schemes, conditions for 160

payment schemes, fixed-term contracts and 174

payment systems, appropriate conditions 159–60; diagnosis of need 159; financial incentives 158–9; group schemes 163; long-term effects of incentive schemes 160–3; profit sharing 163–4; relationship to external market 170; various other developments relating to 174–5

Pedler, M. 15

'performance culture' 239

'performance indicators' 31, 83, 92, 298

performance management, links with appraisal 30, 227, 241–2, 262 ; overlap with human resource management and TQM 242

performance-outcome 144

performance-related pay 22, 66, 158, 175; appraisal situation and 227, 239–41; effect on negotiations 325; effect on unions 240, 305; failure rate of 315; public sector and 83

peripheral work-force 59, 210; training needs of 244

personnel department, role of 298

Personnel Management 230

Peter, Lawrence 12, 208

Peter Principle 12

Peters, Thomas J. 49, 57–8, 151–2

Philips 152

Piper Alpha oil rig fire 311

'plan-do-check-act' cycle 64

politics, leaders in 103

Ponting, Clive 281

power culture, small organisations and 57

Powers, Gary 194

Practice of Management 204

presentational skills, check list 195

Prison Service Agency 125

private and public sector, developments in 79

private sector, effect of competitive pressures 39, 79–80

privatisation, UK and 81, 300, 305

process control 330–1, 333

productivity levels, influences on 76

product life cycles, information technology and 68

'product-type' teams 57

Property Services Agency 85

provincial police forces, changes planned 92

psychometric tests 211–12

Public Accounts Committee (1994) 70, 85

Public Appointments Commissioner 86

public sector, changing shape of 80–2 ; the Civil Service 86–8; comparisons with the private sector 82–4; contracting out 60; devolution of authority 300; local government and 88–91; merit pay in 239; National Health Service 91–2; performance-related pay and 83, 241; pressures for economy in 39; problem of boundary-crossing 74; quangos and government agencies 84–6; various other changes in 92

public sector funding, restrictions on 295

purchaser-provider relationship, in local government 90; National Health Service and 91

quality circles, critical factors in 62, 151

quality gap 65
quality kitemark, commercial advantage of 65
quangocrats, checks for 'political acceptability' of 85–6
quangos, 82, 84, 89; Nolan Report and 86; politicisation of 85

Race Relations Act (1976) 219
Railtrack 302
rate-capping 88
ratings in appraisal, criteria for 232; methods used in recording 233
Reagan, President 37, 81
'reasonable behaviour' by employer 268, 272, 274
'reasonably foreseeable' disaster 125
recession 58; quality initiatives and 66
redundancy, ex-employee arguments about 268; substantive agreements about payments 316
Redundancy Payments Act (1965) 267
reference for employee 209–10
Regan, Donald 37
religion, as cultural variable 112
Reluctant Managers 15
remedies and developments for securing effective management, further developments 20–2; training and monitoring 19–20
'representatives of the workforce', employers required to consult 269
resource allocation, targeting of 92
restructuring, organisation and 248
Ridley, Dr. Tony 125
'rightsizing' 134
Robens, Lord 124
robotic technology, effects of 67
Rodger, Professor Alex 206
role behaviour, personality versus 53, 77–8; reducing conflict and 78–9

role set analysis, for head of personnel of professional organisation 33; manager's job and 32–9
Rothwell, Sheila 247
Royal Air Force 6, 56, 110
Royal Commission on Trade Unions and Employers' Associations 138
Royal Society of Arts 248
Royal Statistical Society 300

St Bartholomew's Hospital 119
sale of council houses, freezing of revenues from 90
'sapiential authority' 97, 121
Savage, A. 230
Savundra, Dr. Emile 124
Scase, Richard 12, 15, 153
Schmidt, Warren H. 106
Scientific Management School 53, 80
Scotland 85–6, 89
Scottish assembly 82
Scottish companies (electronic industry 1953–7) 56
'screened out' crime 36.
selection interview 212; being interviewed 221–3; interviewing skills 214–15; and other common problems 215–16; planning for 212–14
Selection panels 213, 217–19
selection processes, and equal opportunities 219–21
selection of staff 22–3, 202–3; and assessment centres 211–12; collection of information about candidates 209–11; criteria for 206–9; defining the job 203–4; interview assessment form 226; and short and long-term needs 204–6
'self-actualisation', motivating factors for 141–2
self-appraisal 236–7; informal guidance and 237
'self-regulation' 134

'service level agreements',
departments and 90
Sex Discrimination Act (1975) 219
Shell 19, 48
Shewart, Walter 64
Shimmin, Sylvia 15
signal workers dispute (1994)
301–3
Singapore 73, 186
skill pyramid 146–**147**
skill shortages, and lack of
training investment 302
'slotting-in' jobs 172–3
Social Protocol, UK and 309
software packages, automation
and 68
South Korea 73
Soviet block, collapse of
communism 81
specialist career structures,
limitations of 6–8
Stalker, G.M. 55–6
Stewart, Rosemary 29, 178
structure of organisations, factors
that determine 66
subcontracting 60–1
Subject Access provisions
(operative from 1987) 234
'subsidiarity' of business in
organisation 48
substantive issues, chair and
331–3, 337, 344
successful group, roles needed for
107–8
Sunday Times 187
supervisor 'captured' by work
group 159, 161
'supervisory control' 16, 317–18
'SWOT' analysis 47

Taiwan 73
Tannenbaum, Robert 106
Taylor, F W. 53, 80, 106
teleworking 60
'ten day rule' 317
Tenerife air disaster (1977) 191
testimonial for employee 209–10
Thatcher, Margaret 81, 84, 86,
307, 338

'the disposable work-force' 152
theories of organisation 53–5;
mechanistic and organic
structures 55–9
theories X and Y, approaches to
work 104–6, 138
Tiananmen Square (1989) 198
time management, critical path
analysis 42–3, **44**; fatigue 43–5;
general points 45; identifying
priorities 40–1; sequencing work
42
'top of the range' excellence 63
'total quality of life', audit of 154
Total Quality Management
(TQM) 20, 59, 136, 151, 304;
Deming's approach to 194, 243;
empowerment and 133; human
resource management and 242;
interdepartmental co-operation
and 76, 90; key preconditions
for success 63, 97; objectives of
31–2; organisation and 62–6,
298, 315; Theory Y assumptions
and 105; training and 243
'total' scheme 30
Trade Union and Employment
Rights Act (1993) 84, 310
Trade Union and Labour
Relations (Consolidation) Act
(1992) 307
Trade Union Protection
(Consolidation Act) (1992)
268
Trade Union Reform and
Employment Rights Act (1993)
84, 168, 268–9, 307–8
trade unions, health and safety
and 310; job evaluation and
168; local bargaining and 306;
performance-related pay and
240; reductions in collective
rights 307–8; role of 304–6
traffic wardens 78
training 22, 227; evaluation and
follow-up 251–2; identification
of needs 243–4; and the
learning organisation 246–8;
management training and

development 250–1; meeting needs 245–6; NVQs and related developments 248–50

Training and Enterprise Councils (TECs) 249

'trait' theories 102

transnational organisations 73

Treasury, de-layering in 87

Treaty of Rome 17 1, 269

'Triple I Organisation' 99

trust hospitals, local bargaining machinery and 91

'tunnel vision' 320, 326

UK 115, 142; comparison with Japan 113; concept of mentoring in 251; Conservative administrations since (1979) 81; European Commission and 168, 171, 269; European Union employment legislation 308; Exchange Rate Mechanism and 125; Japanese and American companies in 299, 303–4; 'mandarin approach' to management 19, 87; privatisation in 81, 300, 305; Protestant ethic of 112 ; Social Protocol 309; Treaty of Rome and 171; unemployment levels 300; Working Hours Directive and 309

Understanding Organisations 110

union power, effect of decline in 174–5, 295–6, 301, 304

UNISON (1993) 305

'unitarist' view of organizations 31–2, 299

urban decay 91

USA 80–1, 83–4, 112, 152

valence 144

'value for money' 85, 88, 90

Vehicle Inspectorate (1988) 86

Voss, R.C. 66

Wages Councils, abolition of (1993) 300

Wales 85–6

Walker, John V Northumberland County Council 155

Wandsworth, borough of 89

Waterman, Robert H. 49, 57–9, 151

Welsh assembly 82

Wessex Health Authority 71

West, deregulation in 81, 112

Western Electric Company (Chicago) 54

West Germany 112

Westminster, borough of 89

'Whitley' system 87

'Winter of Discontent' (1978/9) 307

'witch-hunting' by employers 288

Woodward, Joan 67, 72

'workaholism', dangers of 154

Working Hours Directive 309

work performance 136–7; assumptions about why people work 137–9; reasons for poor 137, 175; variables in 139

workshops, value of 38

'wrongful dismissal' 266

Yes Minister 187

Zeebrugge disaster 311